CHINA

An Introduction

CHINA
An Introduction

LUCIAN W. PYE
Massachusetts Institute of Technology

With the collaboration of Mary W. Pye

LITTLE, BROWN AND COMPANY
Boston

The translation of the poem on page v is from Lin Yutang,
The Gay Genius (New York: John Day, 1947), p. 171.

To A. Doak Barnett, Charles T. Cross, Harold R. Isaacs,
and to the memory of John M. H. Lindbeck,
friends who have shared my China.

The affairs of men are in a turmoil,
The lonely scholar's spirit is vexed.
Why should the melody of the lute
Be drowned in the noise of the kettle drum?
Three cups can drown ten thousand worries,
And after waking up my spirit is cleansed . . .

Su Tung-Po
A.D. 1036–1101

Preface

I resolved to write this book after my colleague Harold R. Issacs remarked to me that "what we really need is a simple, straightforward introduction to China." I have not sought to advance novel theses or excessively unconventional interpretations, for the rapid expansion in the numbers of monographs on China provide ample opportunities for these. Now, more than ever, there is a need for better understanding of China and its historical evolution. In international politics there is debate over whether it is possible to have "two Chinas," but in intellectual circles there have been for several years an ever growing number of Chinas as different kinds of specialists analyze China from their particular vantage points. Quite often specialists on contemporary Communist China have little feeling for the Confucian traditions, and conversely scholars of old China and even Republican China may have little understanding of Mao's China. Growth of knowledge calls for specialization, but public understanding also calls for an initial perspective that is broad enough to include all the main forces that have contributed to the making of modern China.

Thus my purpose in writing this book has been to introduce students and laymen to the many dimensions of Chinese politics and history. Surely there is a place for an introduction to China that brings together the Confucian, Republican, and Communist periods, and examines them in the light of China's physical characteristics and vivid cultural forms. The need seems particularly great at this time. China is becoming increasingly involved with the international community, and we must seek to understand this distinctive one-quarter of mankind. For too long China has been an abstraction — a devil for some and a utopia for others.

My writing was greatly facilitated by Alison Huey, who collected data and criticized my drafts. I am deeply indebted to Edwin O. Reischauer for helping me immeasurably with the chapters on the Confucian order. William E. Griffith checked my analysis of Communist relations and ideology; Takashi Inoguchi and James L. Foster carefully reviewed my summary of domestic development during the Communist period. Molly Morell and Joanna Hill skillfully and cheerfully deciphered my illegible hand and typed the different drafts. The assistance I received from Mary W. Pye went beyond that of an editor, and therefore she is rightfully recognized as my collaborator.

Contents

CHINA

An Introduction

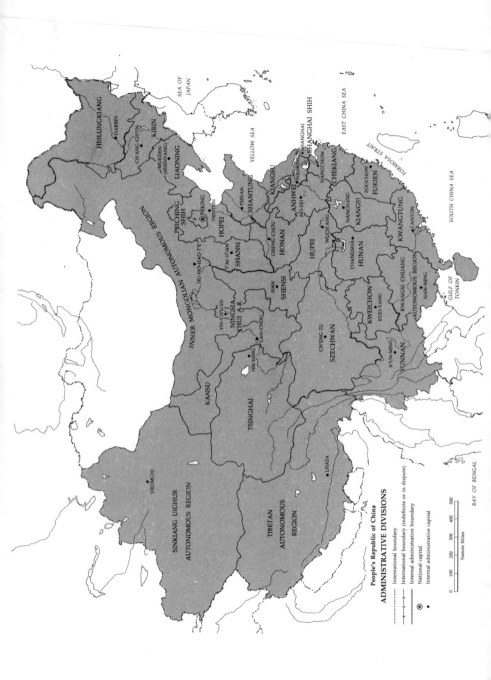

People's Republic of China
ADMINISTRATIVE DIVISIONS

	International boundary
+-+-+	International boundary (indefinite or in dispute)
	Internal administrative boundary
⊛	National capital
•	Internal administrative capital

0 100 200 300 400 500
Statute Miles

CHAPTER ONE

An Abundance of Questions

During the turmoil of the Cultural Revolution, journalists, scholars, and diplomats spoke of the isolation of China and of how one-quarter of mankind had turned its back on the rest of the world and was absorbed with itself. Red Guard youths captured the Chinese foreign office, attacked foreign diplomats in Peking, and generally denounced all manifestations of foreign as well as traditional Chinese influences on contemporary Chinese life. Strange events were these, yet China has always in a sense been alone, and the rest of the world has always viewed it with a mixture of fascination and revulsion. The mysteries of Cathay, the Middle Kingdom, the warlords, the Nationalists, and Mao Tse-tung's revolutionary visions have each in their time attracted and repelled the imagination of all whom the Chinese designate simply as "foreigners."

Now China is a member of the United Nations, and for the first time in history an American president has visited Peking, the ancient center of Chinese civilization. The fascination of China spreads, but so does the awareness of our ignorance about the most populous and oldest country in the world.

Chinese civilization is one of the great achievements of the human spirit. Although many of its ancient forms and traditions are gone, the fact remains that the people most touched by it — the Chinese, the Koreans, the Japanese, and the Vietnamese — continue to show remarkable vitality in comparison with most non-Western societies. The grandeur and the pretensions of the Confucian Way have crumbled, and the Confucian family system is no more, but the basic cast of personality that made China great still exists. To the extent that the character of the Chinese has persisted, China's potential for greatness has been continuous.

1

The puzzle that has been China grows more perplexing with the decades. Recently whenever China has demanded our attention it has confused and dumfounded us. Yet China in all its various forms has much to teach the rest of the world. Traditional China perhaps reveals more about social order and political stability than any other society. The Chinese imperial system was the most enduring major political system in world history. For over two millennia, from the second century before Christ until 1911, the Chinese adhered essentially to one form of government and, with only modest modifications, one political philosophy. Why did this most amazing system of public order persist for so long?

In contrast to the theme of stability that characterized traditional China, the story of modern China is that of revolution — profound, intense, violent, and protracted. Like most of the countries of the non-European world China has been caught up in the complex problems of modernization, but the challenge has been on a more massive scale for the Chinese. For over one hundred years they have been experiencing profound social change, and for decades they have lived through violent political upheaval, civil wars, and foreign conquests. Behind the political and military turmoil have been deep intellectual and moral issues; the Chinese have grappled with the perplexing questions of how they should relate their traditions to modern experiences.

Just as traditional China had one of the most stable and persistent social orders in history, so the Chinese revolution has been one of the longest, most far-reaching, and fundamental of all times. The fact that China embodies these two extremes explains in part why it is so confusing. The stereotypes of the "changeless Orient" and the "revolutionary East" persist precisely because China continues to surprise us by holding to continuity when we expect change and changing when we expect inertia.

Today the Chinese in their communism stand in a class by themselves. When the Communists first came to power in Peking it was widely assumed by westerners and by intellectuals in China that they would be more rational, less ideological, and more flexible and accommodating than the Russians; possibly they would be mere peasant reformers. Now, of course, people everywhere in the world call their most radical, ideological, and unreasoning elements their "Chinese," their "Maoists." How was it possible for Chinese communism so completely to change its character, and to do so under the leadership of one man, Mao Tse-tung?

In every age the story of China has been filled with fascinating questions and perplexing contradictions. Traditional China in its solid stability extolled harmony and, more than most systems, emphasized morality and ethical precepts as the basis for legitimacy and authority. Yet every dynasty in the history of China was founded by military force, and to this very moment armies have been key factors at every critical turn of events.

Chinese political philosophy was elitist, sanctioning the rule of autocratic philosopher-kings, yet it praised the common man and the simple virtues. Among all the state ideologies of the ancient world Confucianism was unique because it was precociously secular, making no assertions of divine revelation or mystical origin. The greatest figure in the Chinese tradition, Confucius, was a mere mortal. Yet in the last analysis, reason and morality — the ultimate foundations of Chinese imperial authority — were sanctified in the concept of the Mandate of Heaven, which suggested an element of divine influence in governmental affairs, and thus the Chinese confusedly mixed the secular and sacred in still another contradiction.

In a strange fashion elements in the Chinese tradition seem to have given the Chinese unique advantages for establishing a modern state and developing a modern economy. The Chinese originated rule by a bureaucracy based on merit and first recruited men to places of authority on the basis of competitive examinations. At a remarkably early date the Chinese eliminated formal feudalism and the concept of hereditary and landed aristocracy. The spirit of achievement and the virtues of hard work, frugality, and persistence were all central features of the Chinese social ethic. Yet in modern times nation building has been peculiarly difficult for the Chinese, and in spite of their singular economic achievements in other societies the Chinese have failed in their own country to create a modern economic system and to achieve significant economic development. Capitalism never emerged in China, and socialist institutions have yet to prove that they are the answer to China's needs. What are the reasons for these economic difficulties in the face of the manifest sophistication of Chinese civilization?

Furthermore there is the puzzling contradiction that the Chinese achieved many remarkable technological advances at a very early date — the list goes well beyond the obvious items of the invention of paper, printing, gunpowder, and the compass — yet the Chinese failed to develop science. In spite of a tradition venerating the scholar and the role of reason, the Chinese did not significantly advance the art of reasoning, the study of logic, and the development of the physical sciences. Again we are led to wonder about the extraordinary strengths and limitations of the traditional Chinese intellectual achievements.

The challenging questions about traditional China that arise from the perspective of comparative civilization can be matched with equally interesting questions about modern China and particularly the Chinese version of communism. Why was Chinese nationalism so slow to produce effective government? Why did democracy fail in the Chinese setting? Why has Chinese communism presented so many different faces to the world? The Chinese "model" has ranged from the disciplined, well mannered guerrilla, to the orderly and efficient planning and bureaucratic system, to the radical and romantic revolutionary. Thus to know China is to learn about at least three political systems: the traditional, consisting of the remarkably coherent and integrated structures, institutions, and ideologies of the imperial era; the republican or early modernizing, which found China in reaction to the Western challenge and in search of a new destiny in nationalism; and Communist China, in which the theories and practices, the dogmas and disciplines, of Marxism-Leninism-Stalinism and Maoism are being applied to the modernization and development of the world's largest society.

The task of learning about any one of these Chinas would be demanding enough, but in the contemporary world we need to know about all three, for there have been great continuities in Chinese life and the contemporary generation of Chinese is still reacting to its cultural legacies. Mao Tse-tung, today a worldwide symbol of radical revolutionary thought, is unmistakably a product of the intellectual confusion and striving of early twentieth-century China and thus is a man who has taken much from the earlier traditions and legends of China. He is not just a doctrinaire radical. We need to know China in both its Confucian and Communist forms if we are to understand its dynamics.

In looking back to traditional China, we shall be most interested in the distinctive harmony that existed between Confucian thought and Confucian institutions. Confucianism was an ideology of the rulers and of officialdom, but it articulated values that were profoundly meaningful for even the humblest peasants. Confucianism spoke not just to the institutions of government but also to the traditions of the Chinese family system.

The remarkably long period of time in which the formal institutions of the great society meshed with and were mutually reinforcing of nearly all social and private institutions was in part the source of Chinese stability. The dividing line between government and society was blurred. The result was a system of government that was at once humanistic and autocratic. The authoritarian character of the imperial system denied legitimacy to private efforts to make demands on the government: Popular sentiments had no channels for expression, and all forms of individualistic interests, whether economic, social, or regional, were considered improper. Accommodation occurred, but in ways that suggest improprieties and corruption.

The authoritarian spirit of Confucianism lacked the ideological firmness that went with the doctrines of absolutism in the West, and the Chinese, of course, did not have the necessities of competition that accompanied the fragmentation of Europe with its clashes between nobles and nobles, kings and kings, and finally between nation-states. Thus the Chinese state never became as rigid or as mobilized a structure as the European states. According to the Chinese, the greatness of the civilization, and not the reasons of state, shapes history. If we are to understand the heritage that has formed modern China, we must look beyond institutions and ideology in order to capture the spirit of the artistic and philosophical traditions of ancient China.

The story of China's reaction to the West helps to highlight the essential differences between the two civilizations. The clashes illuminate the degree to which the Chinese tradition was based on human considerations, the search for the expression of virtue, and practical moderation and compromise, while Western culture was committed to the principles of law, competition, and individual self-interest. The story of this great meeting of civilizations still needs to be told from a perspective that does not seek to make small moral points about the rights and wrongs of one or the other. In the meantime, however, it is important to see the story as one of the efforts of the Chinese to find new foundations for their society and government. The breakdown of the imperial system caused profound economic and social changes, the rise of new classes, and the impoverishment of old ones; above all it created a sense of self-awareness that produced shock waves of intellectual dissatisfaction and cultural humiliation.

After the revolution that brought down the imperial system, the Chinese began in earnest a search that is still going on. China avoided direct colonial domination but suffered the indignities of the treaty ports and foreign gunboats. It also suffered the humiliation of a period of ineffectual nationalist awakening. Finally and possibly most traumatic of all, China suffered through years of war with and occupation by the Japanese.

The Communist system that emerged from these travails seemed for a while to provide China with a new hope, the prospect for rapid development and an imminent return to world prominence. The turmoils of the Communists have made the future seem more clouded. They have, however, clarified the basic issues of Chinese modernization. The issues that have torn apart the Chinese Communist Party during the periods of the Great Leap and the Cultural Revolution are more than just disagreements of Party factions; they touch the heart of China's modernization.

Does China need to find a new ideological and spiritual identity before it can truly find itself? Or do the Chinese need more the benefits of modern technology and science? The problem of how to modernize the world's largest and one of its poorest populations has challenged Communist authorities. Agriculture, industrial development, education, and national security have in their separate ways created uncertainties that have tended to divide China's leaders. In various fields, basic questions such as whether China's hopes lie in greater ideological commitment or in greater professionalization have set one group of leaders against another. What eventually struck the outside world as the bizarre and unexplainable behavior of the Cultural Revolution was in fact a natural culmination of fundamental differences about how China could best resolve the basic problems of modernization.

We shall examine these subjects and problems in the hope of answering some questions and of raising new ones. In covering the full sweep of Chinese history, we shall be seeking out matters that will reduce the mysteries of China, make that great culture more understandable, and set its current actions in a useful perspective.

Beyond China's remoteness and isolation and the fact that Chinese government has had a variety of political forms, there is the extraordinary record of China's propensity to let down all who have sought to "understand" and champion it. The earliest Western defenders of Confucian and Taoist wisdom were not only ignored by the Chinese but abandoned by them when China turned away from the imperial tradition and sought to become a republic. Those who were the quickest to see democratic potentialities in China were soon let down by events. Westerners with an emotional attachment to the idea of virtuous and decent China being violated by vicious Japan found that the Chinese leaders they had admired were not living up to their ideals. When the Communists came to power, their advocates suggested that they would be more pragmatic, less ideological, than most Communists, but soon the advocates were shown to lack understanding of Mao's communism. When the Chinese seemed to move in the direction of organizational efficiency, they attracted a new group of those who would understand them. These were the ones who spoke unfavorably of the rest of the developing world on the grounds that Peking had a greater sense of economic priorities, technical competence, and disciplined no-nonsense. These apologists of China were soon made to seem completely out of touch with the real China when the Maoist vision of revolutionary commitment replaced the Chinese "model" of development. Now it is the turn of radicals throughout the world to wonder whether Mao's China is about to turn its back on them.

The problem, of course, has always been that friends as well as critics have persisted in making China an abstraction and treating it as a symbol of good or evil. Subjective images have blurred objectivity. What is forgotten is that China has physical characteristics, that behind its veil of mysteries is a reality. Before turning to the social and political puzzles of China, we need to be introduced to China as a physical entity.

PEOPLE'S REPUBLIC OF CHINA

Area

Total area (square miles) — 3,691,500
Cultivated acres per person — .5
Percentage that is arable — 25%

Population (millions)	1972	1953
Total nation	850.0	582.6
Total cities over 1 million		
Peking (the capital)	4.0	
Shanghai	7.5	
Tientsin	4.0	
Canton	3.0	
Mukden (Shenyang)	2.5	
Wuhan	2.0	
Chungking	2.0	
Harbin	1.5	
Nanking	1.5	
Sian	1.3	

Population Density and Distribution

Per square mile — 233
Percentage in cities — 15%
Percentage of working age — 59.7%
Percentage of workers in agriculture — 69%
Percentage of workers in industry — 5.4%
Average annual growth rate (1950–1970) — 2 to 2.5%

Economy

Total GNP — $50 billion to $80 billion
Per capita — $60 to $100
Defense expenditures — 3.6%
Foreign trade — 9% (world rank: 79)

Communications

Newspaper circulation — 20 per 1,000 people (world rank: 79.5)
Television sets — .03 per 1,000 people (world rank: 67.5)
Cinema attendance — 2.2 per capita per year (world rank: 75)
Physicians — 1 per 8,700 people

Education

Students in higher education — 69 per 100,000 people (world rank: 74)

Elementary and secondary-school age children in school — 41% (world rank: 65)

Literacy — 47.5% (world rank: 65.5)

(Source: United Nations Economic and Social Affairs Office, Department of Statistics, *Statistical Yearbook,* 1970; and Bruce M. Russett, Hayward R. Alker, Karl W. Deutsch, Harold D. Laswell, *World Handbook of Political and Social Indicators* (New Haven: Yale University Press, 1965).

CHAPTER TWO

Meeting China

The physical characteristics of China defy generalization. South China lies in the subtropics and blends into the world of Southeast Asia, while at the other extreme northern Manchuria and western Sinkiang are on a line with Newfoundland. On the east and south, China has over four thousand miles of coastline marked by excellent harbors, yet the country has always turned its back to the sea and contented itself with being a continental society. In looking inward, however, China has tended to ignore or treat with disdain the desolate mountainous reaches of its western interior, the extent of which makes China the third largest country in area, following Canada and the Soviet Union.

The tremendous population of China, which totals over 800 million — making China nearly twice as large as India, the next most populous country — seems to deny China's physical size, for it is overwhelmingly concentrated in the eastern third of the land. Only about one-quarter of China's territory is arable. Perhaps 300 million acres are in cultivation — an average of less than half an acre per person — and these farm lands are concentrated along the eastern and northern coasts, the Manchurian and the north China plains, along the main rivers, and on the Szechwan plateau.

Over six thousand years ago Chinese civilization emerged along the Yellow River valley and spread across the north China plains. This region, with its vividly defined seasons and rich, good earth, has been the heart of the Mandarin-speaking region of China. The winters of north China, which begin in late November with the freezing of lakes and ponds, are dry and cold and sharply intensified by persistent and penetrating winds from across the Gobi Desert and out of Mongolia. By mid-February signs of spring appear.

People's Republic of China

AGRICULTURE

Percent in cultivation

Non-cultivated 0 50

Agricultural boundary

Administrative boundary

Statute Miles

0   100   200   300   400   500

Northern Chinese, like all people, talk much about the weather, but possibly to more purpose because they believe that every winter is made up of two "large colds" and three "small colds" — that is, two major and three minor cold spells — and therefore every change in temperature calls for judgments and classifications to determine what lies ahead. Men gather to compare impressions and test their judgments about what has been real and what mere illusion in the passing of the winter.

Spring in north China brings the crop of winter wheat and an early sowing of the *kaoliang* (capricorn), millet, and barley crops, which farmers hope will be helped by light spring rains. Summers are intensely hot, fueled by air that has moved across a whole continent. The rains arrive in July and August, but they are not as dramatic in their beginnings nor as continuous as the Indian monsoons. Sudden and intense storms, particularly in the mountains on the edges of the plains, cause flash floods but provide water for irrigation. About one-half of all the cultivated land in China depends on irrigation. Every mountain stream and river is tapped to feed the fields . Electrically powered pumps exist, but frequently when water must be lifted the method remains the old one of manually working a bucket attached to a balanced pole that is weighted with a rock at the other end. In the past, the desperate shortage of water tended to be a principal cause of feuds within and between villages; farmers clashed over the "stealing" of a few minutes of the flow of irrigation streams. Throughout the growing season the quiet night of the Chinese countryside would often be broken by shouts of violence and pain and the ring of picks and shovels smashing together as one group of peasants attacked another caught in the act of trying to surreptitiously change the direction of a sluice. Long ago the requirements of irrigation taught the Chinese the need for cooperation and for a higher authority to adjudicate disputes and solicit fair shares in maintaining the dikes. The peasants also learned from the preciousness of water that one man's advantage was always another's loss and that believing that all could benefit from a steadily improving situation was naïve.

In central and south China water is less of a problem. There the brown flat plains of north China give way to a lush green and far more mountainous countryside. China is physically divided by the Yangtze River, which in west China moves through spectacular gorges and then races into the rich rice lands of central China feeding numerous lakes before reaching the sea near Shanghai. In May and June the lower Yangtze has continuous rains called *mai-yü*, or plum rains, and the fog, clouds, and mists along its entire course have been the source of the great Chinese landscape painting tradition. Along the lower reaches, river traffic includes sizable steamboats, but on the upper river the boats and barges have to be towed by men straining in harnesses as they plod along the rocky path by the churning water's edge. The scene enforces the impression that man is small and insignificant in contrast to the majesty and clouded mystery of nature.

Until recently the Yangtze could be crossed only by boats, and the principal north-south railroad was disrupted because the train cars were ferried across the river and reassembled on the other side, a procedure requiring from two to three hours. One of the great prides of Communist China is a bridge over the Yangtze at Nanking under which 10,000-ton ships can pass.

In south China the countryside is far more broken up with mountains. Although Canton has plains for its immediate hinterland, other principal south China cities such as Foochow, Swatow, and Amoy back right into mountains. The isolation of the population in China south of the Yangtze is reflected in the great variety of mutually unintelligible dialects spoken in the different communities.

Contrasts between north and south China exist in nearly every aspect of life. In the north farms are large, and a farmer working with a donkey or mule can cultivate as much as twelve acres of wheat, millet, or *kaoliang;* in the south, working with a water buffalo and planting rice by hand, a farmer can at most cultivate three acres. In north China herdsmen tend flocks of sheep and goats on the hilly slopes of the loess valleys and on the mountainsides surrounding the main plains. In south China livestock is limited to work animals and scavengers such as pigs, fowl, and dogs.

Beyond the agrarian regions of north and south China lie the mountainous plateaus of Tibet and the deserts and mountain ranges of northwest China, where in the past nomads roamed. Today the scenery of Tibet is much as it has always been, in spite of the destruction of the Lama theocracy and the construction of military roads. The Kunlun Mountains separate the Tibetan plateau from the deserts of northwest China, which in recent years have received several million migrants from east China but still have vast empty areas marked by isolated settlements at water spots along the recently extended railroad from Lanchow through to the Soviet Union and Alma Ata.

The physical features of China have created great social differences. People near the mouths of the Yellow and Yangtze rivers live in some of the most crowded rural conditions in the world; those who live beyond the atomic test site near Lake Lop Nor in Sinkiang are part of one of the most sparsely settled regions in the world. These differences have probably increased over the centuries and continue to do so in spite of major efforts of the Peking government in recent years. Before Buddhism came to dominate Tibetan society and cause over one-quarter of its males to practice celibacy, Tibet supported a larger and more militant population, which spread out and conquered much of the rest of northwest China and Mongolia. From Roman times to the last Chinese dynasty, the desert regions of the northwest were the site of extensive trade caravans and restless, raiding nomadic peoples. The sharp upsurge of population in east China has occurred mostly in the last two hundred years.

The confusing diversity of China is further accentuated by the fact that although eighty percent of the people live close to a rural setting, Chinese civilization was built out of a great urban tradition. Thirteen of the fifty largest cities in the world are in China, and because most of these cities emerged in response not to industrial development but as administrative and trading centers, they generally reflect an orderly scheme and a responsiveness to comfort and beauty. The bustle of life in Chinese towns is largely directed toward the marketplace and to consumer interests. Matters of taste and choice, of novelty and quality, are important to the Chinese, and it is striking today that Communist China, with a poorer economy, surpasses the Soviet Union in the production of goods that can compete in international consumer markets.

Peking is unquestionably one of the greatest — some would say the greatest — cities of the world. It evokes a strange blend of majestic orderliness and comforting unexpectedness that possibly only Washington, D.C., is able to suggest. The majesty of its broad avenues and open squares, the massive paved courtyards and golden roofs of the palaces in the Forbidden City, all of which succeed in humbling the individual, are juxtaposed with the intimacies of parks and narrow, wall-lined, and sharply turning residential streets called *hutungs*. The main streets such as Hatamen and Chiang An are broad far beyond the needs of their limited motorized traffic, and they have equally generous sidewalks, which at certain points become markets of curbside stalls.

A city of four million people, Peking has peculiarly little need for public transportation. People live near their places of employment. A system of buses and streetcars supports the principle but not the reality of mass transportation (as in Los Angeles), but the bicycle is the main means for getting about. Whereas old Peking had a low architectural profile, with only Coal Hill and the walls of the Forbidden City and the Tartar City breaking the skyline, Peking in the 1950's was filled with massive government buildings and high-rise apartments for the legions of clerical workers, who still give Peking its slightly superior and quasi-intellectual tone. During the republican years many of the old imperial buildings of the capital were converted into museums and public parks, yet when the peasant armies of the Communists captured power their leaders quite readily transformed the Forbidden City into their natural habitat. In much the same way as the Russian revolutionaries took to the Kremlin, the Chinese Communist leaders have turned the majesty of the imperial scene to their advantage, and indeed they have expanded on what went before by clearing a massive square for huge parades.

Although the traffic on Peking's streets is not dense, it is, as in all Chinese cities, diversified. The absence of automobiles is more than made up by the prevalence of other forms of transportation — pedicabs, bicycles, animal-drawn carts, and human-drawn carts often massively loaded and pulled by teams of men. The scene in Peking is very like that in Nanking described by Alberto Jacoviello, editor of an Italian Communist paper:

> The first thing that strikes one in this city is the large number of carts pulled by men. There are large and small ones. Some of them are pulled by one person, and others by five, ten, or even fifteen men, old men, young people, and women. One is guiding the shaft while the others pull. The men are almost naked to the waist. It is an impressive sight.[1]

[1]Alberto Jacoviello, "Clash Between Two Lines on the Nanking Bridge," *L'Unità* (Rome: January 9, 1971); Peking Radio carried by Foreign Broadcast Information Service (January 21, 1971).

With little effort Peking retains cultural superiority to the rest of the country. The Peking accent is the model for the national language, and consequently the common and even unschooled people of Peking often sound more cultivated than the educated from elsewhere. Chinese accents reflect geography far more than class or social distinctions do.

The opposite extreme to Peking is Canton, a massive, formless city, which abounds with streets teeming with constantly moving people. In recent years it has been the scene of annual trade fairs at which China displays its products to buyers from abroad. Historically Canton was China's gateway to the sea, and it retains a tradition of fishing and a sizable population of "boat people," families who live on sampans. Canton is not on the sea but is up the Pearl River. Along the waterfront are old buildings once associated with the foreign traders. Among other Chinese, the three million people of Canton are thought of as industrious traders and merchants and as hot-blooded revolutionaries always ready to challenge central authority.[2]

Before the Communist regime, Shanghai, the largest city of all, was a strange blend of East and West, cosmopolitan and provincial, exciting and vibrant to some, depressing and degrading to others. From one perspective its International Settlement was a ghetto where Europeans and Americans huddled together, isolated from the main currents of the larger Chinese community. From another perspective it was a place where haughty foreigners showed their scorn for the Chinese. In contrast to the International Settlement, which was dominated by the British but accommodated the pretensions of several nationalities, the French Concession in Shanghai reflected a Gallic spirit of shabby dignity and of preferring to go it alone.

After the arrival of the Communists, Shanghai experienced more of a shock than any other city in China. Shanghai and its Bund, which used to welcome cargo and people from all over the world and was once the sixth busiest port in the world, now receive only a few ships at a time. With the arrival of the Communists, Shanghai's

---

[2]For the full story of Canton in modern times see Ezra Vogel, *Canton under Communism: Programs and Politics in a Provincial Capital, 1949–1968* (Cambridge, Mass.: Harvard University Press, 1969).

industrial life was no longer entirely dependent on foreigners. The exodus of Chinese capital from Shanghai not only depressed the city but was so great that it started Hong Kong on its course as one of the most dynamically growing cities in the world. Over the years the Communists have steadily worked to change the character of Shanghai, to break it of its old cosmopolitan and decadent ways, and to disperse its massive population back to the countryside. Today there is a blend of functional puritanism and elegant decay in the parts of Shanghai that were once centers of international activity. Politically, Shanghai is more radical than any other Chinese city; it was from Shanghai that Mao Tse-tung launched the Cultural Revolution. The neon lights and huge advertisements of the pre-Communist period have been replaced by equally huge "large character posters," or *tatzepao*, that carry political slogans and quotes from Thoughts of Mao Tse-tung.

Other cities of China have distinct qualities only partially affected by the changes of government and politics. Hangchow as in the past is attractive because of the graceful and restful beauty of its lakes. Swatow, Foochow, and Amoy bring together mountains and harbors and hilly cobblestone streets. Nanking on the Yangtze has a refreshing new aspect because of its public buildings; the Sun Yat-sen mausoleum on a hill overlooking the city is the ultimate example of orderly neatness, a virtue to which the Chinese are attached.

In contrast to these cities, which reflect administrative, trading, or international traditions, is a group of nondescript, depressing industrial cities, which at best have small sections of uniqueness and charm but generally seem to be massive company towns bringing together railroad yards, factories, and workers' living quarters in a sooty gray sprawl. The archetypes are Hankow and the Wuhan complex, Tientsin, Tsinan, Taiyuan, and in Manchuria the cities of Mukden, Harbin, and Dairen.

Hankow and its companion cities of Wuch'ang and Hanyang, which make up the Wuhan complex, have the spectacle of the Yangtze to relieve the gray, industrial tone. In Tientsin, the old British Concession, surrounded by the dilapidated buildings of the former French and Japanese concessions, gave to the heart of an otherwise undistinguished industrial complex a nest of European town houses and some winding residential roads that originated at a country club and racetrack (now a military barracks), and terminated at a neat, orderly Victorian park, adjoining which was a town hall and clock tower built of imported stone. At the edge of the British Concession there was once the gray, soot-covered barracks of the Fifteenth Infantry Regiment of the United States Army, the "Can Do Regiment" posted to China during the Boxer troubles of 1900, only weeks after it had been coping with the Philippine insurrection.

Mukden and Dairen, in escaping from their essentially industrial dimensions, offer innumerable examples of what might be called Japanese colonial architecture, large boxlike buildings, plain in form and decorated at best with unnaturally small towers — buildings like those found in Taipei.

Harbin is much more distinctive, for over one-quarter of the city was once occupied by Russian refugees, and its public buildings were once churches and synagogues with onion spires and arched domes. Its streets are wide and empty, and its buildings are now run-down.

The principal Chinese cities blend, in different amounts, tradition and cosmopolitanism. Although the "barbarian" has always been scorned by the Chinese, the foreigner has been able to leave his mark on China more indelibly than might be supposed in an essentially isolated culture. Especially in absorbing the impact of the West, scars were left.

The provincial cities of China that had less foreign influence tend to be low-built, with little design or plan, and possess at best a historic center formerly contained within high city walls. The heart of such cities is generally divided between the area around the railway station and a central market. The Chinese practice is to congregate similar shops and businesses and to have entire streets (Silk Street, Jade Street) devoted to a single activity.

Historically the distinctive feature of provincial cities and the large district towns was the high city walls, each broken only with huge gates closed each evening and guarded from above by towers in which a company of men could be stationed. The walls of the small towns were generally straight and brick faced, broken only at the top with ramparts; such walls averaged from forty to sixty feet in height and were about twenty feet wide at the top. In the large towns the walls were higher, reaching in some cases nearly a hundred feet, and had battlements crenellated so that the troops at the top could cover all possible angles of fire. The tops of such walls were as wide as modern two-lane roads. The rectangular lines of the walls tended to give an orderly pattern to the streets of the towns. Even now, many streets in provincial and district towns are unpaved. Except where shops open onto them, most streets are lined by the walls of private residences, government offices, and other establishments.

Throughout China rural life centers around villages — not isolated farmhouses. Farmers must travel to their fields, starting the day early but usually ending it with a long period of chatting with neighbors. The men often bring their chopsticks and bowls of noodles out to the roadside where, squatting together in groups, they have their evening meal.

In physical appearance Chinese villages are remarkably similar regardless of the region they are in. However, in south China the houses are slightly more crowded together, and there is more use of bamboo and straw in the construction. In north China the walls tend to be higher, and construction is of adobe brick. In parts of Manchuria, Hopei, and Shantung, houses are made of baked brick. In all areas villages traditionally had something of public or collective concern, such as a common well, an ancient shade tree, or even a small grove. They also had a tablet or shrine to the local gods or to the ancestors of the dominant clans. If the village was large enough or thought to be auspiciously situated, it might have a temple, usually without priests or monks but possibly with an aging caretaker. Periodically such temples would serve as a marketplace and would be the scene of annual festival celebrations, such as the Autumn Festival on the fifteenth day of the eighth lunar month or the Dragon Boat festival on the fifth day of the fifth month. From time to time, if things were not going well for the village or for individuals in it, villagers would refurbish their (generally dilapidated) clay idols, which originally had been painted in vivid colors and occupied secluded positions of honor in the temple.

Since the arrival of communism the temples have been quite run-down and devoted to secular concerns. Frequently they have become the storehouses for a collective's grain, the administrative center of the commune, or the location of a visiting clinic. Shrines and tablets have been replaced by bulletin boards, which first began to appear in villages during the Kuomintang days and now are ubiquitous wherever people live. Such conversions of temples convey little sense of sacrilege, for in Chinese culture the separation of sacred and secular was never sharp and there was no need for reverence among worshipers.

In northwest China, through parts of Shansi, Shensi, and Kansu, where the loess plains have been eroded by rivers to produce cliff-lined valleys, there are villages of caves. The most famous of these is Yenan, where Mao Tse-tung established his headquarters after the Long March and throughout the years of the Japanese war. In this region cave villages are quite the equal in livability and status to the adobe ones. The caves are usually in a neat line part way up the cliff, well above the high-water line of any floods. Most dwelling units consist of a single cave dug into the rockless, brownish yellow soil, with an arched ceiling from twelve to fifteen feet high, a width of fifteen feet, and a depth of from twenty to thirty feet. The front of the cave is filled in with an adobe brick wall, the frame for the door, and possibly a window or two. At night a wooden door is pulled shut, and during the day the doorway is covered, in the coldest weather by a quilted mat and in summer by a bamboo curtain.

The chambers of the caves tend to be of uniform size, and therefore the only difference in dwelling units is the number of parallel chambers linked together. The largest units might have additional rooms whose doorways connect them to the main chamber, which has the only exit. The secondary rooms, which generally serve as bedrooms and storage rooms, often do not have windows, the front facing the cliff being either entirely filled in with adobe brick or the original wall of the cliff, with the room being dug out through the door to the main cave. If the caves are close to the top of the cliff, they have a chimney drilled through to the surface above, which has to be roofed to prevent seepage. When the caves are at mid-cliff level, the stove pipe comes out through the front wall. Ventilation is generally poor, but the caves are snug in winter and the earth is cool in summer. In adobe and brick houses in the northern part of China there tend to be few windows, and when windows do exist they usually cannot be opened and more often than not are covered with sheets of glued paper rather than glass.

Village life is geared to the rhythms of agriculture, but historically Chinese villages have not been quiet pastoral places. There was enough movement in the fortunes of families to create tensions. Clashes and rivalries between clans were often intense, and since primogeniture did not prevail, hostilities could arise over the division of family holdings. In north China more often than in the south, landlords and tenants had to live as neighbors. The children of rich and poor peasants had the same schooling, but in the past and probably still those who were inclined to command and those who were destined to obey found their respective roles at an early age.

Compared with other underdeveloped countries, China has respectable agricultural technology. In the Chinese countryside animal power is more conspicuous than it is in Southeast Asia, India, and Africa. In north China farmers customarily employ oxen, mules, and donkeys for plowing and for carrying loads. In Manchuria and a few parts of north China the state farms use tractors. In south China plowing of the flooded rice fields is done with water buffalo.

Chinese farmers have long appreciated differences in quality of seeds and the advantages of fertilizers. In the south the pattern of planting is relatively static, but northern farmers rotate their crops and respond quickly to changes in market and weather developments. Above all it is of great historical significance that Chinese farmers were able to keep pace with population growth. They have long understood that they can benefit by working beyond mere self-sufficiency and by producing for larger markets that may be far away.

Indeed, rural China was never just a series of isolated, autonomous villages. Its villages tended to fit together around a marketing center, and the centers in turn were parts of larger regional marketing systems. Such centers moved rice from south to north along the Grand Canal and, after the introduction of the railroads, tied together not only regional grain markets but also the distribution of fresh fruits and vegetables.

Although today it might seem that the Chinese have an inadequate and antiquated system of transportation, in fact they have always, within the limits of their technology, invested enough in transportation to have a fairly complete national network. In modern times the system has been built around roads for animal-drawn carts and the railroads. Little attention has been given to roads for motorized vehicles.

One of the extraordinary historic developments of China is that the "first unifier," Emperor Ch'in Shih Huang-ti, decreed that the axles of all carts should be the same length so that the ruts in the roads throughout the empire would have the same width and thus military transport would have no difficulty reaching every area. In the plains of north China, over the centuries, the carts cut away the soil, encouraging erosion, and many roads have sunk. Heavily loaded carts pulled by as many as four teams of mules can move along such roads and be lost from the sight of a farmer plowing the adjacent fields. The peculiarities of such sunken roadways have had some interesting consequences. They have made ambushing and banditry relatively easy. They pose problems for the passing of carts going in opposite directions and have given rise to the Chinese rule of the road that the lighter loaded cart must give way to the heavier — a principle the Chinese carried over to the motorized era, so that pedestrians must give way to bicycles, bicycles to cars, and cars to trucks. The bigger the vehicle, the more haughty the driver.

China severely lacks paved roads for automobiles and trucks; consequently such vehicles are mainly urban-bound and are used only along a few well established intercity routes. In the 1950's the Chinese claimed only 160,000 miles of usable highways, most of which were of dirt or gravel, and by the end of the 1960's about 225,000 miles of "all weather" roads. Until the Japanese conquest of north China, the road between Peking and Tientsin was unpaved. Because of the problems of flooding in the north, motorized roads tend to be raised, almost dikelike structures. Today the principal means of road freight transport is still big carts pulled by either, and at times both, animals or men. According to Chinese Communist statistics, in 1958 the total amount of highway freight in China was 1,200 million tons, of which only 280 million were carried by motor vehicles.

Modern China is closely tied to the life of the railroad. The most elementary and most commonly recognized test for distinguishing the modern and the traditional parts of China is ascertaining the reach of the railroads. Cities and towns connected by trains have a distinct character that sets them off from the rest of the country.

The railroads did not, however, come to China as a coherent system. On the contrary, and quite different from Ch'in Shih Huang-ti's unified rut system, different sections of China's railroads were capitalized by different sources and thus used different equipment, including different gauges of track. For example, the railroad from Shihchiachuang to Taiyuan was built by French capital. Its *wagon-lits* had French signs and pictures of the Seine and the French Alps, and its narrow, one-meter gauge gave it a miniature appearance. From Shihchiachuang to Peking the railroad used British equipment and a wide gauge. The Chinese Communists have continued to build railroads with different gauges largely because they have encouraged the construction of local lines with narrow gauges. Yet in spite of such technical differences there has been a relatively uniform Chinese culture of the railroads. Railroad stations have tended to be central to Chinese cities. Working on a railroad carries considerable status; hardly a man who has any connection with the railroad is too lowly not to have a uniform.

From the outset Chinese railroads followed the European pattern of providing different classes of passenger service. Most lines had three classes. First class consisted of compartments with seats convertible to berths; second class consisted of less-luxurious compartments; and third class generally had wooden seats and no privacy. The Communists have maintained these class differences, and indeed in upgrading the services for first class they have possibly accentuated them.

Foreigners first pressured the Chinese for rights to build railroads in the 1860's when the Taiping Rebellion was being crushed and when developments in America after the Civil War and in Latin America seemed to set off worldwide interest in the promise of railroads. From the outset the Chinese reacted with caution: Li Hungchang, at the time governor of Kiangsu, rejected a joint British and American request in 1863 to build a railway from Shanghai to Soochow, saying that "railways would only be beneficial to China when undertaken by Chinese themselves and conducted under their management."[3] Chinese officials, without a tradition of eminent domain, immediately sensed the possibly insurmountable problem of building roads through fields dotted with ancestral graves. Nearly three percent of China's arable land was given over to the mounds of graves, for the Chinese did not have separate graveyards but rather buried their dead in their own fields and then built large mounds of earth over the grave, ten to fifteen feet high depending

---

[3]Hosea Ballou Morse, *The International Relations of the Chinese Empire*, 3 (London: Longmans, Green, 1918), p. 74.

upon the importance of the person. Family fields were always marked with grave mounds.

The first railway in China was constructed in 1876 by subterfuge. British authorities claimed that a tramway was being constructed at the edge of the International Settlement in Shanghai, but then a locomotive was brought in. For a little over a month, six times a day the train, loaded with passengers, covered the five miles of track until a pedestrian was killed, under conditions that to the British mind suggested "either extreme dense stupidity or a malicious intention to commit suicide and thereby create a prejudice against railways"[4] — a not untypical example of how the Western mind thought the Eastern mind operated. Probably the unfortunate coolie was merely trying to use the locomotive, as countless later Shanghaiese have used motor cars, to run over the evil spirit he believed was bearing down from behind, and he simply played it too close. In any case, public wrath forced the line to be closed down; Chinese authorities bought the track and the rolling stock and shipped them off to Formosa, where they were never reassembled.

The first successful railroad was a Chinese venture inspired by Tong King-sing, the head of the China Merchants Steam Navigation Company, who wanted to get the coal from the Kailan mines in T'angshan, Hopei, to the seacoast and his ships. An Englishman, C. W. Kinder, was hired to construct the line, and he first laid the tracks and used mules to pull the carts while he went about building a locomotive out of odd parts and scrap iron. In 1881, on the hundredth anniversary of the birth of George Stephenson (the founder of the railroad), Kinder's steam engine went into operation and was christened "Rocket of China."

A few years earlier another English engineer had tried to convince the imperial Chinese authorities that they should engage in railway building only on the basis of a coherent general plan. He submitted such a plan: Hankow was the hub, with trunk lines going east to Shanghai, south to Canton, north to Peking, and west to Szechwan, Yunnan, and Burma, with spur lines connecting Shanghai and Ningpo, Foochow and the interior, Peking and Tientsin and Nanking. Eventually much of the plan was completed, but at the time it was rejected. It provoked a split within Chinese officialdom

---

[4]*Ibid.*, p. 76.

between those who supported an expansion of Kinder's efforts in order to link up Tientsin and eventually Peking with the Great Wall and Manchuria, and those who rejected such military security arguments by saying that railroads that could carry troops north toward Korea could be used by an enemy to go in the opposite direction, toward the capital of the empire. The latter faction pressed for an interior system radiating from Hankow, which was far from the capital.

The imperial court saw merit in both arguments and allowed both to proceed. Li Hung-chang had by then been transferred to the north and strongly supported Kinder's design, and when the line had reached into Manchuria he used his appointment as ambassador-extraordinary to the coronation of Tsar Alexander III to work out a secret agreement bringing Russian capital into the south Manchuria program and to direct Russian construction of the Chinese Eastern rail line across northern Manchuria to Vladivostok. So began the complex schemes whereby European capital, working through special banks and under agreements with the imperial government, competed to build railroads. Money carried influence, though not always decisively. The Russian ambassador sought unsuccessfully to have Kinder removed, "not because he is an Englishman, but because he is not a Russian."

The central China program, and in particular the Peking-Hankow railway, began as a completely Chinese effort in terms of both capital and materials, but eventually foreign capital was sought, first from America and eventually from Belgium. In time, capital and engineers from Britain, France, Germany, and America produced other lines, but control and management of all lines in China proper remained constantly with the Chinese.

By the first decade of the twentieth century the spread of railroads was beginning to significantly alter Chinese society and politics. The traditional system of transportation, involving networks of canals and riverways, could be maintained by local and provincial authorities with limited central direction. Railroad revenues, though collected locally, had to be passed on to the central authorities in order to service the foreign loans that had provided the initial investment. Imperial authorities were thus compelled to penetrate more deeply than ever before into the domain of provincial authorities. In fact, a controversy over precisely this issue of railroad

THE CHINESE LANGUAGE

Mandarin Chinese (Kou-yü) is spoken by more people than any other language in the world. There is greater variety of dialect or "accent" among Mandarin speakers than among English speakers. In addition, there are in China a number of non-Mandarin dialects, such as Cantonese, Hakka, Foochow, and Shanghai, which differ from each other as much as Italian, French, and Spanish do. All Chinese dialects employ the same written characters, so Chinese who cannot speak to each other can still communicate with no difficulty in writing.

Mandarin is essentially monosyllabic; every character is a single syllable. Because certain compounds or pairs of characters do frequently stand for a single word, the language is not strictly monosyllabic. All words end in a vowel or in n, ng, or r (which may be written with the letter h). All Chinese words have a single immutable form; there are no declensions of nouns and conjugations of verbs, for in Chinese grammar there are no distinctions between object and subject, for example, and there are no tenses. "I come today." "I come yesterday." "I come ten minutes": Time must be indicated by a specific qualifier and not by inflectional endings.

Chinese abounds with homonyms. In the spoken language distinctions between words are indicated by tones or musical accents. In Mandarin there are four tones. The first is even; the second is a quickly rising tone similar to English "who?"; the third is a brokenly rising or longer note that dips before rising; and the fourth is a falling tone, much like the last word in an ordinary English sentence. It is necessary to distinguish quite different words merely by their tone; for example, there is chù (pig), chú (bamboo), chǔ (master), and chù (to dwell). The same sound with the same tone can also mean different things. For example, the sound yi in the fourth tone has over ninety characters, all representing different words. Context, sentence structure, and the coupling of words are used to reduce the confusion.

Chinese script was originally ideographic, or picture writing, and not phonographic or according to sound. In the evolution of characters the step beyond the picturing of concrete nouns, such as "man," "sun," and "mouth," involved combining elements of concrete pictures to express abstract concepts. For example, the pictograph for "pig" was placed under that for "roof" to give the character for "house," "home," "family." The character for "good," "right," and "excellent" combined the characters for woman and child. The next step was to use pictographs of concrete nouns to represent abstract words of similar sound. For example, "to come" (pronounced *lai*), being abstract, was hard to depict. However, the word for "barley" was also pronounced *lai,* and thus originally the scribes simply used the pictograph for "barley" whenever they needed to write "to come," confident that anyone who read "king barley" would understand it to mean "king comes."

The development of phonetics meant that characters could be formed with part giving a sense of the sound and part the meaning. For example, the word for "mouth," which is simply written as a small box, is pronounced like the word for "to beat"; because "to beat" is done with the hand, the character for "hand" was combined with that for "mouth" to give the character "to beat."

There are more than forty thousand Chinese characters, but most Chinese literature has used only six or seven thousand, and the knowledge of two or three thousand is enough for general purposes. Hoping to make literacy easier to acquire, the Chinese Communists have sought to simplify the characters.

The strokes used in writing Chinese characters are precise and follow a set order. The art of writing, calligraphy, was a greatly appreciated feature of traditional Chinese culture. There are two basic styles of calligraphy: clear and bold, the equivalent of printed letters in English; and fluid and less legible, the equivalent of cursive writing.

The use of Western alphabets to write Chinese words has produced several systems of "romanization." The most conventional is the Wade-Giles system, and the most recent is a Communist system that uses some modified Russian letters. The Wade-Giles system is complicated by the use of apostrophes after certain consonants to indicate that they should be aspirated. Thus, *p* is pronounced as *b* as in the English *be*, while *p'* is *p* as in *pig;* so Pei-p'ing is pronounced *Beiping*. Similarly *t* is sounded as a *d*, while *t'* is *t* as in *tea;* therefore T'ang sounds as though it begins with a *t*, but Taoism is correctly pronounced as though it begins with a *d*. The Communist system replaces the unaspirated *t* with *d*, the *p* with *b*, and the *k* with *g*.

The Wade-Giles system has other peculiarities. One is the use of *j* for a sound much like *r*, and another is the use of the ending *-ih* for the sound *-er*. For example, the official organ of the Chinese Communist Party, the *People's Daily,* is written *Jen-min Jih-pao* in Wade-Giles but pronounced "Ren-min Rer-bao." Another complication in Wade-Giles is the distinction between *sh* and *hs:* *sh* is sounded like *sh* in *shore; hs* is like *sh* in *she.*

With respect to vowels it is important to note that *a* is an *ah* sound. Therefore Wang sounds like Wong, and T'ang is like Tong and neither rhymes with the English "sang." The vowel *o* is approximately the same as the English *aw* in *saw; u* is an *oo* sound as in *food; ü* has no English equivalent but is close to the French *u.*

Because Chinese has so few sounds, correct pronunciation of the most common words is not difficult to learn.

revenues was the catalyst for the 1911 revolution, which overthrew the Manchu (Ch'ing) dynasty and brought the Republic.

Although the railroads brought change to China and their network of tracks has tended to hold the country together, there is a danger in exaggerating the significance of any form of transportation for China. The English observer Dick Wilson reported after a visit to Peking, "The sole railway station and only airport of the city for which these 700 million people are administered had respectively, in 1964, two trains and one international flight leaving every day."[5] Indeed, civilian air transportation is still exceedingly limited. In 1967 China had four British Viscounts and nine Soviet Ilyushin-18's, plus an assortment of older Soviet models and their own plane, the AN-2, which is a biplane.

China is not geographically homogeneous, as we have seen. Diversity abounds, the pulls of regionalism are real, and national institutions, aside from government, hardly exist. Yet China is a cultural entity. The diversities of language and dialect that separate northerners from southerners and southerners from each other are as great as the divisions of European tongues, yet the Chinese have held together. Behind the physical realities of China lies a deeper reality, that of Chinese tradition, an extraordinary tradition that con-

---

[5]Dick Wilson, "Where China Stands Now: An Introduction," in *China After the Cultural Revolution: A Selection from the Bulletin of the Atomic Scientists* (New York: Vantage Books, 1970), pp. 6–7.

tinues to provide a sense of national unity for China's massive population.

The physical differences of China have precluded the development of a homogeneous culture. The wheat-growing peoples of the arid north and the rice-growing peoples of the semi-tropical south follow quite different life styles. The key to their sense of common identity has been the existence, at times quite fragile, of a superior culture, a great tradition, which has been spread throughout the land largely through the requirements of government and has provided a thin bond of cohesion for otherwise parochial peoples. At one time the bond consisted of the mandarinate and all the literary and artistic and artisan traditions that went with the Confucian order. Now it is communism and the Maoist order.

The fundamental story of China is about how all the diversities of a continental society have been kept in check but have also challenged the authority of unifying forces, first of Confucianism and then of communism. The drama has intensified because the problems of modernization have increased the strains and posed perplexing questions about how China should take its rightful place in the modern world. With this sense of the physical reality of China, we are ready to consider the Confucian tradition.

CHAPTER THREE

The Confucian Tradition

For over two thousand years, without interruption, the evolving Chinese civilization was shaped by a distinctive political system and based on a humanistic ideology. Beginning half a millennium before Christ and extending into the twentieth century, the Chinese functioned within a social and institutional framework that was the most enduring and stable in history. In the world of traditional societies, Chinese civilization ranks at the forefront in enlightenment and sophistication, in artistic achievement and ethical sensitivity, and above all in the imaginative development of the arts of government and the harmonious conduct of social life.

The stability and success of the traditional Chinese order stemmed from the preeminent place the Chinese gave to a remarkable ideology — Confucianism. Confucianism was remarkable because it was secular and was considered valid and appropriate for the problems of everyone, whether emperor, bureaucrat, gentry, or ordinary subject. It spoke to authority and for the common concerns of all who, like fathers, must look after their children. Other societies have in their time been bound together by the authoritative hold of religious beliefs. Indeed the grip of custom throughout most of the traditional world was stiffened by an awe for divine authority that was never far removed from temporal authority. China is unique because its social order was based on a secular ideology. Although the emperor was called upon to perform critical rituals of a religious character and his rule was identified with the Will of Heaven, the government set humane and decent standards and acted according to ethical principles based on learning rather than on divine revelation.

It is hard to say why the Chinese were inclined to give up the advantages for ruling inherent in the principle that the ruler's will, whether just or unjust, is coequal with divine authority. For unexplainable reasons the Chinese, as early as the first millennium before Christ, during the Chou dynasty, developed a consciousness about government and began to ask what the ideal form of the state would be. The fact that so early the Chinese had thinkers who articulated a sense of social malaise and proposed tactical and strategic ways for altering conditions made them unique among ancient peoples.

At an early stage in their history, the Chinese also abandoned the traditions of an aristocracy based on birth and invented the great principle that those who manage government should do so because of merit and individual attainment in competitive examinations. In developing, by the second century before Christ, the great technique of bureaucratic rule by men of superior education, the Chinese created a form of centralized government that the West was not to use until the nineteenth century.

According to the Confucian ideal, government is the core of civilization. For the Chinese the most exalted task for mankind was the devising of proper and just government. They were concerned not only with the problems of rulers; their ideal also involved a sense of cultural and political unity for all members of their civilization. The result was an early and powerfully enduring sense of cultural identity and a profound sense of the unity and greatness of the Chinese people.

The Chinese people's sense of greatness was historically justified not merely because of their cultural and material superiority to all their neighbors in Asia but also because they were constantly reminded by their dealings with non-Chinese that they were unique in holding to the principle that government was basically a matter of ethics. While others believed in gods or sought the advantages of crude power, the Chinese thought of government as a moral force and suggested that princes should rule by example through the force of their superior moral conduct.

The Confucian tradition also linked government to scholarship. The Chinese early developed a profound faith in education and held that human nature could be perfected. Running throughout Chinese civilization has been the ideal that all individuals ought to perfect themselves, find virtue in performing their allotted roles, and contribute to the general good. Whenever the Chinese have sensed that all is not right with the collective state of affairs, thay have reacted by believing that their troubles may be overcome if everyone will try to improve his conduct, work harder at achieving cultural ideals, and conduct himself more properly in his relations with others. This tradition has outlasted the Confucian era and has been constantly appealed to by both Chiang Kai-shek and Mao Tse-tung in seeking to motivate modern Chinese.

Although the Confucian ideals favored an elitist view that stressed the responsibilities of rulers, Chinese civilization also gave to its members a belief that virtue and merit will be rewarded and that hard work and striving for achievement provide the proper approach to life. Thus the Confucian emphasis upon stability and order was tempered by an insistence that, ideally, those who held superior positions should have worked to obtain their advantages and should subsequently display more merit and more virtue than those beneath them.

The Confucian ideal was eminently appropriate for an agrarian society but was detrimental to the development of commerce and industry. Eventually the Confucian tradition of distrust for all that might unsettle the agricultural order worked against the Chinese in their confrontation with the modern industrial and technologically oriented West. In the weighing of history, however, this final failure of the Confucian system should not obscure the remarkable greatness of China's polity in comparison with that of other traditional systems.

THE BEGINNING OF CHINESE CIVILIZATION

Chinese civilization originated in the Yellow River valley, first spread through north and east China, and only gradually extended into the southern regions. Substantiated Chinese history begins about 1500 B.C. with the Shang dynasty. The history of the earlier Hsia dynasty is based more on legend than on fact. Archeologists have been able to reconstruct much of the Shang culture through excavations and the analysis of "oracle bones," which had been used for divination. Questions scratched on the bones are an early version of the Chinese script. The bones were heated and the cracks that formed were "read" to give answers to the questions. Shang society

CHRONOLOGICAL CHART

Principal Dynasties		Western Developments	
c. 2000 B.C.	HSIA		
		CRETE	c. 3000–1400 B.C.
c. 1500	SHANG		
1122 (?)	CHOU		
	Feudal states		
	Confucius		
	Taoist school		
	Legalist school		
	Warring states		
		GREECE REACHED ITS GREATEST HEIGHT	c. 500–300
211	CH'IN		
206	HAN		
	Centralized rule		
	End of feudalism		
	Establishment of Confucianism		
		ROME AT GREATEST PERIOD	100's
A.D. 222	SIX DYNASTY PERIOD		
		FALL OF ROME	A.D. 476
589	SUI		
618	T'ANG		
	Bureaucracy		
	Examination system		
		CHARLEMAGNE	800
907	SUNG		
		CRUSADES	1096–1291
1127	SOUTHERN SUNG		
	Neo-Confucianism		
1278	YUAN		
	Conquests of Genghis Khan and Kubla Khan		
		RENAISSANCE	1300
1368	MING		
	Model Chinese period		
		REFORMATION	1517
		THIRTY YEARS WAR	1618–1648
1644	CH'ING		
1912	REPUBLIC		
1949	COMMUNISTS		

was agricultural; it had a dominant ruler or emperor and a class of feudal nobles. The most striking feature of Shang culture was the creation of magnificent bronzes. Shang craftsmen developed techniques of bronze casting that exceeded anything in Europe until the time of the Renaissance.

The Shang dynasty fell in 1122 B.C. to the conquering Chou ruler who emerged in the northwest and established a dynasty that lasted until 211 B.C. The Chou conquest did not bring about a sharp break in social organization. The feudal aristocracy continued, and the Chou emperor could not effectively control his vassal lords, whose domains eventually became semi-autonomous kingdoms and city-states.

In reaction to the decline of the Chou and the rise of aggressive competition among the kingdoms, the Chinese experienced a great awakening about the need to question what constitutes proper government. The philosophical awakening in the later years of the Chou dynasty, during the era of the "contending states," was marked by such self-awareness that the Chinese spoke about having "one hundred contending schools" — the phenomenon Mao Tse-tung referred to when he used the metaphor about allowing "one hundred flowers" to grow and contend. The Chinese mood was one of deep disquiet that there should be such confusion and uncertainty about the political order. The emergence of the Chinese reliance upon ideology came in response to what seemed to be basic disorder. The authority of the Chou emperor had declined, and at the same time numerous city-states and petty kingdoms had emerged with separate rulers.

Western historians might view the period as unexceptional because it seems to be characterized by princes seeking security through diplomacy and alliances and generally participating in a competitive multistate system. The Chinese, however, thought there was something improper in such an unruly scheme of things, and wisemen and prophets emerged to express their deep feelings of dissatisfaction and suggest different routes to a better set of arrangements. The intellectual and ideological differences were great and the arguments were subtle. In the end, however, three principal views emerged about how Chinese, or rather Chou, society could escape its difficulties: the Confucian, the Taoist, and the Legalist schools.

According to the Confucian school, which ultimately dominated China, society was in disarray because standards had deteriorated and people were not living up to their highest ideals. All would be improved if each person would work more conscientiously to fulfill his historic role in society. The ideal state of affairs that had once existed could be restored by the use of moral persuasion to make everyone be on his best behavior. Confucianists reasoned that if each individual were perfect in his behavior, society as a whole would likewise be perfect.

The Taoists called for almost the exact opposite course of action. They rejected the Confucian view that society was in trouble because standards had declined and suggested instead that the basic trouble lay in the concept of standards. The fundamental problem was that society had become too artificial. They thought the Confucianists were introducing artificiality into life and were working against the Taoist ideal of harmony with nature. According to the Taoists, people should ignore the ethics and etiquette that the Confucianists preached and seek only to come to terms with nature, to become one with the natural forces of the universe. The Taoists contended that it was quite easy to deal with the Confucian problem of how to reduce evil and increase virtue. All that had to be done was to lower standards for defining virtue, and immediately there would be an increase in virtue and a decline in sin. Since for the Taoists all was relative, they insisted that the Confucianists were increasing the amount of evil in the world by attempting to raise standards for defining virtue.

The response of the Legalist school was that the others were champions of nonsense and that the only way to deal with a disintegrating and confused social order was to rely upon the powers of law. The Legalists argued that the problems of the day could be readily swept away if the ruler would establish clear and unambiguous laws and strictly enforce them. When people saw that violation of the laws would be dealt with severely, they would quickly and quite naturally change their behavior, thus ensuring a tranquil and orderly society. The laws could be quite arbitrary; indeed, there was a certain advantage in making laws arbitrary, for the people would constantly be reminded that power ultimately rested with the state and not with their personal notions of what was just and reasonable.

In the confusion at the end of the Chou dynasty, the Legalists triumphed. In the longer flow of Chinese history, the Confucianists became the champions of orthodoxy. The Taoists persisted, however, and provided a vital ingredient to Chinese popular thought and an escape valve for officials and bureaucrats who needed some balance to the heavy and unsubtle moralism of Confucianism.

THE SHORT VICTORY OF THE LEGALISTS

The _Fa Chia_, or Legalist school, made its great but brief contribution to Chinese institutional development when Shang Yang, Lord Shang, became prime minister in the state of Ch'in and set about putting into practice the theories of Han Fei-tzu. Lord Shang convinced his ruler Ch'in Shih Huang-ti that he would be able to reunite China and establish a centralized dynasty if he would commit all his powers to a rule of law based not upon moral law or justice but on state fiat. The combination of Ch'in Shih Huang-ti's military prowess and his reliance upon the uncompromising legalism of Lord Shang was successful, and China was united in 221 B.C. under its first great centralizing emperor, who initiated the practices that were to evolve into bureaucratic rule.

In establishing his capital at Hsien Yang on the Wei River near present-day Sian in Shensi province, the "Great Unifier," Ch'in Shih Huang-ti, gave a sense of physical grandeur to his rule, which was continued by all succeeding emperors. His palaces were not as densely concentrated or grand in size as those of later dynasties, but they did extend over twenty-five miles and all the connecting roads and paths were covered against rain. Ch'in Shih Huang-ti, particularly as he got older, was obsessed with fear of assassination and the idea of death. He never slept on consecutive nights in the same chamber or with the same woman. He insisted that the most influential people in the empire maintain residences at the capital so that they could be kept under surveillance while participating in a ceaseless round of parties and extravagant social life.

To his great credit, Ch'in Shih Huang-ti established numerous lasting features of Chinese civilization. He is credited with standardizing weights and measures. He introduced the concept of a uniform currency, contributed to the building of the Great Wall, established a set of written characters, and standardized the length of axles on carts.

A major accomplishment of the Ch'in regime was the destruction of the feudal aristocracy of ancient China. Out of the Legalist philosophy, Ch'in Shih Huang-ti derived the idea that he should abandon the practice of rewarding loyal lieutenants with holdings of land that they and their families might hold in perpetuity. Lord Shang impressed upon him the dangers of such a policy, which would create within the empire self-contained power centers, each with its own resource base. Lord Shang suggested that loyal officers be given territories to govern, not to own, and that they should continue in office only so long as their behavior was consistent with the emperor's wishes and the rule of law.

In this unique way, feudalism, as a system of hereditary local rulers, based on a combination of independent estates and loyalty to the emperor, was abolished in China because of military rationale and legalistic demands — two elements of the Chinese tradition that Confucianists always thought to be of secondary importance. Elsewhere in the world the forces that eliminated feudalism, such as an emergent commercial class and the strength of kings, dominated the next phase of their societies' history. Not so in China, for the causes of the elimination of feudalism were soon replaced by the new institutions of bureaucratic government.

The Legalists failed to survive the death of Ch'in Shih Huang-ti. In no small part this was because Lord Shang had been excessively vigorous in pressing Han Fei-tzu's doctrine that all, including emperor and ministers, should be equally obedient to the law. He had, it turned out, offended the emperor's son, so when the latter succeeded his father, he quickly put Lord Shang to death. The dynasty could not long survive this double loss, and it was succeeded by a brief period of conflict during which the previously deposed feudal lords sought to reassert themselves. The idea of a unified empire had, however, been effectively established in the Chinese mind, and therefore the issue during the interregnum after the fall of Ch'in was who would be the man to establish the next dynasty.

Eventually the struggle became one between the colorful, romantic Hsiang Yü, who represented a revival of feudal traditions, and the cautious, doughty Liu Pang, who had a peasant background and mobilized a massive army of commoners. Although Hsiang Yü and his dashing knights won battle after battle, they failed in the campaign and could not consolidate political power. Liu Pang, on establishing the Han dynasty, had to turn to others for advice and assistance, and he soon discovered the usefulness of those who had sustained the traditions of Confucius, Mencius, Hsün Tzu, and others of the same scholarly and ethical persuasions. The stage was thus set for the emergence, under an emperor of peasant origins, of a government of gentlemen and scholars who were quick to develop both a bureaucratic tradition and the concept of an orthodox ideology.

China became a powerful empire during the Han dynasty, which lasted from 206 B.C. to A.D. 222. The institutions of Chinese imperial rule evolved, and China expanded its empire, particularly to the north and west, and engaged in extensive foreign trade through central Asia. During this period Confucianism became the state ideology, and the traditions of Chinese scholarship that provided the basis for the remarkable examination system for recruiting officials were established.

CONFUCIANISM: THE ETHIC
OF MORALISTIC GENTLEMEN

Although eventually Confucianism became the essence of Chinese civilization, it was almost obliterated before it had a chance to shape Chinese institutions. Ch'in Shih Huang-ti sought with all his autocratic vigor to destroy the emerging Confucian tradition once he had conquered the Chou. He went so far as to declare that all the scholars' books should be burned. Yet clearly the words and sentiments of Confucius spoke to the majority of thinking Chinese. Indeed, the unsystematic but pithy statements of a relatively obscure and modestly successful scholar-official of Lu, one of the smallest and least significant Chinese states under the Chou dynasty, became one of the most influential doctrines of human history.

Strangely little is known about the man Confucius, who lived, according to tradition, from 551 to 479 B.C. What is known is wrapped in myth, for later generations sought to give him a divine dimension. It is generally believed that he was brought up by a domineering mother who wanted him to rise above his deceased father, a low official. Another interpretation, however, is repeated by Fei Hsiao-t'ung: "Confucius' origins were quite doubtful. He was said to be the child of an illegitimate union. His mother would not tell him where his father's tomb was, and only when his mother died did he learn from someone else where his father was buried so that he could bury his mother also in that spot."[1] Both versions provide an interesting psychological background for speculating about the man who made ancestor worship and filial piety the keystones of Chinese civilization.

In addition to stressing the vital importance of the family for society, Confucius concentrated on the arts of government. Yet his personal record of governmental performance was unimpressive. After he left the service of the ruler of Lu, he wandered about from state to state seeking employment as an adviser to local rulers. In his travels he attracted a following of disciples who transcribed what are believed to be his sayings. Possibly the fate of Confucianism was determined by Mencius, a later disciple also from the state of Lu, who lived from 373 to 288 B.C. and who also had a determined mother. He too wandered from state to state, preaching good government, seeking to advise rulers, and helping to establish the legitimacy of Confucian doctrines. After Mencius came Hsün Tzu, who also taught that education was the basis of good government. But, unlike Mencius, who believed man to be inherently good and only needing exposure to education to bring out latent virtues, Hsün Tzu believed man to be inherently bad and needing education to tame his immoral and violent qualities.

Early Confucianism was a humanistic and pragmatic moral system. It dealt with worldly problems and assumed that its powers of persuasion rested entirely upon its self-evident reasonableness. Over the centuries and especially after the appearance of Buddhism during the T'ang dynasty (A.D. 618–907), when the Chinese learned more about sophisticated metaphysical systems, Confucianism became more than just an ethical system, especially during the Sung dynasty (1127–1279), when neo-Confucianism emerged.

Both early Confucianism and neo-Confucianism were less im-

---

[1]Fei Hsiao-t'ung, *China's Gentry* (Chicago: University of Chicago Press, 1953), p. 38. Copyright 1953 by The University of Chicago.

pressive as formal philosophical systems than as guides for elite behavior. Confucianism was a powerful force in shaping attitudes and giving a common orientation to generations of leaders, but it was not a vigorous or elegantly logical system of thought. In a sense, the starting point of Confucianism was the requirement for proper philosophical definitions before discussion and action could begin. The Confucianists argued that trouble in human affairs began whenever there was confusion over the definition of roles. Thus the first step toward good government and the realization of a harmonious society was for each person to know his role and perform it well according to the strictest interpretation of that role. Confucianism identified five key role relationships — between ruler and subject, neighbor and neighbor, father and son, husband and wife, and brother and brother. If everyone involved in any of these roles adhered to the highest standards for that role, the country as a whole would achieve a condition of collective perfection.

The stress on the achievement of perfection in role relationships, rather than the search for individual salvation or self-realization, gave to Confucianism and to Chinese culture its distinctive emphasis on human and social relationships, at some expense to the individual and his autonomy. Confucianism taught that people should be sensitive to what others thought of their behavior, that they should seek always to act with an eye to how others might respond and above all never be shameless but rather be constantly anxious to do the right thing.

Confucianism treated man as a social being whose identity is determined by where he stands in relation to others in the web of social relations. Each individual had his unique place in the total scheme, and each individual's behavior differed according to his station and according to the particular person with whom he was dealing. An elder brother had responsibilities different from those of a younger brother, and one's manner toward an individual changed according to whether the other person was older or younger, a stranger or a member of one's community.

The importance of correct behavior was related to the need for education and the imperative of sincerity. Confucianists assumed that people naturally crave to do right and will spontaneously seek education and guidance in how to find the Way or the correct path of the upright man. By the same token, they assumed that people will inevitably act in the wrong way if they are not properly trained. Thus whether one took the view that men are inherently good or basically evil, the absolute importance of education was stressed. This carried with it the corollary that educated men are inherently superior to the uneducated, and therefore that rulers and governors should be educated.

The key to correct behavior was sincerity, but the Confucian concept of sincerity had nothing to do with spontaneity or open good-heartedness. Confucianists believed that what keeps people behaving properly is their inner sense of sincerity. The test of whether one was sincere was one's willingness to pay the price of practicing good manners. The sincere man obeyed absolutely all the requirements of proper etiquette. Bad or crude behavior suggested a lack of sincerity.

Partly as a reaction to the earlier, Legalist, views and partly as a logical extension of their own views, the Confucianists argued that officials should be allowed considerable freedom and that as long as they displayed sincerity their small faults could be condoned. Toleration and understanding of anyone who was sincere led to an easy acceptance of corruption in government. By assuming that officials desired to act correctly and by refusing to be arbitrary or harsh about their behavior, the Confucian tradition arrived at the practice of describing in abstract terms the qualities of the perfect official while tolerating in practice considerable personal corruption.

Confucianism thus raised the issue, which still appears in Maoism, of whether the actual performance or the inner spirit of officials is more important in perfecting government. Neither Confucianist nor Maoist has believed that objective measures of behavior should be the sole basis for evaluating the worth of officials, and both have stressed the importance of the inner state of mind and spirit. In both ideologies the criterion for the sincerity of the inner person has been correct behavior rather than effectiveness or efficiency. Neither the Confucianists nor the Maoists have stressed efficiency of goal attainment over perfection of the inner man.

Correct behavior was closely associated with five Confucian virtues — goodness or benevolent compassion (*jen*), righteousness (*i*), propriety (*li*), wisdom (*chih*), and faithfulness (*hsin*). Confucian scholarship was an endless process of discussing all the possible meanings and connotations of these and other words, such as virtue (*te*), filial piety (*hsiao*), princely or superior man (*chün-tzu*), and of course sincerity (*ch'eng*). Over the centuries the meanings of these terms have changed. For example, in earliest times *jen* was identified with the notion of free man, in contrast with *min* or subject, but in time *jen* became associated with gentlemen and thus with benevolence and goodness. (In modern times, and particularly with the establishment of the Republic, *min* became the word for citizen — a reflection of the positive concepts of nationalism and people's democracy.)

Much of early Confucianism dealt with what were presumed to be the official problems of government. In the main, these were questions of the proper behavior of rulers, the correct rituals or manners for all situations, and the correct moral perspective for officials. The Confucian assumption was that if rulers and officials behave in a model way, all who are exposed to them will act with equal propriety. Personal behavior was considered decisive in public events.

The belief that emperors and fathers could rule by example gave to the Chinese the view that virtue and any public manifestation of virtue result in power. Contrary to the Western view of the conflict between morality and power, the Confucian idea was that goodness produces power. To show a concern with moral issues suggested that one had power. Rule by example also encouraged the view that superior people were obliged to strive for virtue (*te*) and could expect deference from all who recognized this virtue.

Neo-Confucianism incorporated mystical concepts from early pre-Confucian texts and religious formulations from Taoism and Buddhism. The increasing complexity of Confucianism called for more authoritative interpretations, resulting in the rigid orthodoxy that came to dominate Chinese thought from Sung times down to the Western impact. Neo-Confucian orthodoxy led to the identification of sacred texts, and the Four Books and the Five Classics became the basis of all education and of the examination system. This stultification of knowledge produced the classical Chinese concept of the "eight-legged essay" which was required in many examination answers. It was thought that all subjects were best dealt with as eight points; every idea introduced called for a balancing opposite idea; and sentences should alternate between being four and six characters long.

THE MATURE TRADITION
AND HIGH SCHOLARSHIP

After the fall of the Han dynasty in A.D. 220, China experienced a prolonged interregnum, lasting more than three and a half centuries. A series of local dynasties rose and fell in north and south China, central government disappeared, and nomadic bands (called "barbarians" by the Chinese) of central Asia penetrated the agricultural domains of the north. The lack of central authority left the country open to outside influences, the most prominent of which was Buddhism, rapidly introduced from India. Chinese monks traveled overland to the subcontinent to bring back sacred texts, and some of the local "emperors" accepted Buddhism as their dynastic religion.

The reunification of China followed the pattern of a short dynasty being succeeded by a great one, as the Ch'in was followed by the Han. In A.D. 589 the Sui dynasty was established, but in 618 it fell and was replaced by the T'ang, which lasted until 907. The Sui emperor established an examination system and sought administratively to extend central control to the local level by dividing the provinces into districts (*chou*) and counties (*hsien*), divisions that persisted into modern times.

The T'ang was a high point of Chinese culture. Reunification and peace brought a flourishing of commerce and a growth of urban culture. The T'ang was the last dynasty to have its capital in the Wei valley in the northwest. In the realm of government the T'ang was notable for giving China a codified legal system and the most formal ordering of the bureaucracy. When Japan and Korea sought to adopt Chinese institutions, their model was the T'ang system. During the period came the development of a form of lyric poetry called *shih*, which stressed a mood of tranquility and remembrance of pleasures, in contrast to *fu*, the didactic poetry of the Han period. T'ang military conquests carried Chinese civilization toward the southwest.

The high point of the T'ang was the reign of Hsüan Tsung (712–756), during which the court in Ch'angan (present-day Sian in Shensi) became the center of scholarship, art, music, and high cultural style. At the same time, however, court intrigues became intense; the emperor became involved in scandals, especially when he took his son's wife Yang Kuei-fei, the most famous courtesan in Chinese history, as his favorite. Intrigues led to revolts. In the meantime the military commanders on the frontiers had become semiautonomous; they had established alliances with the Turkish frontier people whom they were supposedly opposing. By the T'ang period Chinese traditions and institutions were firmly formed and would change little until the end of the imperial system in 1911.

The half century after the fall of the T'ang, called the Five Dynasties period by the Chinese, saw a series of petty states struggling for power. During the Sung period (960–1279) there were additional innovations in philosophy and the arts, and neo-Confucianism with its metaphysical dimensions developed. Printing became widespread, and great numbers of historical writings and encyclopedic compilations were produced. Artistically the dynasty was most notable for advances in landscape painting and the production of porcelains — especially celadon and figured white porcelains — and the rough brown *tien-mu* ware.

By the end of the Sung the Confucian tradition was so firmly entrenched in Chinese life that even when alien rulers from central Asia and later Manchuria conquered China, they could bring little change to Chinese society and in fact had to accommodate themselves to Confucian institutions and ideals in ruling the Chinese. Evidence of the remarkable strength of the Confucian system is shown by the fact that during the 632 years from the fall of the Sung to the fall of the Ch'ing dynasty in 1911, the Chinese controlled their own empire for only 276 years; yet because the alien dynasties had to employ Chinese scholar-officials, there was little basic change in the Confucian tradition.

The vitality of the scholar-official class in China stemmed from the cultural ideals they embodied from generation to generation. Their commitment was to a moral view of power, to a personal search for artistic sensitivity, and to intellectual excellence in a highly disciplined form of scholarship.

In some respects, Confucian scholarship resembled medieval European scholasticism, except that the Chinese worked with a far larger body of literature. In addition to the Four Books and the Five Classics, which might be compared to the New Testament, and eight other classics, which in a less accurate analogy could be thought of as the Old Testament, the traditional Chinese library contained several other categories. A feeling for the volume of Chinese literature can be gained from noting that one of these categories consisted of the *lei shu*, or encyclopedias, which reached huge proportions and consisted mainly of selections from other books rather than original articles. The *Yung Lo Ta Tien*, which was not strictly an encyclopedia, was compiled in the Ming dynasty (1368–1644) and ran to nearly twelve thousand volumes; because of the cost only three sets were produced. During the Ch'ing dynasty (1644–1911) under Emperor Ch'ien Lung, scholars compiled the *Ssu K'u Ch'üan Shu*, which sought to reproduce or excerpt all books of the time and was followed by an annotated bibliography that included more titles than had been published in the entire Western world up to that date (about the time of the American Revolution).

During the Sung dynasty the neo-Confucianists sought to "canonize" certain texts as works that had a particularly close relationship with the Master. The Four Books, which consisted of the *Analects or Sayings of Confucius (Lun Yü), Great Learning (Ta Hsüeh), Doctrine of the Mean (Chung Yung),* and *Mencius,* did have a somewhat closer association with the spirit of early Confucianism. The Five Classics reached back earlier into history and brought to Confucianism an element of mysticism. The five were *Book of Changes (I-Ching), Book of History (Shu Ching), Book of Poetry (Shih Ching), Book of Rites (Li Chi,* of which the *Ta Hsüeh* and the *Chung Yung* of the Four Books were parts), and *Spring and Autumn Annals (Ch'un Ch'iu).*

The *Analects* is presumably the sayings of Confucius transcribed as he discussed problems of good governance with his disciples. Much of it, however, includes statements about the Master's views as well as his sayings. The style of *Mencius* is much the same, using the device of disciples or straight men asking questions or making incorrect statements to set the stage for Mencius' wise responses.

Great Learning and *Doctrine of the Mean* were two parts of the *Book of Rites* that Confucius had supposedly identified as being the most significant. The first is a rather brief text filled with Chinese aphorisms and sequential reasoning. For example:

> What a man dislikes in a superior, let him not display in the treatment of his inferiors; what he dislikes in inferiors, let him not display in the service of his superiors.

When the ruler, as a father, a son and a brother, is a model, then the people imitate him.

Let the producers be many and the consumers few. Let there be activity in the production and economy in the expenditure. Then the wealth will always be sufficient.

Great Learning also contains a classic example of Confucian logic:

The ancients who wished to illustrate illustrious virtue throughout the kingdom, first ordered well their own states. Wishing to order well their states, they first regulated their families. Wishing to regulate their families, they first cultivated their persons. Wishing to cultivate their persons, they first rectified their hearts. Wishing to rectify their hearts, they first sought to be sincere in their thoughts. Wishing to be sincere in their thoughts, they first extended to the utmost their knowledge. Such extension of knowledge lay in the investigation of things.

Things being investigated, knowledge became complete. Their knowledge being complete, their thoughts were sincere. Their thoughts being sincere, their hearts were then rectified. Their hearts being rectified, their persons were cultivated. Their persons being cultivated, their families were regulated. Their families being regulated, their states were rightly governed, the whole kingdom was made tranquil and happy.

The *Doctrine of the Mean* stresses the great Confucian and traditional Chinese value of harmony. It was attributed to the grandson of Confucius and could be seen as an effort to reconcile Mencius' concept of the inherent goodness of men with Hsun Tzu's skepticism. For example:

When we have intelligence resulting from sincerity, this condition is to be ascribed to nature; when we have sincerity resulting from intelligence, this condition is to be ascribed to instruction. But given the sincerity and there shall be the intelligence; given the intelligence, and there shall be the sincerity.

Much of the rest of the *Book of Rites* is given over to instructions about ceremonial behavior, including, for example, how one should hold the bow and finger the arrow while engaged in the gentlemanly art of shooting. The *Book of History* was supposedly edited by Confucius and therefore was profoundly important. It is in fact an odd collection of speeches, oaths, rituals, and observations of how rituals were more precisely performed in earlier ages. *Spring and Autumn Annals,* which was also attributed to Confucius, deals with affairs in the state of Lu from 722 to 481 B.C. and makes observations about how rites and rituals were performed, the conduct of officials and sacrifices they performed, and their manners in various relationships. It lists numerous historical events, ranging from diplomatic meetings to natural phenomena such as eclipses and the birth of two-headed lambs. Confucian scholars did not have an easy time figuring out what to make of such a collection, and since they had to assume that Confucius would never have wasted his time with trivial and irrelevant matters, they produced the *Commentary (Tso Chuan),* which sought to interpret the deeper meanings of *Spring and Autumn Annals* but goes off in enough directions of its own that it seems to have been written independently of any interest in *Spring and Autumn Annals,* and it certainly can be read without reference to it.

The *Book of Poetry* also caused great trouble for the later moralistic Confucian scholars, who felt that because the Master had read and commented on it, it must have meaning deeper than its obvious rustic simplicity. In a sense it occupies a place comparable to the Song of Solomon in the Bible. The poems are early folk verses that were popularly sung before the days of Confucian moralizing, and generally they describe boys and girls frolicking and playing erotically in the spring and at harvest time.

The *Book of Changes,* a mystical text dealing with divination and the forces of destiny, was an early work, elevated to classical status in later periods. Its key feature is the *pa kua,* or eight trigrams, that since earliest history have been used by Chinese fortune-tellers. Another classic was *Erh Ya,* an early dictionary, which seeks to explain the obscurities of the *Book of Changes* and the *Book of Rites* but, like the *Commentary,* seems only to muddy the waters.

In identifying the literature that shaped the Confucian mind, mention should be made of the *Book of Filial Piety (Hsiao Ching),* upon which countless generations of Chinese children have been raised and which taught them that others with parents far worse than their own had displayed exemplary behavior toward these awful parents.

Another dimension of the Chinese scholarly tradition was the writing of history, which produced above all the *Standard Histories*

(*Cheng Shih*). These cover twenty-six dynasties. The first history, *Historical Records* (*Shih Chi*), deals with the pre-Han and early Han periods, and the last covers the Ch'ing and was completed in T'aipei in 1961. The tradition was established by a father and son combination of Ssu-ma T'an and Ssu-ma Ch'ien, who wrote the *Shih Chi*. The son in particular, who took over after his father's death, set the style of straightforward, unambiguous, terse statements with a minimum of moralizing.

The pattern of the *Standard Histories* was clear-cut. Each history was written by the court historians of the succeeding dynasty; each describes the dynasty beginning in glory and ending in disgrace as its successor rightfully takes over the Mandate of Heaven. The *Standard Histories* is in four parts: annals, tables, treatises, and biographies. The annals follow very much the style and content of the *Spring and Autumn Annals*. The chronology was often incomplete, and considerable attention was given to natural events. The tables are a compilation of genealogies (which unfortunately record only the eldest son and are therefore of no help in providing demographic statistics) and lists of who held what office at what time. The treatises are essays on a wide range of subjects. They include significant imperial documents (the Chinese called such official papers "memorials"), impressive imperial decrees, as well as dissertations on foreign travels, calendars, rituals, music, administration, punishments, and other topics relating to state affairs. The subjects are generally interesting, but often the essays turn out to be lists of names and identifications of little substantive value.

The final section of the *Standard Histories*, biographies, are generally the most useful for modern scholars. They tell about the lives not only of great public officials of the dynasty but also of various virtuous and exceptional individuals, such as an exceedingly dutiful son, a virtuous widow, and even a butcher exceptionally skilled in cutting thin slices of meat. Although the biographies provide almost no sense of individual human development and portray most subjects as rather stiff and stuffy paragons, they do reveal career patterns and social practices and thus give some feeling for the times.

Confucian scholarship produced a rich and demanding intellectual tradition. Men had to spend years exploring its different reaches, and it was not supported by anything resembling a formal educational system or religious institutions such as monasteries. The individual with the help of a tutor had to work his way through the classics, memorizing long passages and striving to interpret obscure meanings. Since the language of the classics was not the same as the spoken tongue, this endeavor was much like engaging in scholarship in a foreign language.

Study of the classics provided a shared experience for that thin layer of men who held Chinese civilization together. Regardless of where they came from in the empire or their native accent or dialect, they could all speak to each other in the official's language, which was also the scholar's language. They used the same metaphors and aphorisms and could use the same allusions in making their points to each other. They were in much the same situation as products of traditional British public schools and of Oxford and Cambridge, with their classical education, as background before entering government service.

The limits of the Confucian world view, its smugness, its self-centeredness, its noninquisitive approach to all that lay outside its immediate concerns, became dramatically self-evident once it confronted the dynamic spirit of modern science and technology. Yet in comparison with other belief systems of the ancient world, Confucianism was most sophisticated and enlightened. In making morality a central feature of government, it not only tempered the autocratic propensities common to ancient governments and gave to Chinese rule a humanistic dimension, but it also mobilized the great social powers of reasoned morality for service to the political system. Many systems of government have tapped the human sentiments of parochialism, nationalism, and religious convictions to strengthen the basis of the ruler's authority; Confucianism was outstanding because it insisted that government could be based on ethics and man's instinctive desire to avoid shameful behavior.

TAOISM AND BUDDHISM: THE UNCERTAIN RELIGIOUS TRADITIONS

In all formal respects the Confucian scholarly tradition concentrated on the ethics of government, the moral behavior of citizens, and a pragmatic, conservative view of the importance of the secular social order. Yet as neo-Confucianism demonstrated, the scholar-official could not entirely divorce himself from other-worldly, mystical, and metaphysical considerations. Thus, although the Chinese talked of different schools of belief, particularly in early periods, the divisions were not particularly sharp, and Confucian scholars casually indulged in Taoist speculations and took an interest in Buddhist metaphysics. Over time distinctions between the traditions became increasingly blurred, and in many respects all three became vulgarized.

Early Taoism did present some of the most sophisticated blending of philosophy and metaphysics in Chinese history. The Taoist concern with how man could go beyond the confines of reason and achieve identification with the central forces behind nature went far beyond the Confucian search for meaning in man's existence. However, much in early Taoism bordered on the merely clever. For example, Chuang Tze awakens from a dream that he is a butterfly and then finds that there is no way to answer the question of whether he was really a butterfly dreaming that he was Chuang Tze or Chuang Tze who had dreamed that he was a butterfly.

The great contribution of Taoism to the Chinese political tradition was its stress on the value of "nonaction" and the argument that much can be accomplished by it — a belief that became a justification for a laissez-faire view of the role of government. Essentially the Taoist position was that most actions are counterproductive because things will occur in their own time; much of the tension and confusion in life come from people's pressing for specific objectives when the time for them is not ripe. When conditions are appropriate, the desired outcome will occur automatically.

A contemporary Taoist argument might be that although individuals assume they have complete freedom to decide the time of their marriage, aggregate marriage statistics clearly show a uniform time when marriages have occurred and seem to deny the significance of personal choices.

After the introduction of Buddhism to China, Taoism became more a religion and less a philosophical system. Taoist monasteries spread, and in time a pantheon of Taoist gods came to be recognized and depicted in paintings and statues. The highest Taoist god was usually called Yü Huang, or the Jade Emperor, and beneath him came an array of holy men (*sheng jen*), ideal men (*chen jen*), and finally and possibly most popular of all, the Eight Immortals (*Pa Hsien*). The Taoists also had a spiritual leader, known in English as the Taoist Pope, who was presumed to be the lineal descendant of an early Han believer in Lao Tzu who codified his writings and helped to establish *The Way and Its Power* (*Tao Te Ching*) as the classic of Taoism. The current Pope is now a young man on Taiwan who succeeded his uncle, who fled with the Nationalist remnants from the mainland when it fell to the Communists.

Both Taoism and Buddhism were more popular with the common people than Confucianism, and in many respects their sacred texts became the basis of learning for those who could not aspire to a Confucian education. For those who had no hope of making the civil service, it was still possible to find security by joining a monastery. Some of the tensions between Buddhism and Taoism on the one hand and the Confucian mandarinate on the other stemmed not just from conflicting doctrines but possibly even more from class tensions and an awareness that as the monasteries grew they could become centers of power and wealth.

The political and cultural influences of the Taoist and Buddhist monasteries were, however, always limited by the fact that the clerical life and celibacy never had great appeal to the Chinese. Consequently, Taoist monks usually were only part-time religious practitioners and often were married, had their own secular occupations, and performed their priestly roles for supplementary income on special occasions such as weddings, funerals, the opening of new enterprises, and when people had deep personal needs ranging from rainfall to a change in luck and the restoration of health.

An indication of the basically secular spirit of higher Chinese culture, China never produced any great religious spokesmen. Historians have not recognized any great spiritual leaders; priests were not a part of the established elite; and the Chinese spirit was never profoundly influenced by the inspirational example of any man of God. But this does not mean that religion had no place in the lives of Chinese, and particularly the common people.

Although Taoism and Buddhism, and Confucianism in its ancestor-worship aspects, were the principal formal religions of traditional China, the vast majority of the Chinese were also responsive to pervasive but local forms of animism. Cults of gods, spirits, and ghosts were never organized to the point of becoming institutionalized, but they did provide most Chinese with a feeling for the supernatural. Shrines, temples, and tablets dotted the Chinese countryside. At frequent intervals along Chinese roadways, and particularly beside mountain paths, there were piles of stones tossed one on top of the other by travelers concerned with their own fortunes and the moods of the local spirits. Travelers approaching the piles would pick up a slate or stone and toss it on the pile. If it stayed in place their trip would continue in peace, but if it slid off there would be trouble.

Hardly any event of significance could take place without an attempt to placate the appropriate spirits. In particular, the construction of a sizable building called for the calculation of *feng shui* (wind and water) — the supernatural forces and spirits of a location, which had to be reckoned with in order for a building for human occupancy to be safe and unhaunted. Within each household, in addition to tablets or paintings placed in reverence to the ancestors, there were usually signs of respect for the kitchen god at New Year's time and to other spirits at the appropriate festival periods.

The conventional Western interpretation of Chinese civilization has tended to suggest a sharp division between the secular philosophical tradition of the Confucian elite and the religious superstitions of the uneducated common people. Modern Chinese scholars have contributed to this view by insisting that the Chinese were basically rational and unreligious. In particular they have pointed to several quotations of Confucius to support their claim that the tradition he initiated was essentially agnostic:

> Since we do not know all about life, how can we speculate about the afterlife?

> While we are not able to serve men, how can we serve the spirits?

And of course there was a long Chinese tradition of poking fun or raising commonsensical objections to the antics of ghosts or *kuei*. Thus, for example, Ssu-ma Kuang dismissed the concept of Hell: "When the body has decayed, the spirit fades away. Even if there be such cruel tortures in Hell as chiseling, burning, pounding, and grinding, whereon are these to be inflicted?"[2]

[2]C. K. Yang, *Religion in Chinese Society* (Berkeley: University of California Press, 1961), p. 247.

The distinguished Chinese sociologist C. K. Yang has, however, shown how limited this agnostic current was and how much it has been exaggerated by Western and modern Chinese scholars who were themselves agnostics. In fact the Chinese were neither devoid of spiritual interests nor particularly embarrassed about their supernatural concerns. Chinese social conventions meant that they did not generally talk about their beliefs any more than they would discuss their sex lives. A careful review of all aspects of Chinese life reveals that concern about the supernatural and correct ritual behavior was ubiquitous, but not glorified.

Probably more significant than the question of the extent of agnosticism in traditional China is the lack of severe tensions between the sacred and secular domains and between the various religions. The ease with which Chinese accepted Taoism, Confucianism, Buddhism, and animism has been frequently mentioned, and the Chinese practice of hedging bets about eternity by inviting priests of all religions to participate at funerals is equally well known. In the essentially isolated and self-contained conditions of traditional China the culture probably was able to accept certain contradictions and feelings of dissonance. Secular philosophical views and religious and supernatural beliefs could be as easily held by the same man as, say, the modern social scientist holds his different economic, psychological, and sociological theories without demanding total coherence.

STABILITY AND THE DYNASTIC CYCLE

Western characterizations of Confucian society have often stressed negative features such as the emphasis on the past, the opposition to innovation, and the failure to develop science and industry. It is true that the Confucian order valued continuity more than novelty and placed great importance on filial piety and ancestor worship and the maintenance of a division between the cultured and ethically concerned elite and the humble and hard-working masses. The Chinese were concerned more with social relationships than with exploring the physical world; their imagination turned more to poetry and painting than to science and inventions. Yet the Confucian order succeeded in establishing the most stable and enduring culture in human history. It set forth the remarkable ideal that government should help the individual to realize his full moral potential. The Confucian concept that government should be involved in seeking the perfectibility of man has persisted into the present with Chiang Kai-shek's New Life Movement and, even more dramatically, with Mao Tse-tung's massive attempts to inspire the Chinese with his version of the puritan ethic.

The Confucian stress on continuity and orthodoxy did not snuff out all attempts at innovation in China. For example, during the Sung dynasty, Wang An-shih, a prime minister, sought to bring about fundamental structural changes in Chinese polity and economy. His proposed reforms were ambitious and remarkably farsighted. He proposed a state budget that would control expenditures, a system of state purchases of grain designed to maintain an "ever normal granary," a system of loans to peasants, a form of graduated taxation and land reform, a limited system of military draft and militia organization, and changing the emphasis of the examination system from the classics to current problems. The proposals were far too radical for the mandarins in his government, but they are evidence that Chinese officials were capable of innovative thinking. Although dramatic changes did not take place, the Confucian order was far from static. There were vigorous political struggles in the bureaucracy and significant incremental changes in practices.

There was also a rhythmic cycle in Chinese history, reflected in the rise and fall of dynasties. Chinese historians traditionally attributed the success or failure of the dynasties to the moral character of the emperors and the behavior of their officials. The first emperors of each dynasty were seen as vigorous, conscientious, and virtuous; their officials were diligent; the land prospered. The last emperors of the dynasty were venal, lazy, and not interested in ruling, and their officials were corrupt and lacking virtue.

The moral theory of the dynastic cycle was encouraged by the concept of the Mandate of Heaven, by which emperors could legitimately rule so long as their conduct was consistent with the Will of Heaven. When heaven was displeased with the quality of rule or the character of the ruler, the mandate to rule could be revoked and revolt was then legitimate. Evidence in support of such a theory was readily provided by classical historians who were commissioned to write about the preceding dynasty. They were inclined to be generous in their praise of the founders of the former dynasty because that was long ago and they needed to establish a contrast with the later emperors. They had to picture the last emperor as an evil force, justifying his removal and setting the stage to legitimize the new dynasty, in which they always wrote.

Modern historians have rejected the view that Chinese history was governed by "good" and "bad" emperors. Yet the need to account for the differences between the early stages of a dynasty and its eventual decline still exists. This historical problem has produced the theory of the dynastic cycle, for which evidence is most convincing for the most recent dynasty and somewhat weak for several of the earlier ones because of the absence of adequate data.

The theory of the dynastic cycle begins with the period of disorder between dynasties and notes that when military force succeeded in establishing a new ruling house most of the people were anxious for peace and order and thus each dynasty began with a honeymoon period characterized by great vitality. The disorder before the establishment of the dynasty had produced sufficient chaos to have reduced the population so that with peace the ratio of people to land was relatively favorable and the land could be fairly evenly divided among the rural peoples. However, peace brought change. The population grew and the officials began to accumulate wealth. This produced an increase in the numbers of landless peasants and absentee landlords. It also reduced the size of the tax base, for officials skillfully avoided taxing their growing holdings. This meant that the tax burden became heaviest on the poorest peasants, who eventually had to sell out. Concentrations of holdings grew, as did the peasants' frustrations. Under these conditions natural disasters would have particularly disturbing effects because so many people lived a marginal existence. The scene was set for rebellions, which generally began at the fringes of the poorest areas. The need to suppress the rebellions resulted in tax increases in the loyal areas, and these would cause the rebellion to spread. The emperor would then have to squeeze his shrinking domains harder and harder. During the last years of the Ming dynasty the government needed more than four times its normal amount of resources to fight rebellions and foreign conquerors. The Ch'ing dynasty never recovered financially from the strain of putting down the Taiping Rebellion.

Finally the dynasty would be overthrown, and a period of strife and civil disorder would reduce the population and equalize holdings. The estates of the corrupt former officials would be re-divided, and the stage would be set for another dynasty to emerge and for the cycle to repeat itself. Such changes in response to social and economic forces had little effect on the ideals of the culture. To appreciate the dynamics of the Confucian tradition, it is necessary to examine in detail the specific institutional arrangements that managed Chinese political and social life.

CHAPTER FOUR

Imperial Institutions
and Practices

Chinese behavior did not always achieve Confucian ideals. In their personal lives emperors were not the paragons they were supposed to be. Officials could be crass and self-seeking, lacking ethical sensitivity. In examining the institutions of traditional China, one must keep in mind that although they did not always meet the ideals of Confucianism, those ideals did inspire both rulers and subjects.

Important also is the fact that much of the stability and endurance of Chinese civilization came from the extraordinary compatibility and integration of public and private institutions. The subtle meshing of philosophical ideals, family practices, controls on social advancement, formal arrangements of government, and career patterns that sustained public institutions was the basis of Chinese greatness. Indeed, when the separate parts of Chinese civilization are examined independently, out of context, weaknesses and flaws are all too apparent. Chinese emperors often seemed much too arrogant and remote to meet the test of providing leadership for such a vast society. Chinese mandarin officials were often far too dedicated to acquiring irrelevant knowledge to effectively manage the great enterprises of the empire. Chinese fathers were generally so repressive and demanding that one might have expected them to produce deep alienation and rebellion in their sons. Yet the system worked with little tension and great stability. The contradiction between the parts and the whole makes it difficult to describe the traditional Chinese order, for attention to the separate institutions tends to exaggerate difficulties.

The parts of the government were the emperor and his court at the apex of a hierarchical establishment composed of a civil bureaucracy of scholar-officials, balanced by military authorities and their troops. The three basic elements were thus the emperor and his court, the bureaucracy of mandarin scholars, and the military. The emperor was supreme in his capital, and the viceroys and governors-general were comparably powerful at the regional and provincial levels; in the local district the dominant official was the magistrate. This structure based its claims of legitimacy on Confucian ideals.

In theory the great masses of the people were controlled by and benefited from the system of distant government by their betters, but in practice they were kept in line primarily by the extremely demanding and immediate institutions of family, clan, and community. Parental power and imperial power preached the same doctrines and upheld the virtues of obedience and loyalty to authority. As the rulers and opinion makers of China, the scholars and philosopher-kings who adhered to Confucius ceaselessly stressed the need for harmony in all aspects of life and the legitimacy of classes and a priority of occupations that rewarded compliance and penalized anti-social behavior.

THE EMPEROR AND HIS COURT

Although the institution of a supreme emperor began only with unification in 221 B.C., when the state of Ch'in conquered its neighbors and set the stage for the Han dynasty, the Chinese have never been able to think of themselves as being without an emperor. Thus, in seeking to imagine the origins of their civilization, they have assumed that at the start there must have been great emperors, and they have always measured time by the reigns of emperors and their dynasties. For the Chinese not gods or mystical beings but the images of emperors dominated legends of how life and culture began and history unfolded.

Emperor P'an Ku was supposed to have separated heaven from earth. Of the nine Human Sovereigns (*Jen Huang*) who ruled 45,600 years, Yu Ch'ao taught people how to build houses, Sui Jen showed the Chinese how to start fires, Fu Hsi invented the technique of fishing with nets, and Nu Kuan introduced the regulations for marriages. Another mythical emperor, Shen Nung, taught the people agriculture. Musical instruments, ox carts, the development of silk, and other useful inventions were attributed to Huang Ti, the Yellow Emperor. The succeeding Five Sovereigns (*Wu Ti*) were identified with the five elements of traditional Chinese science. Finally, there were three great legendary Model Emperors (*San Huang*): Yao, who passed over his incompetent son to pick Shun as his successor; Shun, who subdued the barbarians and divided the empire into provinces; and Yu, who drained the world of water after the great floods and founded the Hsia dynasty.

The mythical emperors, and particularly the Model Emperors, or Three August Ones, were depicted as doing things for the common people or acting as highly moral and virtuous rulers, thereby setting an example for all subsequent emperors.

The institution of the emperor and his court was to a remarkable degree shaped by the first emperor of a unified China, Ch'in Shih Huang-ti of the Ch'in dynasty. He established the tradition of the autocratic supreme ruler who relied not upon autonomous lords and nobles but upon technically competent officials to carry out the tasks of government.

After Ch'in Shih Huang-ti the Chinese evolved doctrines that placed the emperor in a unique and interesting relationship to sacred powers. The Chinese emperors never had close ties with centralized religious authorities whereby ruler and priest reinforce each other. In Chinese theory the emperor, representing the benevolence of heaven, ruled according to the Mandate of Heaven. This doctrine legitimized the right of rebellion. If the emperor's conduct violated celestial norms, the anger of heaven might be expressed in natural disasters. People might regard floods or droughts as signs that heaven was withdrawing its mandate to the current ruler. In practice the doctrine was useful for justifying the overthrow of a dynasty and for legitimizing a new one without requiring any structural or organizational changes. It tempered the behavior of emperors and made them sensitive to the importance of correctly adhering to ceremonies. It also no doubt reminded them that they were mortal and might be destroyed if they failed to use their power correctly and effectively.

The throne was surrounded with ritual, and the emperor had to perform many religious tasks even though Confucianism was a secular ideology. For example, every spring at precisely the right moment the emperor would go to the Temple of Agriculture and plow the first furrow of the year. From Ming times, when the capital was moved from Nanking to Peking, until the fall of the Ch'ing dynasty in 1911, every emperor faithfully performed ritual sacrifices, which first required imperial abstinence from food and women for a whole day, at the blue-tiled Temple of Heaven and the yellow-tiled Altar to Earth a few miles south of the outer wall of Peking.

It is not easy to evaluate the significance of individual emperors in Chinese history. The Western mind, with little more to go on than the age of absolutism and the grandeur of Louis XIV, has never known anything to compare with the powers of the Chinese emperor. The fact that the imperial court was concerned with ceremonial duties, acted as the arbiter of manners, and contributed to the arts — much as the European courts did — should not obscure its tremendous political and economic power. Indeed, it is exceedingly hard for the modern mind to grasp the breathtaking scale of the imperial enterprise.

The Forbidden City in Peking, now the seat of the Communist government, was once the private inner domain of emperors. Immediately outside its two miles of walls and moats were a series of parks built around large lakes and an artificial mountain with pavilions and rest spots where the emperor and his favorites could enjoy themselves. Next in importance was the Tartar City, where those who had duties within the court or who were related to the emperor resided. Outside Peking and toward the Western Hills was the Summer Palace, with its marble boat and its outdoor theaters.

The imperial establishment involved far more than grand buildings. The number of retainers and personal household attendants surrounding the emperor placed him clearly above all others and in a sense removed him from easy contact with his government and his officials. The emperor's household was headed by his consort and usually four or five other recognized wives. In it were also concubines and maidservants. All the imperial offspring were formally recognized as the children of the consort, who held the title of empress. The number of palace women was always impressive. By the end of the Ming dynasty there were over nine thousand concubines in the Forbidden City, and during the Ch'ing there were over twelve thousand. By accepting as completely reasonable the idea that the emperor needed and could use so many women to satisfy his personal and sexual needs, the Chinese demonstrated their belief in the natural superiority and hence legitimacy of their emperor.

The development of a class of nobles was deterred by the refusal of Chinese emperors to dilute their power by allowing marriages to elevate the in-law families. Most of the consorts and palace women did not come from powerful families but were usually daughters of lesser, even humble, families. The emperor did not need alliances by marriage to enhance his power; rather he had to counter the danger that consort families would exploit their imperial connections. He did this by having such numbers of women that no one of them could claim special advantages.

Within the Forbidden City there were also eunuchs, whose duties, like those of the palace women, were entirely directed to the person of the emperor. In theory the eunuchs had no role in the management of government and the making of public policy, but the fact that they had access to the emperor and controlled his appointments — even to the extent of holding off ministers and pre-

---

TITLES OF EMPERORS

Emperors generally had several designations, a practice that led to many complications. A Chinese taboo forbade the mention of the personal name of a reigning monarch. Scrupulous scholars would in fact never put on paper any of the characters used in the emperor's name as long as he was alive. During other dynasties scholars might use such characters, but they would interrupt the column of their writing and place the character at the top of the next line, one space above all the other characters on the page. When the emperor died, he received a temple name, or posthumous title, such as "Grand Progenitor," "Martial Ancestor." During their lifetimes emperors would assume reign names, or reign titles, called *nien hao*, which were used to reckon dates. They were generally of an auspicious nature so that people could speak, for example, of the seventh year of "Eternal Contentment." Starting with the Ming, emperors were known by their *nien hao* and not by their temple names; in the early dynastic histories temple names were generally used.

venting them from seeing the sovereign — meant that in practice they had great power. The theory for surrounding the emperor with castrated men was that this would not only ensure that all children of the palace women were his, it would also surround the emperor with men, who, not having families of their own, would be relatively uninterested in amassing fortunes. Nevertheless, during periods of dynastic decline the chief eunuchs freely used their powers for self-enrichment.

When the capital was moved to Peking during the Ming dynasty, the emperor had about ten thousand eunuchs. By the end of the dynasty there were seventy thousand eunuchs in Peking, and during the Ch'ing the number exceeded one hundred thousand. Surprisingly little is known about who the eunuchs were. As far back as the T'ang dynasty it was illegal for an adult to be castrated, but fathers could have it done to their sons. Presumably this meant that family lines were not threatened, for only fathers with several sons would sanction the castration of one. Most eunuchs came from very humble backgrounds and were usually illiterate. For no obvious reason, a few districts in Honan seem to have produced a disproportionate number of them.

In addition to the palace women and eunuchs, the emperor's inner court was composed of expositors-in-waiting and readers-in-waiting, who drafted imperial proclamations and helped the emperor peruse the memorials sent to him. The one formal and disciplined institution in the inner court was the Hanlin Academy, whose members maintained the Confucian ideology and assisted the emperor in making sure that the imperial examinations singled out the best scholars to serve in the state bureaucracy.

There is some debate over how tyrannical the emperors were with their public officials. For example, writers as different as Fei Hsiao-t'ung and Karl Wittfogel claim that even the highest bureaucratic officials were essentially helpless before their tyrant emperor and that all policies came from the emperor, who could crush his subordinates. Others, including Wolfram Eberhard, believe the officials and emperors worked together to maintain the interests of the landed gentry. There were frequent struggles between emperors and bureaucrats to control state resources, and certainly the bureaucrats could protect their interests, if in no other way than by being excessively incompetent. Indeed, Fei Hsiao-t'ung argues that the tyranny of the emperors drove the civil service to develop the fine art of inefficiency as a means of self-protection. Much of the time, however, emperors were absorbed with their own concerns, and their officials were left free to conduct public affairs in their own manner.

On occasion emperors would be arbitrary and humiliating in their treatment of senior officials whom they seemed to feel they had to intimidate in order to control. Charles Hucker describes how frequently the Ming emperors brutally treated their officials — arbitrarily imprisoning and torturing them or executing them for very little reason: "On one occasion, 107 officials of the central government were even sentenced to kneel outside the palace gate for five successive days. What was most humiliating of all was that officials could be seized in open-court assembly, stripped naked, and flogged with bamboo poles, sometimes to death."[1] Officials were thus in much the same position as courtesans, trying to please every whim of the emperor and avoid his wrath, and in spite of Confucian rhetoric about how compassionate rulers should be, in practice they were frequently autocratic and arbitrary.

The autocratic behavior of emperors did not, however, produce an administrative or executive style of ruling. At times the clashes between emperor and scholar-bureaucrats were over policy issues, but just as frequently they were of a more personal nature. As a consequence the basic style of emperors was a blend of ruling and reigning, of projecting personal influence upon decision making at one moment and of withdrawing into supreme isolation the next. Emperors could display their ultimate powers by frantically working their officials and by ignoring them and forcing them to wait upon the imperial pleasure. Sometimes they would leave everything to an official, and at the next moment they would have every detail of that official's life and work checked by other subordinates. The intensity with which emperors at times attended to the affairs of state is documented by Hucker's statement that during the Ming dynasty, "In one ten-day period late in T'ai-tsu's reign, 1,660 memorials dealing with 3,391 separate matters are reported to have been presented for imperial decision."[2]

---

[1]Charles O. Hucker, *The Traditional Chinese State in Ming Times (1368–1644)* (Tucson: University of Arizona Press, 1961), p. 98.

[2]*Ibid.*, p. 48.

In the contemporary world both Mao Tse-tung and Chiang Kai-shek, though acting far more civilly than the dynastic emperors, have tended to blend ruling and reigning, to intervene in the details of governing at one moment and then to pull back into aloof isolation for prolonged periods. Mao, much like an emperor, has depended on his bureaucracy, yet he has felt compelled to clash with it and to distrust its most professional members. To be sure, the tradition of castigating bureaucratic behavior is as old as the bureaucratic tradition itself. But in China, unlike the West, it was a tradition that came from above, from the court itself, and not from below.

THE CIVIL SERVICE

The concept of a professional civil service, based on competitive entrance examinations, regularized evaluations, and systematic promotions, was possibly China's greatest contribution to the modern world. While European states were still relying on ancestry, aristocracy, and patronage, the Chinese had several times refined their competitive and merit-based civil service. When the American and the British governments felt the time had arrived to professionalize their services, they looked into Chinese practices.

In developing a professional civil service, the Chinese as early as the Han dynasty hit upon the remarkable idea that officials should be regularly transferred from place to place and never serve in their own home districts. The object was to reduce crony-ism and opportunities for corruption and free officials from the awkwardness of dealing with the problems of friends and neighbors. Impersonal posting did, however, have some practical disadvantages. Officials did not build up long-range interests in the welfare or economic development of particular regions.

The Chinese civil service was based on a body of shared knowledge and ethics — Confucianism — which gave its members a common approach to problems and to life. Members of the civil service had all proved themselves in national competitive examinations, which tested their scholarship and the depth of their knowledge of the Confucian tradition. Since the Chinese social structure was essentially monolithic and government service was the principal avenue of advancement, competition was intense and men would study for years and keep coming back for reexamination in the hope of gaining admission to the service. The rewards were so great for those who passed that families, clans, and whole villages were willing to invest in years of education and tutoring of bright young candidates.

The starting point in the examination system was certification, which occurred every three years when examiners from the capital went out into the provinces to identify the people who had done the proper studying and were of good character and certified them as *Hsiu Ts'ai*, or as having the bachelor's degree. Certification qualified the candidate to take additional examinations and was good for three years, after which it could be revoked if there was no evidence of further intellectual progress and continuing moral virtue. Full provincial examinations took place every three years and involved three days of continuous writing. Only one percent of those who went through this ordeal received passing grades. They were designated *Chü-jen*, or Licentiate (M.A. level), and were qualified for lower positions in government service, but unless they continued their scholarly progress and passed higher examinations they could not hope to reach the top grades and hold the highest posts.

The ultimate imperial examinations were held every three years at the capital. The candidates were locked into small, isolated cubicles with slits under the door through which food was passed. The cubicle had a single high window and contained a desk at which the candidate stood while writing and a brick bed where he slept during the seven days of the examinations. Each candidate was given a number, which he put on his examination papers so that the graders would have no hint about his identity. Those who passed became *Chin-shih*, or Doctor, and were admitted to the higher service and could hope to reach the topmost positions in the government and become ministers and grand counselors. During the 267 years of the Ming period only 24,874 men became *Chin-shih*.

Failure in the examinations could be shattering and resulted in many suicides. Disappointed candidates often became rebels, the most famous of whom was Hung Hsiu-ch'üan, who became the leader of the Taiping Rebellion, the most disastrous conflict anywhere in the nineteenth century, taking twenty million lives. Most men who failed merely went back to study more in preparation for the next round of examinations. Their education, of course, had not taught them to be rebellious, and its content was essentially useless except for a career in government: Confucian knowledge made no concession to practicality except in the realm of governing.

A much-debated issue about Chinese history is the extent to which the examination system was vigorously applied and whether it brought a significant flow of new blood into Chinese ruling circles. Certainly during many periods, especially near the end of a dynasty such as the Ch'ing, corrupt practices developed and men were allowed to buy office. The quest for office in such cases was not inspired solely by a search for greater wealth; it often signified a craving of the newly rich to gain the stamp of culture, for government service was the mark of the cultured gentleman throughout Chinese history. The system was also compromised from time to time by the open designation of categories of special candidates. For example, during the Ch'ing dynasty Manchus and Chinese did not take the same examinations, and in several of the earlier dynasties the heirs of the founding family could take separate, and presumably easier, examinations.

These exceptions aside, the system was on the whole highly competitive, and it certainly succeeded in impressing upon most people the idea that they were being ruled by their intellectual and cultural superiors. It is hard to answer the question of whether the examination system facilitated or impeded elite mobility and recruitment. There are no comparative criteria for determining the norm for the "circulation of elites" in a genuinely open society. Bright fathers sometimes do have bright sons, and in a society in which there was only one channel for advancement a high proportion of exceptional sons would have had to enter their father's professions and compete to enter the ranks of officialdom. Moreover, in traditional China the sons of mandarins obviously had cultural and psychological advantages because they were brought up in a home environment in which education and the achievement of official status were stressed. Children of nonmandarin families, on the other hand, had little exposure to the classical literary traditions. It is therefore not surprising that during the Ming and Ch'ing dynasties sons of elite families outnumbered sons of nonelite families in holding official office.

However, few families had more than two generations in

office.[3] E. A. Kracke has found that during the Sung dynasty, of those who passed the examinations in 1148 and in 1256, fifty-six percent and fifty-eight percent respectively were "new men" in the sense that for three generations in their families there had been no officials on the paternal side.[4] On balance, it would seem that there was more mobility throughout most of Chinese history than in even eighteenth- and nineteenth-century England.[5]

The examination process instilled a cast of mind blending the amateur ideal of the gentleman-scholar and a general feeling of superiority over all others. The Confucian tradition developed no sense of professionalism or specialization. It encouraged people to think about their life styles. For the best men this meant reflecting on the humanistic values desirable in government; for the rest it meant thinking about careers in a bureaucracy.

The civil service was divided into nine grades, each of which was divided into two parts, making a total of eighteen steps. It is not clear why the Chinese bureaucrats (and subsequent European bureaucrats) found it natural and reasonable to divide authority and careers into eighteen stages. The pattern seemed to fit the life cycle rather well. The individual's final promotion usually came shortly before his vigor declined. Retirement was not institutionalized. Men stopped working either when they had the inclination or when their superiors no longer had an appropriate post for them. A unique feature of the Chinese career pattern was the break of about three years for mourning after the death of one's father. According to Arthur Waley:

> This was a sort of "sabbatical," occurring as a rule towards the middle of a man's official career. It gave him a period for study and reflection, for writing at last the book that he had planned . . . , for repairing a life ravaged by official banqueting, a constitution exhausted by the joint claims of concubinage and matrimony.[6]

[3]Ping-ti Ho, *The Ladder of Success in Imperial China: Aspects of Social Mobility, 1368–1911* (New York: Columbia University Press, 1962).

[4]E. A. Kracke, Jr., *Civil Service in Early Sung China, 960–1067* (Cambridge, Mass.: Harvard University Press, 1953).

[5]Rupert Wilkinson, *Gentlemanly Power* (London: Oxford University Press, 1964), ch. 12.

[6]Quoted in John K. Fairbank, *The United States and China* (Cambridge, Mass.: Harvard University Press, 1948), p. 103.

The Chinese imperial bureaucracy averaged ten thousand officials. The trend during each dynasty was Parkinsonian. There were only forty-nine hundred officials at the beginning of the Ming dynasty, but there were fifteen thousand at the end: These were only senior mandarins. In addition, however, vast numbers of government employees supported these officials and were in some degree participants in official decision making. John Fairbank has estimated that there were as many as one hundred thousand such men.[7] This is not a large number, for these men were managing a country of 100 million people — a population that became nearly 400 million by the end of the imperial era.

Thus as large as the imperial court was and as extensive as the bureaucracy became, when it came to control at the local level, there were exceedingly few officials. During the Ming dynasty the magistrate at the *hsien* or county level had on the average fifty thousand people to rule, and by the Ch'ing period the magistrate at the *chou* or district level was responsible for an average population of nearly a quarter of a million.

It was possible to have so few officials at the point of contact between government and people because Chinese society had built into it powerful forces for self-regulation. The traditions of the family and clan and of other associations and occupational groupings made government intervention to maintain routine order rare. Most disputes were settled informally and by appeal to middlemen and village elders, and as little recourse as possible was made to courts of law.

In spite of the early role of the Legalists and the impressive body of administrative codes developed by the T'ang, the imperial tradition did not identify government with law. The Chinese did little about civil law, stressing instead the virtues of accommodation, mediation, and compromise. The Confucian emphasis upon ethics and reason precluded the adversary approach of Western law, and above all the Chinese rejected the idea that the law should protect the individual. For the citizen law meant punishment — the degrees ranged from prescribed numbers of strokes with the heavy or light bamboo to death by strangulation, with little use of incarceration — for officials law meant administrative practices and punishments that ranged from demotion to exile.

[7]*Ibid.*, p. 104.

The Chinese generally accepted a theory of collective rather than individual responsibility. When a crime occurred, it was not necessary to ensure that the perpetrator of the evil act was apprehended and punished; the government had only to identify the community or the family to which the criminal belonged and then hold the group responsible. Fathers were not inclined to accept punishment for their sons' deeds and hence vigorously sought to make sure that their children did not misbehave. Since one brother could be punished for the act of another, there was a tendency for all to be their brothers' keepers. Patricide in a town would bring lasting shame to all: in the short run higher taxes and, far worse, the perpetual stigma of having one corner of the city's walls rounded rather than at the normal ninety-degree angle. Any traveler approaching such a city could instantly recognize its moral shame, even though the ignominious event might have happened generations earlier.

Although informal social pressures were powerful forces easing the tasks of government, there was also a somewhat more formalized system of community and family controls called *pao-chia*. Although the numbers varied according to population and the natural size of the community, the *pao*, or community, usually consisted of 110 households. The heads of the ten most prosperous or established families were the community chiefs, and under an annually rotating leadership they would deal with the county (*hsien*) magistrate and the tax collector and haggle over how to reduce and divide their collective tax burdens. They decided whose sons would be sent off to military service and answered the imperial decree for corvée labor.

The remaining hundred families were divided into ten *chia*, a unit of ten households. In theory the head of each *chia* was also selected on an annual rotating basis, but the position tended to rotate only among the few family heads who were deemed competent. At the *chia* level pressures could be extreme and painfully conflicting because the leaders had to live closely with their neighbors and enforce some of the most biting regulations of government. For example, the tax collector at the county level usually did not care to decide on his own the individual tax bills of each family but would present the *pao* or the *chia* with its collective quota and allow the people close at hand to deal with problems of equity.

THE SWEET AND SOUR CHARACTER
OF GOVERNMENT

By now it should be clear that there was ambivalence about government and authority in imperial China. On the one hand, government was manifestly society's principal industry and elite activity. The higher the level one reached, the greater were one's rewards. Regardless of what one wanted in life — money, prestige, art, social refinement, action, leisure — the best career to follow was in government. On the other hand, the emperor could brutally mistreat those who were most successful, and the routine of service meant assignment to communities where one had no ties, did not know the spoken language, and would be seen by the local people as an agent of suppression.

The same ambivalence about power existed for those outside of government. There were advantages in being recognized as a negotiator with government, for one could look after one's personal interests while representing the community. Yet there was also the awful pain of having to serve as the government's agent in bringing bad news to one's neighbors.

These features of the hierarchy of authority in China produced schizophrenic behavior among those who were in any way involved with government. They had to learn how to display complete and abject servility toward all who were above them and to be harsh and repressive toward those beneath them. The highest officials in the land had to show degrading self-abasement before the emperor, and thus quite naturally they were gloriously haughty in their dealings with lesser figures. And so it went down the hierarchy. Local magistrates at the bottom had few face-to-face contacts with their superiors, and most of their time was given to showing their superiority over ordinary citizens. These attitudes, carried over into modern China, have contributed to what has been called the bicycle complex — that is, bending the knees to those above and kicking those below.

The sweet and sour character of government service was also to be found in the lack of material reward and the need to live constantly in the shadow of illegality. The official pay scale provided negligible salaries. Fairbank has estimated that a governor-general responsible for two provinces, often with populations exceeding the populations of modern France or Germany, was paid the equivalent of $300 a year plus an expense account, or "anti-extortion allowance," of $41,000.[8] Nevertheless he was expected to maintain a household and staff of several thousand people and to conduct himself in a style appropriate to the imperial representative. The result was a system of government by corruption, in which those who had dealings with officials tended to pay for services with "gifts." Just as the formal flow of tax monies was extracted out of the people at the bottom of the hierarchy and passed up each step of the bureaucratic ladder to the imperial court with vague amounts taken off at each level to maintain government operations, there was a private flow of resources, with subordinates' seeing that superiors were taken care of. Fairbank tells of one Manchu official who, on falling from favor, was revealed to have had an estate of 425,000 acres, $30 million worth of gold, silver, and precious stones, and shares in ninety banks and pawnshops. The fact that all officials had to breach the line of corruption whether they amassed such fortunes or not meant that any official who displeased the emperor could be readily charged with misconduct in office and severely punished.

The basic logic of the system was that officials at every level of the hierarchy wanted tranquility and peace beneath them while they extracted enough from below to keep those above satisfied. Model magistrates were those who could keep their people from publicly complaining or disturbing the peace while they were passing to those above them gratifying amounts of revenue. Their third concern was to satisfy their own entourages and their own private needs. The strains could be considerable, but that was the essence of government.

Fei Hsiao-t'ung has mentioned the Chinese tradition of poetry in which officials, in spite of their lofty estate and the grandeur of their offices, bemoaned their conditions, as for example T'ao Yuan-ming:

> Why should I be an official?
> I bend my back

[8]*Ibid.*, p. 105.

For only three piculs of rice.
Why should I not go back to till the land.[9]

Although the material benefits of office sufficiently out-weighed the hardships so that people strove to get into the bureaucracy, the sour qualities of service were sometimes strong enough to inhibit their efficiency in carrying out their duties. Fei Hsiao-t'ung probably overstates the degree to which officials consciously or effectively fought back by doing a poor job and thereby frustrating the will of the emperor, but his words are helpful:

> Inefficiency and parasitism, on the one hand, remoteness of imperial control and a do-nothing policy by the emperor, on the other — this has always been the ideal. Yet this ideal of government, of a "good emperor" as one who presided but did not rule, has rarely been attained. As far as the officials were concerned, the next best thing, then, could only be to protect themselves, to keep a back door open for their relatives, and to be able to use their position as a shield against the emperor's whims. To protect not only themselves but their relatives and their whole clan from the unchecked power of the monarch, and to do this not by constitutional or by legal means but by personal influence — this is what they sought. Not by challenging the emperor's authority but by coming close to him, by serving him and from this service gaining an advantage in being enabled to shift the burden of the emperor's demands onto the backs of those lower down, did the propertied class attempt to neutralize the emperor's power over them and to avoid the attack of the tiger.[10]

The careers of officials were not specialized in function or committed to particular policy goals. Instead, officials followed a lifetime of moving from post to post, accumulating contacts and friendships, trying not to make enemies, and picking up subordinates who would be willing to throw in their lot with them. As an official's seniority increased, he accumulated a larger and larger following of staff assistants who accompanied him from one post to the next. Eventually, if he faltered, his staff might split and his principal lieutenants would become figures in their own right and would in their turn begin to accumulate followers.

[9]Fei Hsiao-t'ung, *China's Gentry* (Chicago: University of Chicago Press, 1953), p. 29. Copyright 1953 by The University of Chicago.
[10]*Ibid.*, pp. 26–27.

THE STRUCTURE OF OFFICIALDOM

For members of the bureaucracy tensions existed at two extremes: at the top in their relations with the emperor and at the bottom in dealings with the citizens. It is remarkable that within the bureaucracy, except for certain superior-inferior relationships, there were almost no institutionalized points of conflict. The reason that differences of interest among the ministries or boards did not often come into the open was the lack of professionalism and specialization. The bureaucrats were all generalists, trained only in the Confucian tradition, and they did not have strong loyalties for particular offices. For example, what might be assumed to be a natural clash between the interests of the Board of War and the Board of Revenue or between the Board of Public Works and the Board of War would never develop. If an official became excessively skillful and aggressive in obtaining funds for the Board of War, the ministers would transfer him in a year or so to the Board of Revenue or to the Board of Public Works so that he could argue the case against the Board of War. The combination of the amateur's ideal and constant movement among ministries kept officials from becoming personally specialized even though the government itself was organized by functional divisions.

Organizationally the imperial government can be visualized as having three layers. At the top were the highest officials who were closest to the emperor and concerned with general policies. The nature of their offices changed from time to time in response to relations with the personal power of the emperor. Next came the operational offices, which to an amazing degree hardly changed after they had been fully institutionalized into six boards or ministries early in the T'ang dynasty. The third level consisted of the hierarchy outside of the capital, at the provincial and local levels.

When the Chinese bureaucracy first took shape, during the Ch'in and Han dynasties, the emperor was surrounded immediately outside his inner court by his three consultants (*san-kung*): the chancellor (*ch'eng-hsiang*), who was closest to being a chief administrator; the imperial secretary (*yu-shih-ta-fu*), who promulgated decrees and thus had legislative functions; and the grand commandant (*t'ai-mei*), who commanded the military. By the early Ming dynasty these top officials had formed the Grand Secretariat (*nei-ko*). Emperor T'ai-tsu discovered that they were becoming so powerful that they were usurping some of the imperial prerogatives. In 1380 he abolished the Grand Secretariat and suggested that bureaucrats of the capital might improve their claim to merit if they got out into the countryside.

Under the Ch'ing rulers the most powerful group was the Grand Council (*chüh chi chu*), of which half were Manchus and half were Chinese, which acted as a cabinet or advisory council to the emperor. This body of the most august men in the empire was expected to conduct its business early each morning, starting before sunrise — a tradition that made it easy for those below to observe when standards were slipping and decline was setting in — which may help to account for emperors' petulance toward their ministers, for meeting with them so early in the morning after the active imperial nights could not have been easy.

As important as the officials around the emperor were, the hierarchy of Chinese officialdom did not point to any particular office as the commonly acknowledged goal of all careerists. Not all mandarins aspired to become members of the Grand Council or the Grand Secretariat. On the contrary, for most officials the preferred position was that of viceroy; one could rule with great autonomy as "little emperor" over sizable domains.

The Six Boards (*liu-pu*) were the principal ministries of the government and administered basic policies. The Board of Civil Appointments (*li-pu*) handled the personnel of the civil service, controlled appointments and promotions, and evaluated the performance of all officials. The Board of Rites (*li-pu*, but a different Chinese character) was responsible for ceremonies, sacrifices, and relations with foreigners, the rationale for the last responsibility being that visitors would not know proper etiquette and would appreciate guidance from specialists. This board had extensive and critical duties; the Ming administrative code devoted 75 of its 228 chapters to its responsibilities.[11] The Board of War (*ping-pu*) controlled the military, which, in spite of the Confucian scorn of soldiers, was never an insignificant force. For example, early in the Ming dynasty there were 15,000 officers and 1,100,000 men, and by the end of the

---

[11]Hucker, p. 68.

dynasty there were 100,000 officers and 4 million troops.[12] Throughout their history the Chinese have maintained a remarkably high
proportion of the population under arms even when not engaged in
conquest or defense against invaders.

The Board of Finance or Revenue (*hu-pu*) supervised the collection of taxes, set general quotas on what was expected from each
province, managed census taking, handled the financial accounts of
the entire government, and managed state enterprises such as the
granaries. The amateur spirit of the entire bureaucracy ensured that
businesslike methods were not closely followed even in this apparently technical ministry, and the style was one of getting along as
well as possible. For example, the land tax in the Ch'ing dynasty,
which lasted until 1911, was fixed on assessments made in 1713 that
provided the baseline for all subsequent haggling. The amount of
revenue collected depended largely on the urgency of the emperor's
concerns and the avariciousness of the particular officials involved.
The Board of Public Works (*kung-pu*) had some duties that came
close to those of the finance board, such as the management of some
state manufacturing, but specifically it was responsible for water
control and irrigation schemes, canals and transportation systems,
the construction of public buildings, and the mobilization of manpower for state services.

The Board of Punishment (*hsing-pu*) administered justice by
codifying the laws, managing courts, and capturing and punishing
criminals. Magistrates had considerable discrimination in decreeing
punishments, but the most serious sentences were supposed to be
reviewed by higher officials in the ministry. The review process
helped to ensure standardized policies throughout the empire.

Outside of the capital the highest officials were viceroys or
governors-general (*tsung-tu, chih-chun,* or *chih-t'ai*), who as "little
emperors" presided over two provinces. At the provincial capital
there were two governors, the provincial judge, the salt comptroller,
and the grain intendant. Provinces were subdivided into circuits
(*fu*), districts (*chou*), and finally counties (*hsien*).

Officials moved about every two or three years among all these
offices. Their ranks were proclaimed to all by the size of their en-
tourage, by the number of banners they flew, by the color of the

buttons on their skull caps, and by the square insignia they wore in the middle of the front and back of their state robes.

THE CENSORATE

Possibly the most novel feature of the Chinese institutional arrangement was the Censorate (*tu ch'a yüan*), which served as special watchdog over the entire civil service and performed as a blend of inspector-general and secret police. The institution was formed because of the suspiciousness of Ch'in Shih Huang-ti, but its development eventually reflected the personal styles of many emperors. In general its task was to keep a sharp eye on the performance of all officials and to criticize any deviation from established norms. It reported to the emperor any misconduct of any of his officials. It could also, however, criticize the emperor himself, which some censorates did. In return for that action they gained in the long run immortal recognition for their courage and honesty, but in the short run they generally lost their jobs if not their heads. The concept of the Censorate might have brought a remarkable corrective influence to the Chinese system, restraining emperors and punishing evil officials. In practice, members of the Censorate were relatively lowly officials who were outside the flow of policies and revenues and thus their influence was usually marginal. Officials might worry about a censor's finding them adhering to the wrong forms, making a mistake in a document, or violating official etiquette, but generally they did not expect the censors to take up more fundamental matters. Consequently the Censorate was generally staffed with low- and middle-grade officials of little personal influence who were always vulnerable to the emperor's wrath.

THE SCHOLAR, THE GENTRY,
AND THE MERCHANT

The boundary between state and society in imperial China was quite imprecise. The government dominated the society, and much of its authority was used to enforce and punish people for what in the West would be private matters. Exemplary moral conduct was also a matter of state concern. Authority thus could be humane and highly paternalistic.

However, the citizen had no claim on government, and there was not the slightest inkling of an idea that government should respond to the competitive forces among the people. The emperor's rule was supposed to bring tranquility and universal contentment, and officials were expected to support justice and decency, for all government rested on ethical considerations.

Because citizens had no legitimate mechanism for organizing and openly pressuring the government, influential people outside of government sought to have their interests protected by officials. The lack of any formal machinery for registering the demands of special interests meant that they took on a subversive character, and the officials who responded to the realities of competing interests had to act in ways that were essentially corrupt. In the gray area beyond governmental jurisdiction there existed a wide range of organizations that lacked respectability, were not honored in the formal histories, but did give protection to collective and special interests.

The most extensive and best organized of these groups were secret societies, the most famous of which included the White Lotus, the Elder Brother, the Triads, the Yellow Turbans, the White Lily, and the White Cloud. Each had its elaborate rituals and its areas of special concentration. The members looked after each other and took care of funerals and bereaved widows and children. Most of these secret societies cut across class lines; their membership included not only representatives of the rural gentry but also ordinary peasants and even a few thugs who could be called on for the physical protection of the collective interests.

Most analysts of Chinese social classes observe that in a predominantly rural society there are always distinctions between landlords and rich peasants on the one hand and tenant workers and lowly peasants on the other. However, in China those who were better off were not really an aristocracy. Early Western observers of China were struck by the lack of a formal aristocracy based on landholdings, and many of the contemporary interpretations of the collapse of the imperial system identified its weakness as precisely its lack of a hereditary class committed to aristocratic values.

More recent studies of Chinese society have focused on the existence of a gentry class that may not have had much sense of style or collective identity (in comparison to such classes in the rest of the world) but was a force for stability and even repression. Whether the gentry identified its interests with those of the government or whether it was victimized by the officials, it is clear that most of the scholar-officials came from this class. The gentry's values were Confucian, and they did tend to see the good life in much the same terms as the scholar-officials. In general, the gentry had pathetically small landholdings, and only those who got into government could hope to amass fortunes significant by any standards.

In contrast to the rather tense closeness of gentry and officials, there was a relatively unambiguous feeling of contempt and animosity among gentry and scholars toward merchants. As has so often been the case in agricultural societies there was distrust of those who dominated the marketplace and sought wealth without regard to sentiment and tradition. The Chinese had a great tradition of trading, and from the early Han dynasty they traveled extensively across central Asia. Yet those who ruled the empire never accorded status or recognition to the merchants. Instead, social and political pressures encouraged successful merchants to abandon money making and enter government, even if they had to buy office. If they were not so enticed into the ranks of officialdom, it was still likely that their sons would be given a Confucian education and instilled with anti-mercantile views.

Social values were a prime reason for the failure of capitalism to develop in China. Government policies further impeded economic development by controlling much of the foreign trade on the pretense that it was really an exchange of tribute and gifts between the emperor and foreigners. The government also controlled certain critical commodities and industries, such as salt and iron in the early period and liquor and tea at later dates. In a sense the Chinese always had a "mixed economy" in which the "public sector" restrained the "private sector."

CHAPTER FIVE

The Sweep of Change

The collapse of the stubbornly durable structure of traditional China and the effort to erect in its place a modern Chinese nation-state is the central theme in the history of modern China. A system that had lasted for over two thousand years and had experienced several periods of alien conquest, each time absorbing its foreign rulers, was unable to withstand a century of Western contact.

So long as the outside world reached China by land, its traditional society and economy were well protected. For many centuries the Chinese had coped with the probes and the raids of nomads, and at times the "hordes" beyond the Great Wall were well enough organized to conquer the agricultural Chinese. But power relationships in central Asia generally favored the Chinese, and they had few reasons not to cling to their belief that those beyond their cultural reach were mere "barbarians."

The challenges of the nomads to the agrarian Chinese had strengthened Chinese civilization. In reacting to the need to defend themselves, the Chinese developed their centralized empire and also their sense of cultural identity. However, the impact of the West was of a completely different order, for it represented a political and military threat based on modern science and technology. As long as China was threatened only by familiar forces, Chinese civilization was secure. The collapse came when China was confronted with enemies who had advantages of science and modern forms of military, economic, and political organization.

Western civilization, when it first reached China, was not a major threat; only after the modern age of science and industry did it become a profound problem for the Chinese. Once British ships with advanced forms of firepower began to appear off the China coast in the early nineteenth century, the balance of power between China and outside "barbarians" began to change, and the Chinese became aware that they were facing a challenge unknown in their previous history.

Steadily throughout the eighteenth and nineteenth centuries the West became more effective in producing military power. The modernization of Europe generated a capacity for organizing large economic enterprises, which could pressure the Chinese to adhere to Western terms for conducting trade. Although Europe was divided into nation-states competing for special advantages, Europe nevertheless confronted the non-European world with the demand that European norms govern all interstate relations.

The West challenged China at many levels. In addition to presenting a military challenge its impact created a historic confrontation between a traditional, agrarian society and a modernizing, urban-industrial one. For the first time China was confronted with enemies who were not isolated but were in close communication with each other. The traditional Chinese diplomatic technique of "playing one barbarian off against the other" by the careful management of favors backfired, and the granting of a favor to one European power resulted in all demanding similar concessions.

The fundamental balance between China and the rest of the world began to change, and inevitably Chinese domestic society began to experience the profound effects that always accompany the decline of a traditional order and the creation of a modern, technological society. The old order was threatened, but there was no clear indication of what the new should be. The self-assurance of the emperor was broken, and members of the civil service found their skills and cast of mind were irrelevant to the new problems of the day. Throughout China by the end of the nineteenth century, human relations were to undergo wave after wave of upheaval as new forms of urbanization pulled people in from the countryside and as rural life reacted to the broadening of the monetized economy. Members of once-despised classes such as soldiers and merchants were to find new opportunities, while previously secure classes such as the scholars and gentry were to have their most basic values and their self-esteem threatened. The Chinese family was to experience great stresses and fundamental changes.

CHINESE VULNERABILITIES

It would be wrong to give the impression that the sweep and the rate of change in Chinese society resulted only from the military effectiveness of the Western impact. Certainly China, like all the rest of the world, would probably in time have had to accommodate and absorb the essential features of the modern world based on the scientific and technological revolution. However, China in the mid-nineteenth century at the moment of Western impact was experiencing a phase of domestic decay and was therefore peculiarly vulnerable to outside influences.

By the middle of the nineteenth century the imperial system was displaying many characteristics typical of dynastic decline. Conceivably even if there had been no Western impact the Ch'ing dynasty might have been nearing its end. Such speculation aside, the policies and practices of the imperial court and the mandarinate were exceptionally inefficient and ineffectual at the very time that the system was experiencing its greatest challenge by outside forces.

China was also experiencing some historically unique developments that made the country peculiarly vulnerable to basic social change. There was a peculiarly sharp rise in Chinese population in the eighteenth century, before China had even faced the impact of the West. The doubling of China's population between 1740 and 1790 and its continued growth by another third in the next fifty years fundamentally changed the historic man-land ratio and in doing so may have greatly weakened the fabric of Chinese society.

The basic patterns of Chinese social and economic life had evolved under conditions of a population that numbered well below 100 million, and indeed most of the time the population was closer to 60 million people. Although slight technological changes and particularly the introduction of new crops (potatoes, sweet potatoes, peanuts) provided some basis for a growing population, the inescapable fact is that China's resources barely expanded as fast as its population, and thus Chinese society was under considerable stress on the eve of its exposure to the challenge of the West.

The growth of population had brought about an expansion of urban centers long before there was any industrialization. Chinese cities had emerged as administrative rather than as trading centers, and most of the people who lived in them were artisans and those engaged in service functions. Increase of population without a concomitant increase in investment in productive enterprises tended to debase the old handicraft trades and make service activity servile and degrading. Even before industrialization, Chinese urban culture was based on a surplus of labor that reflected a spirit of abject poverty. When China began to industrialize in the early twentieth century, there was an overriding tendency to exploit the cheap labor, and there was less compulsion than in Europe and especially America to substitute machinery for manpower.

Also, at the beginning of the period of intense contact with the West, the Chinese government, though too weak to deal effectively with foreign pressure, was strong enough to play its classic role of obstructing China's merchant and commercial classes. Those active in the Chinese economy could not react on their own terms to the challenge and stimulus of Western traders. The pressures of internal, arbitrary taxation prevented the natural development of a more integrated national economy. Trade within China was impeded by a variety of internal taxes and tariffs called *likin*.

In later years even a weak government was able to delay the growth of a modern intellectual class because it still served as the major employer of the intelligentsia. A weak government could also allow traditional standards of scholarship to decline and tolerate the practice of buying degrees and admission to the bureaucracy. Those who were in government service by the end of the Ch'ing dynasty were second-rate by traditional Chinese and Western standards of scholarship. For the first time in Chinese history the stage was set for the development of an intellectual class that was divorced from government and increasingly came to reflect the frustration of imaginative but powerless and inadequately employed intellectuals.

AN ABUNDANCE OF THEORIES AND A SHORTAGE OF FACTS

Chinese intellectuals and officials were not alone in being puzzled about the broad sweep of change that came to China after the impact of the modern West. All thoughtful observers of the Chinese scene have felt it necessary to seek fundamental interpretations of the causes and the character of the prolonged "Chinese revolution" that eventually brought the downfall of the old order and massive turmoil in all attempts to establish the new. As might be expected, interpretations of the "causes" of such a major historical occurrence have been numerous, reflecting individual points of view and preferences in theories of history. Until recently most students of China accepted all theories as partial explanations of what happened. Thus they believed that the Western impact challenged the traditional Confucian order in all spheres: The immediate diplomatic and military confrontation of the mid-nineteenth century merged with fundamental economic and sociological changes, which in turn contributed to intellectual and cultural confusion and tension.

Recent scholarship, however, has shown that the process of Chinese modernization was not so coherent and has raised doubts about the two most sophisticated theories. According to the first, the breakdown of the Confucian order resulted from the undermining of the agricultural economy and the rise of rural discontent. According to the second, the breakdown of the Confucian order stemmed from the collapse of the Chinese family system as a consequence of urbanization.

Doubts about the validity of these economic and sociological interpretations led to the view that modernization in China has been outstanding because of the central importance of intellectual conflict. Although military and political considerations dominated China's initial reaction to the challenge by the West, the issue soon became a choice between reconciliation and replacing traditional Chinese values, views, and practices with the ideas and values of a modern scientific and technologically oriented society.

Because the economic and sociological interpretations have been so popular it is appropriate for us to examine them and comment on the evidence in their support.

THE BANKRUPTCY OF CHINESE AGRICULTURE

Since both the society and the economy of China were agricultural, it would seem logical to assume that developments in the countryside were basic to the breakup of the traditional order. Thus a conventional interpretation of the economic history of China traces the collapse of the Confucian order to changes in tenant-landlord relationships. According to this view, which ignores the demographic mysteries we have just mentioned, the processes set in motion by the Western impact began with a rise in population, which increased the supply of cheap labor. At the same time those who made money in the cities as a result of new developments tended to cling to old practices and invest in land. This meant that land prices were driven steadily upward. Consequently there was a disturbing increase in both landless peasants and absentee landlords. The gentry, which had once been a stabilizing feature in the countryside regardless of whether they acted as allies of a domineering government or as a force that opposed the bureaucracy, were compelled to become more distant and exploitative. The lot of the peasant thus became desperate, and increasingly rebellion seemed his only hope. In time, class lines became more sharply drawn, and eventually the entire social and political order was toppled by the frustrations and demands of the landless and poor peasants.

This theory is challenged by facts suggesting that the processes of change were much more complex. Undoubtedly the rich took advantage of the poor when they could. However, the facts that are available do not suggest any dramatic increase in tenancy and landlessness, and there is no solid evidence that the size of the largest holdings increased markedly from the 1850's to the 1950's.

Dwight A. Perkins has shown that China's agricultural production grew at a rate consistent with the growth in population. This growth was achieved largely because the opening of new areas and the expansion of irrigation increased the amount of arable land. During the eighteenth and nineteenth centuries publicly and collectively owned lands were steadily transferred to private ownership. Lands once owned by the imperial family, the government, the army, the temples, and clans were transferred to individuals. At the beginning of the Ch'ing dynasty the entire area of Manchuria was reserved for the Manchus, and in theory Chinese were not allowed to own land "beyond the Wall." But even before the end of the dynasty there was a flow of migrations, particularly from rural Shantung and Hopei, and they greatly increased after the revolution of 1911.

The expansion of acreage and the reduction of lands reserved for tenancy meant that during the nineteenth century there was a rise in the proportion of independent small holdings and a decline in the percentage of peasants who rented rather than owned their fields. These facts do not support the view that the changes that might have followed the Western impact on the Chinese economy produced a significant increase in tenancy and landlessness among China's peasant populations.

There is no evidence that after the Western impact there was an expansion in the size of landholdings. The Chinese never practiced primogeniture, and with the passing of each generation individual holdings were invariably broken up among all the heirs. Indeed, because of the Chinese insistence that all sons should receive equal shares, the tendency was to fragment holdings in order to ensure that each got the same amount of good as well as of poor land. Wealthy people tended to have large families, and the general Chinese pattern was that increases in the number of heirs ran ahead of increased accumulation of land. As a result holdings were broken up almost as fast as they were accumulated as in each generation sons split up what their fathers had put together.

Consequently Chinese "estates" were rather trivial by the standards of most agrarian societies. A 1935 government survey of eleven provinces revealed that there were only 1,545 "big landlords," and these averaged less than 350 acres per family. In 1937 the largest holding in Hopei province, which contains Peking and Tientsin, was only 165 acres. In south China the size of the "estates" was even smaller, and holdings of four and five acres were enough to make one a member of the "gentry" with tenants.

Although there is little evidence to suggest that the landlords were becoming either more numerous or possessed larger holdings, some facts suggest the peasant owner was having more trouble avoiding bankruptcy. By the early twentieth century rural indebtedness had become endemic. In part the difficulty stemmed from the tenacity with which the Chinese peasant clung to traditions and customs more appropriate to an earlier period of less intense population pressures. He persisted in living well beyond his means in his observances of weddings and funerals and festive occasions. Years of indebtedness generally followed such major events. Possibly in earlier ages it had been easier to maintain the customs because they were supported by a larger collective, either the extended family or the clan. The trend toward individualized agriculture meant that many peasants who owned their own land were not able to maintain elaborate customs.

More importantly, the peasant was increasingly driven to indebtedness because the expansion of the monetized economy and

LAND TENANCY

Statistics on land use and tenancy over time and for the different parts of China do not exist. At best we have isolated figures for different locations at different times. The problem of tenancy is further complicated by the great variety of land rights and forms of ownership. In some areas sharecropping was practiced. In others peasants had permanent rights to the land they worked. They could will the rights to their sons, but they could not sell their rights, and the "landlord" could not evict them. In other areas the general practice was for a high proportion of "tenants" to also be owners of part of the land they worked. In many areas the relation between landlord and tenant was that of a clan organization to one of its members.

Size of holdings differed greatly according to population density, crops raised, and general economic conditions. These factors in turn influenced the tenancy picture.

A study[1] by Dr. R. T. Ts'ui of the University of Nanking College of Agriculture showed for central China the following historical pattern:

	Percentage of Total Number of Farmers		
	1912	1934	1937
Tenants	28%	29%	30%
Part owners	23	25	30
Owners	49	46	46

The last report in the *China Handbook,* the semi-official statistical abstract, before the Communists came to power stated that in

[1]Report in Gerald F. Winfield, *China: The Land and the People* (New York: William Sloane, 1948), p. 279.

---

closer trade linkages with the cities meant that he had more fixed and inflexible obligations and fewer possibilities of relying on handicrafts for additional income. Traditionally the peasant could pay his taxes or rents in kind, as a proportion of his crop. In bad years he would pay less, and furthermore he could bargain for special considerations that might further lighten his load. The historic Chinese pattern was that government, landlord, and peasant all took a loss during bad harvest years, and the peasant, being closest to the situa-

1947 about one-third were tenants, one-fourth were part owners, and from forty to forty-five percent were full owners.

Dr. John Lossing Buck found that in a sample of 16,796 farms taken in the mid 1930's only seventeen percent were tenants, and "only 28.7 percent of the total Chinese farm area was rented (12.7 percent in the wheat region and 40.3 percent in the rice region)."[2] Compared with American, European, and South Asian patterns of tenancy, the Chinese situation was not in any sense extreme, according to these studies.

Other studies, particularly those by the Communists, suggest that there was greater inequality in distribution. One non-Communist study suggested that from ten to fifteen percent of the farm population owned from fifty-three to sixty-three percent of the land.

Equality certainly did not exist, for even though China lacked the large-scale estate holdings common to many other agricultural societies, there were always differences in wealth among village families. What is less clear is how stable the inequality was. In Chinese folk culture there is a strong notion of the constant rise and fall of family fortunes. In America "shirt-sleeves to shirt-sleeves in three generations" and "rags to riches" stress upward social mobility; similar Chinese concepts have emphasized the idea that when one family rises another must go down, and the notion of social decline and decay is more vivid in China. Inequalities did not imply security for some. The search for equality did appear in the Chinese practice of dividing inheritances equally, both with respect to size and quality, and thus the tendency toward fragmentation of plots was traditionally a more serious obstacle to productivity than excessive concentration.

[2]*Ibid.*, p. 280.

---

tion, could often look after his own interests so as not to suffer proportionally more. By the end of the nineteenth and the beginning of the twentieth century peasants had more standardized taxes and rents because governments needed predictable incomes, particularly as they borrowed more and had to meet their schedules of debt payments. This was also true of the landlords, who not only had to pay their taxes in cash but also had more fixed obligations. For example, they once had been able to educate their children by supporting a tutor-teacher in their households, but now they had to pay tuitions at schools and universities. The process of moving toward more impersonal and generalized practices tended to hurt the peasant most because he was confronted with increasingly rigid obligations although nature remained unpredictable.

The indebtedness of the Chinese peasant was rarely related to investments to increase production; the weight of his debts tended to erode only his position as landowner. Yet the fact that concentration of landholdings and the ratio between owner-operated and rented lands did not appreciably change, and certainly did not change at a rate proportionate to the rising level of indebtedness, suggests that those who owned their lands were somehow able to survive economically in spite of their indebtedness. No doubt the main explanation is that these people tended to maintain some personal contacts, including family connections, so that indebtedness brought help from friends and relations. This might mean that relatives who had moved to the city were sending back some of their earnings. Thus for these families the generally unfavorable terms of trade between countryside and city were balanced by private remittances.

The tenant farmer had the greatest problems with indebtedness. To borrow the money he often needed to get from one harvest to the next he would usually turn to his landlord. The result was that even when rents formally remained constant, the proportion of the crop that went to the landowner could be increasing. Since tenants usually did not have family connections as economically effective as those of the landowners, they could only mortgage their future earnings.

These patterns suggest that the only way in which it would have been possible for indebtedness to increase without an increase in the amount of rented land was for there to have been a significant turnover of tenants — as those who collapsed under their burden of debt were replaced by new tenants who would soon be likewise indebted. But this plausible theory is contradicted by evidence from village surveys, which show that until the Japanese occupation Chinese villages were extremely stable. Landowners tended to rent only to long-established tenants and rarely to strangers. In neither north or south China was there any significant tendency toward the creation of an impersonal market of tenants. If a peasant wanted to rent land, he could hope to do so only if he were known and trusted by

the landowner. Indeed, the trend toward more absentee landlords —
which grew as landowners moved to larger towns to take part in
new economic activities or people from the distant cities invested in
land — increased the need for reliable tenants. The farmer who
worked part of his land and rented out part was more likely to rent
to a stranger than would an absentee landlord who could not keep
his eye on the tenant.

Thus although indebtedness probably increased, and life certainly was not easy for the Chinese peasant who worked his own
land, the basic structure of the rural economy was not severely
shaken, and the proportion of landless to peasant owners probably
did not greatly change during the decades in which the traditional
Confucian order was decaying.

The thesis that Chinese political changes stemmed from a
sharp rise in rural economic discontent is also put into doubt by the
pattern of rebellions. The great peasant rebellions that shook imperial China took place in the nineteenth century. However, they
occurred either before the Western impact could have produced extensive economic changes — as was the case with the Taiping Rebellion which lasted from 1851 to 1864 — or in the areas least affected
by the Western impact — as was the case with the Muslim rebellions
in Yunnan province from 1855 to 1873 and in Sinkiang from 1877
to 1878. In the twentieth century, when the effects of rural bankruptcy should have been increasingly intense, there were no significant peasant rebellions until the emergence of the Communists, who
did not rely solely on rural economic discontent but appealed to
Chinese nationalism during a period of Japanese war and occupation.
In short it is not possible to establish a clear connection between
peasant rebellions and the accumulative consequences of rural
bankruptcy.

Another historic indicator of the condition of the Chinese
countryside has been the frequency of famines. From 108 B.C. to
1911 1,828 famines of significant proportions were recorded. In
1921 there was a major famine in north China, in the relief of which
the International Red Cross played a significant role. But, interest-
ingly, in the next decades there were no famines of such proportions.
Although not a particularly reliable measuring rod, the reports of
travelers in the Chinese countryside do give the impression that the
most obvious forms of human suffering seemed to be declining with
each decade from the turn of the century. Female infanticide was

widespread in the first two decades of the twentieth century, but it was rarely noted by the 1930's. Daughters were sold into various forms of bondage in the first decades, but this practice had largely disappeared by the 1940's. The quality of textiles and of clothing improved during the very period when, in theory, conditions were deteriorating.

We are thus left with a complicated story filled with contradictions. The most plausible theory, that of steady rural pauperization, is not fully supported by the facts. No unambiguous measure shows the landlords getting richer and the peasants getting poorer as China was exposed more and more to the international commercial world. On the contrary, the more objective the data and the more precise the study, the greater is the doubt about the validity of what in general terms seems to make sense. From a distant perspective that sees only the collapse of the traditional order and the emergence of Communist China, the theme of increasing exploitation of peasants by landlords seems so reasonable as hardly to require accurate data for its validation. Yet in village studies made before World War II little evidence was uncovered to support such a pattern of change in economic relationships. Scholars currently examining the voluminous economic and social surveys conducted by the South Manchurian Railroad are discovering that although the work was done by Japanese social scientists personally inclined toward Marxism, the results were almost identical to those of some Kuomintang-supported studies done in Shantung and Hopei, and both groups of studies show that not until the mid 1930's did tenancy and size of landholdings begin to change. The proportion of the people who were landless showed almost no increase until the eve of full-scale war with Japan, and by then other political and social factors were at work.

The best available evidence thus demands different speculations, for no direct correlation between economic factors and the fact that the Chinese social and political order did collapse can be established. There must have been something more to the story; something tempered the economic trends and intensified the degree of political and social change. In looking for such intervening considerations, it would seem reasonable for sociologists to begin with the institution that traditionally was the most decisive in giving shape to Chinese society — the family.

Perhaps the Chinese family moderated and accommodated the

stresses in Chinese life, for a long time preventing them from becoming too explosive but eventually collapsing itself, thus opening the way to the final disintegration of the old Confucian order and the advent of Communism.

FORM AND SUBSTANCE
OF THE CHINESE FAMILY

The conventional account of the transformation of the Chinese family is even more established than the conventional account of the breakdown of Chinese agriculture. Available facts about the Chinese family, however, seem to contradict this second major interpretation even more emphatically than the facts bring into doubt the theory about agricultural bankruptcy being the prime cause of the disintegration of the Confucian system.

The standard view, held by Chinese and foreigners alike, is that historically the Chinese family consisted of three, four, or even five generations living together as a social and economic unit. The Confucian ideal of filial piety was presumed to translate itself into children looking after parents in such an unbroken line that the extended family, in which a son brought his wife to live with his father and the grandfather, was a cultural ideal violated only by extreme economic necessity.

In a society dominated by extended patrilineal families, an individual had unquestioning obligations to look after his relatives and to share with them whatever good fortune might befall him. The strength of the Chinese extended family presumably gave stability to the entire society. The conventional wisdom about Chinese society has generally held that only with modernization did the traditional family structure begin to break down and be replaced by the stem or the nuclear family consisting of parents and children or just husband and wife.

This theory, just like that of increasing repression by landlord or peasant, is not easily defended by the data. Wherever it is possible to find solid evidence of how the Chinese actually lived, the facts uniformly suggest that they rarely achieved their cultural ideal of the extended family. The Chinese family, even during the Ch'ing dynasty, often consisted of no more than parents and children. As soon as sons could support themselves, they were expected

THE TRADITIONAL CHINESE HOUSE

Chinese architecture, particularly of upper-class homes, accommodated the extended family. Old, large houses in Chinese
cities had a series of courtyards, each of which could house one
or more family units. A high wall and a large gate separated
the compound from the street. Immediately inside and usually
to the left was a gate house or room or two where the gate-keeper
lived and slept. The rest of the first courtyard was usually given
over to the servants and to stables and storerooms. The courtyard
was a perfect square and in its center there was likely to be a
well and maybe a tree. The passage between the first and second
courtyards tended to be in line with the front gate. Just within
the front gate there was likely to be a large screen or wall directly
behind the gate so that when the doors were opened one did not
have a direct view inward. The Chinese believed that evil spirits
could move only in straight lines and thus the screen protected the
living quarters from them and gave privacy and a break between
living units. The second courtyard repeated the first, but on a
grander scale. On both sides were two or three rooms, usually
accessible only through the center room. The roof extended over
the front to give a covered walkway or narrow veranda on three
sides of the courtyard. This courtyard might serve as quarters for
the staff and personal servants. Then depending upon the size
of the total establishment, the next, or in some cases the fourth,
courtyard, would be the living quarters for the junior members
of the family.

Depending on the wealth and station of the family, each son and
his family would occupy either a side of a courtyard or a total
courtyard. Certain courtyards might also be the quarters for the
master's concubines. The innermost courtyard belonged to the
master. Domiciled here was the first wife and often the second
and third wives, who occupied the rooms along the sides.
The eldest son's courtyard would be immediately before
the master's and, depending on whether he had a second wife
or concubines, the second and third sons and their wives might
occupy the rooms on the two sides. Questions of precedent were
important. Hurt feelings could result from decisions about whether
the younger son or the unmarried daughters should rank above
favored concubines, the issue being less the status of the concubines and more the physical convenience of the master, who
might prefer not to stumble through too many courtyards on a
dark night.

Traditional Chinese House and Courtyards

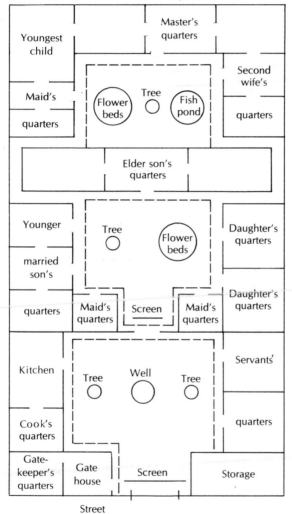

to go out and seek their own fortunes. Moreover, there is little evidence that during the last 150 years the most prevalent pattern of family institutions changed dramatically. In villages elder sons did tend to stay close to the family enterprises and the younger sons did drift away a bit more, but the pattern was little different from that in Europe. Indeed, the fact that the Chinese did not practice primogeniture meant that there was possibly less difference in the treatment between eldest and youngest sons than in Europe.

The ideology of the Chinese family was indeed severe. There were no conceivable grounds for challenging the institution. Children were expected to be unquestioningly dutiful regardless of parental behavior. Divorce was exceedingly rare and was never to be initiated by the wife. The husband had seven possible grounds: if the wife was disobedient, excessively talkative, stole, had a reputation for loose morals, displayed jealousy, had a contagious disease, or was childless. However, like the structure of the extended family, the ideology of marriage was more firmly embedded in the culture than the practices.

Modernization seems not to have brought quick changes to the structure of the family and to practices of marriage and divorce; rather the Chinese became increasingly conscious of not meeting their cultural ideals. Strains made the Chinese aware of the gaps between their ideology and their practices. Economic stress from increased monetization of the economy and the increasing population competing for a limited amount of land did cause the Chinese to turn to their families for help. Faced with immediate problems, the Chinese, responding to their own sense of isolation and insecurity, often tended to believe that earlier Chinese generations had not had the problem they were having. They idealized the security of the past by suggesting that the extended family had once been very widespread, although it never really had been.

The general impression that great changes were taking place in the Chinese family was heightened by changes in marriage practices. During the 1920's and 1930's the number of Chinese who did not accept marriages arranged by their parents but selected their own mates grew. Independence in such a decision was a bold act, limited in the 1920's largely to the urban and educated segments of society. By the time of the Japanese war, however, it was far more common at additional levels of society. This trend made the Chinese believe the nature of the Chinese family was changing. As significant as this development was for creating a sense of autonomy among modernized Chinese, it did not greatly affect the prevalence of extended families.

Wherever we have solid facts about Chinese social life it is clear that the composition of families did not change very much. Attitudes, sentiments, and cultural ideals were changing far more than the actual family structure. The "breakdown of the Chinese family" was thus more a change in attitude than in behavior. There was little statistical change in the number of extended families, but the number of people who felt threatened because they lacked the protection of an extended family significantly rose.

The key to the collapse of the traditional social order was not a significant rise in economic dislocations or a perceptible change in family patterns. Rather it was fundamental changes in political attitudes and emotional commitment. Statistics about landholdings and family practices show that physical changes lagged behind changes in beliefs and feelings. During the nineteenth and into the early twentieth century life in China did not undergo great changes, but there was an increasingly widespread belief that conditions were in fact different. In particular, Chinese intellectuals were frustrated because they believed conditions had severely deteriorated — more than the facts suggested they had, we now know. Others were disturbed because they wanted changes to be more rapid.

THE DECLINE OF IDEOLOGY

A comparison of the intellectual and economic history of the period reveals that far-reaching changes in the status of Confucianism and in the acceptance of foreign ideas occurred before there were significant changes in the economy and in basic social institutions.

Within a few decades after the Opium war (1839–1842) the Chinese were experiencing profound self-doubts and wondering whether they should incorporate Western technical knowledge to protect what remained of their Confucian system of values. Mary C. Wright, a most careful historian of modern China, identified the T'ung-chih Restoration, the remarkable effort of the throne to modernize China on Confucian terms after the Taiping rebellion, as "the last stand of Chinese Conservatism," by which she suggested that thereafter there was no effective defense of the Confucian order.

Certainly by the end of the nineteenth century the "traditionalists" as so ably described by Joseph Levenson, were self-consciously defensive and haunted by doubts and were thus no longer true Confucianists.

China's intellectual vulnerability to Western ideas can be seen from the fact that the ideological basis of the bureaucratic system — the classical examinations for the civil service — was completely eliminated by 1905, long before there had been significant structural changes in the economy. In the 1860's leading officials were arguing that the traditional amateur and belletristic ideals would have to be supplanted by more professional and technical skills. In the next two decades there evolved a fundamental debate on issues about knowledge that are still plaguing the Chinese Communists. Within the leading circles of the mandarinate there tended to be general agreement that it was possible to distinguish between basic values, of which the Confucian tradition presented the supreme examples, and technology, in which the West had significant advantages.

Chinese intellectuals tried to make a sharp distinction between fundamental values, including their Confucian ideals, and utilitarian and practical knowledge. The scholar-officials debated about "controlling the barbarians through their own superior technology," and many advocated that Chinese students learn Western science and use foreign technical knowledge to defend Confucian civilization.

The debate itself, however, began to spread doubt about the superiority of Confucian knowledge. By the 1890's the most vigorous reformers in the government were pressing for the all-out adoption of foreign knowledge in order to protect Chinese culture. In the summer of 1898 these reformers had one hundred days of complete control during which they sought to open the way to making China a constitutional monarchy supported by modernized governmental and educational systems. The reformers went too far, and a group of conservatives began to challenge the validity of the distinction between cultural values and utilitarian knowledge. They advanced the extraordinarily sophisticated view that Western technology could not be separated from the underlying values of Western Judeo-Christian civilization, and similarly Confucian values depended on the integrity of all aspects of Chinese civilization. Their concern was that if Western science and technology were accepted as the basis of the new Chinese education, Chinese students would soon come to doubt Confucian values and turn to foreign values.

Even though some of the conservatives recognized the superiority of Western technology, they felt that it would be better for Chinese civilization to go down to defeat honorably clinging to the Confucian world view, than to insist that the old could be defended by incorporating select elements of the new.

The conservative argument, which was defensive and lacked the easy self-assurance of the traditional Confucian view, sowed doubts among the reformers, causing some to become pessimistic about any hope for China and others to become even more radical to the point of rejecting the need to defend Chinese "civilization" and favoring the idea of preserving the Chinese "nation."

The clash between values and knowledge became a central ingredient in the development of Chinese nationalism. It has in a strange fashion survived to this day, appearing now as the "red and expert" problems of Mao Tse-tung, in which "redness" is political correctness and values and "expertness" is technical knowledge and skills. The fact that Chinese nationalism was shaped by questions about values and knowledge reflects the degree to which the Chinese in a few generations experienced the most fundamental intellectual changes that any society ever experienced in so short a time. It has been argued that the mental climate of China changed more during the first half of the twentieth century than that of the West changed between the thirteenth and twentieth centuries.

The clashes of values did not occur in a calm, intellectual atmosphere; often they were at the vortex of considerable violence. For example, the reformers, led by K'ang Yu-wei, who gained the support of the young Emperor Kuang Hsü for the hundred days of reform in 1898, realized they might have to counter the reactionary forces by assassinating Jung-lu, the close adviser of the Empress Dowager Tz'u Hsi. The chosen agent for the act, Yüan Shih-k'ai, who later became the first president of the Republic of China, informed the Empress Dowager of the plot, and she quite ruthlessly had the young emperor seized and placed under house arrest in the palace, while she executed several of the reformers. K'ang Yu-wei fled the country. In the following years the incompetence of reactionary leaders and the fiasco of the Boxer Rebellion encouraged more and more Chinese to think of the need for change, and reformers became revolutionaries as the spirit of national self-consciousness made more Chinese resentful of Manchu rule.

The extent to which Chinese intellectual life was breaking out of the Confucian mold can be seen from the spectacular rise in the number of students studying in new-style, westernized schools as soon as the examination system was changed. In 1905, when it was decreed that the Confucian classics were no longer the basis for the examinations, only slightly more than one hundred thousand students were in new-style schools. By 1907 the number had increased more than tenfold, and there were over a million students in nearly thirty-eight thousand schools. At the time of the 1911 revolution there were over 1.5 million students and 52,650 schools, and by 1916 the number had risen to nearly 4.3 million students in 129,739 schools. By 1923 there were over 6.6 million students learning modern sciences and mathematics instead of the Confucian classics. During this period numerous universities were founded by both foreigners and Chinese; some floundered and failed while others became noteworthy centers of knowledge. By 1931 there were thirty-four universities and sixteen technical institutions of higher learning in China.

In addition, large numbers of Chinese students, starting with Yung Wing, who had graduated from Yale in 1847, began studying abroad. At the time of the 1911 Revolution there were eight hundred Chinese students in America, four hundred in Europe, and from ten to fifteen thousand in Japan. By 1930, nearly two thousand students left the country each year for university work in America and Europe. The speed with which the Chinese turned to modern education reflected not only their rejection of Confucianism and their continuing faith in education but also the remarkable efforts of foreign missionaries to establish schools and universities along the east coast and in the interior. The first major schools and universities were missionary supported. Many of the people trained to teach at these schools were encouraged to spend some years abroad. By the 1930's twenty-one Protestant societies and a dozen American universities were supporting a dozen or so Chinese universities and colleges that ranged from Yenching, near Peking, to Lingnan, near Canton.

In 1919 the intellectual ferment in China became highly politicized with the May Fourth Movement, which was occasioned by the announcement of the decision of the Allies at the Paris Peace Conference to give Japan rights in Shantung province which had once belonged to Germany. Since China had declared war on Germany as a consequence of American persuasion there was a strong feeling that China had been most unjustly treated by Woodrow Wilson. Over three thousand college students demonstrated in Peking; the home of one cabinet member was burned; and two other ministers had to escape over their back walls. In the days that followed, students poured down to Shantung in commandeered trains. The government sought to restore order, but by mid-May the students had called for a general strike and there was widespread sympathy on the part of merchants who were anxious to boycott Japanese products and workers who were fired by the spark of nationalism.

John Dewey happened to be in China at the time and inspired the intellectuals with his views of the pragmatic and utilitarian focus appropriate to modern education. Ts'ai Yuan-p'ei, the chancellor of Peking National University, and Dr. Hu Shih, a former student of John Dewey and China's leading philosopher, gave constructive intellectual leadership to the students' movement. Student unions were established in the major cities, and a variety of new journals, such as *Young China, The Construction,* and *Young World,* made their appearances and, along with such more-established journals as *The New Youth, The New Tide, Weekly Review, The Modern Critic,* gave the Chinese intellectual scene a heavy dose of utopian idealism that stressed the purity of youth and nationalist sentiments.

With the May Fourth Movement the Chinese intellectuals decisively deserted the faltering regime of the warlords and set the stage for the founding of both the Kuomintang and the Communist Party as mass movements heavily influenced by students in search of allies in the rest of society. These developments carry us well ahead of our story. However, these trends demonstrate the degree to which intellectual currents came to dominate the fate of China as the old imperial structure crumbled.

We must now review how the Western impact politically challenged the Ch'ing dynasty by questioning the legitimacy of that dynasty and set in motion the currents of nationalism, which at first was strongly anti-Confucianist and pro-modern but in time became increasingly anti-foreign in spite of (or because of) its dependence on foreign knowledge. These observations may be of some help in guiding our survey of the political dimensions of the Western encroachment on China because they suggest that the dynamic element in China's modernization was primarily the problem of attitudes and intellectual perspectives and less one of material or economic changes. Joseph Levenson, Benjamin Schwartz, and other intellectual historians unquestionably discovered what was both critical and distinctive in China's modernization when they focused on the clash of ideas.

THE MYSTERIES OF CHINA'S POPULATION

There are several mysteries in the history of Chinese demography. First it is startling that the first census taken in A.D. 2 when the population was still concentrated in the Yellow River Valley reported 59.5 million people, which compares with the estimated 54 million in the entire Roman Empire at about the same year. But in the next 1500 years there was apparently very little change as the Malthusian balance must have been at work:

A.D. 2	59.5	million	1651	60	million
742–755	51		1741	143.4	
900	53		1775	264.5	
1200	45		1793	313	
1292	53.6		1849	413	
1393	60.5				

These figures probably underestimate the actual population by at least 20 percent; as the census was the basis for establishing tax quotas, both households and districts benefitted by understating their sizes. Official estimates often vascillated greatly from year to year: the figure for 1774 was only 221 million and for 1775, 264.5 million. The deepest mystery of China's population is that it more than doubled between 1741 and 1793, before the Western impact, industrialization, or any changes in public health standards. The explanation seems to lie in a combination of minor technological innovations in agriculture and the introduction of new crops.

The mystery of China's population continues today. Between 1849 and 1949 the assumption was that the population was growing slowly and at the most totaled only some 450 million. The first Communist census, however, revealed a figure of 580 million, but since then no further figures have been published. Speculation now places the population at anywhere from 750 to 850 million.

CHAPTER SIX

Confronting the West

A paradox of China's external relations is that in spite of prolonged periods of alien rule, the Chinese throughout most of their history felt secure, to the point of complacent smugness. Far richer and stronger than their nearest neighbors and exposed only to "barbarians" who might conquer but who could never rule without employing Chinese ideas and personnel, the Chinese understandably developed a deep sense of cultural superiority. Others might be rude and militarily vicious, but the Chinese had no reason to doubt, in spite of some unfortunate experiences, that they were culturally the center of the world, the Middle Kingdom, as they called themselves.[1] Although during the last thousand years of the imperial order all or part of China was ruled by alien conquerors, the Chinese persisted in feeling supremely self-assured.

The first contacts of the Chinese with the West were not threatening and indeed reinforced the Chinese view of themselves as the center of civilization. As early as Roman times the balance of trade with Europe heavily favored China. The Chinese were able to export tea, silk, chinaware, paper, and art objects, while the Romans could supply only such exotic and unlikely objects as "ostriches' eggs and jugglers; dwarfs and musicians; horses that sweat blood; parrots; peacocks and apes; incense, perfumes, and aphrodisiacs; ivory, rhinoceros horn and tortoiseshell; and even pretty girls for concubines."[2] And above all there was gold and silver bullion.

[1]The Chinese word for their country is *Chung-kuo,* which means central or middle country. The Western word *China* may have come from a faulty transliteration of *Chung-kuo* or more likely it may have been derived from the Ch'in dynasty that briefly ruled prior to the Sung.

[2]George B. Sansom, *The Western World and Japan: A Study of the Interaction of European and Asiatic Cultures* (New York: Knopf, 1950), p. 18.

Indeed, the drainage of gold to China during the period of the Roman Republic was so great that a decree was passed that Romans should no longer wear silk togas (and thereafter they could only surreptitiously wear silk under their outer garments, which may have been the beginning of silk lingerie).

The arrival of Christianity in China created little disturbance. The Nestorian Christians who wandered into China from Europe by way of Central Asia during the T'ang dynasty were hardly noticed by the Chinese. The emperor T'ai Tsung apparently welcomed some Christians to his capital of Ch'angan as early as 635 and had parts of their sacred book translated for the enlightenment of his people. Some six hundred years later William of Rubruck made his way across central Asia to the Mongol capital and sought to convert Mangu, the grandson of Genghis Khan. Mangu welcomed him warmly and gathered a great audience for him to preach to. After the performance Mangu commended the good friar for his high fervor and his manifest sincerity but told him if he were to succeed in his divine mission he would have to drop implausible doctrines such as the Virgin Birth and the Resurrection.

By the Ming dynasty (1368–1644) more Westerners, particularly Portuguese, were reaching the celestial empire. In the middle of the sixteenth century the Portuguese had established a colony at Macao, where they have remained to this day. The Spaniards and the Dutch soon followed on the seacoast, and the Russians began to make their appearance to the north. The most remarkable achievement during this period was the patient and highly successful mission of the Jesuit Matthew Ricci, who arrived in Macao in 1582 and then set about carefully analyzing Chinese society and Confucianism. After twenty years of study he came to the conclusion that Confucianism was not a religion, that one could be both a Christian and a Confucianist, and that it should be possible for Jesuits to compete in the examination system and become mandarin officials and so gain the emperor's attention. The strategy was to convert the emperor so that he in turn might decree that all Chinese should embrace Christianity. Eventually the dedicated and tolerant Ricci made his way to Peking and the Imperial Court. He became a tutor to the heir to the throne, helped develop Chinese astronomy, and wrung from the emperor the concession to establish a church near the palace. Before he died in 1610 he had won two members of the

Hanlin Academy — the height of the Confucian elite — and an imperial prince to his faith. The commitment of the Jesuits to the Chinese court was tellingly demonstrated when they served as the chief negotiators for the Chinese in arranging the Treaty of Nerchinsk with the Russians in 1689. This first modern treaty involving the Chinese was drafted in Latin, and because of Jesuit determination it was truly a treaty of equals and lacked the humiliating features that became a part of subsequent Chinese treaties with the European seapowers.

The Jesuits' commitment to the Ming court also appeared when they helped design and direct artillery in the last battles against the conquering Manchus. Once the Manchus established the Ch'ing dynasty, the missionaries returned and were usually received with tolerance. Once again the Jesuits found themselves in particular favor in the imperial court. By the early eighteenth century they were joined by Dominican and Franciscan friars from the Philippines, who in the spirit of their mendicant orders were horrified at the elite style of the Jesuits. The new arrivals denounced the Jesuits for treating with the rulers rather than serving the common people and for tolerating Confucianism, insisting that it was indeed a religion and thus incompatible with Christianity. The Emperor K'ang Hsi was amused by the debate and found in favor of the Jesuits, but in the meantime Pope Clement XI had been involved in the "rites controversy" and his legates arrived in China to adjudicate the matter. On the basis of their reports the Pope found in favor of the mendicant orders and against the Jesuits. The Chinese emperor promptly felt that his right to be the sole authority for what took place in his empire had been challenged, so in 1732 he decreed that all missionaries should leave China.

This was the first sign that relations between China and the West would not always be untroubled. The missionaries gradually withdrew. In the meantime the West was developing more effective sailing vessels, which culminated in the development of the clipper ships in the mid-nineteenth century. Once again trade became the main form of contact between China and the West.

Although the clipper ships could make the trip far faster than overland caravans, the balance of trade still favored the Chinese. New England traders from Salem and Boston soon were deeply involved carrying tea, silk, chinaware, and other Chinese products abroad while desperately trying to find enough to send to China in return. Yankee ingenuity led to the shipment to Canton of ice from Massachusetts ponds, roots of trees that New Englanders hoped would be thought of as ginseng (a favored medicine of the Chinese), and furs from Oregon and the Northwest. The balance, however, was so much in favor of China that the Americans had to make substantial shipments of bullion. Indeed, during the first years of the American Republic the export of specie was so severe that one of the first investigatory congressional committees looked into the problem and reported that "the whole amount of our current coin is probably not more than double that which has been exported in a single year to India, including China in the general term." Subsequently the United States Treasury minted a special coin to be used only in the China trade. In time the Americans obtained silver from their trade with Mexico and shipped it to China, and thus the Mexican dollar became the principal unit of currency along the China coast.

Shortly after the turn of the century an item was found that dramatically altered the terms of trade: opium. Very quickly in the first years of the nineteenth century the British East India Company encouraged the production of opium, especially in Bengal and Madras in India. By the 1830's the flow of opium into China had reached major proportions, and China was now beginning to experience an outflow of bullion, for all its exports were not enough to pay for the amounts of opium that were being imported. Long before the trade began to affect the economy the Ch'ing government declared the opium trade illegal. This, however, did not stop the flow because the Western merchants very quickly established working relations with Chinese officials, paying them handsome prices to allow the trade to continue.

At that time the West had no sympathy for China's problems. Western traders took the attitude that opium smoking was beneath contempt, that even the lowliest animal would not engage in it, but the principle of free trade was absolute and all the Chinese had to do was to stop being addicts. They were contemptuous of the Chinese officials they had bribed to keep the trade open, precisely because they were corruptible. The Western view at that time was not too dissimilar to the view of those who today supply the American hard drug market and feel that any society that cannot keep its own people from such awful practices should not expect others to do their policing for them.

The rise in opium trade coincided significantly with a Western, particularly British, movement toward free trade. The case for not interfering with the opium trade rested on the theory of free trade, which logically required that the British government abolish the charters it had once given to certain companies that then had legal monopolies on all trade in a specified area. The greatest of the charter companies was the British East India Company. The principle of free trade finally triumphed in 1833 when the British East India Company was abolished and free competition was allowed to reign.

Before then the "John Company," as the British East India Company was called, had regulated the China trade and assumed full responsibilities for working out the conditions of trade and the adjudication of all controversies associated with it. The Western traders generally accepted the special role of the British East India Company and allowed it to work out all the informal relations with the Chinese officials so that trade could flow. Matters of status and pride were easily handled because the company officials did not have official rank and as private citizens their concern was only with keeping the trade moving. With the ending of the special status of the company there was need for a new basis for regulating relations between the traders and China. For the Westerners, at least, the only logical alternative was the customary legal sovereign-to-sovereign relationship common to the European state system. The fact that the West was engaged in illegal, immoral, but highly profitable trade greatly complicated the problem of arriving at any mutually acceptable basis of official intercourse with the Chinese.

As soon as the British government sought to establish diplomatic relations with China it became apparent that Chinese and Englishmen saw the world completely differently. The English assumed that the Chinese would be anxious to behave according to European standards of international law or that at least they would want to learn what those standards were. The Chinese on their part were convinced that Britain was merely another "barbarian" country that should welcome the opportunity to partake of Confucian culture.

The problem of establishing workable diplomatic relations was nearly made insurmountable by the Western notion that official acts and private commercial contacts were completely separate matters and the Chinese sense that as far as the Middle Kingdom was concerned trade and tribute were the same. According to the Chinese view, all trade with China was a political act; "barbarian" countries showed their reverence for the Son of Heaven by sending him "tribute," while he in turn showed his magnanimity by giving gifts in return. Thus foreign trade for the Chinese was really just a way in which others showed respect for the emperor and were rewarded with his bounty. This was why the Imperial Court believed that all dealings with foreigners should be left either to local officials, who did not have to abide by protocol, or to officials of the Board of Rites who would teach the foreign barbarians the correct rituals so they could avoid embarrassment.

By the 1830's an absolutely irreconcilable situation was reached; each side was completely convinced of its unquestionable righteousness. The Chinese were prepared to insist that the opium trade be stopped, and in 1839 the emperor appointed a vigorous and incorruptible mandarin, Lin Tse-hsü, to Canton to see that this was done. The British were equally insistent that the Chinese give up their pretensions of being the center of the world and accept standard conventions of diplomacy. The British were also frustrated by Chinese insistence that trade could legally be conducted only at the port of Canton and with the few recognized Chinese merchants of the Canton guilds, or *co-hongs*.

As early as 1793 the British had sent a mission under Lord Macartney to try to establish official relations with the Imperial Court. That mission, like those that followed, ran into the irreconcilable but essentially ludicrous controversy of the *kowtow*. The Chinese insisted that the ambassador would have to prostrate himself three times before the emperor, touching his forehead to the floor with each prostration. Emperor Ch'ien Lung's responses to Macartney's requests for a straightforward audience gives the flavor of the times (and may help to explain why King George III suffered fits of madness):[3]

[3]Harley Farnsworth MacNair, *The Real Conflict between China and Japan: An Analysis of Opposing Ideologies* (Chicago: University of Chicago Press, 1938), p. 26–27. Copyright 1938 by The University of Chicago.

You, O King, live beyond the confines of many seas; nevertheless, impelled by your humble desire to partake of the benefits of our civilisation, you have dispatched a mission respectfully bearing your memorial. Your Envoy has crossed the seas and paid his respects at my Court on the anniversary of my birthday. To show your devotion, you have also sent offerings of your country's produce.

I have perused your memorial; the earnest terms in which it is couched reveal a respectful humility on your part, which is highly praiseworthy. In consideration of the fact that your Ambassador and his deputy have come a long way with your memorial and tribute, I have shown them high favour and have allowed them to be introduced into my presence. To manifest my indulgence, I have entertained them at a banquet and made them numerous gifts. . . .

Swaying the wide world, I have but one aim in view, namely, to maintain a perfect governance and to fulfil the duties of the State: strange and costly objects do not interest me. If I have commanded that the tribute offerings sent by you, O King, are to be accepted, this was solely in consideration for the spirit which prompted you to dispatch them from afar. Our dynasty's majestic virtue has penetrated into every country under Heaven, and Kings of all nations have offered their costly tribute by land and sea. As your Ambassador can see for himself, we possess all things. I set no value on objects strange or ingenious, and have no use for your country's manufactures. This then is my answer to your request to appoint a representative at my court, a request contrary to our dynastic usage, which would only result in inconvenience to yourself. I have expounded my wishes in detail and have commanded your tribute Envoys to leave in peace on their homeward journey. It behooves you, O King, to respect my sentiments and to display even greater devotion and loyalty in future, so that, by perpetual submission to our Throne, you may secure peace and prosperity for your country hereafter.

Lord Macartney recognized the failure of his mission, but before he left Peking he received another memorial, which said in part:[4]

You, O King, from afar have yearned after the blessings of our civilisation, and in your eagerness to come into touch with our converting influence have sent an Embassy across the sea bearing a memorial. I have already taken note of your respectful spirit of submission, have treated your mission with extreme favour and loaded

[4]*Ibid.*, p. 28–30.

it with gifts, besides issuing a mandate to you, O King, and honouring you with the bestowal of valuable presents. Thus has my indulgence been manifested. . . . But your Ambassador has now put forward new requests which completely fail to recognise the Throne's principle to "treat strangers from afar with indulgence," and to exercise a pacifying control over barbarian tribes, the world over. Moreover, our dynasty, swaying the myriad races of the globe, extends the same benevolence towards all. Your England is not the only nation trading at Canton. If other nations, following your bad example, wrongfully importune my ear with further impossible requests, how will it be possible for me to treat them with easy indulgence? Nevertheless, I do not forget the lonely remoteness of your island, cut off from the world by intervening wastes of sea, nor do I overlook your excusable ignorance of the usages of Our Celestial Empire. I have consequently commanded my Ministers to enlighten your Ambassador on the subject and have ordered the departure of the mission . . . . My capital is the hub and centre about which all quarters of the globe revolve. Its ordinances are most august and its laws are strict in the extreme. The subjects of our dependencies have never been allowed to open places of business in Peking. . . .

The British tried again in 1816 by sending Lord Jeffrey Amherst to Peking. The issue of the *kowtow* again appeared, and the new Chia Ch'ing emperor delivered an equally haughty mandate,[5]

My dynasty attaches no value to products from abroad; your nation's cunningly wrought and strange wares do not appeal to me in the least, nor do they interest me.

For the future, O King, if you will keep your subjects in order and strengthen your national defences, I shall hold you in high esteem, notwithstanding your remoteness.

Once issues of honor, prestige, and relative political importance were compounded with the moral and legal issues of the opium trade, the accommodations that had brought East and West together in Canton began to wear thin. These earlier adjustments had been easier when the British East India Company dominated the trade and assumed the role of informal representative of the traders. Given the Chinese philosophy of collective responsibility, relations were most tranquil when there was a representative of the traders who

[5]*Ibid.*, p. 43–44.

could be held accountable for the behavior of all traders. As more countries entered the trade and the East India Company lost its monopoly, the problem of regulation increased.

The differences between the Western view of individual responsibility and the Chinese view of group responsibility are well illustrated by the Terranova case. In 1821 the *Emily*, out of Baltimore, was at anchor off Canton and surrounded by sampans on which hawkers were selling vegetables and trinkets. Someone threw some garbage overboard and somehow a boat woman toppled into the water and drowned. The Chinese authorities insisted that someone, anyone, be handed over for punishment so that all could see that justice was being upheld. The American captain insisted that the drowning must have been an accident and that in any case the authorities would have to establish proof of criminal guilt before justice could be done. The Chinese threatened to stop the trade of the *Emily* and of all other American vessels. They arrested the Chinese merchants who were the trading partners of the Americans and owed them large sums of money. The American captain then felt he had to yield to necessity, and so he handed over to the Chinese an illiterate Italian seaman who a few days later was executed by strangulation.

During the early nineteenth century Chinese policy was mostly directed toward controlling foreigners in the classic imperial way — by trying to isolate and herd together members of each alien group. The "barbarians" were then ordered to govern themselves according to their own rules in their own circles but to observe Chinese usages in all relations with Chinese. This tradition was extremely important, for it set the pattern for the emerging treaty port system.

In Canton the foreign traders (also called "factors") were restricted to their "factories," which were long narrow buildings of two or three stories and served as both warehouses and living quarters for the traders. The compounds were owned by the Chinese merchants with whom the factory traded. The Westerners were constantly frustrated by Chinese refusal to allow trade with anybody, but the Chinese authorities felt that they could only maintain control over the foreigners by holding the Chinese merchants accountable for the foreigners' behavior. The frustration of the traders was intensified because they were confined to their factories and could not move about within the city, to say nothing of visiting the countryside. The Chinese believed peace would be best maintained if the "barbarians" were kept in their ghettos.

Lin Tse-hsü, a determined and honest official, was working to abolish the opium trade. At the same time the British were seeking once more to force the Chinese to establish diplomatic relations with England. They were particularly annoyed that the representative of their king was being treated as a lowly figure by mere provincial authorities in Canton instead of being received by the central authorities in Peking. Tension quickly mounted when Lin set about confiscating all the opium in Canton, and events soon led to the Opium war, which, in a desultory fashion and with almost no casualties, lasted from November 1839 to August 1842. (When the British frigate *Amethyst*, withdrawing down the Yangtze River in 1949, ran a gauntlet of Communist guns, it sustained more casualties than the British suffered in the Opium war.)

Peking's ability to deal with the British was profoundly hampered by almost complete ignorance of Europeans. The situation was not helped by the flow of memorials from high officials to the emperor. (Often they were as irrelevant as some of the proposals that officials in Washington get from American university professors.) One official, for example, proposed to the Son of Heaven that in order to defeat the British the empire should be searched for men who could stay under water for two or three hours, and when located they should be sent out to pull the plugs out of the bottoms of the British boats. Another official observed that because the British were like locusts large locust traps should be set on the beaches to snare them if they came ashore. Still another mandarin remarked that since the British "barbarians" were peculiarly stiff-legged, all that had to be done was to topple them over and they would not be able to get up again.

The war produced the Treaty of Nanking, the first of the "unequal treaties" that Chinese nationalists over the next hundred years saw increasingly as a principal source of China's humiliation. According to the terms of the treaty, the island of Hong Kong was ceded to England, and the five cities of Canton, Amoy, Foochow, Ningpo, and Shanghai became treaty ports in which British traders resided and conducted business in "concessions" where their own authorities would govern them. The *co-hongs* were abolished and the British received permission to trade with any Chinese merchant.

British and Chinese officials would deal with each other on a footing of equality. A schedule of tariffs was established, and China agreed to pay an indemnity of 21 million taels to cover the opium that Lin Tse-hsü had destroyed, the debts of the *co-hong* merchants, and the cost of the war to Britain.

Immediately, on the heels of the British successes, other Western powers pressed China for comparable treaties. Caleb Cushing, dispatched by President Tyler to negotiate an American arrangement, obtained the Treaty of Wanghai in July 1844. It specifically formulated the rights of extraterritoriality (Americans would be governed by American laws in China) and established the principle of the most-favored nation, which meant in practice that the United States would obtain whatever benefits were given to the European powers, especially the British. In the same year the French obtained a comparable treaty that also contained clauses protecting missionaries. The Belgians signed a treaty in 1845, Sweden and Norway in 1847, and Russia in 1851.

The treaty system that followed from the initial unequal treaties was only gradually and painfully established. The principle of diplomatic representation and of equality in official relations was not easily accepted by the Chinese, who persisted in believing that the "barbarians" were still best handled by the Ministry of Rites, who would teach them civility and proper awe for the Emperor's Way. In 1856 an incident involving a small Hong Kong registered craft, the lorcha *Arrow*, triggered off a second war. British and French troops occupied Tientsin and approached Peking, capturing the Summer Palace. The subsequent Treaty of Tientsin created ten more treaty ports, established the right of foreigners to have embassies in Peking, opened the interior to travel, provided additional protection for missionaries, arranged new tariffs, and ceded to Britain Kowloon, the bit of the mainland opposite Hong Kong island.

By force of arms the Western powers also compelled the Chinese to establish a foreign office and send diplomatic missions abroad. One of the early missions was headed by Anson Burlingame, who had just retired as American minister to Peking but enthusiastically took up the Chinese cause. Washington and London negotiated treaties that provided for the territorial integrity of China and for unrestricted immigration of Chinese laborers into the United States.

In 1861, under constant prodding from the Western ambassadors, the Chinese established the Tsungli Yamen for the management of foreign affairs. Since the new office lacked traditional status and had to deal with unpleasant matters, it was initially staffed by officers who seemed to the foreigners to be peculiarly incompetent. There was suspicion that the Chinese had designed a clever stratagem for dealing with foreign officials — forcing them to conduct their business with the most dim-witted officials in all the empire. Many Western officials were nearly driven out of their minds. The tactics ranged from a persistent tendency of officials to "forget" all that had been agreed to at previous meetings, to the practice of confusing and mixing up the policy demands and interests of the various foreign powers. The diplomatic corps took upon itself the task of trying to educate the Chinese in Western diplomacy, a reversal of the earlier efforts of the Ministry of Rites. The effort was marked by the frustrating ways in which the Chinese repeatedly failed to understand what was involved in "playing the game." For example, the diplomatic corps was completely undone when the emperor ordered some Chinese diplomats executed because a treaty they had negotiated with Russia displeased him: How could one press for advantage in negotiating with the Chinese if they refused to recognize the principle of diplomatic immunity — not just for foreign diplomats but for their own?

CULTURAL CONFLICTS: MISUNDERSTANDINGS AND FRUSTRATION

Detailed analysis of the early nineteenth-century meeting of East and West along the China coast reveals a host of misunderstandings stemming from cultural differences. Each side proceeded to treat the other according to its own perceptions of what was called for, and consequently the behavior of each tended to provoke the other to even more unintelligible acts.

The Chinese frustrations were compounded by the discovery in case after case that traditional techniques that had once worked masterfully in controlling the "barbarians" of central Asia backfired when applied to the Western "barbarians." For example, the cardinal aim of Chinese foreign relations had always been to play off one barbarian against another. In the past the Chinese had been extremely successful in giving and denying favors to nomad groups to pacify them or encourage them to fight another group. The attempt to use the distant "barbarians" to control the nearer ones completely collapsed when the Western countries uniformly insisted on the most-favored-nation principle in all their treaties. Suddenly the Chinese discovered that by giving a favor to one country in the hope of winning its favor or pacifying it, they were in fact giving the same favor to all the treaty powers.

Similarly, the traditional Chinese practice of insisting that alien communities rule themselves according to their own customs — which provided an original rationale for the treaty port system — when applied to Westerners, produced not isolated cells of "foreign bodies" but virulent centers that spread "cultural contagion" throughout the Chinese community. Instead of the treaty ports becoming isolated settlements within which the foreigner was contained, they became the dynamic centers of much of China's economic life and source of humiliation to all Chinese leaders.

By the last decade of the nineteenth century it appeared that China like Africa would be carved up by imperial powers. Parts of the country became spheres of influence of different powers. Russia dominated Manchuria, especially after 1896, when it obtained the rights to build the Chinese Eastern Railroad across the province; in 1898 Russia obtained a twenty-five-year lease for a base in Dairen and Port Arthur. Great Britain sought to counter the Russian advance in Manchuria by demanding a lease to Weihaiwei, a seaport in Shantung across the Yellow Sea from the tip of the Liaotung peninsula of Manchuria, "for as long a period as Port Arthur shall remain in the possession of Russia." The principal British sphere of influence, however, was Shanghai and the Yangtze River valley. Germany in 1898, after the murder of two German Catholic missionaries, obtained a ninety-nine-year lease on the tip of Shantung. In the same year France got a ninety-nine-year lease on the Bay of Kwanchow in southwest Kwangtung, just above the French colony and protectorates in Indochina.

The constant foreign demands for concessions included more than just treaty port arrangements. It has been estimated that between 1842 and 1911 China on 110 occasions had to make indemnity payments to foreign governments. The problem of providing cash for such payments was severe. For example between 1895 and 1900 China had to pay Japan 200 million taels of silver, yet the government's total revenue receipts totaled only about 90 million taels in 1900. The problem of government revenues resulted in odd arrangements whereby the Chinese Maritime Customs Service was organized and staffed by foreigners. China lost control of its own tariffs, but the service did come to provide the government with one of its most reliable sources of income.

In 1900 the Boxer Rebellion, an atavistic, anti-foreign movement that had the tacit support of the Manchu court, provided an occasion for much more severe demands by the European powers, and for a brief period it appeared likely that China would at last be partitioned. Britain, however, was in no mood to assume additional imperial responsibilities because the demands of India were heavy and the Boer war was just commencing in South Africa. The British did not wish to see China divided among other powers, and they were confident of their ability to compete for trade and influence on equal terms.

Immediately before the Boxer uprising, Britain had cooperated in supporting the American declaration of the Open Door policy, under which all countries would recognize the principle that no sphere of influence could interfere with the vested interests of any other state and that therefore there could be no commercial advantage in claiming such a sphere. In 1899 John Hay, the American secretary of state, had sent notes to all interested countries proposing the "open door," and because no country was prepared to answer publicly in the negative, hypocrisy triumphed and compelled all to act more honorably than otherwise they might have, saving China from almost certain dismemberment.

China's problems were not limited to the unruly demands of Westerners. As threatening, if not more so, to the Confucian order was the behavior of China's immediate neighbors, Japan, Korea, Viet Nam, Burma, and even Thailand. At one time they had recognized the Middle Kingdom by extending tribute but, sensing China's weakness, they had become as threatening as the Westerners. Historically, China had been the suzerain of its neighbors; China was considered the "elder brother" and the vassal country was the "younger brother" who had to show proper Confucian deference to the elder. The tribute system called for periodic missions, usually every three years, to the Peking courts. Members of these missions would perform the proper rituals to show their submissiveness to the Celestial Empire and present to the emperor their gifts. The total effect of this practice was to provide the basis for significant foreign trade while not giving power or status to private merchants whom Confucian officials distrusted. It made the Chinese feel superior to all their neighbors and allowed these neighbors to marvel at how vulnerable to flattery the Chinese were.

In theory, in return for sending tribute the emperor would protect the suzerain country and take care of its foreign affairs, while allowing it freedom to manage its internal affairs. In the Chinese mind the relationship was precisely that of the elder and younger brother, but this relationship was not acknowledged in Western international law and could not be easily explained in non-Confucian terms.

According to the Western mind China either was accountable for all the actions of those over which it claimed suzerainty or China forfeited the right to such claims. The French soon sensed that the Chinese were not able to be responsible for what the Vietnamese did. Similarly the Russians challenged Chinese claims in central Asia, in the area of Ili, and proved to their own satisfaction that the Chinese claims of suzerainty were pretentious.

Most shocking was the behavior of the Japanese, who had been influenced by the Confucian ethic but, ever since their exposure to the West, had shown an unfailing ability to demonstrate the faults of the Chinese according to both the Confucian and the Western world view. They vigorously challenged China's claim of suzerainty over Korea and sought to "open" the Hermit Kingdom to contacts with other countries. China was compelled to back up its claims of suzerainty by trying to manage Korea's relations with Japan, but the outcome was a disastrous war in 1894 and 1895, which resulted in a humiliating defeat and the Treaty of Shimonoseki, by which China had not only to give up claims of suzerainty over Korea but also to cede to Japan Formosa, the Pescadores islands, and the Liaotung peninsula in Manchuria.

The fact that Japan felt no awe of the Celestial Kingdom and could handily defeat the Chinese was possibly the most demoralizing blow to China. It opened the way to a flood of Chinese students who were anxious to learn more about Japan's adoption of modern technology. By the end of the nineteenth century no country in Asia still thought of China as the Middle Kingdom, deserving of awe and capable of bounteous protection. Furthermore, increasing numbers of Chinese were questioning traditional Confucian values and were anxious to replace them with assertions of Chinese nationalism.

With the twentieth century came a significant drop in the importance of the China trade to all Western powers. The industrialization of Europe and America made the China market less attractive, for more lucrative possibilities were nearer home. By World War I the dominant impulse of Western contacts with China had become the missionary endeavor, and increasingly the underlying spirit of the relationship became less one of trying to outwit the Chinese and more one of seeking to help them. Americans' image of China was no longer that of a potentially great market but rather that of a country needing great assistance.

Several generations of Americans were brought up thinking China needed the help of missionaries, but few had any idea of the reality of that endeavor. Whereas in the middle of the nineteenth century the focus of Western activities in China was the treaty port and the "factories" of the traders, by the early twentieth century it was the mission compound with its Westernized schools and hospitals.

Scattered throughout China and often far removed from the treaty ports of the businessmen were the compounds of American and European missions. Most contained Western-style houses made of brick with Chinese gray-tiled roofs. The dominant buildings were the school complexes — primary, elementary, and high school, with boarding facilities — perhaps a hospital (often of major proportions), and always a church. The relationship of Chinese and foreigners in these compounds was exceedingly complex, possibly the most complex of any intercultural situation and certainly one that has never been effectively studied. Within the compounds were those who desperately sought to identify with all that was alien to China, from religious belief to secular knowledge; others hoped to gain something of value while not yielding their identity; and many simply sought material benefits from contacts with the foreigners.

Whether from the early trader and the activities of the treaty ports or from the missionaries and their schools, colleges, and hospitals, the incessant message for the Chinese was that others had found a more exciting and significant way of life and that the old Chinese virtues were irrelevant. Young Chinese who attended the new schools dreamed of a new China that would be rich and powerful, fully capable of competing with the West on Western, not Chinese, terms.

The Western impact brought deep humiliation and physical suffering to the Chinese people. More than this, however, it made the Chinese dissatisfied with their historic ways and anxious to prove themselves in modern terms. The stage was set for a profound cultural and political revolution.

CHAPTER SEVEN

Rebellion, Revolution, and Warlordism

The goal of Confucian China was harmony and tranquility; the theme of modern China has been revolution and war, both civil and international. The politics of traditional China was based on the claims of ethics, the pretensions of philosophers, and the accommodating spirit of scholar-officials. Nevertheless, violence occurred, torture was used, and rebels were harshly dealt with. Indeed, every dynasty emerged out of successful military operations, and all relied upon huge bodies of soldiers although in ancient China the source of legitimacy was not military power.

In modern China, once the mystique of Confucianism dissolved, the frantic search for a new basis of legitimacy began. Instead of harmony, sincerity, and virtue, the new modern spirit called for more activist values. Rebellion against what lingered of the old authority blended into aggressive assertions that China had lost its way by being too passive for too long.

The mood of old China was one of siding with age, of revering elders, and of believing that the best of things came late in life. Increasingly in the twentieth century the mood of the new China was one of youthful exuberance and naive innocence. Behind the Chinese spirit of rebellion and revolution was uniquely a search for purity and a higher morality. The old order was judged weak and contemptible because of its decadence.

In the last years of the Ch'ing dynasty the traditions of the ageless imperial system suddenly fell under siege. The West, seeking its own objectives in China, was thrusting new visions into a once closed society. Inexorably long-range trends were picking up force and eroding the Confucian order, and historic domestic processes of rebellion and disintegration were gathering strength.

The Confucian system was no match for this dual challenge. The fact that the old order was toppled by two separate and divergent forces profoundly shaped subsequent Chinese history. The force of rebellion was almost entirely peasant based and reflected the demands and the life styles of the countryside. At times the rebellions, such as the White Lotus Society (1796–1804), the Taiping (1851–1864), the Nien (1853–1868), and the Boxer (1900), took on ideological or pseudo-religious trappings, but they were all partially supported by banditry, which had always been available to Chinese peasants when they found life otherwise insupportable.

The force of revolution, in contrast to rebellion, in modern China was associated almost entirely with the urban culture, and particularly with the educated classes. These people were most responsive to foreign ideas and were most sensitive to the need for fundamental changes in Chinese society. The goals of rebellion were the reduction of suppression, fewer taxes, and more freedom to live out the peasant's traditions; the goals of revolution were the elimination of China's humiliations and the obtainment of greater national power and wealth. Chinese rebellions lacked a creative urge for basic changes but were in tune with the ideal of greater freedom and autonomy for all individuals. Revolutions, on the other hand, idealized the need for greater discipline, self-sacrifice, and the denial of individualistic cravings.

The principal force opposing rebellion was military power. The spread of rebellions during the declining years of the Ch'ing dynasty tended to augment the imperial military forces and to transform civilian authorities into the mobilizers, and even commanders, of armies. Putting down rebellions tended to bring about a structural change in Chinese government, elevating the military over traditional civilian authorities. It is probably accurate to say that since the time of the Taiping Rebellion, armies and those who command them have been the decisive factors in Chinese politics.

Paradoxically, then, the forces of rebellion, which were largely popularistic, tended to encourage the growth of autocratic army rule in China. Although international wars and domestic conflicts also contributed to the growing influence of the military in Chinese society, a basic reason for the persistent escalation of the importance of the Chinese military has, to this day, been the presumed need to react against the spirit of rebellion.

The revolutionary forces in modern China, inspired by reaction to the Western impact, were able to undermine the intellectual foundations of the old regime but did not provoke as physical a counterreaction as did the rebellions. Instead, the thrust of revolution remained the frustrated and ineffectual search for a new order. Eventually, however, the spirit of revolution, first with the Nationalists and then with the Communists, allied itself with military power. To the extent that the revolutionary quest became allied to military power, as it did during the first republican revolutionary years and then with the Nationalists in the late 1920's and early 1930's, it became a force opposed to the spirit of rebellion in China. Only during brief periods have the thrusts of revolution, rebellion, and military power merged into a common force. These have been the periods when modern China seemed about to be finding an appropriate new identity.

Clearly an oversimplification but still a useful first approximation is the notion that modern Chinese history has been marked by a dynamic tension among rural rebellion, urban-intellectual revolution, and pragmatic military power. Over the years there has rarely been a stabilization among these forces. The spirit of rebellion when pressed to the extreme has tended to produce atavism and traditional prejudices completely inconsistent with the modernistic ideals of revolution. The forces of revolution in their purest form have not only been ambivalent toward the older tradition of rebellion but they have distrusted military authorities. The Nationalist revolutionaries never took an interest in the peasants, and Mao Tse-tung, after using the peasants to gain power, sought his revolutionary goals by turning his back upon their desires for autonomy. Whenever those in command of armies have been supreme they have tended to distrust the proponents of both rebellion and revolution.

Chinese nationalism has erratically fluctuated from glorification of the vitality of the ordinary peasantry, to reverence for the idealism of the intellectual revolutionaries, to blind worship of martial practices. With this overview of Chinese modernization in mind, we can more closely examine each of these forces.

THE FORCES OF REBELLION

Repeatedly in Chinese history and most frequently near the end of a dynasty, peasants and dissatisfied members of the gentry tended to band together and assert their independence from imperial control. When the government could no longer collect taxes in a local area, a secret society, with its own quasi-religious ideology, would assert itself as an alternative government. The consequence was rebellion, which eventually would bring to the scene government armies and pacification programs, which were generally a blend of coercion and seductive appeals to rebel elements.

The White Lotus Rebellion, which lasted from 1796 to 1804, was typical of such movements. Based on a blend of Buddhism and an appeal to the most depressed peasants for a life of action, the movement began in the marginal, mountainous areas of the northwest. The hill peoples raided the homes and lands of the richer plains people and banded together to resist the demands of the imperial tax collectors. The lawlessness that the movement produced encouraged more and more people to seek the security of membership in the secret society that initiated the disturbances. Efforts of the government to suppress the rebellion only increased peasant insecurity and drove more and more people to support the White Lotus.

The process by which the rebellion grew and by which it was eventually eliminated by the government is remarkably suggestive of features of the contemporary Viet Nam conflict. Imperial forces called into Szechwan, Shensi, and Shansi to chase the rebel and government armies lived off the remaining peasants who only wanted peace. In time the government broke the White Lotus Society by placing the villagers within walled areas and separating them from all contacts with the rebels. In the late 1930's there were still remnants of some of these walled enclosures, built of adobe or loess and long maintained by the villages so that peasants could flock to them with all their possessions when bandit bands approached their defenseless settlements.

The far more extensive and violent Taiping Rebellion was inspired somewhat by foreign, particularly Christian, ideas. Some scholars argue that it was really the beginning of the Chinese revolution because the Taipings accused Manchu rule of being both foreign and Confucian and sought to satisfy the diffuse rebellious demands of the economically distressed peasants. Its leader was a strange and remarkable man, Hung Hsiu-ch'üan, who was initially committed to becoming a Confucian scholar-official. Three times, however, he failed to pass the provincial examinations. On the last occasion he fell ill, became delirious, heard voices telling him to save mankind, and saw visions of a figure he later was convinced was Jesus Christ. At about this time he had picked up a Protestant religious tract, and subsequently he came to know and even briefly lived in the home of an American fundamentalist missionary, Reverend Issachar J. Roberts, who filled his mind with visions of Christian doctrine and practices. Hung was following the tradition of the frustrated examination candidate, teaching school, but he soon became a local nuisance because his new Christian doctrines inspired him to rove about smashing idols in the temples. He was finally run out of town and took to the hills to organize his T'ai-p'ing T'ien-kuo, or Heavenly Kingdom of Great Peace. Hung had baptized himself and was convinced that in one of his fits he had ascended to heaven, met with God and Jesus, and learned that he was Christ's younger brother, assigned to bring morality to earth.

In very short order, Hung Hsiu-ch'üan surrounded himself with a band of followers who began in the traditional spirit of a secret society revolt but were soon convinced that they were divinely appointed, many of them identifying themselves with the various Apostles. Hung continued to have visions, each of which produced doctrines for the movement, and in time his lieutenants found that they too were having visions that they felt should contribute to the ideology. The issue of what was divine inspiration and what was spurious opportunism eventually split the leadership.

Meanwhile Hung created an enthusiastic and remarkably puritanical movement. All property was to be held in common, no one was to be selfish, material corruption was a great sin, the sexes were to be equal, and people were supposed to devote all their attention to simple homilies. All in all it was remarkably similar to the utilitarianism, anti-sexual puritanism of Mao Tse-tung. Men and women were to treat each other as brothers and sisters, and the women had separate battalions and engaged in combat. Through some strange reasoning, which is still not clear, Hung and his most saintly associates were able to argue that although everyone else should abstain, they were in need of harems.

This unlikely movement caught the imagination of hundreds of thousands of peasants and swept up from south China to take over the Yangtze valley. It sent one column to the outskirts of Shanghai and another nearly to Tientsin. Taipings ravaged the countryside, isolating and starving out cities, so disrupting life that disease and pestilence took their toll. The conventional estimate is that the Taiping Rebellion took twenty million lives, but some careful estimates place the figure closer to forty million.

This rebellion, with its Westernized dimensions, was finally beaten back by a combination of traditional methods and foreign assistance. Initially Western elements looked with some sympathy upon the Taipings and their enthusiasm for spreading a version of Christianity and an ethic of honesty and righteousness, but in time they became increasingly doubtful. Also, as the Manchu court committed itself to more and more treaties with the Western powers, the latter had increasing interests in the preservation of the Ch'ing dynasty. An extraordinary adventurer from Salem, Massachusetts, Frederick T. Ward, organized an army to fight the Taipings when they began to threaten Shanghai. He died during a campaign but his troops, called the Ever Victorious Army, continued under the command of a series of Americans and Europeans until the Englishman Charles George Gordon took over and led them to their final victories. This was the famous "Chinese" Gordon, who later met his end in the siege of Khartoum.

More significant than Westerners in suppressing the Taipings were huge armies organized by some of the most outstanding Chinese officials of the time. In the ancient tradition of the scholar-official, when confronted with rebellion civilians such as Tsêng Kuo-fan and his associate Li Hung-chang, who later became China's ablest statesman, mobilized provincial forces and led them against the Taipings. The technique called for a tightening of taxation and the cooperation of the imperial court in diverting resources from the rest of the empire to the authorities in central China. After victory, however, the technique was disastrously deficient, for it contained no answer to the problem of how to demobilize armies — a problem that has continually plagued modern China. To simply disband the forces would be to create instantaneously widespread banditry.

The armies that were raised by Tsêng Kuo-fan, Tso Tsung-t'ang, and Li Hung-chang were later used to put down the Nien Rebellion and the Moslem rebellions of the 1870's and early 1880's. They became the nucleus for what were to be "model armies" after China's defeat by Japan in 1895. In turn, these modernized forces were made into the Peiyang army, which became the core of the warlord armies that dominated China during the Republican period. Later still the Nationalists had to raise their armies to crush the warlords, and eventually the Communists had to depend on their armies to rise to power. Thus, from the time of the suppression of the Taipings, Chinese politics has been shaped by military power and the fact that large numbers of men have consistently been under arms.

In suppressing the Taipings the practice of raising armies on a personal rather than national basis complicated the role of the military in the modernization of China. In Tsêng Kuo-fan's army each unit took the name of its commanding officer, increasing the tendency of troops to see themselves as private forces. The subsequent effort to modernize the imperial armies did not eliminate the importance of personal ties; it only raised the problem of personalized armies to a higher level and set the stage for warlord politics.

Although the ideology of the Taipings was touched to a degree by foreign influences, the rebellion was basically an indigenous movement that expressed popular discontents and identified the Manchu government as foreign. In contrast the Boxer Rebellion was an atavistic movement, with no taint of foreign concepts, manipulated by the government and directed against foreigners and, more importantly, Chinese who had been influenced or converted by them.

In part the Boxer movement reflected the conservative reactions of some officials who opposed the efforts at moderate reforms in 1898. It exploited famine conditions and popular local reactions to the disruptions that accompanied the introduction of railroads. There were enough problems in China at the time to tap xenophobic sentiments and stir up passions against foreigners. The Boxers emerged out of the local militia in Shantung and Shansi. (These poorly armed forces practiced Chinese "boxing," a form of karate, and hence their name.) The movement grew with official sanction but in time its violent anti-Christian attacks went beyond government control. The high point of the rebellion was the siege of the foreign legations in Peking, which eventually had to be relieved by an international contingent of troops consisting mainly of British, American, Japanese, and Russian soldiers, with representations from the German, French, Italian, and Austrian armies.

To the extent that foreign military contingents remained stationed in Peking from the time of the expedition until World War II, it can be said that the Boxer Rebellion followed the general Chinese pattern in which rebellions evoked rural populist or atavistic sentiments but resulted in an increased role of military force in Chinese politics.

THE THEME OF REVOLUTION

Revolution began with attempts to overthrow the Manchu dynasty and has persisted in Chinese politics to this day. The most active forces opposing the imperial system were the "overseas" Chinese and returned students who were aware of alternative practices and sensed deeply the national humiliation that came from the weaknesses of the Manchus.

The most important early figure in this revolutionary tradition was Sun Yat-sen, who was born near Canton, educated first at a British mission school in Hawaii, then trained as a doctor in British Hong Kong, and later practiced medicine in Portuguese Macao. Sun had limited and generally unhappy experiences in China. He returned from Hawaii as a vigorous Christian and made himself unpopular by smashing idols in his ancestral village. Later he wrote memoranda to Li Hung-chang about reforming the country and became a bore to all who were trying to make Confucianism viable in the modern era. Sun Yat-sen became increasingly revolutionary and secretive, founded the T'ung-meng-hui, an organization of Chinese students studying abroad, especially in Japan, and anti-Manchu intellectuals in China.

In the fall of 1911, while Sun was abroad trying to raise funds and sympathy for the revolutionary cause, and when the clash of interests between central and provincial authorities over the control of railroads was reaching crisis proportions, a bomb accidentally went off in the house of some T'ung-meng-hui members and attracted the attention of the police, who, on searching the premises, found a list of the full membership.

The crisis called for immediate action, and in particular the officers in the imperial army who had been secretly in sympathy with Sun's cause had to act in support of the revolution. They in turn forced their superior, Li Yüan-hung, to declare himself to be with the revolutionaries. The imperial court at Peking promptly responded by calling upon Yüan Shih-k'ai, the general who had informed the Empress Dowager of the ambitions of the reformers in 1898 and who was at the moment out of favor. Yüan responded by cold-heartedly asking what each side was prepared to offer him. When the revolutionaries suggested that he would be made president of their new republican regime, he abandoned the Manchus, thereby undermining the dynasty.

Sun Yat-sen welcomed the developments, accepted Yüan as the new president, and turned his attention to the economic development of China, a subject about which he was both passionate and ignorant. Yüan quickly disposed of the Manchus and professed a belief in republicanism, but he quickly worked to consolidate his own power and began to see himself as possibly the founder of a new dynasty. Before this came about he died in 1916, leaving military commanders with supreme power in all the provinces.

The next two major political groups that sought to reunite China, the Nationalists and the Communists, spoke of "completing the revolution." In contrast to the indigenous quality of the rebellions, the concepts of revolution were cosmopolitan, elitist and above all concerned with giving China strength and unity rather than individual freedom.

The theme of modern Chinese politics has been revolution, but revolution directed by those in command of state power. Both the Nationalists and the Communists on their emergence to power believed that the revolution should overthrow existing authorities and replace them with more effective authorities. The aim of revolution in modern China is not to topple authority but to establish power.

In making power a central feature of the revolutionary mystique, the Chinese in the Republican era tended to merge their revolutionary quests with a heavy reliance upon military force. The tendency to combine the military emphasis with the revolutionary quest followed from the fact that after the death of Yüan Shih-k'ai warlords dominated Chinese politics.

WARLORDISM AND THE PHANTOM REPUBLIC

From 1916 to 1927 China was fragmented and ruled by warlords who had separate provincial bases. For the Chinese this was a period of unrelieved humiliation because all the warlords seemed to be shortsighted, selfish, and unconcerned about the national interest. The experience of the period convinced the intellectuals that China's salvation lay not in competing power centers but rather in the establishment of a monolithic, single-party hierarchy of power.

A case can be made that competition among the warlords opened China to greater ideological and intellectual diversity than it had ever known. It also exposed the country to the challenges of a more pluralistic and competitive form of politics. Although the warlords misappropriated resources and failed to give a sense of national cohesion, the period was intellectually exciting, and the currents of change set in motion by the May Fourth Movement continued to be strong in the universities and among the intellectuals in the larger cities and the foreign concessions. Numerous foreign intellectuals, including John Dewey and Bertrand Russell, made prolonged visits. Dr. Hu Shih pressed on with the drive to give spoken Chinese respectability and to break the grip of classical Chinese as the only language of literature. This was also a period of popular reforms that included the efforts of "Jimmy" Yen to counter adult illiteracy and the programs of some of the warlords themselves to establish "model" provinces and towns. Currents of change seemed to be sweeping the country, and China won much sympathy in the West, for it had the appeal of being a society pulling itself up by its own boot straps. Although the figure of speech at the time was of China's "awakening" (not "developing"), the country was in a sense the first of the newly emerging nations that have been of such interest in world politics since the end of World War II. Socially and intellectually China seemed to be on the move.

Politically, however, the Chinese were deeply dissatisfied by their version of "competitive politics." Seeing power in the hands of the warlords convinced the intellectuals that national salvation lay in some form of one-party or one-man rule. Diversity seemed to offer only divisiveness and the end of the utopian dream of a democratic republic.

After the death of Yüan Shih-k'ai the government in Peking steadily lost its ability to rule; the office of the presidency was filled by a succession of weak military men lacking effective control of the resources of even a single province. The parliament, established immediately after the 1911 revolution and composed of civilian notables and supporters of the T'ung-meng-hui, lacked authority and did not even effectively participate in the selection of cabinets. After the fall of the imperial system the civilian bureaucracy throughout the country lost its dominant power because without the legitimizing force of the Confucian order it had little of utility to offer the new rulers.

The military commanders in the provinces, however, had responsibility for their armies, and their troops had to be supplied, paid, and generally maintained. It might be all right for civilian governors not to pay their bureaucrats, but when soldiers are not paid from the central treasury, they have, with their weapons, the means of getting what they need. The provincial military commanders (_tuchuns_) first sought merely to extract from their territory what they needed to keep their armies intact. Soon they were the actual rulers, for they had the only organizations capable of mobilizing resources and providing order. The problem of maintaining their organizations led them in time to seek alliances with other warlords and to expand their power bases, all in the search for greater security. The politics of warlordism became a complicated balance of power among leaders whose influence depended on their ability to support their armies.

Control of Peking was a prize because it offered the prospect of obtaining foreign loans and the revenues of the customs services. Alliances were formed in order to gain such control, and on other occasions individual warlords sought either by coup or by conquest to take the capital.

The operation of the balance of power among the warlords and their struggles to control the formal institutions of government produced two fairly well recognized factions. The first was the Anfu group led by Tuan Ch'i-jui and supported by such warlords as Hsu Shu-tseng, his immediate lieutenant, Ni Ssu-ch'un of Anhwei, Yang

Shan-te of Chekiang, Li Ho-chi of Fukien, and Lu Yung-hsiang, the commander of the Shanghai Special Area. The Anfu group focused on controlling Parliament and the office of the presidency, and thus sought to become champions of republican legitimacy. It had, however, a questionable reputation, particularly among the intellectuals, who suspected it of being subservient to Japanese interests. It was badly discredited at the outset of the May Fourth Movement because it had been in charge of the Peking government at the time of the Shantung decision at the Paris Peace Conference and thus became the object of attack by the newly awakened student nationalists.

The Chihli faction was the second clustering of warlords. It was first under the leadership of Feng Kuo-chang and then of Ts'ao K'un, a senior commander in the Peiyang army. Its most powerful warlord was Wu P'ei-fu of Honan.

A third major factor in the warlord system was Chang Tso-lin, of Manchuria, who had the largest and most secure power base of any of the warlords. Other principal warlords included Feng Yü-hsiang, the so-called Christian general, who was at times loosely associated with the Chihli faction but generally operated quite independently (executing two coups d'etat and developing a private source of Soviet assistance), and Yen Hsi-shan, the "model governor" of Shansi, who avoided alliances and concentrated on maintaining his autonomy.

In the early 1920's there were two major but inconclusive military clashes between the Chihli faction and Chang Tso-lin's Manchurian forces. The balance of power among the warlords prevented anyone from gaining complete superiority, and generally there was a state of relative equilibrium. The balance operated in such a fashion that even when all the warlords were threatened in 1927 by the Northern Expedition of the Kuomintang they could not band together in a common effort.

Some of the warlords were avaricious and shortsighted, with little sense of public responsibility, but others were exceptional leaders. Wu P'ei-fu, who dominated central China, had great organizing ability and worked effectively with a wide range of people. Chang Tso-lin in Manchuria came from a lowly peasant family and began his career as a bandit before becoming a soldier. Although scarcely educated, he proved to be a skillful negotiator who sensed the international play of forces in his domain and resourcefully balanced relations between Japan and Russia.

Possibly the most colorful warlord was Feng Yü-hsiang, who lacked a definite power base and had to live by his wits. The other warlords distrusted Feng for his unorthodox actions: Twice he executed coups d'etat in Peking. He was supposed to have converted his troops to Christianity (some said by marching them under fire hoses to baptize them) to make his soldiers lead moral lives and abstain from wine, women, and cigarettes so he could pay them less than other warlords had to pay their troops. He was willing to violate the warlords' code and seek help from the Communists. As a consequence of an invitation from Soviet agent Michael Borodin, Feng visited Moscow and received military support from the Soviets, but at the critical juncture when it was expected that he would show his gratitude, he failed to support the Chinese Communists and sided with Chiang Kai-shek. He never became an influential figure with the Nationalists, and on the eve of the Communist takeover of the mainland in 1949, while on a trip to the United States to "study water conservation," Feng declared his support of the Communists. He then took a Russian freighter from New York to return to China by way of Russia, but when the ship was two days out from Odessa the Russians announced that Feng had burned to death when a movie projector caught fire (no one else was hurt). There certainly was no clear future in the Communist scheme for the old warlord, especially since all his old subordinates had already given their allegiance to the new regime.

Other warlords, like Yen Hsi-shan, ended up with the Nationalists on Formosa. For a brief period they had been the main actors on the China scene, but even as they carried out their personal struggles the forces that were to be more enduring in Chinese politics were becoming effectively organized. In the early years of the warlord period the followers of Sun Yat-sen, who by then had organized themselves first into the T'ung-meng hui and then the Kuomintang, hoped they could influence national politics by working through the Parliament in Peking. It soon was apparent, however, that such a democratic and representational institution could have little influence in a situation in which real power lay with those who physically commanded armies. In spite of the important role Sun Yat-sen had played in mobilizing anti-Manchu sentiments, he had been nearly helpless from the time the republic was established. In 1917, Sun accepted the support of the warlord of Canton and became the leader of a regime that was in competition with the Peking government.

In the years that followed Sun again became active in seeking international support for his version of a Chinese nationalist and democratic movement. The Western powers, however, continued to recognize the Peking government, despite its ineffectualness. Although Sun's arguments were often sympathetically listened to by foreign officials, no government felt inclined to intervene in Chinese affairs by withdrawing its recognition of the Peking government and extending it to Sun's southern-based government. So, for nearly a decade, from 1917 to 1927, there were two governments in China seeking international recognition, just as there have been the two regimes since 1949 claiming to be the legitimate government of China.

The reality and the shame of warlord politics convinced Chinese intellectuals and modernizers that the country needed another revolution and that a successful revolution would have to be based on military power. Thus the logic of modern Chinese history, which began with the growth of military influences in order to suppress rebellions, culminated in ideologically oriented revolutionaries being compelled to turn to military power to achieve their goals. The success of the Kuomintang revolutionaries in becoming a national regime depended on the strength of their arms; similarly the Chinese Communists' road to power was by way of military victories.

CHAPTER EIGHT

Kuomintang Rule
and Japanese Occupation

During the decade from 1927 to 1937 it briefly appeared that China might be reunited. The prospect of centralized rule under the Kuomintang was seen by most Chinese political observers as an advance over the warlord period. In actual fact rule by the Nationalists was not as centralized as its leaders pretended it was, and provincial leaders continued to have considerable autonomy. Chiang Kai-shek, however, was seen as a national symbol, welcomed, at least at first, by the modernists and feared by the most idealistic elements.

The period of Nationalist rule was characterized by an attempt to forge a popular ideology out of Sun Yat-sen's writings, create a new structure of national authority, and inspire new loyalties. It was a time when China briefly seemed on the road to greater progress and economic development. The Great Depression and the struggle with Japan, which began in 1931 and became a full-scale war in 1937, meant that the fragile regime had far more problems than it was capable of managing. The war did give the government a great outburst of nationalist support, but the strains of the war years and the increasingly authoritarian character of Chiang's rule gradually weakened his claims of legitimacy.

Although the Nationalist period was a short one, it was significant because it revealed the problems inherent in China's effort to modernize and set the stage for the victory of the Communists. Much that has been happening in China to this day had its roots in those years.

132

THE RISE OF THE KUOMINTANG

In June 1922 Sun Yat-sen was at a low point of his political career, and frustrated by his inability to attract either Western or Japanese help and out of sorts with his Canton warlord host, he withdrew to Shanghai and there contacted the Comintern, seeking Soviet help. Adolf Joffe was responsive and by early 1923 the Sun-Joffe Agreement was announced. The Soviets declared that although China was not advanced enough for a Communist revolution, the Soviets were prepared to aid the Chinese nationalist revolution. At the time there was considerable disagreement about whether Joffe was dissembling by claiming the Soviets were not seeking Communist domination of Sun Yat-sen's revolutionaries. Technically his statement that China was not ready for Communism was entirely consistent with basic Marxist-Leninist doctrine, which maintains that a bourgeois-democratic revolution has to precede a socialist revolution and that a country is only "ready" for Communism after being a socialist system. Be this as it may, the agreement had profound consequences for the subsequent history of China.

The Comintern immediately dispatched Michael Borodin, a former Chicago schoolteacher, to Canton to direct the reorganization of the Kuomintang. The Soviets invited Chiang Kai-shek to Russia for three months before he returned to head the Whampoa Military Academy in Canton. Most important of all, the Comintern decision forced the fledgling Chinese Communist Party to agree that its members as individuals would work within the framework of the Kuomintang, thus bringing together most of the principal actors who have shaped the subsequent history of the country.

As a consequence of Borodin's work the Kuomintang and the Chinese Communists have been organizational mirror images of each other. Borodin sought to make the Kuomintang into a disciplined, purposeful organization, capable of both conducting revolutionary warfare and controlling whatever government it might establish. In addition to party building, the Russian advisers began to plan a military force that would be politically disciplined under officers trained at the new Whampoa Academy (where Chou En-lai was the chief political commissar under Chiang Kai-shek).

Although in retrospect it appears that the Russians moved

rapidly, Sun Yat-sen was impatient and, needing medical assistance, he visited Peking in 1925 hoping to negotiate a reunification of the country. Borodin, accompanying him incognito, had a secret meeting with Feng Yü-hsiang and sought his support. In what must have been one of the most unlikely debates in history, the Bolshevik agent belittled the reformist spirit of the Christian general, while Feng shrewdly defended humanitarian values against the violence of revolutions. Feng was unconvinced at the time but later did take up Borodin's invitation to visit Russia and seek Soviet military assistance.

While in Peking Sun Yat-sen died, leaving an uncertain power situation in Canton. There were the Communists, who were under orders to adhere to the Kuomintang and hence were inhibited from claiming leadership. Also on the left were some less disciplined but assertively aggressive individuals, the most notable of whom was Wang Ching-wei, who felt he had a personal bond with Sun Yat-sen. In the middle, less ideological and most pragmatic, was Chiang Kai-shek, whose strength came from the Whampoa Academy and the military forces being trained to conquer the north and its warlords. To the right of Chiang were several individual leaders, generally older and still sympathetic to elements of the great mandarin tradition. The most notable of these was Hu Han-min, a very close, old friend of Sun Yat-sen. Soon after Sun's death Hu and his associates sought to reunite the country through a conference convened in a major temple in the hills beyond the Summer Palace to the west of Peking, and thereafter they were referred to as the Western Hills clique.

In this confused situation it was Chiang Kai-shek who made the decisive moves and thus became the principal figure in Chinese politics. Acting with authority, he assumed command and declared that the goals of Sun would be realized. He thereupon unleashed his cadets and elements of his army for a series of raids on the leftist elements in the Kuomintang. Some of those chased out of Canton in 1926 scattered to Southeast Asia and, becoming more radicalized, founded the Communist movements in such places as Singapore and Malaya, thereby bringing a Chinese tone to the Communist movements in the region.

In spite of Chiang's sharp attacks on the left, the Communists, and particularly Stalin in Moscow continued to declare that the

Kuomintang was the hope of China and to praise Chiang's leadership. In the next year, 1927, the stage was at last set for the military reunification of China, and Chiang led the Northern Expedition out of Canton. One army under his own command moved to the northeast and approached central China at Nanking and enveloped Shanghai. The other army, to which was attached the Communists and the remaining left-wing elements of the Kuomintang, moved more directly north to central China and occupied Wuhan. Arriving in that major industrial center, they declared that the "capital" had been moved from Canton to Wuhan. Chiang Kai-shek's forces were at the time approaching Nanchang. Shocked by the Wuhan declaration, Chiang tested his own authority by calling a meeting of the Central Executive Committee of which he was nominally chairman, but no one from Wuhan came to Nanchang.

The events that followed were among the most critical for the subsequent development of China. To some degree they are still obscure because all the participants have given different interpretations of what happened. Chiang without question reacted to his rebuff by moving his forces toward Shanghai. Probably (it is hard to prove) he established contact with the Shanghai business community, promising them a combination of order and stability on the one hand and a nationalist, anti-treaty port program on the other.

At this juncture one of the most controversial and confused incidents in modern Chinese history took place. With Chiang's troops on the outskirts of Shanghai, the workers and trade unionists in the city staged a remarkable insurrection, taking power from the police and the militia of the local warlord. With power in their hands they were prepared to welcome Chiang Kai-shek's armies, but when his troops finally entered the city they turned on the workers and soon destroyed that revolutionary power. The drama of these events has been movingly presented in André Malraux's great novel *Man's Fate*.

Since the unions were Communist controlled it was generally assumed that Chiang was retaliating against the Communist-inspired act of setting up the Wuhan government. Chiang's position was that the trade unions had been supplied with arms by the Soviet Union in ships that came down from Vladivostok and that they were supposed to have handed over these arms to him so that his forces could complete the Northern Expedition to Peking. He charged that the unions had refused to carry out the plan because they wanted to conceal their armies and deliver them only to the Wuhan commander.

At this time the Communists in Moscow were being torn by the clash between Stalin and Trotsky after the death of Lenin. The Trotskyites would later claim that Stalin had ordered the Shanghai unions to hide their arms precisely because he wanted Chiang to react by destroying the unions and their leaders. In any case, Chiang acted decisively in crushing the unions and, capturing their arms, confronted Wuhan with the charge of being divisively anti-revolutionary.

Meanwhile in Wuhan there was considerable confusion over what should be done. The Wuhan group included dedicated and disciplined Communists led by Michael Borodin; more romantic and ideological Communists such as M. N. Roy, the Indian representative of the Comintern who had his own channels to Moscow; the radical, undisciplined, non-Communist left wing of the Kuomintang; and the completely un-ideological military officers who were simply seeking to carry out their professional tasks of conquering the rest of the country.

The balance of forces in Wuhan was affected by the struggle in Moscow between Stalin and Trotsky over what should be done about the Chinese revolution. Trotsky was pushing the view that as the armies moved north from Canton they should carry out a social revolution by breaking up significant landholdings and establishing soviets of peasants and workers. Stalin insisted that the Communists should work within the Kuomintang, wait until the entire country had been reconquered, and then by a coup d'etat take over the country and commit it to the socialist world.

In this situation, Stalin was in the awkward position of calling for patience while at the same time wanting to prove that he was a champion of revolution. He sent Borodin impossible instructions, demanding that the Communists continue to accept Chiang and the Kuomintang as leaders but prepare within the Kuomintang army Red Army forces that could suddenly surface and take over.

Borodin recognized that the instructions were irreconcilable and asked Moscow for clarification. M. N. Roy learned of the orders and felt that Borodin was dragging his feet. At this point Borodin showed the Moscow instructions to Eugene Ch'en, a leftist Kuomintang propagandist from the West Indies, who immediately recognized Moscow's cynical game of supporting the Kuomintang with the expectation of taking over everything for itself and the Communists once the country had been won. When Ch'en publicized the instructions from Moscow, he shattered the Wuhan government. The idealistic left wing of the Kuomintang suddenly felt helpless; it was caught between an angry Chiang Kai-shek, who was clearly moving to the right, and an opportunistic Communist Party. Historically this was the end of any non-Communist left of center group in the evolution of Chinese politics.

In his moment of triumph, Chiang was prepared to make any pragmatic adjustment with any force that might thereafter help in the reunification of China. The Communists were driven to desperation. In the fall of 1927 they attempted a series of military operations, known as the Autumn Harvest uprisings, but they were easily crushed. Back in Canton, the Communists sought power by establishing a commune, which was also crushed in a few days. In the meantime Chiang struck an agreement with Feng Yü-hsiang. The Communists had approached Feng and told him that the situation was desperate and that in return for all the help the Soviets had given him he should declare himself against Chiang and in favor of the Communists, for if he did not the Communists would certainly collapse. Chiang's approach to Feng was more assertive and positive: If Feng did not support the Nanking government, he would be opposing a force that would inevitably be triumphant. Feng, never one to support a potentially losing cause, declared himself for Chiang and the Nanking government and was promptly rewarded by being made minister of war in the new regime.

THE NATIONALIST SYSTEM OF RULE

During the decade from 1927 to 1937 Chiang Kai-shek and the Kuomintang achieved the high point of their rule of China. However, at no time were they in full and unqualified command. Domestically, they had to contend with remnants of the Communist forces and a series of challenges from warlords who were not prepared to sacrifice all their autonomy to Nanking. Indeed, during nearly every year the Nanking government had some local revolt or international incident that dramatized the weaknesses of the regime. For example, in the spring of 1929 Li Tsung-jen, the general in Kwangsi, revolted and in the fall of the same year Tang Sheng-chih, also in the south, followed suit. In 1931 Feng Yü-hsiang joined with Yen Hsi-shan in a revolt, and in the same year the military in Canton challenged Nanking's authority. In 1933 the Nineteenth Route Army in Fukien revolted, and in 1936 the generals in Kwangtung and Kwangsi again sought to assert their independence. In all these cases the issue was whether central authority was to replace traditional localized war-lord autonomy.

The Japanese took over Manchuria in 1931, further extended their influence over Jehol province in 1933, and over Hopei and Chahar provinces in 1935, and then on July 7, 1937, initiated the war that lasted until 1945. Thus the Nationalist regime had little peace either at home or abroad during the ten years of its strongest rule.

Nanking's authority never really reached into Manchuria and was limited in northeastern China. Elsewhere Chiang had direct clashes with the Kwangsi generals in 1929, and with Feng Yü-hsiang and his ally Yen Hsi-shan, the governor of Shansi.

Chiang Kai-shek's method of ruling was to balance contrasting elements and seek alliances among all manner of groups. The Kuomintang itself was never a coherent or monolithic party; it contained an array of cliques and notable personalities. Two brothers, Ch'en Kuo-fu and Ch'en Li-fu, headed what was known as the C. C. clique, which pushed a rightist ideology and organized the so-called Blue Shirts, a secret group of Kuomintang activists who employed bullying methods to maintain discipline. At the other extreme were the remaining few left-wing Kuomintang personages who looked to Wang Ching-wei for inspiration. Chiang's power was augmented by his ties with the Soong family through his marriage to Soong Mei-ling in 1927. The oldest Soong sister was married to Sun Yat-sen, and the second to H. H. Kung, one of the wealthiest bankers in China. Their brother, T. V. Soong, was the minister of finance in the Nanking government.

Members of the Kuomintang elite generally came from the urban, educated, and somewhat more cosmopolitan elements of Chinese society. They were not, however, modernized intellectuals with extensive foreign training, as have been the leaders of many of the newly independent states that experienced colonial rule. In the main members of the Kuomintang political class still had their roots in

Chinese culture and society. Many of them wanted China to become a strong power, but they were ambivalent about social changes, for they still valued much in Chinese tradition. This is not to say that they were steeped in the higher forms of Chinese culture but rather that their interests lay with moderate social change.

Kuomintang rule rested on the bureaucratic structures, both civil and military, that the Nanking regime established. The new bureaucracy was quite different from the imperial one: It was not composed of gentlemen-scholars, nor were its members as much the modern technocrats that some of them thought they were; they were functionaries committed to a semi-military ethos. Wearing blue uniforms cut like "Sun Yat-sen tunics," these officials tried to blur individual distinctions and inspire the idea that they were part of an efficient machine of government. However, their technical and administrative abilities were not up to coping with the problems confronting a narrowly based government that had some ideological appeal but no substantial organizational strength.

In the early years, the Nanking regime received most of its support from the merchant and industrial class in the Yangtze valley. This was in the main a newly emerging middle class that lacked a tradition of respectability and seemed to be centrally interested in making money. The industrialists were concerned with China's economic development, and they were forward looking and technologically progressive in their outlook. They could accept the idea of change. Many were self-made men: H. H. Kung came from a modest Shansi banking family, and the father of the Soong sisters came from even more modest circumstances.

After the Japanese occupied the industrial centers of east China, these men steadily lost influence within the Kuomintang. Indeed, after the government was driven to Chungking, the problem of collecting revenues to maintain the war effort forced the Kuomintang to become increasingly dependent on the rural gentry, the elite of interior China. Thus during the war years the Kuomintang became dependent on conservative and reactionary elements in China.

Kuomintang rule was based on agreement about China's need for ideological and moral revitalization. Above all, the Party emphasized its commitment to the doctrines of Sun Yat-sen, known as the *San Min Chu I*, or Three People's Principles. Coming out of a series of lectures Sun once gave, they reflect his uneven reading of

Western authors. The first, most emphasized, principle was national-ism. Sun emphasized the extent to which China had been victimized by imperialism and by the unequal treaties. He diagnosed national weakness as the source of most of China's ills.

The second principle was democracy. Sun's interpretation of democracy blended with his concern about China's national power. He had argued that China had had an "excessive degree of liberty" and that "people's sovereignty" called for greater unity and author-ity. The Chinese people were like "loose sand," and they needed greater leadership. Sun rejected the concept of equality and stressed the need for wise leaders. All in all, he professed a version of democ-racy quite different from that generally known elsewhere. Sun did, however, add to his doctrine the idea that the people had four rights — rather modern ones — suffrage, recall, initiative, and referendum. These eventually would be implemented, but in the meantime Sun insisted that China needed "political tutelage."

One feature of Sun's theory of democracy that affected the structure of the Nanking government was his view that government in China should be divided into five powers (*yüans*) — the executive, the legislative, the judicial, the civil service examination system, and the Censorate. The last two were seen as distinctive contributions of traditional China to the organization of government. The Confucian examination system and the independent censorate, which checked on the performance of officials, were thus added to the traditional Western and American three-way division of power.

The Kuomintang established the Nanking government on the basis of the five powers, and it accepted completely the concept of "political tutelage." As for the four rights of the people, it spoke of the desirability of ultimately realizing them.

The third of Sun Yat-sen's three principles was people's liveli-hood, which was a vague form of socialism. Although Sun praised Marx, he was probably influenced more by an obscure American dentist, Dr. Maurice Williams, and by Henry George, the advocate of a single tax system. Sun's livelihood principle did include the ideal that land should belong to the tiller and that people should not make profits from real estate. Although he offered little substantive guidance about how the goal of people's livelihood was to be achieved, he did suggest that the government buy back all the land in the country. The landlords would legally declare the value of their holdings, and the government would have the option of buying the land (if the price was low enough) or taxing the land (if the value was set too high).

The *San Min Chu I* accurately reflects the distinctive blurring of Western ideas and meeting of traditional Chinese virtues that characterized Kuomintang rule on the mainland of China. Strange mixes of foreign ideas were brought together and sanctified into a revered body of political doctrines. The outward forms suggested a commitment to change and modernization; the words evoked concepts of popular involvement and a belief in the sovereignty of the people. The substance of the doctrine, however, was ambiguous and could justify much that was anti-democratic.

Above all the *San Min Chu I* revealed the conflicting state of the Chinese spirit as the country sought revolutionary change. It acknowledged a need to look abroad for ideas and techniques for modernizing the society, but it suggested that the Chinese were not happy in having to do so. Therefore it did not encourage a systematic, hard, and critical approach to the need of examining foreign ways. Similarly it was not explicit about what among traditional Chinese values should be maintained, so that much of the substance reflected the confusion of the Chinese spirit.

In short the doctrines of the Chinese Nationalists went far in teaching the Chinese people that they had to take a broader view of their place in the world. But though they called for a mixture of foreign and Chinese ideas and practices, the doctrines did not capture what was best in each. *The San Min Chu I* tapped much that was second-rate. Sun Yat-sen was not to blame for this. He had thought of his words only as the substance of lectures that he hoped would stimulate a youthful audience. The later Nationalist government decided to elevate his words into a sacred ideology for the Chinese people. The doctrines and the "Last Will and Testament" of Sun Yat-sen were made into articles of faith and were the basis for national loyalty training in all Chinese schools. During the Nationalist period in every school at least on every Monday morning students ceremoniously recited Sun's will and fervently bowed to his portrait.

Ideology aside, the Kuomintang committed itself to a system of government far stronger and more centralized than it was able to realize. In practice, the Nanking regime was relatively ineffectual and not able to penetrate very deeply into Chinese society or give it

the order and new structure to which it aspired. In its rhetoric, however, the Kuomintang consistently stressed autocratic and elitist
themes.

Despite the rising threat from Japan and the instabilities that
came from the lingering warlord forces, China did experience some
significant advances during the decade from 1927 to 1937. The im-
pending international crisis with Japan sharpened the nationalistic
sentiments of students and intellectuals. The national unity achieved
by the Kuomintang set the stage for an upsurge in economic activity,
even under the conditions of the Great Depression.

Against this accomplishment must be set the fact that the
Kuomintang tended, wherever it had control, to become increasingly
authoritarian and antidemocratic. State power often became arbitrary power. Although there were many dedicated and hard-working
lower- and middle-level officials in the government, charges of corruption against higher officials became a major problem, especially
during the upheavals of the Japanese war period. Nor were the specialists and technicians within the specialized departments of government generally effective in using their skills. All government
organizations were under Party dominance, and most Party officials
had little appreciation of technical matters.

THE WAR WITH JAPAN
AND A DIVIDED NATION

By 1936 Chiang, in spite of many shortcomings, was showing
significant accomplishment in increasing national unity. Most of the
remaining warlords had been neutralized and were giving support
to the Nanking government. Chiang had carried out a series of
"extermination" campaigns against Communist guerrilla base areas,
compelling the Red Army under Mao Tse-tung and Chu Teh to leave
Kwangsi and make the Long March that would take them to the
northwest and Shensi province, where they were surrounded by the
Manchurian forces of Chang Hsüeh-liang, the son of Chang Tso-lin.
The Manchurian forces had been driven from their home provinces
by the Japanese and were being used to "suppress the Communist
bandits." The Communists were, however, quite successful in demoralizing the Manchurian armies by stressing the fact that instead
of fighting the Japanese invaders of their home provinces they were

fighting against the only Chinese force that had "declared war" on Japan.

In December 1936 Chiang flew up to Sian in Shensi to press upon Chang Hsüeh-liang the urgency of completing the "annihilation" of the Communists before confronting the Japanese. On arrival he was ignominiously kidnapped by Chang who had been influenced by the Communists' arguments about Chinese fighting Chinese at a time when Japan threatened. The mutinous act shocked the nation and for a few days it appeared as if China was about to lose whatever sense of national leadership it had. At this juncture, according to some reports, the Soviet Union intervened: Stalin sent a telegram to the Chinese Communists declaring that unless they arranged for the release of Chiang he would publicly disavow them as Communists and declare them to be mere "bandits." In any case Chou En-lai did enter the scene and negotiated for Chiang's release.

Finally an agreement was worked out between the Communists and the Kuomintang. Chiang declared that he would firmly lead the national resistance to any further Japanese demands, and the Communists committed their forces to operating under the national command and promised to cease their partisan revolutionary propaganda. Chiang was released on Christmas Eve 1936, and the Chinese nation seemed to be moving toward genuine national unity.

Half a year later, on July 7, 1937, the Japanese officially began the war that was to drive the Kuomintang government out of Nanking, first to Hankow and then to Chungking. The Japanese forces soon occupied all the principal cities of east China and controlled the railroad system. In the early months of the war there was a great outpouring of national sentiment, and thousands of people trekked to west China. Factories were dismantled and the machinery moved piece by piece to the West; entire schools and colleges picked up all that was movable and headed West by foot if necessary and by bus and train where possible. The trains that did move were packed, and refugees clung to the outsides. The country seemed united and committed to a heroic purpose. Gradually over the war years this idealism gave way to greater and greater cynicism as the Chungking government displayed both its ineffectualness and its autocratic proclivities.

Although the brutalities of the Japanese and their policies of exploitation and suppression created widespread hostility and further strengthened the national awakening of China, the Japanese appeal for an East Asian co-prosperity sphere and their series of puppet states did win some converts and spread confusion and self-doubts. The Japanese propaganda approach was in fact rather skill-fully tailored to exploit local and regional sentiments.

In Manchuria, for example, they appealed to the old Manchu loyalties and restored the last Manchu emperor, Henry Pu Yi, to the throne of their so-called state of Manchukuo. In Inner Mongolia and Jehol they appealed to Buddhist sentiments and held out the vision of a theocracy working under Japanese supervision. In north China they appealed to the pride of the greatest of the imperial cities and made Peking once again a capital; they brought out the old five-bar flag that had been China's national emblem during the re-publican, pre-Kuomintang period and put in visible but powerless offices men who had been notable in that era. This set in motion the confusing battle of names between "Peip'ing" and "Peking." When Chiang Kai-shek made Nanking the capital, he changed the name of Peking, or Pei-ching (northern capital), to Peip'ing (northern peace). Pekingese, however, continued generally to cling to their old name and resented their loss of capital status. As soon as the Japanese gave them back their cherished name, they displayed their nationalist ar-dor by uniformly calling their city Peip'ing. This continued to be the practice until the Communists came to power in 1949 and declared the name to be Pei-ching, or Peking, and thereafter the battle of names became one between Communists and Nationalists, with the United States State Department adhering strictly to Peip'ing, until President Nixon announced in 1971 his planned visit to Peking.

In central China the Japanese made Nanking a capital. They shamelessly adopted the Kuomintang flag and the *San Min Chu I* ideology, placed Wang Ching-wei in a position of nominal leader-ship and surrounded him with men, both Chinese and Japanese, who had known Sun Yat-sen well during his years of exile in Japan. The fact that Chungking and the puppet Nanking regimes could both profess to be the legitimate heirs to Sun Yat-sen and hold sacred the same set of symbols tended to seriously undermine all that the Kuomintang seemed to represent.

While in the occupied regions the Japanese were systematically seeking to divide the Chinese among themselves, the Chinese in west China were also becoming more sharply divided. For a brief period at the beginning of the war the Communists and the Nationalists achieved a degree of cooperation and coordination, but it did not last long. The Nationalist armies were short of arms and equipment so Chungking was not inclined to supply the Communist armies as specified in the Sian Agreement following the Chiang kidnaping incident. The Communists, however, were soon operating in north China behind the Japanese lines, running an effective government in the countryside surrounding the Japanese occupied cities. It was no longer feasible for them to take all their orders from Chiang's headquarters, as required by the agreement.

Whatever cooperation existed before December 7, 1941, evaporated after the attack on Pearl Harbor, for all politically conscious Chinese knew from that moment that Japan would certainly be defeated by the United States regardless of what the Chinese did. Thus, while Americans were concerned with how and when the war might be won and expected everyone to do his all in the cause, the Chinese were beginning to worry about what was to be the balance of domestic forces in the country once the Japanese were beaten.

Before World War II ended, the stage in China was set for a civil war. The Communists steadily expanded their guerrilla base territories, built larger armies, and extended their capabilities for civil rule. The party also engaged in a major self-disciplining campaign, the cheng-feng, to raise its ideological level and improve its revolutionary spirit.

The Nationalists were equally concerned with maintaining and strengthening their domestic political position. Although the Nationalist armies carried on the main war against the Japanese, they seemed increasingly less concerned with pushing back the foreign conquerors and more with husbanding their resources for the postwar period. The strain of prolonged war and the realization that victory depended little on what the Chinese did and almost entirely on the Americans created a pervasively cynical and depressed mood in Chungking. Authority tended to respond with increased repression and dependence on military rather than on political or ideological power.

The final defeat of Japan left China deeply divided — between Nationalist and Communist, and between those who had collaborated or lived accommodatingly with the Japanese in east China and those who had gone to west China. Immediately following the surrender of Japan to the Allies, the United States helped move

Nationalist armies from west China to the major coastal cities, and soon the Nationalists were in almost exactly the same situation that the Japanese had occupied — in command of the cities and the railroad lines while the Communists held the countryside.

During the next four years the country gradually slipped toward civil war. The Communists steadily grew in strength and benefited from the confusion while the Nationalists just as steadily lost morale and the capacity to rule. The division between city and countryside, the inability to unite the country into a single economy, and the tremendous costs of maintaining huge armies contributed to an acute inflation that hurt, above all, the civil servants and the urban middle classes, the very groups whose support was most critical for the Nationalists. Probably inflation was the most critical immediate cause of the fall of the Kuomintang on the mainland. It not only wiped out the middle class but also encouraged ever more flagrant corruption among higher officials.

During this period the United States was involved in seeking to bring about a truce and some form of national integration. Shortly after the Japanese surrender President Truman sent General George C. Marshall to China to try to bring together the Nationalists and the Communists. Negotiations aiming at some form of coalition government broke down because of the mutual distrust of both sides. The effort to freeze the military situation also failed, largely because both armies were drawn into Manchuria to fill the void created by the withdrawal of Russian forces, who had conquered the Japanese during the last week of World War II. The fighting that became intense in Manchuria gradually spread to north China, and by 1948 the country was in a major civil war. Peking was surrounded and finally fell to the Communists in 1949, and by autumn the Communists had crossed the Yangtze.

Finally Chiang was driven to the island of Formosa, or Taiwan, where gradually the remnants of the Kuomintang armies and Party were able to reorganize themselves and establish a more efficient regime than they had had on the mainland. The Nationalist government and the Kuomintang Party remain the principal foe of the Communists and an alternative government to Peking's that aspires to return to the mainland but in practice concentrates on ruling its island country, achieving impressive economic development but only limited civil liberties.

CHAPTER NINE

The Rise of the Communists

The Chinese People's Republic was established on October 1, 1949, but for the previous twenty years the Chinese Communist Party had controlled territory in various parts of China. It thus had had the unique experience of being a governing force before coming into national power. Before the Party captured national power it had had more experience in ruling than in being a revolutionary party without governmental responsibilities. The early history of the Chinese Communist Party was almost from the outset one of tactical judgments, and it never experienced a period, comparable to that of the early Russian Marxists, when ideological disputations were all-absorbing.

The speed with which the Communist Party became a major force in Chinese politics was truly amazing. Before the Russian revolution of 1917 there was almost no awareness of Marxism in China even within intellectual circles. By 1921 the first congress of the Chinese Communist Party had been held, and by 1927 the Party seemed to be on the brink of capturing national power. Thereafter, for over twenty years the Chinese Communists were a military force, beyond the ability of the Nanking government to eliminate. They controlled territories, ruled over citizens, collected taxes, and even issued their own postage stamps and currency.

The initial spectacular spread of Communism reflected both the craving of intellectuals for ideas that might revive China and the Communists' ability to act when they felt they had found their answer. The upsurge of Chinese nationalism after the Paris decision to give Japan the former German rights in Shantung (the May Fourth Movement) was most intense among the students and faculty of Peking National University. Its sprawling, unimposing campus of gray brick buildings located to one side of the Forbidden City was an intellectually vital scene where students returned from Japan, America, and Europe sought to share their new knowledge with younger compatriots who were equally anxious to find answers for China's impotence. Peking National University (or Peita as it was conventionally shortened in Chinese) became the preeminent intellectual center of China. It was also a center of Chinese nationalism largely because of the qualities of chancellor Ts'ai Yuan-p'ei, who encouraged independent and unorthodox thinking among his faculty and political activism among his students.

Ts'ai, a highly competent philosopher, was interested in synthesizing Chinese and Western intellectual traditions. As a young man he had been one of the last of the Hanlin scholars, but after China's ignominious defeat by Japan in 1894 and 1895, Ts'ai gave up his concentration on Confucian learning and vigorously sought out Western knowledge. Before the 1911 revolution he visited Japan, spent four years studying at Leipzig, and then, after a brief return to China during the presidency of Yüan Shih-k'ai, he returned in disillusionment to France, where he helped organize the Société Franco-Chinois Education, which sponsored a work-study program that brought to France over two thousand Chinese, including Chou En-lai, who became one of the leading figures of Chinese Communism. Indeed, participants in this program became in time an important channel of recruitment to the fledgling Chinese Communist Party.

After Ts'ai Yuan-p'ei became chancellor of Peita in 1916, he recruited a talented faculty that included Hu Shih, who, as a disciple of John Dewey, pressed for pragmatic approaches to Chinese ills, and also Li Ta-chao and Ch'en Tu-hsiu, two leading figures both in introducing Marxism into China and in founding the Chinese Communist Party.

Li Ta-chao was educated in Japan. As a student at Waseda University in Tokyo he had become a politically active publicist who was soon recognized as a passionate champion of Chinese nationalism. In 1918 Ts'ai invited him to become chief librarian at Peita, and two years later he became professor of history, economics, and political science (in those days discipline differences were not great). He and Hu Shih and other leading intellectuals devoted considerable energy to literary and cultural movements focusing around *The New*

Youth magazine, which was founded by Ch'en Tu-hsiu, dean of social sciences at Peita. In the fall of 1918 Li Ta-chao hired a young man from provincial Hunan who had just graduated from the Changsha Normal School, Mao Tse-tung, to serve as an assistant librarian. Mao was strongly influenced by Li's enthusiasm for a better China, and he sought contacts with both Hu Shih and Ch'en Tu-hsiu.

In the spring of 1919 when the May Fourth Movement swept the campus bringing all classes to a halt, Ts'ai, Li, Ch'en, and Hu Shih all adopted strong positions in support of a student strike and in opposition to the Peking government that financed their university. Ts'ai's threatened resignation helped gain the release of imprisoned students and faculty, including Ch'en Tu-hsiu, who, however, had to resign and withdraw to the security of the International Settlement in Shanghai as a condition of his release.

During the rest of the academic year and into the following fall the confusion continued. When funds were cut off, Ts'ai Yuan-p'ei and Hu Shih sought to turn the momentum of the strike into more constructive directions. They proposed that students and staff return to their home districts to spread the message of the May Fourth Movement and help illiterates learn to read. Hu Shih's proposal to replace classes with a politicized work-study program sent Mao Tse-tung back to Hunan to study rural conditions.

In the following year the radicalizing of the university continued with the introduction of Marxist-Leninist study groups under the leadership of Li Ta-chao. Early in 1920 Li was approached by Gregory Voitinsky, an agent of the Comintern, to see what help the Chinese intellectuals might need if they were to become serious Communists. Li suggested that Voitinsky contact Ch'en Tu-hsiu in Shanghai and provided a letter of introduction. Ch'en at that time was busily contacting former students and colleagues and welcomed any help that would facilitate his organizational work.

Within a year's time cells had been established in Shanghai, Peking, Changsha, and other cities by former associates of the Peita leaders, and the first group of Russian-language students, including Liu Shao-ch'i, had been sent to Moscow. In January 1921, Ch'en Tu-hsiu left Shanghai for Canton to become the head of the education department of Kwangtung province and to establish Communist cells in the area of the southern government.

Voitinsky was joined by a Dutch Comintern agent, Sneevliet, who operated under the name of Maring and before World War I had brought Marxism to Indonesia. The time seemed right to link the separate cells into an organized party. In the previous spring the Chinese work-study group in France had formed the Communist Youth Corps, which included Chou En-lai, Li Li-san, and others destined to become important figures in the Communist Party. When Maring arrived in Shanghai, he sent out the call for an organizational meeting that would establish the Chinese Communist Party.

THE FIRST CONGRESS OF THE CHINESE COMMUNIST PARTY, JULY 1921

There has been some confusion over who was present at the creation of the Chinese Communist Party, but it is generally recognized that there were twelve Chinese, Maring, and either Voitinsky or an agent named Nikorusky. Ch'en Tu-hsiu was not able to be there because of his new duties in Canton, and Li Ta-chao was busy in Peking so he sent Chang Kuo-t'ao to represent the Peking group. Mao Tse-tung and Ho Shu-heng came from Hunan. Some of those present at the initial meeting later turned against the Communists or dropped out of politics. For example, Chou Fo-hai later became the personal secretary to Chiang Kai-shek and a leading propagandist for the Kuomintang before going over to the Japanese, while Li Ta drifted away from disciplined communism to become a university professor and intellectual Marxist. Ch'en Kung-po also left the Communist Party after a few years and became closely associated with the left wing of the Kuomintang and finally helped Wang Ching-wei to establish the Japanese puppet regime in Nanking. Liu Jen-ching became a Trotskyite in the 1930's and only came back to the Party he helped establish after the Communist victory of 1949. Tung Pi-wu spent much of the rest of his career as a liaison man between the Communists and the Kuomintang and was the only Chinese Communist representative on the Chinese delegation at the founding conference of the United Nations at San Francisco. Ch'en T'an-ch'iu spent several years in Moscow and was finally executed by the warlord of Sinkiang after serving as the Communist liaison officer in that province bordering the Soviet Union. In the 1927 disorders

Li Han-chün also met a violent death. The last two, Wang Chin-mei and Teng En-ming, had relatively undistinguished careers in spite of being present at the founding of the Party.

The meetings took place on Perbalu Street in the French Concession in a private girls' school whose custodian allowed the delegates to use the rooms vacated for the summer vacation. On the evening before the last meeting the delegates were crowded into Li Han-chün's apartment when a suspicious man wandered in, claiming he was looking for someone. As soon as he left, the meeting adjourned and a few minutes later police raided the apartment but found nothing incriminating. To find a safe place to finish their business, the delegates retired to Neihpu Lake, away from Shanghai, where, posing as a group of vacationing sightseers, they rented a boat, provided themselves with a picnic lunch, and finished their deliberations in isolation on the lake but still in public view.

The group had not found it easy to arrive at any form of ideological agreement. The various delegates had divergent interpretations of history and of the current state of the world. They did, however, decide that Ch'en Tu-hsiu should be chosen secretary-general of the Party, and by this decision the fledging organization avoided intellectual disputes and came to focus on action programs. Ch'en was an extremely articulate intellectual as well as a straightforward believer in the need for change and the importance of science. He was ready to be pragmatic and to do what had to be done to make the Chinese Communist Party into a significant political force.

Ch'en immediately left Canton and returned to Shanghai to take command of the Party. Maring worked closely with him, and during the next year they both concentrated on help ing Chang Kuo-t'ao establish the secretariat of the Chinese Labor Union and carry out railway and seamen's strikes, which were relatively ineffectual.

THE SECOND PARTY CONGRESS, MAY 1922

When Ch'en took office as secretary-general, the Party had possibly fifty members. By the following May it had nearly one hundred, when the Second Party Congress was held on West Lake, in beautiful Hangchow. The growth in numbers was not impressive, but there had been significant political changes in China and the stage was set for a momentous decision by the Party. The Kuomintang was becoming a significant force in Canton and had successfully carried out a seamen's strike in Hong Kong. Chang Kuo-t'ao had also early in the year attended the Conference of the Toilers of the East in Moscow and learned of Soviet interest in creating a broad nationalistic force in China that could drive out the warlords. The currents of revolution seemed to be running high in Asia.

When the Second Congress met, Maring shocked the delegates with the proposal that the Party seek to cooperate with the Kuomintang. Most of the delegates were committed to the belief that the Party should not compromise its proletarian integrity by allying with the Kuomintang, which had clearly bourgeois and even "semifeudal" elements. There have been conflicting statements about what transpired. Maring, many years later, told Harold Isaacs, leading chronicler of the period, that he had no trouble convincing the delegates of the wisdom of simply entering the Kuomintang and using its organization as a means of reaching a larger public and that the only uncertainty was whether the Kuomintang was in fact a potentially effective organization. Ch'en Tu-hsiu, years later when he was in disgrace, insisted that Maring had forced the decision of the first united front upon the Chinese Communist Party by asserting the authority of the Soviet Comintern.

The ultimate decision was clear: The members of the Chinese Communist Party would enter the Kuomintang as individuals and, while maintaining their Communist Party discipline, would seek to shape the Kuomintang into a force that would unite the country and lead to a socialist revolution. This decision was unambiguously ratified in August 1922 at a special plenum of the Central Committee of the Chinese Communist Party called by Maring at Hangchow.

THE THIRD PARTY CONGRESS, JUNE 1923

In the last weeks of 1922, at the Fourth World Congress of the Comintern, Karl Radek, the German socialist and close supporter of Lenin, publicly called for closer collaboration between the Kuomintang and the Communists, and this was followed immediately by Moscow's encouragement of the Sun-Joffe Agreement in which the Soviets pledged to help the Kuomintang while claiming that China was not ready for communism.

By June 1923, when the Third Congress of the Chinese Communist Party met in Canton, membership had grown to possibly three hundred persons and Maring was still having trouble making the twenty delegates support the Comintern line of working within the Kuomintang. Ch'en Tu-hsiu, who had just returned from the Comintern Congress, strongly defended the Kuomintang-Communist alliance. At this stage Chang Kuo-t'ao began to advocate a more independent line. The final manifesto of the congress supported the alliance but included some criticism of the Kuomintang and called for closer ties with the world proletariat. Ch'en Tu-hsiu was again confirmed as secretary-general.

In September 1923, Michael Borodin arrived in Canton, replacing Maring as Comintern representative. By January 1924, he had reorganized the Kuomintang to the point of calling for its First National Congress. At the congress the Kuomintang accepted the Communists to membership, declared an alliance with the Soviet Union, and elected three leading Communists to the Central Executive Committee and six as alternate members, including Chang Kuo-t'ao and Ch'ü Ch'iu-pai.

THE FOURTH PARTY CONGRESS,
JANUARY 1925

During the next year the Kuomintang established the Whampoa Military Academy and commenced serious planning of a northern expedition from Canton that was to reunify the country. The Communist members within the Kuomintang were beginning to encounter resistance and suspicion. When the Fourth Party Congress of the Chinese Communist Party met in Shanghai, the delegates, who now represented over one thousand members, eagerly pointed out that the Kuomintang was composed of several factions and that the Communist Party members should join the left wing of the Kuomintang to try to weaken the right and center factions. At the same time the congress called for some activities that would go beyond the Kuomintang. The congress urged the development of workers' unions and peasant associations in central and north China. The Central Committee also set up two regional offices that went beyond Kuomintang territories: one for north China headed by Chang Kuo-t'ao, and one for central China under Ts'ai Ho-shen.

Opportunities for political action outside of the Kuomintang framework were becoming increasingly tempting. When Sun Yat-sen died in Peking on March 12, 1925, many Communists called for more independent action. In October, Ch'en Tu-hsiu told an enlarged session of the Central Committee of the Chinese Communist Party in Peking that actions independent of the Kuomintang were to be welcomed. The Party was also having apparent success among laborers, which was particularly gratifying to the intellectuals who had little experience with the working classes. Li Li-san was organizing strikes in Shanghai, and the Comintern was enough impressed with the labor unions to supply them with arms so that they could cooperate in the northern expedition of the Canton forces.

The Communists were also quick to exploit a clash between the Shanghai police and students, which became known as the May Thirtieth Incident. They were able to call for a brief general strike. In the meantime in the Hunan countryside Mao Tse-tung was beginning to organize the peasants. For the first time Party membership was growing at a pace that suggested that the Chinese Communist Party might become a mass party. In the two years between the Fourth Congress in 1925 and the Fifth in 1927 the Party increased from a little more than one thousand to more than sixty thousand members.

These substantive advances by the revolutionary leaders strained relations with the Kuomintang and hence relations between the Chinese Communists and Moscow. Stalin and the Comintern still insisted that the character of the Chinese revolution demanded that the Chinese Communist Party continue to work within the Kuomintang. The anomalous feature of the relationship was dramatized after Chiang Kai-shek staged his military coup against the Communists and left wing of the Kuomintang in Canton on March 20, 1926. Even with the Soviet advisers under a form of house arrest, with leading revolutionaries having to flee the country, Moscow blindly continued to insist that Chiang was a hero of the working classes whom all Communists should continue to support.

Ch'en Tu-hsiu and the other Communist leaders were beginning to learn the true meaning of revolutionary discipline. Borodin
continued to display the required loyalty to the Kuomintang and
was soon again helping with plans for the Northern Expedition. In
July 1926, the armies began to move out from Canton. In the meantime in the Soviet Union, the struggle between Stalin and Trotsky
was centering increasingly on interpretations of the Chinese revolution. Trotsky impatiently argued that as the Canton forces moved
toward the Yangtze they should set up soviets along the way,
initiate land reform, and carry out a social revolution. Stalin persisted in his view that although the Chinese Communist Party
should encourage peasant rebellion, it would have to contain "peasant excesses" and continue to operate within the Kuomintang until
the country had been united. To introduce a social revolution as an
adjunct of military operations would be a disruption certain to bring
about failure.

THE FIFTH PARTY CONGRESS,
APRIL 1927

In November the left wing of the Kuomintang moved the "government" from Canton to Wuhan. The act signaled a challenge to
the leadership of Chiang Kai-shek, who was leading his troops
toward Nanking and Shanghai. In spite of the strains in China
among the revolutionary forces, in Moscow at the Seventh Enlarged
Plenum of the Executive Committee of the Comintern, Stalin's views
about the need to continue to support Chiang dominated, and criticism of the Kuomintang was declared counterrevolutionary.

Early in 1927 the Chinese Communists joined the left Kuomintang government in Wuhan. Meanwhile the Communist trade unions
in Shanghai launched a series of remarkable attacks on the warlord
garrisons in Shanghai, facilitating Chiang's ultimate conquest of the
city. On April 12, however, Chiang turned his troops against the
workers, stating that they had failed to hand over their arms to his
command.

Only fifteen days later the Fifth Congress of the Chinese Communist Party met at Hankow, one of the three cities that made up
the Wuhan complex where the left-Kuomintang government was lo-

cated. The debates at the congress were confused, and there was even disagreement between Borodin and M. N. Roy, the watchdog of the Comintern. Borodin was pressing for new ties with Feng Yü-hsiang, which would carry the Party into the northwest, while Roy argued that if there was further trouble with the right-Kuomintang, the Party should return to its base in the south and strengthen its revolutionary forces there. The discussion also revolved around the issue of mobilizing the peasantry by encouraging land confiscation. In the previous year Mao Tse-tung had actively worked to organize peasant associations in Hunan, and he was anxious for the Party to take a strong stand legitimizing the destruction of "local bullies and bad gentry."

The Fifth Congress acknowledged Chiang's attack upon the Shanghai workers but insisted that the Chinese Communists should continue to work with the left Kuomintang in Wuhan. Wang Ching-wei, the leader of that government, attended sessions of the congress and heard M. N. Roy expound the theory that the Communists should continue to work within the Kuomintang to be in position to take it over at the appropriate moment of revolutionary success.

Mao's more extreme views about peasant confiscations did not win the day, and when the Central Committee established the first Politburo in the Party's history, he was not on it. The members were Ch'en Tu-hsiu, Chang Kuo-t'ao, Chou En-lai, Ch'ü Ch'iu-pai, Li Li-san, Li Wei-han, Su Chao-cheng, T'an P'ing-shan, and Ts'ai Ho-shen.

While the congress was in session Chang Tso-lin, the warlord in control of the north, sanctioned a raid on the Soviet embassy in Peking capturing large quantities of documents revealing the extent of Soviet involvement in both the Chinese Communist Party and the left wing of the Kuomintang. The raiding troops also captured several Communist leaders, including Li Ta-chao, on the embassy grounds, and they were summarily executed. The stakes were clearly rising for the Chinese Communists. At this juncture, June 1927, Borodin received his contradictory instructions from Stalin ordering both continued cooperation with the Kuomintang and the building of an anti-Kuomintang force from below. Roy showed the communication to others, and Wang Ching-wei finally recognized what the Communists had in mind. Shocked, he expelled them from the Wuhan government and from the left Kuomintang. Soon after this, the Nanking forces under Chiang Kai-shek turned toward Wuhan, spelling the end of the left Kuomintang.

On the night of August 1, 1927, the commanders of forces that were part of the Northern Expedition under the Kuomintang carried out an uprising in Nanchang. The revolt was quickly put down and the troops scattered, but the remnants became the nucleus of the entirely separate Red Army, which eventually would conquer its Kuomintang foe. The commanding generals, Ho Lung and Yeh T'ing, were secretly Communists and they were supported by Chu Teh and Lin Piao. In the confusion at the time, however, it seemed that suddenly total disaster had struck a party that only months before was calculating on taking over total power in the largest country in the world.

On August 7, 1927, the Central Committee of the Chinese Communist Party held an emergency conference, and Ch'en Tu-hsiu was charged with right-wing "opportunistic deviations." He was removed as secretary-general and replaced by Ch'ü Ch'iu-pai. The Comintern, and particularly Stalin, was unwilling to share responsibility for the disaster that their policies had brought upon the Chinese Communist Party, so Ch'en was made the scapegoat. Stalin's inherently contradictory orders made it easy to say that Ch'en had not followed all instructions. The charge that he had been engaged in "right deviation" — that is, that he had been excessively cautious and unprepared to push the more revolutionary elements — was peculiarly unfair because Stalin's emphasis had been on conservative tactics and he had picked up Trotsky's theme of peasant insurrections only after defeating Trotsky.

It was soon Ch'ü Ch'iu-pai's turn to be made the victim of Moscow's inability to understand the Chinese situation after the removal of Ch'en. Stalin insisted that the time was ripe for armed uprisings, and even after the failure at Nanchang he insisted on additional revolutionary acts. Consequently during September and November Mao Tse-tung led the Autumn Harvest uprisings in Hunan, but when these failed Mao was blamed and dismissed from all important Party posts. By December the Party was still trying to carry out Moscow's wishes and attempted a disastrous uprising in Canton under the general direction of the German Comintern representative, Heinz Neumann. For several days revolutionaries did hold ground in the southern city and declared the establishment of a commune, but soon they were scattered by troops loyal to Chiang Kai-shek.

THE SIXTH PARTY CONGRESS, JULY 1928

After the Canton commune, Moscow could no longer ignore the declining fortunes of the Chinese Communist Party, and at the Ninth Plenum of the Executive Committee of the Comintern, in February 1928, Stalin declared that the Chinese Party was guilty of "putchism" — improper use of military power — and a series of "left deviationist" errors, all stemming from insufficient planning. Whereas Ch'en Tu-hsiu had been removed for "right opportunism," Ch'ü Ch'iu-pai was under attack for the "left deviation," or "putchism." Yet both had merely sought to carry out the Comintern's unrealistic instructions.

On July 9, 1928, at the Sixth Party Congress in Moscow, Ch'ü Ch'iu-pai was removed as secretary-general and replaced by Hsiang Chung-fa, who held the office in an administrative capacity until he was arrested and executed by the Kuomintang in June 1931. He never was the actual political leader of the Party. The role of the Party leader went from Ch'ü Ch'iu-pai to Li Li-san, whose formal title was head of the Party's propaganda bureau.

The Sixth Congress decreed that "the degree of consolidation of the reactionary regime in different regions is uneven; therefore the revolution, in a general new rising tide, may succeed first in one or more provinces." For some members of the Party, including Mao and Chu Teh, this meant that an effort should be made to consolidate rural base areas for the Red Army. Even before the congress met, Mao and Chu Teh had joined forces to establish the Fourth Red Army. Li Li-san, however, discounted the possibility of revolution by military means and instead compelled the Party to emphasize labor organization and agitation. He believed that only the proletariat could lead a successful revolution, and in this belief he thought he was carrying out the highest principles of Marxism-Leninism. By the time that Li Li-san became the dominant figure in the Chinese Communist Party, the Party was down to only fifteen thousand members, and he was devoting all his time and energy to meeting with secret cells in Shanghai, Hankow, Tientsin, and other industrial centers.

After the Sixth Congress a significant split developed within the Chinese Communist Party between those who were in close contact with the secretariat in Shanghai and those who were in isolation in a mountainous retreat in Kiangsi. During 1929 one part of the Party was vigorously seeking to expand within the urban workers' environment, and the other faction was becoming increasingly militarized and allied with the peasantry in some of the most backward and isolated parts of China. By August 1930, at the Third Plenum of the Central Committee at Lushan, there was widespread criticism of the "Li Li-san line" because it expected too much of the labor movement. In November 1930 Li Li-san was disowned by the Comintern. In January 1931 the Fourth Plenum of the Central Committee met secretly in Shanghai and formally declared that the Chinese Communist Party was abandoning the Li Li-san line because it was, like the Ch'ü Ch'iu-pai line, too "putschist" in stating the revolutionary potential of the working classes. Li confessed his errors and agreed to retire to Moscow to study and improve his capacity for revolutionary analysis.

At this point the leadership of the Chinese Communist Party in the urban areas passed to a group of young Communists who had been trained in Moscow and were generally identified as the "returned students group." They included Ch'en Shao-yü, alias Wang Ming (who replaced Hsiang Chung-fa after he was executed and became the next secretary-general), Chang Wen-t'ien, Shen Tze-min. Chou En-lai, who was always with whatever group seemed dominant at the moment, joined briefly with the Shanghai group.

THE KIANGSI SOVIETS

While the Party leadership, with its Comintern connections, continued to operate out of an unimportant office in Shanghai, the other element of the Party was busily building actual governmental power in the mountains of Kiangsi. After Mao Tse-tung and Chu Teh were driven out of Hunan, they crossed to the east and sought safety in the mountainous isolation of Kiangsi. There they established the Chinese Soviet Republic with Juichin as the capital. Until 1932, the Politburo continued to operate out of Shanghai, but it commanded only a handful of people, while in Kiangsi there was evolving a system of government and a military force. In the fall of 1932 Ch'en Shao-yü, Chang Wen-t'ien, Liu Shao-ch'i, and the other members of the Central Committee left Shanghai and escaped to Juichin.

Chu Teh was the recognized military commander in Kiangsi, and all the resources available to the Communists went into building his army. Mao Tse-tung steadily emerged as the political leader. The anomaly of the time was that the Comintern in Moscow continued to pretend that revolutionary currents were running high in China and that the only reason the Communists had not taken command of the country was the incompetence of the various Chinese Communist leaders. In fact the organization of the Chinese Communist Party was exceedingly weak as a national institution, and whatever power existed lay with separate and isolated groups, whether in cells in the cities or in the separate soviets in Kiangsi. Even in the mountains there was not a single command structure.

In addition to Chu Teh and Mao Tse-tung there was a group under the command of Chang Kuo-t'ao, who thought of himself as the senior Party representative in Kiangsi. Thus Moscow assumed that the Chinese Communist Party had greater revolutionary potential than it in fact had, and furthermore Moscow was least aware of the developments that would in time give the Party its greatest advantages — the growth of the Red Army forces in Kiangsi.

The Kiangsi soviets were a blend of civilian and military rule. Party cadres served as both military commanders and political commissars. By 1931 a clearly established tradition of political officers paralleled the military chain of command. The troops were subjected to daily propaganda sessions, and everyone sought to prove in the almost daily self-criticism sessions that they were unequivocally committed to the revolution. Peasants who lived on some of the poorest land in China easily abandoned their farms and sought service and community in the new army that Chu and Mao were building.

In the meantime Chiang Kai-shek was directing his armies against the remnant warlord forces and was beginning to meet the threat of Japan, which had invaded Manchuria in 1931. Chiang did, however, devote some of his troops to Kiangsi and began a series of five "extermination" campaigns, each of which was expected to annihilate the Communists. Thus, in between his campaigns against Feng Yü-hsiang, the Kwangsi generals, and the Japanese, Chiang moved against the Communists.

Finally in 1934 the pressures in Kiangsi became too great. With the soviet areas encircled, the decision was taken to abandon the Kiangsi base and seek security elsewhere. Thus began the Long March, which was to be the most significant experience in the history of Chinese communism. In the autumn of 1934 Moscow radioed Juichin to advise the Chinese to seek safety as far away as Outer Mongolia if necessary. The Red Army, which broke out of the Kuomintang ring and started the Long March, totaled about 120,000 men. At the end, in Yenan in Shensi province, it was down to about 10,000 men.

From the outset there was a blend of heroic, romantic, and tragic elements to the Long March. When the troops set out, they left behind Ch'ü Ch'iu-pai, who was politically discredited and physically consumed by tuberculosis. Captured by the Nationalist troops, he was dramatically executed. According to a story then current, Ch'ü was carried on a stretcher from prison to the place of execution. He drank a glass of whiskey, asked for a brush and paper, and wrote this poem:[1]

> The colorful splurge of the setting
>   sun etches the mountains of Fukien.
> The rustle of the falling leaves and
>   the sound of the running streams
>   show that winter is near.
> These are eternal.
> Ten years I have passed in
>   worldly undertakings, and now
>   I am prepared to join heaven,
> But I leave with desires unfilled.

Then "he met his death singing the 'Internationale' in Russian, a cigarette drooping languidly from his fingers."

[1]Reprinted from *Moscow and Chinese Communists*, Second Edition, by Robert C. North with permission of the publishers, Stanford University Press. Copyright © 1953, 1963 by the Board of Trustees of the Leland Stanford Junior University.

The story may have been a bit romanticized by the Communists because while Ch'ü was a prisoner he wrote a remarkable introspective essay, quite un-Chinese, in which he suggested that it had been a historic misunderstanding for him to have been involved with communism: "My basic nature, I believe, does not make for a Bolshevik fighter, or even a revolutionary novitiate. But because of pride, I did not have the courage, after joining the group , to recognize my own self and ask them to wash me out."[2]

THE TSUN-YI CONFERENCE
AND MAO'S RISE TO POWER

As the Long March columns moved out of Kiangsi and entered Kweichow, their leaders were consumed with debates about what had gone wrong. The political leaders close to the Red Army were convinced that the "returned students" led by Wang Ming had failed to understand the revolutionary potential of the countryside and of the Red areas. The fact that they had been faithfully following Moscow's orders was ignored. In time, however, those who left Kiangsi began to clash as they in their turn sought to follow Moscow's instructions, even to the point of the routes to be followed.

In later years the Communists would idealize the Long March, but much that happened during its course is still obscure. There was, for example, a conference at Tsun-yi, in Kweichow, at which, according to some accounts, Mao Tse-tung was recognized as the leader not only of the military operation but of the Chinese Communist Party. Others have suggested that the leadership was more diffuse and collective. In any case, there was a major break between Mao Tse-tung and Chang Kuo-t'ao. Chang had long been a major figure in the Party and had begun the Long March with more men under his command than Mao Tse-tung had. When Mao asserted his leadership at Tsun-yi, Chang Kuo-t'ao refused to recognize the legitimacy of his decisions. By the time the two leaders reached Yenan in Shensi, however, it was clear that Mao had established his superiority in the eyes of such important figures as Chu Teh, Chou

[2]Chester C. Tan, *Chinese Political Thought in the Twentieth Century* (Garden City, N.Y.: Doubleday, 1971), p. 322.

En-lai, Lin Piao, and P'eng Te-huai. Chang Kuo-t'ao at this juncture broke with the Party. Thus during the course of the Long March Mao Tse-tung became the great symbolic leader of the Chinese Communists.

YENAN AND THE SECOND UNITED FRONT

The decision to settle in Shensi was influenced in part by Stalin's increasing concern about the rise of Japanese power in the Far East. The Russian leader was anxious to have as strong and unified a China as possible to serve as a balance to Japan and provide security for the Soviet Union. On August 1, 1935, during the Long March, the Chinese Communist Party issued a "declaration of war" against Japan and called for all Chinese to unite in opposing the nation's principal foreign threats. The decision was made to seek a base area in the northwest of China from which the Party could continue to appeal for national unity in opposition to the Japanese.

An unexpected opportunity presented by the kidnaping of Chiang Kai-shek, in December 1936, gave the Communists the additional leverage necessary to extract from Nanking the agreement for the Second United Front of the Chinese Communist Party and the Kuomintang. In Communist tactical jargon the first united front (1922–1927) had been "a bloc within a bloc" and a "united front from below" — that is, it involved Communists working as individuals within the Kuomintang. According to class analysis this meant that the Communists worked directly with workers, peasants, petty bourgeoisie, and big bourgeoisie — that is, from "below" — to lead them into support of the Kuomintang. The result of such a united front should have been a bourgeois-democratic revolution, which would set the stage for a subsequent socialist revolution as the workers' and peasants' powers grew. The Second United Front was in Communist theory an alliance and thus a "united front from above." It involved Chinese Communist Party leaders arriving at limited agreements with the leaders of other parties and classes to pursue certain common but highly restricted goals. The distinction is significant. Neither form of united front was seen by the Communists as demanding a merging of interests or complete cooperation. Under their understanding of a "united front from above" the Party was bound only to adhere to the formal conditions of the alliance. It could still build its own class base and subvert the power of enemy classes.

In short, with the First United Front the Communists had been seeking power and advancement in any way possible; with the Second United Front (1937–1945) the relationship was more one of alliance between two mutually suspicious governments, each of which had its own territorial bases and constituencies.

During the Yenan war years Mao emerged not only as the symbolic leader of the Chinese Communist Party but also as an ideologue in the tradition of Marx and Lenin. Although Chinese communism sprang from the activities of intellectuals and some of its earliest champions were among the liveliest minds in the nation, the early years saw few doctrinal disputes and nothing in the way of memorable ideological writing. The Party leaders were far too engrossed in learning the intricacies of Comintern logic and tactics to treat Marxism as a subject of intellectual challenge. Men who had once been trained in philosophy and philology concentrated only on learning about "left" and "right" deviation, "adventurism," "putschism," and the other sins that beset the way of the Bolshevik revolutionary.

In the relative security of Yenan, Mao Tse-tung was able to devote more attention to larger questions about communism in China. This was the time when Mao was most productive, and his essays ranged from military affairs (*On Protracted Warfare*) to political analysis and propaganda (*On New Democracy*), basic Marxist theory (*On Contradiction* and *On Practice*), and sermons and attacks (*Talks at the Yenan Forum on Literature and Art* and *On Liberalism*). Mao was also busy meeting with foreign visitors and managing the public relations of the Yenan regime.

Other leaders, especially Chu Teh and Liu Shao-ch'i, assumed the principal responsibilities for military operations and civil administration. Even before the Japanese conquests had reached their greatest limits, the Chinese Communist Party had organized "border" governments that straddled provincial lines and made it possible to jump from jurisdiction to jurisdiction and thus exploit the federal or provincial traditions of China. After the Second United Front was established, the Chinese Communist Party was supposed to end its propaganda and revolutionary efforts, but it continued to maintain the Shensi-Kansu-Ninghsia Border Region government and as early as December 1937 it also established the Shansi-Hopei-Chahai Border Region government. These "governments" organized the peasants behind the Japanese lines and provided support for the guerrillas. The civilian populations were formed into various organizations that collected intelligence on Japanese troop movements, provided food and funds for the guerrillas, and produced uniforms, equipment, and even munitions. In the rural areas the Communists controlled, they introduced their own currency and stamps and collected taxes. When the Eighth Route Army moved about it had to live off the countryside, and when it obtained food and supplies it generally gave in exchange a form of IOU that would be honored once the war was over and the People's Republic was established. The Red Army thus left in its wake large numbers of people who felt their interests lay with the establishment of a Communist government, for only then could they hope to be reimbursed.

During the war years the Chinese Communist Party grew not only in numbers but also in political sophistication and discipline. Early in 1942, after America had entered World War II and the defeat of Japan was assured, Mao Tse-tung initiated the *cheng-feng* movement, which sought to instill in the Chinese Communists the Bolshevik traditions of party discipline. The target of his ideological attack was political liberalism and bourgeois democratic sentiments. The goal was to create a monolithic party, advanced in the use of political indoctrination, that regularly employed self-criticism and mutual criticism to eliminate deviationist tendencies.

By 1943 the Chinese Communist Party controlled millions of people in north China, and through increasingly professional activists it was disseminating new attitudes and styles of behavior. The line between soldier and civilian was blurred, and all were expected to lead a frugal and austere life. Workers who labored long hours and asked for no extra pay were idealized as heroes. Army units were expected to support themselves, as were schools and administrative organs of government. Soldiers, students, and officials divided their time between raising food, making handicrafts, and carrying out their primary functions.

During these years the Party gained extensive experience in both warfare and ruling a rural population. It introduced new guerrilla practices to China, and it upheld new ideals of civilian and military relationships. But much of its energy still had to be focused on reacting to the initiatives of others and coping with immediate circumstances. To a surprising degree Mao and the other Communists had little to say about the kind of China they were seeking to build. In his *New Democracy* Mao made it clear that, as a good Marxist, he did not expect that government by the Chinese Communist Party could bring communism to China because China had not experienced the bourgeois-democratic revolution that must precede a socialist revolution. Yet he did say that because socialism existed in Russia the process might be speeded up in China. His discussion, however, dealt with historical generalities and not with programmatic considerations.

Although during the early years of the Communist movement in China Mao Tse-tung was identified with the most radical view toward land reform, strangely during the Yenan period, when Mao was more clearly in authority, questions of confiscation were muted. In the base areas it was important to emphasize unity and avoid potentially divisive issues, so extreme forms of social change were avoided. At the same time there was no mistaking the direction of Communist policies. Owners of large landholdings knew they had little to gain from the Communists while the poor peasants saw the Communists as their natural ally.

The Communists' emphasis during the war years was thus less on social and economic issues and more on appeals to nationalism. Nationalism was not only opposition to the Japanese conquerors; it also involved a historic process by which the rural and interior parts of China were being brought into the national political spotlight. The Communists were extremely successful in establishing contacts with villagers and making them feel that their actions could influence the fate of their country. The years of foreign, particularly Japanese, pressure on China had produced a general awareness of China's limitations, which the Nationalists' propaganda had further highlighted. The Communists at last offered the people something constructive to do: They could support the anti-Japanese war by helping the guerrillas and becoming model, hard-working, unselfish citizens in the Communist-controlled areas.

By the time the war ended, the Communists had greatly strengthened their popular and their political positions. The Chinese Communist Party was at last highly disciplined, well organized, and extensively distributed. It had cells not only in the countryside but also in all the major east coast cities, where its underground had been active during the entire Japanese occupation. The Red Army had a dual structure of authority with political commissars paralleling the conventional military command chain. The Party's propaganda organization was talented and constantly provided the people with plays, dramas, speeches, newspapers, and radio programs that stressed the themes of nationalism and the worth of the common man.

The Party, however, said little about what national policies would be under its rule. Many people assumed therefore that communism would bring to China a system more democratic and less authoritarian than Kuomintang rule. Even within the Party there was little sense of what victory would demand. Probably few Chinese, either in or out of the Party, expected the extreme version of totalitarian rule that emerged. The Communists had produced idealism and the mechanism of mass organization, but they had only the model of Stalin's Russia to tell them how to build socialism.

CHAPTER TEN

The Means of Ruling

In the summer of 1949, with the Kuomintang armies in demoralized retreat toward the island of Taiwan and Chiang Kai-shek in temporary retirement, Mao Tse-tung moved his government from the caves of Yenan to the yellow-tiled Forbidden City in Peking. In June he had gathered the leading Party members and notables who were prepared to support the Communists in a Chinese People's Political Consultative Conference and on July 1 he presented his concept of the Communist government-to-be — a "people's democratic dictatorship." Mao's mood and his words were confident to the point of being aggressively self-assured as he dismissed the rhetorical criticisms he made of himself:

> "You are leaning to one side." Exactly . . . All Chinese without exception must lean either to the side of imperialism or to the side of socialism. Sitting on the fence will not do, nor is there a third road. . . .
>
> "You are too irritating." We are talking about how to deal with domestic and foreign reactionaries, the imperialists and their running dogs, not about how to deal with anyone else. . . . We must not show the slightest timidity before a wild beast. We must learn from Wu Sung on the Chingyang Ridge. As Wu Sung saw it, the tiger on Chingyang Ridge was a man-eater, whether irritated or not. Either kill the tiger or be eaten by him — one or the other. . . .
>
> "Victory is possible even without international help." This is a mistaken idea. In the epoch in which imperialism exists, it is impossible for a genuine people's revolution to win victory in any country without various forms of help from the international revolutionary

forces, and even if victory were won, it could not be consolidated. . . . Internationally, we belong to the side of the anti-imperialist front headed by the Soviet Union, and so we can turn only to this side for genuine and friendly help, not to the side of the imperialist front.

"You are dictatorial." My dear sirs, you are right, that is just what we are. All the experience the Chinese people have accumulated through several decades teaches us to enforce the people's democratic dictatorship, that is, to deprive the reactionaries of the right to speak and let the people alone have that right.

"Who are the people?" At the present stage in China, they are the working class, the peasantry, the urban petty bourgeoisie, and the national bourgeoisie. These classes, led by the working class and the Communist Party, unite to form their own state and elect their own government; they enforce their dictatorship over the running dogs of imperialism — the landlord class and bureaucrat-bourgeoisie, as well as the representatives of those classes, the Kuomintang reactionaries and their accomplices — suppress them, allow them only to behave themselves and not to be unruly in word or deed.

"Don't you want to abolish state power?" Yes, we do, but not right now; we cannot do it yet. Why? Because imperialism still exists, because domestic reaction still exists, because classes still exist in our country. Our present task is to strengthen the people's state apparatus — mainly the people's army, the people's police, and the people's courts. . . .

"You are not benevolent." Quite so. . . .

To sum up our experience and concentrate it into one point, it is: the people's democratic dictatorship under the leadership of the working class (through the Communist Party) and based upon the alliance of workers and peasants. This dictatorship must unite as one with the international revolutionary forces. This is our formula, our principal experience, our main program.[1]

On October 1, 1949, at three in the afternoon, Mao stood on the reviewing platform at Tien An Men (Gate of Heavenly Peace) Square, declared the establishment of the Chinese People's Republic, and hoisted the new flag. Government at that time — and for the

[1]Mao Tse-tung, "On the People's Democratic Dictatorship," *Selected Works of Mao Tse-tung* (Peking: Foreign Languages Press, 1967), vol. 4, pp. 415–22.

most part ever since — involved three closely related institutions: the Chinese Communist Party, the People's Liberation Army, and the state bureaucracy.

Since that day Communist rule has gone through several phases. Initially the chief task of government was to restore order and legitimize the new system. The search for order caused an early reliance on the army for administering the country. The problem of legitimacy produced numerous populist policies, the recognition of minority political parties (that in time had no independent powers), the creation of large mass organizations for mobilizing specific segments of the society, and above all extensive propaganda campaigns to influence individual citizens.

The Korean war facilitated the restoration of order and the legitimation of the new regime. In the next phase the principal problem of government was to take up the tasks of socialist construction and economic development. The government had to strengthen its administrative and technical capabilities. The result was the rapid growth of the civil bureaucracy. From about 1952 to 1958 the Communists made their most impressive achievements in bringing effective centralized government to China. The bureaucracy that emerged under Party control was the most efficient institution in Chinese history. The government reached down further into society than any previous government, penetrating into villages and urban neighborhoods where officials had tolerated a great deal of autonomy. Government reached out to encompass all phases of life. Never before in Chinese history, or for that matter in world history, had a government sought to rule more completely and involve itself in so much.

The third phase of Communist rule was the brief period from 1958 to 1960 when the leaders sought to achieve total mobilization of all segments of the Chinese population and go beyond the limits they believed the bureaucrats could reach in achieving economic and socialist development. This was the period of the Great Leap and the communes. Whereas in the first years the government had used mass organizations to mobilize public support, beginning in 1958 cadres focused on activities in people's places of employment.

Since 1960 the Chinese Communist system has vacillated between depending on bureaucratic controls and seeking to go beyond administrative measures in mobilizing mass activities. Because of these vacillations it is difficult to characterize the processes of government in Communist China. Nearly every general statement has to be qualified because of the limited time period for which it is valid.

In this chapter we shall describe the formal structures of government that have emerged under Communist rule. These generally have been most obvious during periods of relatively systematic national development and have been weakened during periods of revolutionary agitation such as the Great Leap and the Cultural Revolution.

THE ARMY AS RULERS

The field armies that brought the Communists victory in the civil war provided the initial administrative capabilities for the Party. As the armies advanced and "liberated" rural areas and cities, they established military control commissions that maintained public order, arrested former Kuomintang officials, and provided political and ideological guidance to the population. These commissions in turn were dependent upon the organization of the People's Liberation Army. Quite naturally the military jurisdictions of the five field armies and of the central army command in the area of the capital became six administrative regions, which provided the critical dimension of government during the first five years of the regime.

Elements of the Fourth Field Army were responsible for the Northeast Peoples' Government, headed by Kao Kang, which included the Manchurian provinces and Jehol. This region became autonomous, and Kao Kang went so far as to conduct his own relations with the Soviet Union before he was purged and said to have committed suicide. The majority of the Fourth Field Army was under the command of General Lin Piao and administered the Central and South China Regional Committee, which included Honan, Hupei, Hunan, Kiangsi, Kwangtung, and Kwangsi. The Third Field Army was responsible for the East China Military and Political Committee, headed by General Jao Shu-shih, which contained the coastal provinces from Shantung down to Fukien and in theory Taiwan. The First Field Army, under the command of General P'eng Te-huai, ruled the northwestern provinces from Shensi and Kansu to Sinkiang. The Second Field Army handled the Fifth Administrative region in the southwest, under Liu Po-ch'eng, and included Szechwan, Kweichow, Yunnan, and Sikang provinces. The sixth region was the Suiyuan Military and Political Committee's jurisdiction, which included Suiyuan and Inner Mongolia. The Central Government in Peking, the Central Military Headquarters under Chu Teh, and officers of the former North China Field Army under Nieh Jung-chen administered Hopei, Shansi, Ping Yuan, and Chahar provinces.

Although in theory the Chinese People's Republic was supposed to have a highly centralized government, in practice the great regional administrative councils were quite autonomous and in their separate ways sought to translate the general policy lines that emanated from the Party and the Politburo into practical administrative policies. In the early years of Communist rule the administrative regions were declared to be temporary subdivisions, existing only until the government was fully centralized. However, by 1954 the leaders acknowledged that practicality favored decentralization. In June 1954 the administrative regions were abolished, and effective control was brought down to the level of the province. The number of provinces was reduced from thirty to twenty, the number of counties set at slightly more than two thousand, and the number of villages came to two hundred fourteen thousand. Increasingly in the years that followed, the Chinese Communists were compelled to follow the practice of all previous rulers of China; they had to treat the province as the key unit beneath the capital. Co-equal with the provinces (_sheng_) were special cities (_t'e-pieh shih_), which included Peking and Shanghai.

In Communist China the provinces are divided into counties (_hsien_), districts (_ch'ü_), and villages (_hsiang_). The village is the smallest administrative unit, and after the Great Leap it became in many cases a commune. On the average a village has about seven thousand inhabitants, and a few Party activists manage it. A county is considerably larger, with an average population of two hundred twenty-five thousand. From even the earliest days of Communist rule, and more so in recent years, there has been a considerable clustering of technical specialists at the county level. Agricultural specialists, medical officers, visiting nurses, special police, and propaganda groups are county officials.

THE STATE APPARATUS

In September 1949 the Party convened the Chinese People's Political Consultative Conference, which in turn legitimized the establishment of the National People's Congress. This body, which in theory was to be elected by county representatives, established the Central People's Governmental Council or, as it soon came to be called, the Government Council. The chairman of the council was Mao Tse-tung. It contained an executive body called the Government Administration Council, or State Council, which has consistently operated as a cabinet under the guidance of its premier, Chou En-lai.

The State Council has been composed of a variety of ministries, generally grouped into three categories: political and legal, financial and economic, cultural and educational.

From the beginning Communist rule was characterized by two practices: The incessant use of committees and liaison groups and the integration of rule by giving many offices and posts to the same man. In theory the administrative regions were run by committees that included military officers (who were, of course, Party officials) and civilian officials. The ministries in Peking were staffed with specialists but were constantly being "coordinated" by various sub-cabinet committees. Coordination and integration were achieved by giving individuals high status in the Party hierarchy, definite commands in the army, and specific governmental responsibilities.

The practice of wearing several hats started with Mao Tse-tung, who was called "chairman" because he was chairman of the Central Committee of the Chinese Communist Party, chairman of the Governmental Council, and also chairman of the People's Revolutionary Military Council, which controlled the People's Liberation Army. Thus in theory Mao was in command of the three basic institutions of the new regime, the Party, the government, and the army.

In practice, however, during the first fifteen years the management of the government went to the premier, Chou En-lai, and management of the Party to Liu Shao-ch'i, the vice-chairman of the Central Committee and of the Politburo. When the regime was established in 1949, considerable care was taken to separate the state apparatus from the Party organization. During the early years the principle was well established that the state apparatus was to be given over predominantly to technical specialists and not to political policy makers. Thus the State Council has never performed as a cabinet, and the heads of the various ministries are implementers of general policies and not figures of power.

The extent to which the state apparatus was made into a narrowly technical and administrative institution reflects a distinctive characteristic of the Chinese Communist style of rule: Policy making and policy execution are clearly separated. In making this separation, the Communists emphasize the distinction between general policy, or the "line" (fang-chen), made by the Politburo, and administrative policy (cheng-ts'e), arising out of officials' efforts to implement the general line.

Because the state apparatus has been devoted entirely to the implementation of policy, the ministries lack distinct characters. During the first five-year plan several separate ministries dealt with different parts of the economy. Since the Cultural Revolution the number of ministries has been reduced by nearly half. Government officials in state offices have tended to become increasingly specialized, in contrast to the gentlemen amateurs who filled the bureaucratic posts in the imperial system. Officials are expected to implement policies although Communist rhetoric stresses the need for initiative and for everyone to be an activist. Over the years officials in the state bureaucracies have had to learn to uphold ideals of loyalty and obedience while creating the impression of being imaginative in figuring out how established policies can be carried out more efficiently. They have had to worry about the sin of bureaucratism (kuan-liao-chu-i), the tendency to lose touch with the masses and become absorbed with questions of rank and status. Government officials must engage in constant study sessions to ensure that they do not develop wrong attitudes.

PARTY ORGANIZATION

The key to the processes of government and the behavior of officials is the role of the Party. Although descriptions of the mechanisms of rule have stressed the state organs, and although the army was the most conspicuous institution of government during the first years and after the Cultural Revolution, the critical factor in the Communist system of government has been the Party and the individual cadre.

During the Yenan period the Party had been exposed to a stern rectification campaign (*cheng-feng*), but as the Communists moved toward victory there was an upsurge in the number of candidates for Party membership and in the need for skilled and trusted people. In 1945 the Party had 1.2 million members; by 1948 the number had grown to 3 million; by 1950 it reached nearly 7 million; 12.7 million in 1956; and 17 million by 1961. Since 1961 accurate figures are not available. The Cultural Revolution nearly destroyed the Party, which is only now being gradually reconstructed.

Historically Party membership has required the candidate to demonstrate his loyalty and competence during a probationary period. In rural areas Party members are a distinct elite, numbering no more than two or three percent of the population. In urban areas, where there are more educated and technically skilled people, the number of members can be as high as one out of every seven or ten people. In the army officers with the rank of company commander and higher are likely to be Party members.

The basic unit of the Party is the branch (*chih pu*) committee, and in theory every Party member belongs to one. In any governmental organization or other large institution (factories, research institutes, universities) there has generally been a Party branch that provides guidance to and surveillance of the actual hierarchy of officials. The Party chain of command constitutes an invisible inner framework for formal institutions. Each Party member must combine the duties of the office he holds with the higher obligation he has to his position within the Party. In this sense the Communist Party, even after the victory of 1949, remained a submerged organization, following semi-clandestine practices.

In theory the leadership of the Party rests with the Central Committee, but in fact it is in the hands of the Politburo and more particularly in its standing committee. According to the Party Constitution the Party Congress is supposed to meet every year. Its members, elected by the Party congresses of provinces and the special cities, have terms of five years. However, the Eighth Party Congress held its first session in September 1956 and was not reconvened until May 1958, and the Ninth Party Congress was not called until April 1969, in the wake of the Cultural Revolution.

Since Yenan the Party congresses have generally been less significant than the meetings of the Central Committee and the various plenums at which policy lines have been announced. At various times there have been strong policy conflicts in the Central Committee, which is not always a rubber stamp for the Politburo. However, most of the time it is docile.

The Central Committee is composed of leading Party members, who manage not only the Party but also the army and the government. Although it rarely acts as a decision-making body, it is the symbol of established authority and its members derive considerable power and prestige by being identified with it. For these reasons the chairmanship of the Central Committee is the most prestigious office in Communist China, followed by the position of senior vice-chairman.

The Central Committee is a sounding board, a legitimizer of policies, and a device for indicating relative rank and status. Real power in the Party rests with the Politburo. In 1949 when the Chinese People's Republic was established, the Politburo had only eleven members. With the new Party constitution of 1956 the Politburo was expanded to seventeen full members and six alternates; at the time of the Cultural Revolution there were twenty-one full members. The Politburo runs the county and provides policy guidance for all institutions. Operationally it is too large, and thus its standing committee of five members is its most powerful decision-making part.

Beneath the Politburo and responsible for the actual administration of the Party is the Central Secretariat. Until he was purged during the Cultural Revolution, Teng Hsiao-p'ing was the long-standing first secretary of the Party. The number of secretaries at any one time has varied from four to ten. The major task of the Central Secretariat is to communicate Politburo decisions and receive reports from all the offices of the Party. Yet in practice much of its power flows from its management of the personnel of the Party.

Separate from the Central Secretariat is the Party's Military Affairs Commission, which directs military policy, controls the People's Liberation Army, and supervises the work of the political commissars in the army structure. Although in theory the commission deals with military and security policies, it has in fact been an important political decision-making force, especially in light of the role of the People's Liberation Army in governing China in the early days of the regime and after the Cultural Revolution.

The secret of the strength of the Chinese Communist Party is not its Leninist discipline or its hierarchy of unbending authority. It is the concept of the dedicated individual member, the Party cadre. Liu Shao-ch'i stated in his essay *On the Party*: "The cadres of the Party are the nucleus of the Party leadership and of the Chinese revolution. Everyone knows that cadres decide everything. . . . They are as Comrade Mao Tse-tung puts it, 'the treasures of the nation and pride of the whole Party.' "[2]

The most startling development that took place as the Kuomintang retreated in the civil war was the sudden surfacing of dedicated cadres in organization after organization. Suddenly on university campuses janitors and technicians, students and maintenance workers, asserted themselves and revealed that they were long-standing Party members. In government offices, hospitals, and business concerns people who had previously appeared to be uninvolved stepped forward to become spokesmen of the new regime. In urban neighborhoods, in schools and factories, cadres emerged to guide their associates and colleagues in learning the new work styles demanded by the new rulers.

The ideal cadre *(kanpu)* is a Communist Party member who with endless vigor and complete self-sacrifice works for the goals of the revolution. As an activist he is a part of the elite, sensitive to the rationale of the correct Party line. At the same time he is completely in tune with the masses, aware of their interests and their problems. He is a paragon of Communist virtues, always striving to improve himself, constantly sensitive to his failings, and completely obedient to the demands of the Party. Increasingly over the years the good cadre has become one who is absolutely devoted to the Thoughts of Mao Tse-tung and an unquestioning worshiper of the demi-god who leads the Chinese Communist Party.

There are two kinds of cadre: Party and non-Party. Non-Party

[2]Liu Shao-ch'i, *On the Party* (Peking: Foreign Languages Press, 1952), p. 101.

cadres are activist officials or military officers who lack official status in the Party but are leaders in their respective spheres. They are presumed to have a deep personal commitment to the Communist system. Under no condition would a cadre question policies or discount the goals of the revolution.

The outlook of a cadre is supposed to be that of a professional revolutionary inspired by ideals of voluntary dedication. He works for promotion and is aware that he is part of a system that recognizes seniority and provides a career ladder. However, he works more for an honorarium than for a meaningful salary and is prepared at all times to sacrifice his own interests for those of the organization. He is in a sense the perfect "organization man" precisely because he denies that he is striving for material rewards and wants only to work for the good of the collectivity.

In the early years of the regime there were possibilities for advancement in the Party, but increasingly the hierarchy became frozen and cadres had fewer opportunities to improve themselves. A symptom of the tendency toward rigidity is the practice of referring to cadres according to cohort groups. There are "old cadres" and "new cadres," "Long March cadres" and "Yenan cadres." Promotions within the Party have been exceedingly slow because expansion of the Party brought in mainly young people. There has been a major telescoping of generations within the Party hierarchy.

Partly because of decreasing promotion possibilities and because the pay is so low, cadres have been transferred quite freely from place to place to do any required task. The cadre is like a member of a modern army or large bureaucracy in which personnel is frequently assigned and reassigned.

The quality of the cadre's work is supposed to be related to the intensity and regularity of his study and his participation in indoctrination sessions and theoretical study (*li-lun hsüeh-hsi*). During drives and special campaigns the cadre may have to spend almost all his free time attending struggle meetings (*tou-cheng hui*) at which all engage in criticism (*p'i p'ing*), self-criticism (*tzu-wo chien-t'ao*), and mutual criticism (*ho-hsiang p'i-p'ing*).

The ultimate discipline of the cadre has been expulsion for being found to be an anti-Party and anti-progressive person. A less drastic threat has been criticism about one's inadequate work style. A unique Chinese form of discipline and retraining has been the practice of demanding manual labor of all cadres and of periodically "transferring downward" (*hsia fang*) — that is, moving cadres to rural areas. Since 1950 nearly forty million cadres and young people have been sent to isolated rural communities where they are expected to improve their outlook by learning from the peasants. This procedure has interjected into the most stagnant and tradition-bound rural villages of Chinese millions of young and ambitious men and women who are anxious to prove themselves as leaders. Whether this has been effective in raising the ideological level of the Party

---

PROPAGANDA SONGS

Sailing the Seas Depends on the Helmsman

> Sailing the seas depends on the helmsman,
> Life and growth depend on the sun.
> Rain and dewdrops nourish the crops,
> Making revolution depends on Mao Tse-tung's thought.
> Fish can't leave the water,
> Nor melons leave the vine.
> The revolutionary masses can't do without the Communist Party.
> Mao Tse-tung's thought is the sun that forever shines.

The East Is Red

> Red is the east, rises the sun.
> China has brought forth a Mao Tse-tung.
> For the people's happiness he works,
> *Hu erh hai yo,*
> He's the people's liberator.
>
> Chairman Mao loves the people.
> Chairman Mao, he is our guide.
> To build a new China,
> *Hu erh hai yo,*
> He leads us forward.
>
> Communist Party is like the sun,
> Bringing light wherever it shines.
> Where there's the Communist Party,
> *Hu erh hai yo,*
> There the people win liberation.

---

may be questioned, but there is no doubt that it has indirectly served to reduce slightly the gap between the backward villagers and the more politically conscious urban people.

The Chinese Communists have gone beyond the Russians in making class distinctions less a sociological phenomenon and more one of personal attitudes and convictions. A cadre can by his words and deeds prove himself to be a model proletarian revolutionary, and even people with no working-class experience can prove themselves ideologically. However, the Chinese have certainly made more over the values of manual labor than have any of the other Communist parties. Factory managers are expected to spend one day a week working as common laborers; government officials are called upon to engage regularly in physical labor; and all cadres are believed to benefit from a systematic regime of some form of manual work. A. Doak Barnett has suggested the interesting hypothesis that the Chinese Communists' near-reverence for manual labor may be related to the work-study program in France that played such an important part in founding the Party. Certainly the intellectuals who founded the Party were very much in awe of workers, and all modernizing Chinese have tended to feel that a basic flaw in the ethic of the Confucian scholar-official was his contempt for working with his hands. Whatever the explanation, the fact is unmistakable that the Chinese Communists believe that physical labor is important for creating and maintaining correct political attitudes.

MASS LINE AND DEMOCRATIC CENTRALISM

The stress on cadres' maintaining close contact with the common people, both workers and peasants, relates to the Chinese Communists' concept of the mass line, which in turn is based on the principle "from the masses, to the masses." Cadres are supposed to collect individual and general views of the masses — their complaints and their wishes — sum them up, relate them to policies, and finally take integrated ideas back to the masses and explain them so that the people will see their correctness and will also accept them. The cadre is then expected to get people's reactions to the explained policies, transmit the reactions upward so that they can be reintegrated and expressed in modification of policies that are then once again explained to the people. The process is supposed to go on endlessly: Cadres tap public attitudes, report them, and seek to present policies in the light of the public attitudes they have discovered.

The concept of the mass line does mean that policies are presented in ways that take some elements of public opinion into account. The mass line evolved while the Chinese Communist Party was a guerrilla movement and had to live close to the rural people. When the Party came to power, communication "from the masses, to the masses" became far more complicated. National policies had to be made from a national perspective, and increasingly the mass line became a means of instructing people about their responses to given policies. Paradoxically the concept of the mass line, which made a virtue of cadres' contacts with the population, provided the bases for the practice of "transferring downward" or *hsia fang*.

The mass line is a generalized form of democratic centralism, to which all Communist parties adhere in theory. Members of the lower branches of the Party are encouraged to discuss possible policies and pass up their views. When decisions are taken at higher levels, all subordinate levels must strictly obey. The Common Program, approved by the Chinese People's Political Consultative Conference on September 29, 1949, carried the concept of democratic centralism beyond the limits of the Party and the entire government. Article 15 stated:

> The organs of state power at all levels shall practice democratic centralism. In doing this the main principles shall be: the People's Congresses shall be responsible and accountable to the people; the People's Government Councils shall be responsible and accountable to the People's Congresses. Within the People's Congresses and within the People's Government Councils, the minority shall abide by the decisions of the majority; the appointment of the People's Governments of each level shall be ratified by the People's Government of the higher level; the People's Governments of the lower levels shall obey the People's Government of the higher levels and all local People's Government throughout the country shall obey the Central People's Government. . . .[3]

[3]*The Common Programme* (Peking: Foreign Languages Press, 1952), p. 7–8.

THE PROCESS OF GOVERNMENT

In the first years of the Peking regime most people's contacts with authority came not through dealings with the Party, army, or state bureaucracy but through a series of drives or campaigns in which mass organizations were established to mobilize various segments of the population. Specialized organizations such as the New Democratic Youth League, the All China Democratic Women's Federation, the All China Federation of Trade Unions, and the All China Federation of Industrial and Commercial Circles were established to link the new government with different groups. Cadres took the lead in organizing the mass organizations, which eventually became critical channels of communication between leaders and the Chinese people.

During the early 1950's much time and energy was expended in building the mass organizations, and it appeared as though the regime would seek to rule permanently through these institutions. However, gradually and then quite abruptly after the Great Leap there was a trend away from the mass organizations; greater reliance was placed on the basic structures of the Party, the army, and the state. Since the Cultural Revolution, mass organizations have nearly disappeared.

During the first years of the regime, most observers were extremely impressed with the ease of coordination among Party, army, and state. It was universally assumed that the coordination resulted from the fact that the top Communist leaders knew each other well and had worked together for a long time. Their personal relationships seemed to ensure that all the institutions of government worked smoothly.

Since the Cultural Revolution we have learned that there were more stresses and strains among the leaders than appeared on the surface. Policy differences emerged among the top rulers, and some of the erratic behavior of the regime was probably due to such conflicts. Indeed, one of the persisting characteristics of the Communist system in China has been conflict over the relationship between ideological commitment and technical specialization — the "red and expert" problem, as the Chinese call it. This tension has contributed greatly to the retardation of institutional development in China. As procedures tend to become routinized, they are likely to be disrupted by the clash of ideological requirements with technical or pragmatic considerations.

The revolutionary legitimacy of the regime has not been effectively routinized. In the early years the continued use of mass campaigns and special drives to accomplish objectives prevented the institutionalization of administrative routine. Later Mao's personal views about the need to maintain revolutionary ardor by opposing bureaucratic rule prevented standardized procedures.

The conflict between ideology and technical specialization has steadily intensified. Year by year the policies and programs of the Chinese Communist leaders have been changing in reaction to conflicting trends within the Chinese People's Republic. One trend has been toward increased institutional stability and order; the other involves the forces that led to the Cultural Revolution.

CHAPTER ELEVEN

The Vintage Years
of Chinese Communism

Nothing suggests more vividly the restless uncertainty of the Chinese Communists than the year to year vacillations and at times violent oscillations in policies. More than inconsistency, there has been an almost frantic pattern of change. Merely to mention specific years is to evoke quite different images of Chinese activities: 1951 — mass organizations absorbed with the Three-Antis Movement and the Resist America, Aid Korea Campaign; 1955 — Chou En-lai advancing the Bandung spirit, while at home rational and vigorous programs to socialize industry and agriculture; 1958 — the Great Leap and the frantic efforts to "catch up with Great Britain" and create communes everywhere; 1961 — China afflicted with famine but aggressively denouncing the relative prosperity of the Soviet Union; 1966 — the Cultural Revolution and the madness of the Red Guards.

Each year since 1949 has been distinctive. Instead of following trends and counting on incremental developments, Chinese leaders have been striving for dramatic solutions. Or, we can hypothesize, instead of the apparently unified leadership there has all along been a series of struggles.

The Chinese Communists speak of distinct stages in the history of their regime. The first, "Reconstruction," commenced with the founding of the government and the end of the civil war in 1949 and lasted until the end of 1952 when order was established. From 1953 to 1957, in the second stage, the "Period of Transition to Socialism," occurred the collectivization of agriculture, the start of the first five-year plan, and the beginning of state-supervised industrialization.

The third stage, "Socialist Construction," extended over the Great Leap years of 1958 to 1960 and witnessed the introduction of

communes. The fourth stage is least discussed in Communist literature. It is referred to as the "Period of Readjustment," in which the
country after the Great Leap experienced an extremely severe depression and confronted the prospect of having to strive for
economic development alone, without Soviet or any other foreign
assistance. Finally, the Chinese talk of a stage of "Renewed Class
Struggle and Socialist Education Campaigns," which began in 1962
and lasted throughout the Cultural Revolution.

The amount of vacillation in Communist policies and practices
was far greater than the number of stages and is best revealed in
a year by year review of the Communist era.

1949: THE EXHILARATION OF CONQUEST

In their moment of victory the Communist leaders appeared in
two, quite contradictory, guises to the Chinese population. People
were ready for change after years of turmoil but were not sure
whether they could trust their new rulers. In their search for legitimacy the Communists sought to be paternalistic and constructive
toward those who would support them and ruthless and unforgiv-
ing toward all who persisted in supporting the old order. During the
first year the Party had to greatly increase its membership, and so
one emphasis of the regime was on recruiting and welcoming new
people, who were almost without exception young. Students and
young people were identified as the natural supporters of the regime, and they were encouraged to assume leadership roles and to
"correct" the thoughts and behavior of their elders. At the same
time the regime, in spite of the unquestioned victories of the People's Liberation Army, was constantly uncovering "enemies" who
had to be exterminated so that they might not destroy the new order.
There was a blending of expectation and fear throughout China.

The militant spirit of the new regime was heightened by the
fact that administrative powers in the local areas were largely the
responsibility of political cadres in the People's Liberation Army
who for years had been providing political guidance to soldiers.
These cadres greatly appreciated the importance of disciplined organizational behavior. They were inclined to see the problem of
ordering Chinese society as being the same as maintaining morale
and professional discipline within the army.

In the first year membership in mass organizations and united front groups was encouraged. In its search for legitimacy and acceptance the Party constantly emphasized that "minority" and "democratic" parties were supporting the new government, which they characterized as a coalition of Communists and non-Communists. In less than two years most of the concern for "minority" parties disappeared, but during 1949 the Communists went to great lengths to suggest that non-Communist elements would have a political future in China.

Domestically the most significant issue was land reform. In the rural areas "liberation" involved the establishment of "people's courts." Landlords were brought before them and in highly emotional scenes were charged with all manner of private sin. The assembled crowd would decide if their land should be taken. Cadres indirectly manipulated these proceedings and usually could claim that in punishing the landlord they were only carrying out the passionate will of the people. In theory land redistribution was based on regulations that classified rural residents into five categories: landlord, rich peasant, middle peasant, poor peasant, and farm hand. Rich peasants worked part of their land and rented part; middle peasants owned all the land they worked; poor peasants rented some or all of the land they worked. People's tribunals were established to help in classifying people and to right previous wrongs.

By beginning with land redistribution and only later moving toward agricultural collectivization, the Chinese avoided the trauma that the Soviets experienced in eliminating the kulaks. The regime seemed to be promising that the tillers of the soil would indeed own their own land and that the Peking rulers were land reformers and not dedicated Communists. Between one and two million landlords, few of whom could have owned more than a dozen or so acres, were executed during the land reform movement, which lasted into 1952.

1950: THE KOREAN WAR
AND THE FOREIGN ENEMY

Only one year after the regime was established, Chinese troops were fighting in Korea in support of the North Korean government. Chinese intervention against American troops marching toward the Yalu River gave the Communists' prestige a great boost. For the first time in modern history Chinese armies were able to engage in a great-power conflict beyond Chinese soil. The war also marked the high point of Chinese dependence on the Soviet Union. Internally the regime was seeking to emulate Soviet practices in nearly every phase of life. At the universities Russian textbooks and Russian procedures replaced Western ones, and in government and industry Russian advisers were active. The Chinese army, resupplied with Russian equipment during the war, was transformed from an overgrown guerrilla force into a modern army.

During 1950 the Party instituted intensive programs of thought reform, particularly among the intellectuals. Professors at the major universities were required to write detailed autobiographical confessions in which they exposed their former anti-social and bourgeois thoughts and pledged to change their views. Indoctrination programs were established for all who were in any way identified with the Nationalist regime. Self-criticism and mutual criticism sessions were introduced into schools, neighborhoods, and places of employment.

Domestically the land reform program continued to dominate attention, but in addition to it were various bandit suppression campaigns against Kuomintang remnants and spy cases against individuals identified as inadequately loyal or found in suspicious circumstances. In the spring of 1950, before the Korean war, the regime promulgated the marriage reform law, which provided equality for women, granting them the right to divorce and to consent to marriage. Marriage reform was accompanied by extensive programs of involving women in all manner of public activities.

1951: THE MASS CAMPAIGNS

Although Peking maintained the posture that only Chinese "volunteers" were fighting in Korea, throughout China there was a sense of national mobilization for war. On every occasion Chinese leaders professed their complete dedication to the Socialist bloc, under the leadership of the Soviet Union. Within China the number of Soviet technicians increased, and the Party pressed its cadres into every community. Probably at no time in modern history was China as united as it was during the years of the Korean conflict.

However, the rapidity of the Communist advances within the country began to cause some internal problems. In March 1951 the leadership initiated the Party rectification campaign to tighten discipline over cadres, many of whom were being carried away with self-importance. By December 1951 the problem of maintaining standards of leadership had become so severe that it was necessary to expose all ranks of officialdom to vigorous self-examination. The result was the Three Antis Movement, directed against corruption, waste, and bureaucratism. The basis of the Three Antis Movement was the assumption that newly elevated officials were prone to act in selfish and anti-Socialist ways. The attack on Party and government officials was balanced with a continuing campaign against counter-revolutionaries who were presumably infiltrating the Party.

In the meantime the country as a whole was caught up with the Resist America, Aid Korea Campaign. Each day in every school children were exposed to political instruction and dramas that accentuated the themes of nationalism, world Communist solidarity, and anti-Americanism. In factories and offices time was devoted to daily political sessions. In the evenings in the neighborhood or the city block there would be further sessions at which people could manifest their feelings of solidarity with the government.

Near the end of 1951 the regime started the Five Antis Campaign, directed at individuals from whom money was extracted to help pay the costs of the Korean war. The attack was specifically directed against merchants and manufacturers who had been allowed to continue operations. Their capital was expropriated in the name of justice for violations of one of the five sins of bribery, tax evasion, theft of state assets, cheating in reporting labor or materials costs, and stealing state economic information. Company books were examined, and officials were publicly humiliated. Nearly half a million commercial and industrial establishments were attacked, and the businessmen found guilty lost their assets to the state. Nationalization and expropriation of business, particularly small businesses, was justified not in ideological terms but by moral and ethical criticism and by appeals to nationalism at a time when the country was at war.

1952: THE BEGINNING OF PLANNING

Truce talks for the Korean war began in July 1951 and continued throughout 1952. Fighting also continued, but at a reduced level. The excitement of the war and the shrill propaganda campaigns, such as that of accusing the United States of germ warfare, died down by 1952. The Five Antis Campaign continued, however, and internal control in the form of indoctrination techniques and self-criticism sessions became standardized. People were learning to use the vocabulary of Communist rhetoric.

The drive against intellectuals intensified, and reforms in education were designed to eliminate any remaining attraction of the liberal arts. Education was expected to be functionally relevant for the building of state power.

Above all, 1952 was notable for the new emphasis on economic policy. At the end of the year the first Five-Year Plan was announced. All the propaganda and agitational capabilities of the Party were directed to increasing production. The earlier emphasis on social and economic equality and justice was replaced by the theme that everyone should sacrifice for the economic growth of the state and not expect a higher individual standard of living. The Five-Year Plan was modeled on the Soviet pattern of giving primacy to heavy industry at the expense of agriculture and consumer interests.

Prior to 1952 the Communists were considered by their supporters to be dedicated primarily to eliminating the evils of traditional Chinese social life and providing equality. Their enemies believed them to be totalitarian rulers striving to remold Chinese society. After 1952 a new image began to emerge. Communist China was seen by all as offering a "model" for rapid economic development to the rest of the underdeveloped world.

1953: PEACE AND STEPS
TOWARD COLLECTIVIZATION

By July 1953 the Korean truce was agreed upon, and Chinese troops began to return to their country. With peace came a dramatic rise in self-confidence. The process of bringing order and integration to the country after so many years of internal division and war gave the Chinese economy the opportunity to benefit from the abilities and motivation of the Chinese people. Trade between cities and countryside was fully restored and factory production began to rise rapidly. The first part of the year was given over to the enthusiastic welcoming of the first Five-Year Plan by the regime's public opinion mobilizing capabilities. By June, the new spirit of getting down to work and away from excessive propaganda demonstrations manifested itself in the Five Too Manys Campaign — against too many meetings, too many organizations, too many concurrent posts for cadres, too many documents, and too many forms to be filled out.

In 1953 advances toward the full collectivization of agriculture were substantial. At the end of 1951 the regime initiated a three-part process for reversing the effects of land reform and removing the redistributed land from individual ownership. The first step involved the establishment of mutual aid teams consisting of from five to ten households that would pool their efforts on a seasonal basis. Membership was to be voluntary but considerable social pressure was applied to ensure near-universal conformity. In practice the mutual aid teams gave legal form only to patterns of cooperation that had traditionally existed in the rice-growing parts of China. The individual still owned his own land, tools, and animals.

The second step was the establishment of lower producers cooperatives, which consisted of from twenty to twenty-five households that pooled their land, tools, and animals but were paid in proportion to their contribution of capital as well as of labor. The principle of ownership continued to exist, but state decisions governed production. During 1953 much of Chinese agriculture was transformed from mutual aid teams to lower producers cooperatives.

Dissatisfaction among the peasants began to arise in 1953, especially over the decision that all surplus grain had to be sold to the state at fixed prices that did not favor the peasant. By the end of 1953 and during most of 1954 there were signs that the Party was becoming less enthusiastic about collectivization. Production declined and Party cadres in the rural areas lost much of their earlier enthusiasm. There might even have been a decision to delay further collectivization in 1955 had it not been for the personal intervention of Mao Tse-tung in July 1955. He ordered the cooperative movement to be pushed and the Party to quickly prepare for the next stage of collectivization. There was an economic basis for going ahead because 1955 was a good crop year, the best since the Party had come to power.

The third step in the Chinese plan was advanced or higher producers cooperatives in which all property was collectively owned and people were paid for their labor according to work points and work days. Advanced producers cooperatives were like Russian collective farms. They were large units, involving whole villages or even counties. During 1956 nearly three-quarters of the countryside was brought into advanced cooperatives. Production was poor and peasant discontents again surfaced.

In 1953, as the momentum for collectivization was beginning to build, centralization of authority increased considerably. Although the administrative regions were not abolished until the next year, there was tension between Peking and some of them, particularly Manchuria, culminating in the first significant purge of senior Party officials. Kao Kang and Jao Shu-shih were accused of being involved in an anti-Party alliance against Peking. It appeared subsequently that part of the difficulty was that Kao Kang was engaged in autonomous relations with Soviet officials and was allowing Russian influence to rise in Manchuria. He had been a senior Party leader and was one of the six vice-chairmen of the Central People's Government Council. He was head of the northeast bureau of the Central Committee while Jao Shu-shih headed the east China bureau. They were charged with plotting to oust Liu Shao-ch'i. Kao Kang reacted to the charges against him by allegedly committing suicide. Jao was imprisoned and never heard of again. The case was handled with so little disruption and publicity that it reinforced the impression that the Chinese leaders were united and free of the internal conflicts so characteristic of the Russian leaders.

1954: CONSOLIDATION

Domestically 1954 was a year of increasing centralization and consolidation of political control. The leaders seemed to have a clear sense of direction, and the people showed they had learned what was expected of them. During the year a new constitution was

adopted, and over 150 million people were supposed to have participated in discussion meetings about the draft that Mao Tse-tung submitted. The Constitution reaffirmed the dual structure of Party and
government. Foreign observers tended to agree with Peking's claims
that the political revolution was complete and the regime in firm
control.

In 1954 Peking became more actively engaged in foreign affairs. The Chinese were an important element at the Geneva Conference that arranged for the French withdrawal from Indochina and
the establishment of the governments of North and South Viet Nam.
After Stalin's death in 1953 relations between Peking and Moscow
for a time remained close. They began to change when the Chinese
started to assert the principle of equality, being no longer content
with the position of "younger brother."

Then in 1954 came the Chinese military advances in Tibet and
the first Quemoy-Matsu crisis. Tibet had been historically recognized as a part of modern China, but it had always had considerable
autonomy. The country was a Buddhist theocracy, and the Dalai
Lama at Lhasa ruled in a feudal manner. In 1954 the Communists
began to assert their political domination of Tibet and posted troops
in the capital. They left the monasteries and the Dalai Lama free to
perform their religious and some secular duties. The fact that the
Chinese did not insist on an immediate social and political revolution
encouraged the view that they were willing to accept a degree of
Tibetan autonomy. During the next few years tensions gradually
increased, and in 1959, in the wake of the Great Leap, the Chinese
finally demanded that the traditional Tibetan authorities be swept
aside. The result was the tragic Tibetan revolt, which culminated in
the flight of the Dalai Lama to India. The reception given to the
Tibetans by the Indians, including Prime Minister Nehru, marked
the beginning of Sino-Indian tensions, which culminated in the
border clashes of 1962.

The Quemoy-Matsu crisis raised the question of the extent to
which the United States would protect the Chinese Nationalists on
Taiwan and specifically whether the United States Seventh Fleet
would defend the offshore islands. The Quemoy islands, located in
the harbor of Amoy, and the Matsu islands, in the harbor of Foochow, were held by Chiang Kai-shek's troops. In August 1954 the
Peking leaders, including Chou En-lai, intensified their public state-

ments about liberating Taiwan. On September 3, Communist troops began heavily shelling Quemoy, and an attack appeared imminent.

There was great uncertainty about what the United States would do. In December the United States and Nationalist China signed a mutual defense treaty, which clarified the American commitment to defend Taiwan but left uncertain what might be done about the offshore islands. In the meantime the Nationalists so greatly reinforced Quemoy that the Communists would have to pay a high price for it.

The first crisis passed when it became clear that the Nationalists were well entrenched and could not easily be removed. It also passed without the United States revealing the extent to which the Seventh Fleet was prepared to assist in defending the offshore islands. Three years later the second Quemoy crisis also ended in Communist frustrations, but that setback was much more damaging to Peking's security because of the context in which it took place.

1955: THE SPIRIT OF BANDUNG AND THE SOFT LINE

From 1949 to 1955 the Peking regime maintained a high level of physical and psychological mobilization throughout Chinese society. The mood of the country was that of struggle and of vigilance in distinguishing friends from enemies. In early 1955 the tone of government pronouncements changed, becoming more relaxed, more reasonable. In foreign policy China adopted a far softer and more accommodating position. The leaders appeared to be buoyed up by their accomplishments. However, by the end of the year the domestic scene was once again tense as collectivization was accelerated, but the benign approach still dominated foreign relations.

By 1955 the new regime had achieved considerable success in transforming industry and commerce. The Five Antis Movement had cowed the remaining industrialists who had hoped to cooperate with the new government. It was clear that all industries would be transferred to state control and the old managers could aspire at best to be employed as executives in state industries.

In the summer the weather was kind to the Chinese, and they had the best crop since the Communists came to power. Party leaders were prepared to rejoice over their good fortune and not press ahead toward further collectivization that might only disrupt production. At this juncture, however, Mao personally and quite abruptly intervened and challenged the entire leadership by insisting that the only correct policy was to press ahead immediately to the formation of advanced producers cooperatives regardless of peasant opposition or the dangers of a decline in production.

This was probably the first conspicuous demonstration of Mao Tse-tung's propensity for allowing the government to proceed under its own initiative until he felt he must intervene, whereupon he would interject his own ideas even at the cost of upsetting the entire process of government. Mao was prepared to be shrill, to insist that no alternative course of action was acceptable, and to make the issue one of ultimate values and loyalties. The Politburo and the Central Committee had to give in to Mao's wishes and press ahead with total collectivization.

The collectivization drive in the countryside was matched in urban areas by intensification of controls over intellectuals, publicized by the campaign against Hu Feng. Hu Feng and his associates were writers who professedly supported the government but were inclined to question the excessive single-mindedness of the authorities. The attack on Hu Feng was intense and aggressive, and he and his associates were summarily purged.

These domestic developments did not in any way compromise Chinese efforts at projecting a benign face to the outside world. In the early years of the regime the Chinese Communists insisted that the cold war was the absolute reality of international politics, that there could only be two opposing camps, and that the posture of neutralization adopted by India and other developing countries was merely continuation of support for the imperialists. After Stalin's death, as the Communist bloc countries evolved toward more complex and flexible relationships, the Chinese saw that they could enhance their own position of leadership by identifying with the neutralists and turning neutralism into a broad united front in opposition to the United States and the principle of imperialism.

Accepting the sponsorship offered by Nehru of India, the Chinese, largely in the person of the skillful diplomat Chou En-lai, took the initiative in courting the leaders of the newly emerging states. Chou En-lai vigorously stole the show at the Bandung Conference

of Afro-Asian states in 1955. He attracted attention at the conference partly because China had been feared as a dangerous and evil
force only a few years before and there was novelty in the innocent
presence of Chinese officials at an international gathering. In
addition, however, Chou acted with considerable grace and ease,
suggesting to all that Peking was about to become a reasonable and
constructive member of the international community, anxious only
to eliminate the lingering evils of imperialism.

China, emerging as a leader of the underdeveloped world,
seemed to have a new answer to the problem of speeding change
and progress. China also found that there were advantages in appearing to act somewhat independently of the Soviet Union. The
Bandung Conference did not result in any substantive changes in
international power relationships, but it did highlight the aspirations
of the newly emerging states and provided China with an arena for
leadership. Although India had been one of the principal forces behind the planned meeting of Afro-Asian states, Bandung resulted in
the beginning of the decline of India's influence among the emerging
nations and the rise of China as a competitor.

1956: CONFIDENCE AND DOUBTS
AND ONE HUNDRED FLOWERS

The public relations successes of China at Bandung encouraged Mao to attempt a bolder role in foreign affairs. The Chinese initiated in 1956 a major cultural campaign, inviting delegations
from all the developing countries to visit Peking and to view the new
factories and farms that were the showpieces of the new government. The Chinese also became more active in Communist bloc
affairs. Mao Tse-tung increasingly spoke out as the senior Communist ruler in the world and offered advice, particularly to the Soviet
Union to be tolerant of the liberalizing tendencies in Poland.

In February 1956, at the Twentieth Congress of the Communist
Party of the Soviet Union, Khrushchev made his secret speech
attacking Stalin's memory. This was a shattering event for the Chinese, who still saw much merit in maintaining the memory of a great
Stalin. The effects of the repudiation of Stalin were soon felt
throughout the Communist world. Mao, showing his first sign of

serious dissatisfaction with Khrushchev, began to champion liberalization within the bloc while still upholding the virtues of Stalin at
home. A serious crisis developed in Poland, and in January 1957
Chou En-lai interrupted his goodwill tour of Asian capitals, where
he was seeking to build on the spirit of benign friendship he created
at Bandung, and went to Moscow and Warsaw to mediate between
Wladyslaw Gomulka, who was pushing for increased autonomy for
Poland, and the Russian leaders, who sensed anti-Soviet aspirations
in Polish developments. Chou encouraged the Poles to seek to follow
their own road to socialism.

This posture of relative liberalism toward Polish developments
had been matched domestically in China by Mao's appeal in May for
the intellectuals to express their criticisms of his government.
Alluding to the late Chou dynasty period when "one hundred
schools" of philosophy, including the Confucianist, Taoist, and
Legalist, had clashed with each other in seeking to give Chinese
society direction, Mao proclaimed: "Let one hundred schools of
thought contend; let one hundred flowers bloom." Since during the
previous five years the intellectuals had been forced to undergo self-
criticism sessions and to confess their anti-proletariat sentiments,
they were extremely cautious in responding to Mao's invitation, suspecting that he was not sincere in his protestation of liberalization.

By the end of the year, however, more and more intellectuals
began to work up their courage to express critical views, most of
which were that the regime was not achieving its professed goals. It
soon became apparent that there was widespread and deeply felt
resentment against the regime. Mao must have been shocked at the
intensity of the criticism. Instead of mentioning failings of the system that could be quickly put aright, the intellectuals began to raise
fundamental questions about Communism.

In June 1957 Mao issued his essay *On the Correct Handling of
Contradictions Among the People,* in which he stated that some
forms of conflict were healthy and could be expected even in a completely socialist and classless society, while others reflected class differences and had to be sharply repressed. He drew a line on criticism
and initiated the Anti-Rightist Campaign, which brought all critical
intellectuals under severe attack for being counter-revolutionaries.
The Hundred Flowers period ended and repression against all forms
of criticism was again the order of the day in China. Many Chinese

and foreign observers, including Khrushchev, suspected that Mao might have called for open criticism to induce dissidents to reveal themselves so that he could identify and exterminate them. Another view is that Mao was genuinely surprised by the intensity of dissent.

Moreover, during the fall of 1956 Mao was driven from his liberalizing approach by the shock of the Hungarian uprising, which became so extreme that Soviet troops were required to enter Budapest to crush the freedom fighters. In contrast to his earlier tolerance toward Polish liberalization, Mao strongly supported the Soviet move. He did, however, feel that the "counter-revolutionary" uprising had been encouraged by Khrushchev's faulty and inadequate leadership — faulty because he had turned on Stalin's memory and inadequate because his treatment of liberalization had only confused people about what constituted correct Communist behavior.

Thus 1956 saw a dramatic reversal of China's relatively liberal policies. Mao's conclusion was that greater effort would have to be devoted to the ideological training of the Chinese people. Since 1956 he has constantly worried over whether the revolutionary spirit of the Chinese, particularly the intellectuals and the young, is strong enough for China to achieve Communism.

1957: ADVANCING TO GREATER CONFLICTS

By mid-1957 the Anti-Rightist Campaign, initiated to overcome the weaknesses revealed by the Hundred Flowers disaster, had been absorbed into the larger Rectification Campaign, in which all organizations had to devote time daily to upgrading their ideological study and to weeding out all improper thoughts. The movement toward liberalization was thus absolutely reversed, and the spirit of the Hundred Flowers was dead. In particular the intellectuals became the targets of incessant attack through the Struggle Between Two Roads Movement. Mao acknowledged that complaints against the bureaucracy were legitimate and that the government and the Party were in danger of becoming aloof from the people. However, criticisms suggesting any rejection of the ideals of his revolution had to be forcibly opposed.

Mao was beginning to seek an alternative to the rigid bureaucratic style that had been used by Stalin and apparently was not effectively surviving his death, and an alternative to the liberalization that had caused such trouble in Hungary. His answer was to decentralize administrative controls, increase the activist role of cadres, and strive to mobilize large numbers of people in collective enterprises that would call for little capital but much muscle. He was in search of methods that would replace scarce machinery and money with determined willpower and human energy and ensure political continuity and control without relying on bureaucracy. Mao was unwilling to admit that the ultimate goal of his revolutionary efforts was merely to establish another bureaucracy while allowing economists and engineers to determine the most efficient policies for the country.

During 1957 various experiments were tried in utilizing mass labor. A major campaign, March to the Mountainous Areas, was carried out to expand water conservation. It involved reclaiming wastelands and increasing the amount of arable land. These efforts directed attention to the problems of agriculture and the fact that it was the most likely source of exports to pay for imported materials needed to expand industry.

In foreign affairs, 1957 marked a significant shift away from the themes of peaceful coexistence associated with the Bandung spirit toward a more militant and crusading line. When the Soviet Union startled the world by putting in orbit Sputnik, the first unmanned spacecraft, Mao reacted with elation and proclaimed, "East Wind now prevails over West Wind." He also made his second visit to Moscow, but by the end of the year it was apparent that Peking and Moscow saw the world in quite different ways.

According to Mao's reasoning, a major shift in world power had taken place and it was essential for Khrushchev to solidify and authenticate the gains for the socialist countries. Mao believed that there was a missile gap; he thought the Soviet Union had moved past the United States in strategic arms and that only the personal weakness and folly of Khrushchev prevented the Russians from realizing the political advantages of their technological successes. He was convinced that Stalin would have known what to do with superior power. Above all, Mao was maddened by Khrushchev's decision to seek a relaxation of tension and a détente with Washington, which reached its high point when Khrushchev visited the

United States and met with President Eisenhower at Camp David, the presidential retreat in the Maryland hills.

The Russians, on the other hand, were more realistic. They understood, in spite of journalistic speculation, that there was no missile gap, that Sputnik did not fundamentally alter the realities of power, and that the best they could accomplish was to bluff equality, not assert superiority. It was awkward for Moscow to inform Mao of these facts of international life, for in Moscow's relations with Peking it was helpful for Peking to believe that Moscow was indeed the world's preeminent superpower. The stage was being set for the profound clash that was to destroy the close bonds of the Sino-Soviet alliance, which had come into existence with the establishment of the People's Republic of China.

1958: THE FRANTIC, DRAMATIC YEAR

Events in 1958 were in many respects the most significant and dramatically far ranging in the history of Chinese communism. China attempted the most extreme domestic experiments and failed. In foreign affairs China put itself in the position of having to become the enemy of nearly all its neighbors. Both agriculture and industry were thrown into confusion and turmoil as reason gave way to revolutionary exhortation. In the midst of domestic upheaval, China again confronted the United States on the issue of the offshore islands and became embroiled in Tibet, setting the stage for conflict with India. In 1958 the split with the Soviet Union widened when Mao learned that he could not rely on Soviet nuclear protection.

The most dramatic domestic events of 1958 were the Great Leap Forward and the establishment of people's communes. Mao, in announcing the formation of the communes, suggested that the Chinese were moving ahead of Russia in becoming a truly Communist society and, according to the slogan that went with the Great Leap, would "catch up with Great Britain in fifteen years."

The Great Leap was a supreme attempt to ignore technological and physical constraints and build progress primarily on human willpower. Workers were called upon to work shift after shift with little rest; machines were driven without stopping for maintenance and repairs; and complex but efficient processes were pushed aside in favor of less efficient, more primitive ways that were less capital intensive. The Party line spoke of a policy of "walking on two feet" — that is, using both modern and traditional methods to exploit every means for progress. In part the problem was that there was so much confusion that no methods were effectively utilized. The extreme folly of the Great Leap was the effort to decentralize heavy industry by establishing in rural settings "backyard furnaces" to produce steel.

Within a year it became obvious that the attempt was not working and that Chinese economic development was being severely set back. The damage of the Great Leap extended from the destruction of expensive machines because of lack of proper maintenance to the wasting of natural resources that could never be replenished. Miners, for example, frantically dug out rich veins of ore without shoring up tunnels and did not extract the less rich ores. Consequently mines had to be abandoned before they were fully worked out, or later the costly process of doing the job correctly had to be accomplished although only ores of marginal quality remained.

The introduction of rural communes was most shocking to other Communist countries. Still-backward China was proclaiming that it was introducing a "free-supply system" in which people would receive what they needed and give only according to ability. In theory the communes were to be created by combining several advanced producers cooperatives to form a production unit about the size of a county. Labor was to be mobilized on a large scale, and life was to be regimented according to semi-military practices. In the communes people were to be given free food, barbering, and some clothing. Very soon, however, the Chinese peasant shrewdly figured out how he could get the most with the least effort. The most economically disastrous feature of the communes was the decision that all land and animals would belong to the communes and that people could only earn work points, which would be collectively allocated according to the group's judgment of the appropriate rewards for different activities. It was soon apparent that peasants were not inclined to work hard on enterprises for which they got no personal reward.

To prevent disaster the regime finally had to retreat, even though failure was not publicly acknowledged. The leadership introduced the concept of private plots, which allowed a peasant to manage for himself from five to ten percent of the collective land on his commune. On it he could grow vegetables and raise hogs and chickens. By 1959 private plots had become a vital element in Chinese agriculture. On them are now produced over ninety percent of the country's meat and eighty-five percent of its vegetables. The rest of the land is still collectively worked to produce the country's grain. In 1960 there was severe famine because not enough grain was being produced, and since then the largest import each year has been grain.

As a result of the attempt to establish an extreme commune system during the Great Leap, the Chinese Communist leaders learned that there were limits to how far peasants would go in working without personal incentives. Even during the height of the Cultural Revolution, when the country again experienced a swing to romantic revolutionary views, no major attempt was made to get rid of private plots.

By the end of 1958 there was also a retreat on the communes themselves. Instead of using them as the basic decision-making units on production and as the organizations that decided who got how much in return for what efforts, accounting was passed down to the production brigade and decision making on work went to the production team. In practice the brigade was really the old lower producers cooperative and the team was the group that had made up the mutual aid team. In short, in form the communes continued to exist but in practice the older groups, with different names, again became critical, with the smallest group deciding who would do what tasks at what time and the larger unit marketing the produce and dividing up the returns.

While the country dealt with the problems caused by the Great Leap and the communes, Mao became more publicly and acrimoniously involved in recriminations with Moscow. Khrushchev visited Peking and was not silent about his horror at what he saw. He rudely suggested that Mao had taken leave of his senses, for it was madness to suggest that a country so poor that not everyone had "even one pair of pants" could be entering the golden age of communism.

By September the mood of crisis was heightened by the possibility of war. The regime had been goaded into trying to do something about the offshore islands in the harbor of Quemoy. The impetus behind the second Quemoy crisis was Peking's determination to force the Soviet Union into a hard-line position against the United States. The Chinese wanted Soviet backing during the crisis, and in particular they wanted the Russians to promise publicly that they would give China the protection of Soviet nuclear weapons. Moscow dragged its feet and indicated that if the Chinese got into war out of recklessness they should not count on Soviet assistance. The Soviets said that if they were to give the Chinese protection then there would have to be greater coordination between the two countries and that China should provide Russia with bases in Chinese territories. China was unwilling to strike such a bargain.

Many students of Sino-Soviet relations are inclined to identify the tensions that arose over the second Quemoy crisis as a turning point in the eventual breakup of the alliance. Mao had to face the fact that he disagreed with Khrushchev on more than world communism matters and that he could not trust the Soviet Union to help him in conflicts with the imperialists.

Foreign and domestic crises thus combined to compel Peking to press for greater war preparation by emphasizing the militia and the guerrilla potential of the People's Liberation Army. The Everyone a Soldier Movement suggested that the leaders believed that a new war would utilize the mobile guerrilla warfare practiced during the Yenan days and in the war with Japan. There was clearly resistance within the high command of the army for such planning, and the effort was made to counter this resistance by the movement to "go down to the companies and soldier," under which army officers served periodically in the ranks as enlisted men. At this time Mao Tse-tung made his speech calling the United States a paper tiger, declaring that China was unafraid of nuclear warfare, for the country was prepared to live on without its urban centers.

Little attention was given to the announcement in 1958 that Mao was being replaced as chairman of the government by Liu Shao-ch'i. It was presumed that Mao was giving up these responsibilities in order to devote himself more completely to polemics with the Russians and ideological writing. Later, during the Cultural Revolution, it was revealed that Mao had not welcomed the change and that he was, in fact, ignored thereafter in matters of administrative policies. Indeed, at the time, the problems of 1958 severely disrupted the harmony of elite relations in the Chinese Communist

Party. The factions that were to become the bases for the power struggles of the Cultural Revolution were being formed, and the ideological divisions between the pragmatic leaders, who opposed much of the Great Leap, and the Maoists, who were committed to the spirit of revolution, also began to take shape during that critical year. Communist China was never to be quite as unified or as self-confident as it had been before the year of the Great Leap Forward.

1959–1961: SLOW RECOVERY

By early 1959 the Chinese were engaged in a basic policy retreat on all fronts, except military preparations. There was, however, profound disagreement on precisely what should be done in the military area, and this led in the fall of 1959 to the P'eng Te-huai case. As chief of staff of the army, P'eng had persisted in arguing that the country should maintain its ties with the Soviet Union, not only in order to gain nuclear protection but also because Russia was its only source of modern conventional arms. He believed that China had to advance technologically with the rest of the world and could place no real security in a guerrilla army. Mao won the argument, and P'eng was removed from office for anti-Party activities and was never heard from again.

China's relations with its neighbors were strained by the harsh manner in which the Chinese put down the Tibetan revolt and drove the Dalai Lama into India. During the year there were border incidents with India, Nepal, Sikkim, and Burma.

Mainly, however, China was forced to turn inward in 1959 and continued to do so over the next two years. The country was in the grip of a major depression as a result of the Great Leap. Unemployment was widespread, production was down, and, most serious of all, a series of agricultural disasters resulted in near-famine conditions and widespread malnutrition. The death rate rose as health conditions deteriorated. At the ninth plenum, in January 1961, the decision was made to shift the emphasis of government from industry to agriculture and to legitimize the concept of private plots and a free market for what was raised on them.

The economic crises and China's isolation within the Communist world created a crisis of morale among Party cadres. The regime sent large numbers of cadres to the countryside in order to improve their ideological awareness. However, in the countryside they were not well received because the peasants resented what the Party had done. Control broke down, thousands in Kwangtung fled into Hong Kong, and throughout the country people began to move about to seek their fortunes and the support of their families elsewhere. Lacking papers and work permits, they were called black people because they were in the shadow area of illegality.

The Sino-Soviet split began to be apparent during 1960. Initially the conflict was carried out through veiled criticisms. The Soviets criticized, and the Chinese praised, the Albanian Communist Party. At first the Chinese took a liberal position on the unity of the Communist world, encouraging, for example, the Polish experiments of 1956. However, in time the Chinese moved steadily toward a harder line, against any relaxing of cold war tensions. The Moscow conference of all Communist parties in 1957 resulted in a declaration, which China reluctantly signed, that called for the end of inter-Party attacks. The Soviets were determined to stop Chinese efforts to organize factions favoring their position in Communist parties throughout the world. However, after the Tibetan crisis and the first Sino-Indian border difficulties, when Russia showed sympathy for Indian sensitivities, and after the Soviet Union rejected the Chinese demand for reassurance on providing nuclear protection during the 1958 Quemoy crisis, the polemics between the two parties became intense.

Finally in 1960 the Soviet Union withdrew its technicians and terminated its foreign aid to China. The abrupt withdrawal of Soviet economic help, on top of the disasters of the Great Leap, severely damaged the Chinese economy. Since that time the Peking government has never displayed much confidence about China's potential for rapid economic growth. Instead of suggesting that China might be a model of rapid industrial development for other African and Asian countries, Peking's propaganda began to emphasize themes of equality and revolutionary purity in describing Chinese developments.

It is possible to plot a steady year by year rise in the temperature of the Sino-Soviet conflict. In 1960 on Lenin's birthday the Chinese published in the *People's Daily* an editorial called "Long Live Lenin," which implied that Khrushchev had abandoned the revolutionary ideals of the founder of bolshevism. In 1961 at the Second Moscow Conference the Chinese appeared to be acting more temperately and finally agreed to sign the declaration against inter-Party criticism; but a few months later Chou En-lai felt compelled to walk out of the Russian Party Congress when Khrushchev attacked Albania. In 1962 the Chinese openly criticized the Russians for backing down in the Cuban missile crisis and for being "adventurous" in the first place. From 1963 on, the Chinese ceaselessly charged the Russians with collusion with the United States, especially over discussions about nuclear controls and the test-ban treaty.

In 1961 economic difficulties increased, and during a brief period the Chinese authorities turned their backs and allowed a flood of refugees to leave the country and cross over into Hong Kong and Macao. Domestic difficulties were matched by increasingly bitter exchanges of polemics with the Russians. China mounted an effective campaign among the Communist parties of the world in seeking support for its orthodox Marxist-Leninist position. In general the Chinese were successful in winning over Asian parties and dissident factions in some of the European parties. Peking also sought the support of Castro and the Cuban revolutionaries, but after a brief period of apparent solidarity the Cubans pulled back because of their economic dependence on Russian aid.

China's interest in Africa also dates from 1961, when in competition with the Russians Chinese leaders decided to expand their propaganda and trade fair efforts and began to provide modest amounts of economic aid and technical assistance. Peking's efforts stimulated a rise in American interest in Africa as well as a substantial commitment by the Nationalist Chinese to provide assistance in the hope of preventing the African states in the United Nations from shifting their votes from supporting Taipei's representation to that of Peking.

1962–1963: RECOVERY AND REEDUCATION

By 1962 the Chinese were recovering from the extreme disruptions of the Great Leap and were gradually returning to more orthodox economic practices. The disillusionment and exhaustion caused by the frantic years and the depression had left the Party seriously demoralized. Even within the army there was widespread discontent and loss of faith. It became apparent that while the inertia of normal and routine daily processes was beginning to bring about improvements in living conditions, the maintenance of revolutionary commitment among the people would call for new efforts at political and ideological indoctrination.

At the Tenth Plenum of the Eighth Central Committee of the Chinese Communist Party, an appeal was made to revive the spirit of revolution. Mao Tse-tung called for the initiation of the Socialist Education Campaign, which led directly into the Cultural Revolution. The theme of the campaign was the need to attack all manifestations of revisionism and to learn from the People's Liberation Army. Propaganda cadres began to proclaim the power that came from "Learning from the Thoughts of Mao Tse-tung," which in the next few years would become an endlessly repeated slogan.

The Socialist Education Campaign was directed particularly toward rural cadres, who after the setback of the communes were especially disillusioned. The Four Clean-Ups Movement was designed to revive the revolutionary discipline of the lax and generally apathetic rural Party apparatus. In schools the slogan "From the communes, back to the communes" suggested that rural youth should obtain an education and then return to their rural communities in order to help them progress, instead of remaining in the cities. This was all part of what the Party called the need to eliminate the "three great differences," between town and country, between agriculture and industry, and between mental and manual labor. By August 1963, the effort to increase the flow of talent into the countryside in order to re-ignite the peasants' revolutionary ardor took the form of the Five into the Fields and the Five Fewers campaigns, which were also directed against excessive reliance on the bureaucracy. A major propaganda theme of the time was the need for all people to follow the example of the Tachai farmers in Shansi who, confronted with Mao's appeal for hard work, applied a form of guerrilla warfare to their collective farm. The workers supposedly worked and farmed simultaneously; managers and workers cooperated in making decisions; and everyone sought to put into practice the Thoughts of Mao Tse-tung. Although these features of the Socialist Education Campaign suggested a return to some features of the Great Leap, the management of government was in the hands of pragmatic officials who appreciated the values of modern technology.

We now know that tensions building up within the leadership were soon to explode in the Cultural Revolution. Indeed, by 1964 domestic trends and foreign pressures from both the Sino-Soviet controversy and the prospect of an American military buildup in South Viet Nam had set the stage for the massive convolutions of the Cultural Revolution, a dramatic series of events that we must put off discussing in order first to identify the ideological trends and personal points of view that contributed to causing those amazing events.

EMERGING TRENDS AND PROBLEMS

The first decade of Communist rule was a remarkable period during which the leaders accomplished a great deal and gave the impression that they would be able to achieve far more in the years ahead. Never before in Chinese history had the country been managed so completely, and certainly never in modern times was it as unified. There were mistakes, but the leaders always gave the impression that they were ready to learn and to improve. China, allied to the Soviet Union and after an impressive performance in the Korean war, appeared to be a newly emerging regional, if not world, power. Its neighbors worried about it, and instead of being the power vacuum of Asia, China was seen as a potentially dynamic and possibly aggressive political force.

Yet by 1957 problems were beginning to surface. The country was heavily dependent on Soviet aid in the industrial sectors. Its agriculture, while improving, had not shown that it could provide the surpluses necessary for it to serve as the engine to modernize the Chinese society and economy. China's population was growing at such a rate that all progress was threatened.

The central issue that slowly began to emerge by 1958 was whether China would be able to modernize effectively if it followed pragmatic and technically sound policies. The explosion of the Great Leap in 1958 and that of the Cultural Revolution in 1966 constituted Mao's answer. He had become convinced that China's weaknesses could only be overcome by changing the Chinese character and by tapping the strongest forces of human willpower. Ideological views about how to modernize China had become the dominant issue of Chinese politics, just as ideological and intellectual perspectives had been substantively more important than economic and social changes in bringing down the imperial system. Similarly in the late 1950's the Chinese Communists dramatically changed from coping with objective problems to emphasis on profound ideological disagreements.

In order to understand what happened we need to learn more about the ideological and psychological predispositions of the Communist leaders and the policy problem that came to divide them.

CHAPTER TWELVE

Mao Tse-tung:
Ideology and Personality

The erratic changes in policies and practices that have characterized Communist rule reflect the intractable problems in modernizing China, uncertainties about how modernization should be accomplished, and, finally, disagreements among individuals. In the early 1950's China watchers assumed that the Chinese Communists had a coherent ideology and a monolithic leadership. Over the years, however, it has become apparent that different ideological currents coexisted and that personality differences have been as important as ideology in producing policy changes.

In theory, ideology is supposed to give all Chinese Communists the same world view and the same enthusiasm for achieving a commonly understood objective. Theory and practice are supposed to be so coherent that the appropriate action is always apparent. If the ideological level of the Party is raised, all Party members should most eagerly carry out the actions implied by the ideology.

Ideological variations account for many of the policy changes of the Peking regime. The general drift of change has been toward an increasingly vulgarized version of Marxism, a fanatical belief in the power of the human spirit, and sloganistic puritanism. This trend represents above all the changing attitudes of Mao Tse-tung as he has aged and become frustrated with the pace of developments in China.

In the first years after the Chinese Communist Party was formed, the problem of ideology was little more than learning the subtle nuances of Comintern debate and developing skill in relating the grand theoretical formulations and categories of Marxism-Leninism to Chinese circumstances. Among the intellectuals who first formed the Party there was a peculiar resistance to the idea, which Lenin consistently espoused, that in the "colonies and semi-colonies" (China was an archetype of the latter) the historic class conflicts had been distorted by imperialism and that therefore the fundamental "contradiction" was less the clash between proletariat and bourgeoisie than a uniting of classes in support of nationalism against imperialism. At first the Chinese comrades felt that they were being treated in a patronizing and less than revolutionary way when they were told, for example, that ideology dictated that they should cooperate with the Kuomintang.

Throughout the 1920's the Communist leaders were constantly searching for proletariat-based power in order to become a truly revolutionary force in the traditional Marxist sense. But China had little in the way of an industrial working class. During the time that Li Li-san led the Party a considerable effort was made to strengthen and radicalize the trade union movement, but even then power was most readily available in the countryside where the armies were. Lenin's and then Stalin's insistence on class alliance had produced the combined armies under Chiang Kai-shek and the Wuhan government and the Red Army.

In the meantime Mao Tse-tung in his classic "Report on an Investigation of the Peasant Movement in Hunan" had said that there were considerable tensions in Chinese villages and that they could be exploited for revolutionary purposes. This discovery, plus the fact that armies in China, including the Communist army, depended almost entirely on peasants, raised the Communists' awareness of the importance of the peasantry. It also provoked considerable debate over whether Mao and the Chinese Communists had left the confines of orthodox communism and had become peasant reformers. Lenin had unmistakably recognized the need to build upon the revolutionary potential of peasants while maintaining the "vanguard role of the party."[1]

[1]Whether Mao was a heretic in identifying the revolutionary potential of the peasantry or an orthodox follower of Lenin has been vigorously debated by Karl A. Wittfogel, in "The Legend of 'Maoism,'" *China Quarterly* (1960), no. 1, pp. 72–86, and Benjamin Schwartz, in "The Legend of the 'Legend of Maoism,'" *ibid.* (1960), no. 2, pp. 35–42. Schwartz is correct in saying that Mao was more in tune with peasants than any previous Marxist theoretician had been, but according to strict Communist "logic," Wittfogel correctly stated that peasants would be essential to the revolution in China and hence Mao merely conformed to Communist notions.

Mao fully accepted the Leninist formulation that the "Party is the vanguard of the proletariat," and gradually he carried this to the point of defining "proletarian views" as being "correct Party views." Mao thus contributed to the long-standing tendency of Marxism-Leninism to move away from a strict sociological view of classes; he regarded ideological or intellectual positions as bases of the historical dialectic. In short, just as Marx had turned Hegel upside-down and made materialism more important than idealism, so Mao turned Marx upside-down and reasserted the supremacy of ideas. This feat of Mao was consistent with the historical propensity of the Chinese to attach prime importance to intellectual and ethical considerations.

During the Yenan period Mao made his most substantial contributions to ideology. At that time he was concerned above all with theorizing about warfare and Party development. More than any other leading Communist, Mao sought to identify a category of war that could be called revolutionary and to explain the laws of such warfare. He wrote about guerrilla warfare and the importance of obtaining popular support. He stressed the need for a close relationship between political and military considerations.

In the 1930's, while his armies were engaging in guerrilla warfare behind Japanese lines, Mao was busy writing about Party building and the need to get rid of incorrect attitudes. In books such as *Dialectical Materialism*, *On Contradiction*, and *On Practice* Mao made his most sophisticated efforts to continue the tradition of ideological and philosophical writings established by Lenin and Stalin.[2] Generally his efforts were in the direction of supporting Communist orthodoxy, and indeed from 1938 to 1953 Mao's intellectual contributions were generally consistent with standard Russian Communist positions. He was concerned by the danger that the Chinese Communist Party would be influenced by liberal democratic tendencies that might dilute its professional revolutionary standards. Stuart Schram has uncovered the startling fact that in some of Mao's more theoretical writings of this period he rather

[2]Because of the gross difference in the sophistication of these three works by Mao, there has been some controversy over the order in which they were written and even a suggestion that *Dialectical Materialism* must be forgery because it so clumsily explains elementary features of Marxism. See John Rue, "Is Mao Tse-tung's *Dialectical Materialism* a Forgery?" *Journal of Asian Studies*, 26: 3 (1967), pp. 464–68.

freely plagiarized from the works of minor Russian theorists — no wonder the Russians were later to discount Mao as a Marxist.[3]

Mao specified that the task of ideology was to ensure that Party cadres maintained their revolutionary ideals even as the Party worked with popular nationalistic themes. He recognized that the Party would have to appeal to the masses, which included the bourgeoisie, the intellectuals, and petty bourgeoisie, and the peasantry, who wanted a more just existence though not necessarily a socialist society. He feared that the Party would lose its revolutionary identity as it sought to be all things to all groups.

Thus during the Yenan period Mao developed a keen awareness that a gap existed between appearances and inner convictions, and he worried that cadres' inner convictions would be eroded by pressures toward respectability inherent in propaganda. In a fundamental sense Mao's concern with Party rectification in the 1940's and his fear of revisionism, which became destructively obsessive in the late 1960's with the Cultural Revolution, reflected his basic anxiety about the vulnerability of the revolutionary spirit.

Mao was not the only person who linked ideology with Party building in the 1940's. Liu Shao-ch'i, second in command at the time, was also active in pushing for a more disciplined and ideologically knowledgeable Party. Liu's *How to Be a Good Communist* was a technical manual that made ideology the moral basis of a highly disciplined Party organization.

In recent years, as a consequence of the Cultural Revolution, it has frequently been suggested that as early as the 1940's Mao and Liu had different points of view. Liu Shao-ch'i was predisposed to champion order and Party discipline; Mao consistently favored conflict and struggle. A careful review of the ideological contributions of the two men during the early period, however, does not suggest such consistency. In *How to Be a Good Communist* are sections extolling the virtues of contradiction and the need for ceaseless struggle, and it is not hard to find passages written by Mao Tse-tung in the 1940's and 1950's in which he praises order, patience, and discipline and in which he condemns sins of left deviation and petty bourgeois revolutionary romanticism.

[3]See Stuart R. Schram, "Mao Tse-tung and the Theory of the Permanent Revolution," *China Quarterly* (April 1971), no. 46, p. 223.

After the Communist regime was established, the chief function of ideology went beyond Party building to guiding the reconstruction of Chinese society. During the first years, until the death of Stalin, when the emphasis of the Party was on emulating the Soviet Union, the Chinese developed a new characteristic in their ideological approach to revolution. They displayed an unquestioning faith in the possibilities of converting all people to communism. Regardless of class background, everyone was treated as a potential convert to their viewpoint. The result was a vigorous application of persuasion and the development of the techniques of self-criticism and public confession. Ideology became a highly personal matter. Individuals had to reveal their erroneous views, denounce their past failings, and dedicate themselves to revolutionary ideals.

During this period ideological considerations also focused on the question of loyalty to the regime and commitment to Chinese nationalism. The world was seen as divided between progressive (friendly) people and reactionary-imperialist (enemy) forces. All the subtleties and complexities of Marxism were made to stand for little more than a litmus test for distinguishing good and bad elements in international politics.

China's preoccupation with identifying and distinguishing good and bad in the individual, in domestic society, and in international politics resulted in the late 1950's in Mao's acknowledgement that even in socialist countries there could be contradictions between true revolutionary feelings and inclinations toward bureaucratization, elitism, revisionism, and the restoration of capitalism. During the period of the Hundred Flowers and while Mao was defending the liberalizing tendencies in Poland under Gomulka, China's ideological assumption was that reason could win all intelligent people to the cause of revolution. During the years from Bandung until after the Hungarian revolution, from 1955 to 1957, the tone of China's ideology was reasonable and moderate.

A more constant theme in Chinese communism was the importance of the human spirit in shaping history. Chinese communism has uniquely supported the concept of voluntarism — that is, the idea that revolutionary success is possible if there is unity in commitment and desire. According to traditional Marxism, objective forces of history will inevitably produce the triumph of socialism and then communism. Proletarian leaders were, of course, expected to push history along its inevitable course, but history itself was governed by objective factors and not subjective sentiments. Mao stressed the importance of human willpower in pushing history. For him the dialectic of history was less the clash of class interests than the contradiction between the spirit of revolutionary progress and tendencies toward selfishness, capitalism, and status.

By the mid-1960's, when the clash between Peking and Moscow was being played out in a series of communications and responses, Mao made explicit his view that in socialist countries there was a permanent inclination toward revisionism and the revival of capitalism. Instead of the traditional Marxist view that progress toward communism was inevitable and that attitudes basic to earlier periods could be "consigned to the dustbin of history," Mao, in a Confucian manner, upheld a cyclical view of history in which "feudal" and "capitalistic" attitudes can always reassert themselves regardless of how far a society may have objectively "progressed toward communism." Mao transformed Communist ideology into a morality play between forces of good and evil in which there is a constant danger that evil will seduce even the most virtuous from the straight and narrow path of revolutionary dedication.

Mao has given to socialist morality a sense of omnipresent, if not original, sin. He has suggested that man has a permanent potential for corruption because of selfishness. As long as individuals are ambitious they may be captivated by pride. Pride can lead to egotism, which is only one step from selfishness, which (as the source of corruption) is the principal cause of individual, family, and national decline. Despite his talk about the reconstruction of a new and more virtuous society, Mao has been profoundly pessimistic about the course of history, suggesting that decline, like death, is certain — unless it can be resisted by superhuman efforts — because of the human potential for corruption stemming from man's striving for attainment.

Mao's sense of the conflicting relationships of effort, the search for attainment, and vulnerability to selfish corruption is in a sense analogous to the traditional dilemma of the Puritans. They preached that man should be frugal, hard working, and never slothful and suggested that virtue would produce material success. They had no answer for what would follow if their preachings worked. Would success not bring a decline in the striving for virtue? Mao's problem was not the consequences of material success but rather the consequences of revolutionary and political success. He recognized that the hard-working revolutionary of yesterday, having achieved power, was likely to become self-assertive and corrupt because success results from self-consciousness, which readily becomes egocentrism, which increases one's vulnerability to corruption.

By the late 1960's these contradictory tendencies dominated Chinese ideology. The Chinese belief in the importance of the ego reached its highest point in the extraordinary lengths to which the cult of the personality of Mao was carried. More than any Chinese emperor, Mao was revered, eulogized, and glorified. The central theme of Chinese ideological indoctrination became the praise of Mao and the acceptance of the presumably superhuman power of his words. Mao personally encouraged the most extravagant worship of his person and helped to give a semi-religious character to his political appeal.

At the same time, however, Mao has endlessly emphasized the need for selflessness, for the depreciation of ego, and for sacrificing the personal for the collective. The Thoughts of Mao Tse-tung are simple, moralistic principles stressing the need for self-sacrifice and for heroic self-destruction in favor of collective interests.

According to traditional Marxist precepts, Mao's Thoughts are more a reflection of petty bourgeois sentimentalities than proletarian views. Although by the late 1960's Maoism was recognized throughout the world as more radical and emotionally revolutionary than conventional Marxism-Leninism, it also was considered more utopian, more voluntaristic, and hence more petty bourgeois than orthodox communism. From the classic perspective of Marxism-Leninism the fact that Mao was constantly concerned about the revival of capitalism and endlessly preached against the dangers of bourgeois attitudes is not enough to make his views correctly proletarian. His moralistic belief in willpower is traditionally identified with the petty bourgeoisie.

By the early 1970's, in the wake of the Cultural Revolution, it was clear that the Thoughts of Mao Tse-tung represented a corruption of both Marxist materialism and Leninist operational discipline. Ideology in China had become a form of personal morality instead of a view of the historical transformation of society. In spite of Mao's attacks on the corruption of Soviet society and the spread of revisionism in the "fatherland of socialism," the fact remains that his Thoughts are a deviation from conventional Marxism. Whereas under Lenin the demands of ideology were to advance the revolution and the building of a socialist society and economy, with Mao exemplary ideological conduct has become almost an end in itself. The Maoists insist that they would prefer China to remain materially weak and backward rather than for the Party to lose its spiritual qualities.

The Thoughts of Mao Tse-tung represent not just a break with the traditional style of Marxism but also a change in Mao's intellectual style as he became the dominant, and indeed single, ideologue in the Chinese Communist Party. Although Mao's personal impact has shaped most aspects of Chinese Communism, he has above all dominated ideology. During the Yenan period when others were directing the guerrillas, Mao was busy studying and writing on ideological issues. In the 1950's when others were absorbed in the affairs of state building, Mao in his style of ruling and reigning repeatedly drifted away from administrative concerns to devote himself to theoretical questions. In the 1960's he threw himself completely into polemics with the Soviet Union and proved that he had no equal in the traditional style of Communist ideological debate. From the clumsy discussion in *Dialectical Materialism* of the late 1930's to the Ninth Commentary Letter of the late 1960's, Mao showed tremendous growth in the skills of Communist discourse. Yet his most distinctive writings, especially *Quotations from Mao Tse-tung* (known as the "little red book") reflect an earnest moralism that is not characteristic of traditional Communist writings.

There is a contradictory trend in Mao's intellectual development. As he has become ever more technically competent in the Marxist-Leninist tradition, he has tended to break with that tradition and be a romantic and moralistic revolutionary. The latter development was apparent only later in his life. During his middle years Western scholars assumed that if Mao were to make a new contribution to Communist theory it would be in the direction of pragmatism. Mao was considered less doctrinaire and more humanistic than the Russian Communists. Benjamin I. Schwartz's classic study *Chinese Communism and the Rise of Mao*, published in 1951, analyzed Maoism in great detail but gave no hint that Mao's thinking would ultimately be in the direction of romanticizing the revolutionary spirit and discounting technical and pragmatic considerations.

To find the sources of this revolutionary dimension of Maoism we must look into the personality of Mao and examine his early years, when he revealed many tendencies that were suppressed during his middle years and have reemerged fairly recently.

MAO'S PERSONALITY

Mao was born in 1893 on the day after Christmas in Shaoshan village, in an agriculturally rich part of Hunan province. The same region had produced two of the most outstanding mandarin officials of the Ch'ing dynasty, Tsêng Kuo-fan and Tso Tsung-t'ang, who had been masterful in suppressing the Taiping Rebellion. Hunan had long had a tradition of political activism, producing a disproportionate number of officials and rebels.

Mao's father was the dominant figure in his early life. Mao Jen-sheng, a tough-minded, ambitious, driven man from a poor family, had achieved some success in his community. Like his son, his great break in life came from his use of the army. As a consequence of a few years of service he was able to save and otherwise accumulate enough money to purchase a respectable farm. He owned fifteen *mou* (2.47 acres) of land when Mao was young — enough to make him a rich peasant according to Mao's later classifications. Working hard and displaying all the traditional peasant qualities of avarice and insensitivity to the problems of others, Mao Jen-sheng accumulated land and established a small grain business by buying up his neighbors' rice crops as loans before the harvest. By storing and selling to the mills when the price was best, he worked to his advantage the two extremes of the annual marketing cycle.

Early in his life young Mao showed signs that, like his father, he had a longer horizon and a broader perspective than his schoolmates at the village school, which he attended until he was thirteen years old. He became a voracious reader of adventure and romantic stories. His mind was filled with the exploits of the heroes and clever bandits of the *Romance of the Three Kingdoms (San-kuo Yen-yi)* and the *Water Margin (Shui-hu chuan)*. He was fascinated by stratagems and deceptions and moved by the struggles of the poor and the dispossessed.

Mao Tse-tung was the eldest of four children. Apparently he had little feeling for his two brothers and sister. He never spoke of them except to tell how he mobilized them along with his mother and the hired hands to form a united front against his father. He claimed to Edgar Snow, the American journalist, that in his struggles with his father he learned how to manipulate a united front. Mao's mother, an illiterate, superstitious peasant woman, was overwhelmed by her husband and awed by her eldest son. He considered her warm and generous, in contrast to his father, and as a person whom he could dominate and manipulate because of her fear of controversy.

The relationship of Mao and his father as seen by Mao was one of constant conflict, of a prolonged war that the son was able to win because of his greater stamina, his refusal to struggle according to his father's rules, and his willingness to risk all. Significantly, they clashed over two fundamental issues. The father constantly charged that the boy was lazy and lacked willpower and that he made too much of books, which, according to his father, were of no practical value. It is interesting that Mao will be known to history for his exaggerated faith in willpower and human energy and his determination to prove that books and particularly his "little red book" can solve even the most mundane practical problems.

It is tempting to suggest that throughout his life Mao has been unconsciously struggling to prove that his father was wrong, and if we carefully read Mao Tse-tung's own words this thought may not seem farfetched: "Against [my father's] charge that I was lazy, I used the rebuttal that older people should do more work than younger, that my father was over three times as old as myself, and therefore should do more work. *And I declared that when I was his age I would be much more energetic.*"[4] Mao said of books: "I succeeded in continuing my reading, devouring everything I could find except the Classics. This annoyed my father, who wanted me to master the Classics, especially after he was defeated in a lawsuit due to an apt Classical quotation used by his adversary in

---

[4]Edgar Snow, *Red Star over China* (New York: Modern Library, 1938, 1944), p. 126; italics added.

the Chinese court. . . . *My father considered such books a waste of time.*"[5]

The fact that Mao clashed with his father might not be too significant. But the fact that in a culture stressing filial piety Mao talked openly of his hatred for his father is indeed significant. Mao has admitted that he learned the tactical uses of hate and bluff when challenging his father's authority. He tells of a time when, embarrassed before others by his father's criticism of his laziness, he ran to a nearby pond and threatened to drown himself if his father did not humiliate himself by begging his son not to jump into the lake. (Mao later made much of his prowess as a swimmer.) In Chinese society for a son to threaten to destroy himself, particularly because of displeasure with his father, was an extremely unfilial act; and for a father to have to beg of his son not to act unfilially was the ultimate loss of face. Displaying hatred toward a person and expecting to damage him by threatening or actually harming oneself is also a Chinese cultural practice.[6] In later years Mao frequently used the maneuver of threatening a foe, such as the United States and the Soviet Union, by daring the foe to attack him.

Since we have only Mao's version of his clashes with his father, it is impossible to judge whether Mao's father was particularly unjust. Parents were customarily harsh and demanding of their sons. From Mao's account, his father's demands for physical labor do not seem excessive or out of line with cultural patterns. The pain Mao felt was no doubt excruciating and of the same order as that of a young American boy who is made to mow the lawn. We must wonder if Mao did not exaggerate the extent to which his father mistreated him, particularly when he claimed that his father treated him more harshly than he did his farm laborers: "On the 15th of every month he made a concession to his laborers and gave them eggs with their rice, but never meat. To me he gave neither eggs nor meat."[7] Indeed, in spite of Mao's statement that "I learned to hate him," we must wonder whether the relationship was not more complex, especially when Mao tells about how he and his mother

[5]*Ibid.*, pp. 127–28; italics added.

[6]Nathan Leites has righly documented the prevalence of this Chinese practice in "On Violence in China," D-20517-PR (Santa Monica, Calif.: Rand, July 15, 1970).

[7]Snow, *op. cit.*, p. 125.

were worried about their father's lack of piety and how "We made many attempts then and later to convert him, but without success."[8]

It is easy to find much in Mao's words to support the idea that rather than being damaged by a threatening father, Mao was self-assured and believed he was morally superior to his father. Mao speaks of hating his father and of learning the art of rebellion in his relation with him. What can be inferred from his behavior is that he also learned that those with whom one has an adversary relationship may also be admired and even loved. By threatening to destroy himself by jumping into the lake, Mao learned that his father cared about him. Thus there is some question about how much Mao hated his father, just as there is some question about how deeply Mao hates international foes such as the United States. To have a foe may be more useful than to hate a foe.

What is of unquestionable significance is that when Mao was sixteen years old he defied his father and left home. This action was especially traumatic in Chinese culture. To justify his behavior Mao stressed his desire for more education. He went to nearby Hsiang Hsiang and prevailed on the teachers to admit him to the Tungshan Higher Primary School. A country boy, he felt ill at ease, and because he was several years older and many inches taller than his classmates, he thought they considered him a bit of an oaf.

Mao has never had easy relations with his peers. During his school years and as an ordinary member of the new Communist Party he did not develop close associations with his equals. He was a loner. Later in Kiangsi and Yenan he and Chu Teh shared authority, but in fact they were not personally close and usually were in different areas of China. Mao always tended to set himself apart, and he seemed to feel most comfortable when being treated as a superior, slightly aloof from his colleagues.

Mao as a child and as a young man seemed to be both extremely self-assured and yet highly sensitive to criticism and scorn. Not only did he feel that his classmates were laughing at him at primary school, but years later when he was working as an assistant librarian at Peking National University he said, "My office was so low that people *avoided me.* . . . They had no time to listen to an assistant librarian speaking a southern dialect."[9]

---

[8]*Ibid.*, p. 128.
[9]*Ibid.*, p. 150; italics added.

By the time Mao completed primary school he was thoroughly interested in foreign cultures and recognized the need to modernize China. He walked to Changsha, the capital of Hunan and a center of new and revolutionary ideas, where he entered high school, or middle school as it is called in China. Suddenly he was confronted with the whole of Western knowledge and, dropping out of school, he spent every day for six months in the provincial library reading in translation works such as John Stuart Mill's *On Liberty*, Adam Smith's *Wealth of Nations*, Thomas Henry Huxley's *Evolution and Ethics*, and Charles Darwin's *Origin of Species*.

After returning to school, his high school education was briefly interrupted again by the revolution of 1911. In a state of great excitement Mao cut off his queue and joined the army. A strange feature of his brief army experience — particularly in light of his distaste for physical labor under his father's direction and his subsequent demand when he was in authority that all who work with their minds should periodically be compelled to work with their hands — is that in recounting events at the time he said without shame or apology that carrying water was too much to expect of him because he was a student: "I also had to buy water. The soldiers had to carry water in from outside the city, but I, being a student, could not condescend to carrying, and bought it from the water-pedlars."[10]

In 1913 when Mao was twenty he entered the normal school in Changsha. During the next five years he energetically participated in a wide range of student politics and became secretary and then director of the Changsha Student Association. Mao also came under the influence of a modern and liberal teacher, Yang Ch'ang-chi, whose daughter he later married. In April 1917 Mao published his first article in the new journal *The New Youth*, founded by Ch'en Tu-hsiu, the man who was to be the first leader of the Chinese Communist Party. The article was signed with the pseudonym "Twenty-eight-stroke Student" — the number of strokes in the three characters used in Mao Tse-tung's name; its title was "The Study of Physical Culture" (*T'i-yü chih yen-chiu*).

This article, written in his pre-Marxist period, reveals fundamental features of Mao's thinking, features that became increasingly conspicuous as he became older and less inhibited in expressing

[10]*Ibid.*, p. 138.

his views. In the article Mao tends to assume that national strength and military ability are synonymous: "Our nation is wanting in strength. The military spirit has not been encouraged. . . . The principal aim of physical education is military heroism."[11] Mao reveals his pessimistic inclination to see deterioration as the natural trend of events if not countered by self-conscious human effort and willpower. He observed, "The physical condition of the population deteriorates daily."

Mao expressed his belief that subjective attitudes and willpower are decisive and the correction of the inner spirit is the starting point of all effective programs of action: "*If we wish to make physical education effective, we must influence people's subjective attitudes and stimulate them to become conscious of physical education.*" By merely substituting "revolution" for "physical education," one has a typical statement of the old Mao. One can find the seeds of the basic Maoist spirit of voluntarism in:

> When one's decision is made in his heart, then all parts of the body obey its orders. Fortune and misfortune are our own seeking. "I wish to be virtuous and lo, virtue is at hand." [From the Confucian *Analects.*] How much more this is true of physical education! If we do not have the will to act, then even though the exterior and the objective are perfect, they still cannot benefit us. *Hence, when we speak of physical education we should begin with individual initiative.*

We also find young Mao writing, "*The will is the antecedent of a man's career.*"

The central theme of young Mao's article was that self-cultivation should be a constant concern. If certain elementary steps are taken, all manner of grand outcomes are possible:

> Physical education not only strengthens the body but also enhances knowledge. There is a saying: Civilize the mind and make savage the body. This is an apt saying. In order to civilize the mind one must first make savage the body. [Why? No explanation is given or thought necessary.] If the body is made savage, then the civilized mind will follow. [The assertion is merely repeated in reverse order.] *Knowledge consists in knowing the things in the*

[11]These excerpts are from Stuart R. Schram, trans., *The Political Thought of Mao Tse-tung* (1969), pp. 152–60. Reprinted by permission of Praeger Publishers, New York, and The Pall Mall Press, London. Italics in original.

world, and in discerning their laws. In this matter we must rely on our body, because direct observation depends on the ears and eyes, and reflection depends on the brain. The ears and eyes, as well as the brain, may be considered parts of the body. When the body is perfect, then knowledge is also perfect.

The style of logic here clearly links Mao to traditional Confucian reasoning and also oddly to Stalin's heavy-handed style.

A final basic theme of "The Study of Physical Culture" is that of extolling conflict, rage, and physical violence:

Exercise should be savage and rude. To be able to leap on horseback and to shoot at the same time; to go from battle to battle; to shake the mountains by one's cries, and the colors of the sky by one's roars of anger; to have the strength to uproot mountains like Hsiang Yü and the audacity to pierce the mark like Yu Chi — all this is savage and rude and has nothing to do with delicacy. In order to progress in exercise, one must be savage.

Over the years Mao adopted the language and abstract categories of Marxism-Leninism. However, he continued to preserve the sentiments expressed in his pre-Communist writings. Concern over Chinese national strength, faith in the power of the human will and subjective attitudes, belief in the importance of self-cultivation and self-discipline, and an easy acceptance of the importance of violence and the value of being rude and aggressive have in varying amounts combined to form Mao's basic style.

By the late 1950's Mao's advocacy of policy, with the exception of his polemics with the Soviet Union, tended less to reflect Marxist reasoning and to be instead the views of a man educated in provincial China during the first decade of the twentieth century. The older Mao has freely dipped into Chinese history for examples and often uses earthy phrases and traditional Chinese modes of reasoning. Above all, he has increasingly turned things around and made a virtue of either a necessity or a liability. For example, in a speech at the Supreme State Conference in January 1958, he said:

Our country is both poor and blank: the poor own nothing, and the blank is like a sheet of white paper. It is good to be poor, good for making revolution; when it is blank, one can do anything with it, such as writing compositions or drawing designs; a sheet of white paper is good to write compositions on.

We must have zeal so that the Western world will lag behind us. Aren't we prepared to rectify bourgeois ideology? No one knows how long it will take for the West to discard the bourgeois ideology. If John Foster Dulles should want to rectify his bourgeois style, he would have to ask us to be his teachers.[12]

A most revealing example of Mao's intellectual style was his speech at the Lushan Conference of July 23, 1959, when he was desperately trying to defend his policies of the communes and the Great Leap:

> You have spoken so much; permit me to talk some now, won't you? I have taken three sleeping pills. Still can't sleep.
>
> ... There are three kinds of words; and the mouth has two functions. A man has only one mouth, which is used, first, to eat, and second, to discharge the obligation of speaking. With ears one must listen. He wants to talk, and what can you do about it? There are some who just don't want to listen to bad words. Good or bad, they are all words and we must listen to them. There are three kinds of words: one is correct, the second is basically correct or not too correct, and the third is basically incorrect or incorrect. Both ends are opposites; correct and incorrect are also opposites. ...
>
> No matter what they say, it is muddled. This is also good; the more muddled they talk, the more one wanted to hear it. ...
>
> ... One can't be rash; there must be a step-by-step process. In eating meat, one can only consume one piece at a time, but never hope to be a fatso at one stroke. X consumed one catty of meat daily, but did not even become fat in ten years. That Chu Teh and I are fat is not due to a single day. ...
>
> ... When I was young and in the prime of my life, I would also be irritated whenever I heard some bad remarks. My attitude was that if others do not provoke me I won't provoke them; if they provoke me, I will also provoke them; whoever provokes me first, I will provoke him later. I have not abandoned this principle even now. ...[13]

Countering this tendency of the aging Mao to give expression to undisciplined views have been dramatic efforts to institutionalize

[12]Speech at the Supreme State Conference (January 28, 1958), translated in *Chinese Law and Government*, 1: 4 (Winter 1968–1969), pp. 10–14.

[13]"Speech at the Lushan Conference," *ibid*, pp. 27–43.

the Thoughts of Mao Tse-tung, to make them into the catechism of a new religion. The exaggerated efforts to make the words of Mao into a sacred text go far beyond the usual means of creating the image of a charismatic leader. In a sense Mao's problem of achieving greatness is complicated by the fact that Confucius, China's greatest cultural hero, was a mortal and not a divine being. In other significant cultures, because the supreme figures have been acknowledged as in some measure divine, ordinary temporal leaders have accepted an inferior position without feeling threatened by a divine ideal. But in China Confucius was a mortal and thus able to be supplanted by another mortal. For Mao to achieve comparable greatness he will have to supplant a tradition of more than two thousand years.

The popularization of the Thoughts of Mao Tse-tung reached a high point with the publication of *Quotations from Chairman Mao Tse-tung* in 1964 at the beginning of the Cultural Revolution. Over half a billion copies of the "little red book" were published. Indeed, the entire Chinese publishing industry was given over to the single task of publishing the country's most recognized author. This selection of quotations, which have been ceaselessly studied, memorized, and repeated by millions of Chinese, totals about three hundred pages and includes some stark and aggressive sentiments:

> Every Communist must grasp the truth, "Political power grows out of the barrel of a gun."
>
> We should support whatever the enemy opposes and oppose whatever the enemy supports.
>
> A revolution is not a dinner party, or writing an essay, or painting a picture, or doing embroidery; it cannot be so refined, so leisurely and gentle, so temperate, kind, courteous, restrained and magnanimous. A revolution is an insurrection, an act of violence by which one class overthrows another.[14]

Much of the Thoughts is, however, banal and moralistic. Indeed, the three selections of Mao's works that served as the basis of the Socialist Education campaigns, which led into the Learn from the People's Liberation Army Movement and subsequently the Cultural Revolution, are strikingly similar to Protestant Sunday school

---

[14]*Quotations from Chairman Mao Tse-tung* (Peking: Foreign Languages Press, 1966).

lessons and the moral instruction common to the missionary movement, which educated so many of those who tried to set the moral
tone of modern China. All three selections deal with death, two
being eulogies. One is a memorial statement made at the funeral of
one of the first Chinese officers killed in the war with Japan. Mao
asserts that because a person has only one life he should make
something of significance of it and not waste it on trivial matters.

The second selection is Mao's "In Memory of Norman Bethune" — an extraordinary selection, given the fact that China was in
the throes of extreme xenophobia and isolated from most of the
world at the very time when everyone was called upon to memo-
rize it. In this memorial Mao reminds the Chinese that the Communist Party of the United States helped send the Canadian Norman
Bethune to China, where he died serving as a doctor with the Red
army: "Comrade Bethune's spirit, his utter devotion to others without any thought of self, was shown in his boundless sense of responsibility in his work. . . . We must all learn the spirit of absolute
selflessness from him."[15] Mao's theme is the virtue of selflessness,
of Communist internationalism, and of doing the hard tasks: "There
are not a few people who are irresponsible in their work, preferring
the light to the heavy, shoving the heavy loads on to others, and
choosing the easy ones for themselves."

The third selection is even more strange. It is an allegory involving God and angels. The purpose of Mao's story of "The
Foolish Old Man Who Removed the Mountains" is to preach the
need to "be resolute, fear no sacrifice, and surmount every difficulty to win victory." In Mao's words:

> There is an ancient Chinese fable called "The Foolish Old Man
> Who Removed the Mountains." It tells of an old man who lived
> in northern China long, long ago and was known as the Foolish
> Old Man of North Mountain. His house faced south and beyond
> his doorway stood the two peaks, Taikang and Wangwu, obstruct-
> ing the way. With great determination he led his sons in digging
> up these mountains, hoe in hand. Another greybeard, known as
> the Wise Old Man, saw them and said decisively, "How silly of you
> to do this! It is quite impossible for you few to dig up these two
> huge mountains." The Foolish Old Man replied, "When I die my

[15]Mao Tse-tung, *Selected Works* (Peking: Foreign Languages Press,
1967), vol. 2, pp. 337–38.

sons will carry on; when they die, there will be my grandsons, and then their sons and grandsons, and so on to infinity. High as they are, the mountains cannot grow any higher and with every bit we dig, they will be that much lower. Why can't we clear them away?" Having refuted the Wise Old Man's wrong view, he went on digging every day, unshaken in his conviction. God was moved by this, and he sent down two angels, who carried the mountains away on their backs. Today, two big mountains lie like a dead weight on the Chinese people. One is imperialism, the other is feudalism. The Chinese Communist Party has long made up its mind to dig them up. We must persevere and work unceasingly, as we, too, will touch God's heart. Our God is none other than the masses of the Chinese people. If they stand up and dig together with us, why can't these two mountains be cleared away?[16]

Mao's personality has in many respects overpowered the Chinese revolution. His idiosyncracies have become the basis of national policies and of profound conflicts with his colleagues, whose ideological positions reflect their own personalities.

[16]*Quotations from Chairman Mao Tse-tung* (Peking: Foreign Languages Press, 1966), p. 201–2.

CHAPTER THIRTEEN

The Followers Who Also Lead

In spite of the towering role of Mao, other Chinese Communist leaders have been prominent and not merely as Mao's subordinates. Some students of Chinese communism are convinced that as far back as the Yenan period Mao was more a symbol of leadership than the chief executive. According to this view the management of the war with Japan and the administration of the liberated areas fell to men such as Chu Teh and Liu Shao-ch'i, while Mao stayed in the caves, met with foreign visitors, and absorbed himself with his ideological writing. When victory came, the regime had to popularize its leadership, and this was the beginning of the cult of Mao. Others accepted the cult because it posed no threat to their own domains of power and responsibility.

Numerous men besides Mao contributed to the development of Chinese communism. Paradoxically, the more Mao's personality came to dominate the public image of Chinese communism, the greater the political significance of the personality differences among these men became. During the first decade of the Communist regime the leadership appeared to be integrated and homogeneous in outlook, and questions of relative power did not seem important. However, with the upheavals of the Cultural Revolution came the revelation that there had been clashes and that leaders with considerable autonomy in their own spheres also had different basic approaches to China's problems.

As we learn about the inner workings of the Chinese Communist system, we realize that personal relationships have been quite important. We have recently discovered that the inner councils of the Chinese Communist Party have had complex circles and cliques.

At present we can only sense the complexities of such relationships by examining the character and quality of the men who have been followers of Mao and leaders in their own fields.

Michel Oksenberg, through careful research, has discovered that policy making under Mao Tse-tung during the 1950's and 1960's involved constant struggles among cliques and factions in which personality factors were often important. In many respects the trend under Mao was away from the model of the Bolshevik Party traditions and back to patterns reminiscent of the imperial tradition. Oksenberg has written:

> Intrigue by the emperor's wife, tension between the inner and outer courts, competition between the Grand Secretariat and the Grand Council, the contrast between the remoteness of the emperor and the omnipresence of his influence, the difficulty of distinguishing between loyal and disloyal opposition, the embodiment by bureaucrats of the interests of their constituencies, the inability of the emperor to obtain reliable information, the alleged machination of cliques, and the inability to devise widely accepted methods of handling succession — these were the hallmarks of politics in Peking in the eighteenth and nineteenth centuries. They find ready analogues in Peking in the 1960's.[1]

Over the years as the Peking government had to cope with a wide range of problems of national development and socialist transformation, disagreements began to divide the band of men who had brought the Party to power. These disagreements culminated in the Cultural Revolution and set the stage for competition for the succession to Mao. The leaders who were most important in the power struggle that culminated during the Cultural Revolution and in the conflict over who should succeed Mao were Chou En-lai, Liu Shao-ch'i, and Lin Piao. By 1972 Chou En-lai alone of the three survived the continuous purges that Mao initiated with the Cultural Revolution. The other two, each for a time designated an heir-apparent, contributed greatly to the development of Chinese communism during both their periods of ascendancy and their purging.

[1]Michel C. Oksenberg, "Peking Making Under Mao, 1949–68: An Overview," in John M. H. Lindbeck, *China: Management of a Revolutionary Society* (Seattle: University of Washington Press, 1971), p. 111.

THE POISED SPOKESMAN:
CHOU EN-LAI

Chou En-lai is unquestionably the most cultured and sophisti-cated of all the Communist leaders. Whenever the Party has sought to advance a genial and rational front, Chou En-lai has brought into play his quite considerable social and diplomatic talents. In the early years Chou met with Western reporters and suggested that the Chinese Communists were pragmatic modernizers and not ideologi-cal fanatics. During World War II Chou was stationed in the Kuo-mintang capital of Chungking and carried out public relations activities for the Communists. After the Communists came to power Chou played a leading role whenever Peking sought to beguile others. He emerged in the post-Cultural Revolution scene when Peking was anxious to gain respectability and to suggest that noth-ing was out of order. With equal skill he carried out conversations with young American students and table tennis players, with corre-spondent James Reston and President Nixon's special assistant Henry Kissinger, and with Nixon himself. His personal skills, how-ever, have never been matched by power. His strength has resulted almost entirely from his personality.

Chou En-lai was born in 1898 in Huaian, Kiangsu. His father, a member of the local gentry and owner of a small retail business, had passed the initial provincial civil service examinations but had never served in government. His mother was well educated for a Chinese woman of her generation. While Chou was a small boy his father died, and during the subsequent years of his childhood he lived with various relatives in material comfort but with con-siderable loneliness. First he was sent to be with his grandfather in their ancestral home in Kiangsu, and then he went to Mukden to be with his uncle, a police official. After primary school he was sent to Tientsin to attend middle school. During these school years he be-came increasingly nationalistic and began to write essays about how to make China strong again. When he graduated in 1917, his uncle provided funds for him to go to Japan. He was a special student at Waseda University in Tokyo and then attended Kyoto University, where he first encountered Marxist economic theory.

Chou became an active leader among the Chinese students in

Japan. When news of the May Fourth Movement reached Kyoto he returned to Tientsin, enrolled at Nankai University, and was soon deeply involved in radical student politics. He travelled regularly to Peking to take part in the Marxist study group organized by Ch'en Tu-hsiu and Li Ta-chao. He attracted the attention of the Tientsin police and was arrested, but the president of his university persuaded the authorities to release him on the grounds that it was absurd to take seriously the radicalism of students from good families. Chou next joined a group of students leaving for France on a work-study program. He never enrolled in any school in France but rather became a full-time professional political activist, working among the Chinese in Paris and Berlin and establishing the European headquarters of the Chinese Communist Party. Chou was in Europe, mainly Paris, from 1920 until the summer of 1924, absorbed with the problems of unifying all the factions of left-wing Chinese student politics and propagandizing for the unification of China.

During these critical years in his intellectual development, Chou did some writing of an uninspired nature, but mainly he was learning the art of bringing people together and conciliating different points of view while making sure that egos were not too seriously damaged. These were the skills Chou would contribute to the leadership of the Chinese Communist Party. He developed a strong instinct for practical solutions and for making any position he advocated appear to be eminently reasonable. He learned never to argue from passion or by manipulating the passions of others. His style made it possible for him to work with many kinds of people. When he returned to China he became the deputy director of the political department of the Whampoa Military Academy, of which Chiang Kai-shek was commandant. Just before the Northern Expedition began, Chou En-lai slipped into Shanghai and took the lead in organizing the trade unions who took over the city when Chiang's troops reached the outskirts. When Chiang turned his troops against the workers because they failed to turn their Soviet-supplied arms over to him, Chou was captured. Again he was able to so impress his captors with his reasonableness and decency that they released him. It has been surmised that the Communist hero Kyo Gisors in André Malraux's novel of the Shanghai events, *Man's Fate*, was modeled on Chou En-lai.

During the next few months Chou was consistently half a step behind events. He was never considered responsible for anything that happened but benefited from always having been on the scene. He got to Wuhan just as the government there was collapsing. He went to Nanchang just as the uprising there was being carried out. He was part of the Autumn Harvest uprisings but was not involved in the planning that led to failure. Stricken with malaria and shipped to Hong Kong for recovery, he avoided the issues of the split between the comrades in Shanghai and those in Kiangsi. He recovered in time to go to Moscow as a delegate to the Sixth Party Congress and was thus a member of the Politburo. He spent nearly two years in Moscow and became one of the most knowledgeable of the Chinese Communists on Comintern affairs. He also was in Shanghai working with the Returned Students there, but once again he left Shanghai at the critical moment and went to Kiangsi to join Mao and Chu Teh. He was a new arrival at the Juichin conference of November 7, 1931, which elected Mao chairman of the Chinese Soviet Republic. Chou was likewise on the scene when the Long March took place even though in previous years he had been closer to other factions of the Party. Mao tried to win him over as a spokesman for his role as leader of the Party. Chou had had more experience than any other Chinese Communist in both European and international Communist affairs and was capable of legitimizing and giving professional respectability to Mao's claims of leadership.

Almost as soon as the Red Army reached Yenan, Chou En-lai became "Mr. Outside," the chief negotiator with all non-Communist forces. He was the chief Communist who dealt with the forces of Chang Hsüeh-liang, particularly during the Sian incident, when Chiang Kai-shek was kidnaped. Thus he set the stage for creating the united front to oppose Japan but soon afterward reestablished his orthodox Communist credentials by spending half a year in Moscow. He returned to China in 1939 and went to Chungking to be the principal Chinese Communist representative in dealings with the Nationalist government and Western officials and unofficial representatives.

Unquestionably Chou En-lai's remarkable talent for reasonableness and lack of passion helped to create the impression during World War II that the Chinese Communists were peasant reformers and not professional revolutionaries. After the defeat of Japan, Chou continued to describe the Chinese Communist Party as moderate and democratic in contrast to the backward and venal Kuomintang. Those who observed Chou during the period when General George Marshall was seeking to negotiate a coalition government judged him either a devious spirit or a sophisticated and reasonable man — and in either case a man who could not be a fanatical Communist. Generally people discounted his radicalism just as they had when he had been arrested in Tientsin and Shanghai.

After the Party came to power Chou En-lai regularly sided with strength in Party councils, but publicly he was just as regularly seen as the voice of reason. When the Chinese Communists have sought to create an international image of revolutionary zeal, Chou has been inconspicuous. When the image has been one of wisdom and sound programs, Chou has dominated the scene. During the brief period that China's policies conveyed the Bandung spirit of cooperation with Afro-Asian states, Chou En-lai represented Peking. He carried Chinese diplomacy into Africa. Wherever he appeared it was almost unthinkable to identify him and China with foolish radicalism. People still find it hard to believe that anyone with his poise and genial sophistication could be a fanatical Communist.

In the Party's inner councils Chou has performed much the same role. He has consistently been the conciliator and the unfailing champion of legitimate authority. As premier he has been the spokesman for the administrative departments of the government. Indeed, he has been the leading bureaucratic administrator of the regime. Yet when the Cultural Revolution turned against "bureaucratization," Chou was somehow not selected as a leading target of the radicals, for just as constituted authority has always found it hard to take Chou's radicalism seriously, so have radical dissidents refused to treat him as a serious enemy. Consequently, Chou has had remarkable survival capacity over the years. He added nothing to the ideological development of Communism but has been critical in providing a pragmatic basis for national policies.

More importantly Chou has been the archetype of Chinese professionalism, and if China is to modernize it will have to rely on the technical skills that he represents. Oddly enough, a special mandarin quality in Chou's personal style has made his form of professionalism seem as acceptable and unthreatening as the amateurism that inspired the Confucian scholar-official.

THE PARTY TECHNICIAN:
LIU SHAO-CH'I

In contrast, Liu Shao-ch'i, who was also a professional orga-
nizer and administrator, was always considered a challenge to Mao,
in spite of the fact that he consistently sang Mao's praises more
openly than Chou. While Mao Tse-tung was concentrating on ideological matters and becoming an object of veneration, and while
Chou En-lai was becoming a paragon of wise reason, Liu Shao-ch'i
was learning how to be an impersonal revolutionary, dedicated only
to building the Party in the Bolshevik tradition. Because of his concern with Party matters, he became the administrator of Party policies. His power derived from his appointment of officials. Liu was
the supreme organization man of Chinese communism.

Liu Shao-ch'i was born in 1900 only a few miles from Mao
Tse-tung's native village in Hunan. His father, like Mao's, was a
hard-working and relatively successful owner of a small farm. Liu,
the youngest of nine children, was his parents' favorite. He early
developed a sense of group loyalty and understood the need for
contributing to a collective cause without expecting public recognition.

In 1916 Liu went to Changsha for advanced education and
enrolled in the same normal school as Mao Tse-tung attended. He
was soon caught up in the same radical currents that influenced Mao,
and on graduation he hoped to go to France on the same work-study
program as Chou En-lai. Instead, however, he returned to the Hunan
countryside and worked on the program Mao had worked on. Then
he went to Shanghai to learn more about socialism. In contrast to
Mao, he was soon seriously committed to learning Russian so he
would be able to find out more about communism. The Comintern
recognized his ambition and sent him to Moscow for two years at
the time the Chinese Communist Party was being formed.

By the time he returned to China to work with labor unions
in Shanghai and Canton, he was more knowledgeable about the day-
to-day character of Communist Party life than either Mao or Chou.
He learned the Bolshevik tradition of party discipline and the need
for organization if objectives were to be realized. He soon became
one of the most skilled secret operators in the Party. Using aliases,

he organized workers and students in the Kuomintang and later in Japanese-occupied territories.

During the war with Japan, when Mao was devoting his attention to ideological writings in Yenan, Liu was ceaselessly traveling about, organizing the administration of the guerrilla territories and building the structure of the Party. While Mao was concentrating on making philosophical contributions to Marxism-Leninism, Liu was dealing with the human beings who made up the Party, learning about the capabilities and limitations of each. Mao's attention was on abstract theories of warfare and revolution. Chou's was on public relations with the outside world. Liu's was entirely on the inside problems of Party building and the practical problems of administration and personnel management.

Liu's contributions to ideological writings were in this same spirit. In July 1939 at the Institute on Marxism-Leninism at Yenan he delivered a speech that was later published as *How to Be a Good Communist*. Much of this important book is devoted to nuts and bolts questions of Party membership and indoctrination, but it also included an important theoretical contribution: In an underdeveloped, agrarian society, such as China, with so few industrial workers, it is particularly important to use persuasion and seek to indoctrinate people of all class backgrounds in order to convert them into disciplined Party members. Liu emphasized the endless need for propaganda and indoctrination, for winning over all kinds of people. In this sense Liu provided a theoretical basis for Mao's voluntarism.

At the time the Peking regime was established Liu made a second important theoretical contribution. He suggested that the Chinese revolution was distinct and should serve as a model for the rest of Asia. In doing so, he advanced the idea that Mao had made creative additions to Marxism and should be recognized as a coequal of Stalin. With Liu publicly praising Mao, it was easy for Mao to adopt a modest posture.

Verbally Liu's contribution to Chinese communism was his praise of Mao as a theoretician; pragmatically, however, his greatest contribution was to administer the personnel of the Party with a tight hand. During the first decade of Communist rule his style of vocally glorifying the "Helmsman" while quietly administering the Party worked well. The result was the widespread picture of Chinese communism in the 1950's as a harmonious balance of talents, consisting of the theoretical rhetoric of Mao, the public relations expertise of Chou, and the administrative and disciplinary efficiency of Liu. But by the mid-1960's the strain between ideological aspiration and practical possibilities became great. The Cultural Revolution became, in effect, a struggle between the Mao and the Liu styles of communism.

THE NONCONTROVERSIAL FIGURE
OF THE SOLDIER: LIN PIAO

Given the differences in the approaches of the three leading personalities, it is not surprising that a fourth figure, Lin Piao, emerged briefly as the designated successor shortly after Liu Shao-ch'i lost out as heir-apparent. Lin Piao represented a compromise figure among the top Chinese leaders. Although a leading commander of the People's Liberation Army he always seemed to be less the professional soldier and more the Party representative. But at the same time he was not an ideologue or a Party administrator. By being able to appear to blend many talents while not suggesting any particular biases, Lin Piao became the plausible but uninspiring heir-apparent to Mao Tse-tung.

Lin was born in 1907 in Hupei of a small land-owning family that was well enough off to give him a primary school education and to instill in him ambitions like those Mao and Liu had as a consequence of growing up in much the same circumstances. Lin Piao's father owned a small dye-works, of about the same order as Mao's father's grain-buying business. Just as Mao's father had done, Lin's father left agriculture for a few years to earn money, as a purser on a Yangtze steamer.

Also like Mao, Liu, and Chou, the young Lin Piao left home early in order to get an education and in his school environment came upon the currents of radicalism common to Chinese youth of the early 1920's. Lin was strongly influenced by a cousin, twenty years his senior, who was a professional radical later executed by the Kuomintang. From his middle school at Wuhan, Lin went on to Shanghai to participate in national student activities, but the critical event was his decision, at the age of eighteen, to go to Canton and

enter the Whampoa Military Academy. Soldiering came more naturally to Lin Piao than discussions of student politics. At Whampoa
he soon caught the attention of his teachers, including the Russian
adviser Galen, and was encouraged to blend political and military
training.

After graduation his advancement was entirely within the military, where he was soon associated with Chu Teh. Lin accompanied
Mao on the Long March, and during the Yenan period he was most
notable for his work in training army officers. Although he participated in the war against Japan, his skills as a military commander
became most widely recognized during the civil war against the
Nationalists. He commanded and was also the political commissar
of the Fourth Field Army, which conquered Manchuria and then
captured Peking and Tientsin before driving south to the Yangtze
at Wuhan and finally to Canton.

The steady rise of Lin Piao in the Party hierarchy is not associated with any outstanding ideological or administrative contributions.
By April 1955 he was on the Politburo; by May 1958 he was a
vice-chairman of the Central Committee and the sixth ranking
leader. In September 1959 he replaced the purged P'eng Te-huai as
defense minister. In June 1966 he replaced Liu Shao-ch'i as heir-
apparent to Mao and officially became the second ranking Chinese
Communist. Much of his success can be attributed to his abiding
commitment to the blend of political and military techniques that he
learned at Whampoa and during the Long March. The simple guerrilla style of dealing with problems, which has appealed more to
Mao as he has grown older, was always Lin Piao's basic approach.
When P'eng Te-huai was purged because he felt that China needed
a modernized military establishment to meet the challenge of the
United States, Lin Piao naturally became the spokesman for a more
militia- and guerrilla-oriented People's Liberation Army. The idea of
a politically inspired army making do with primitive technologies
was satisfying to Lin Piao and coincided with Mao's view of what
China needed on the eve of the Cultural Revolution.

In September 1965 Lin Piao made a major statement on
"people's wars" in which he advanced the view that Mao Tse-tung's
strategy, which had brought the Communists to victory in China,
was appropriate for advancing world revolution. He suggested that
Mao's theory of building revolutionary base areas in the rural

countryside in order to encircle the cities and eventually strangle them could be repeated, with the underdeveloped countries of Africa and Asia representing the "countryside" and America and Western Europe the "cities." Lin's doctrine was seen by some people as a declaration of Chinese support throughout underdeveloped areas of guerrilla or people's wars, such as the Viet Nam war. Other analysts, however, have noticed that he also called on the people to employ self-reliance.

In raising again the idea that Mao's theories provide a "model" for other countries, Lin Piao seemed to echo in 1965 the theme that Liu Shao-ch'i had introduced in 1949. In so praising the "Helmsman," Lin seemed to be using the techniques that Liu had used in his relations with Mao. Substantively, however, Lin Piao, as a result of his career and personal development, could blend military rule and political ideology.

Lin Piao's ideological contribution to Chinese communism was the high degree of revolutionary respectability and legitimacy he gave to the idea of the army running the country. In all other underdeveloped countries in which the army has had to assume civil functions, legitimacy has been compromised. In China Lin Piao was able to lead the People's Liberation Army into new political roles without destroying the revolutionary claims of the regime. Yet his very success brought him disfavor with Mao and precipitated his downfall.

THE FRAGILE BASIS OF UNITY

These men and the other leaders of the Chinese Communist Party were able to blend their personal differences throughout the long years of struggling for power and during the first decade of ruling China. There was enough to be done to keep all absorbed, and all were learning how to be dedicated revolutionaries. Their differences in talent and style tended to reinforce rather than compromise the collective effort.

Mao was clearly the supreme figure, the ultimate spokesman, and the charismatic symbol of the new order. Those who ran the day to day operations of government had their separate domains and welcomed the protective symbolism that Mao gave to the entire enterprise. When the Communists came to power, they needed a figure for popular identification and adulation in order to legitimize the regime. The other leaders accepted the need to create the charismatic authority of Mao. In time, however, they were to discover that they had created a figure that could also claim power and influence in their own specialized domains. In the main, however, Mao's authority was diffuse, directed toward generalized policies and postures of government, and his words rarely took the form of providing operational concepts for administrators. Others had to translate his general views into operational programs. This meant that others had considerable practical power, for they could always change the emphasis of general statements as they made them into operational guidelines. Mao thus increasingly became the distant grandfather who had to be listened to, deferred to, but was not expected, except as whim moved him, to interfere greatly with the management of the enterprise.

The personal arrangements among the Chinese leaders provided for easy harmony as long as each was carrying out his separate functions, but the stage was also set for direct conflicts if any leader altered his style and role. Substantive policy problems became increasingly troublesome and eventually forced the differences among the leaders to come into direct conflict. As a result the two men, Liu Shao-ch'i and Lin Piao, who were successively designated as heir-apparent to Mao fell from his grace, and Chou En-lai was finally forced to give up the security of being "number three" and became a polar figure. In the meantime, Mao was driven to become an even more isolated and distrusting leader, who, with a characteristic blending of wit and self-pity, was inclined to picture himself as "a lonely Monk with a leaky umbrella."[2]

[2]Edgar Snow, "A Conversation with Mao Tse-tung," *Life* (April 30, 1971), p. 48.

CHAPTER FOURTEEN

Policy Choices: In General

During the years of its struggle for power, the Chinese Communist Party devoted little attention to what its specific policies would be if it were ruling the country. The Party's propaganda concentrated on the deplorable conditions of Chinese weakness and backwardness and extolled the puritanical virtues practiced in the liberated areas. Programs and policies in these areas did not, however, provide guidelines for what would have to be done once the Party was responsible for managing the whole country. Even during the civil war the Communists emphasized tactics instead of describing ultimate objectives. In fact the stress in those days was so much on power considerations that the Party's political warfare dealt more with the question of coalition government than with what Communist rule by itself would mean.

When the Communist government was established, the first concern of the leaders was to create a sense of legitimacy and convince the Chinese people that they would be able to live on reasonable terms with their new rulers. Gaining political acceptability meant that attention was focused on procedures and particularly on the claim that the regime was a united front incorporating non-Communist minority parties. Ultimate goals were left vague, and there was some question about whether the Chinese were true Communists.

The Korean war, coming so soon after the establishment of the new regime, facilitated the growth of national unity and pushed the government toward policy programs. The leaders pointed to the dangers of a foreign foe and, using appeals to national security, attacked critics as traitors. The need to put the country on a war footing justified a rapid movement toward increasingly centralized control of all aspects of life. Movement toward totalitarianism began with the requirements of war mobilization.

For the Communists, as for all recent Chinese leaders, the goals of policy have been to modernize China, build up its economy, and reestablish China as a major world power. Because modernization and national power have been the common themes of all Chinese leaders, the degree of their implementation provides a basis for measuring the relative successes and failures of the Communists' policies in various fields. The initial appeal of communism for the Chinese intellectuals who first formed the Party was that it offered a program to satisfy the universal Chinese desire for national power and wealth. Those who came to the Party after the civil war were eager to believe that communism might bring China back to its rightful place as a major world power.

When the regime was finally established, the leaders came to realize that communism did not offer as clear-cut answers to China's problems as had been presumed. A host of practical problems pressed in on them: What was to be done to restore the economy? How was industry to be regulated? What would be the relationship between the cities and the countryside now that they could be reintegrated into a single economy? In the face of such confusion, ideology provided valuable guidelines, for it made the Party discriminate between friends and foes, both domestic and international. In area after area the Chinese sought to emulate Soviet practices, and they enthusiastically cast themselves in the role of "younger brother" following the ways of "elder brother."

Gradually, however, the Chinese had to search for their own path. It is still not clear that they have found it in many areas of life. The almost yearly vacillations and the ease with which they could move to the leftist, radical extremes of the Cultural Revolution and then swing toward a rightist course confirm the difficulties the Chinese have been having.

In addition to the guidance they received from their ideology, Peking's new rulers relied on their military organization to give them administrative direction. The army provided not only the structure for administration and for conveying orders but also a tradition for establishing priorities. The army's approach to matters such as public order, the mobilization of materials, logistics, and even production became the approach of the new regime.

From time to time Chinese spokesmen, Liu Shao-ch'i in the early 1950's and Lin Piao in the late 1960's, have spoken of a Chinese or Maoist "model" of revolution, appropriate for the other underdeveloped countries of Asia and Africa. Yet Peking's policy vacillations have made it increasingly difficult to perceive what that "model" is supposed to be. At times Chinese policies have been pragmatic, down to earth, and based on science and technology; at other times they have been highly idealistic, rhetorically revolutionary, and based on anti-scientific faith in the human spirit. During the first decade of the regime some Asian and Western leaders thought that China might become a significant model for underdeveloped states seeking rapid economic development and modernization. Indeed, one of the forces behind American foreign aid was the belief that vulnerable new states need viable alternatives to the Chinese approach to development. However, after the failure of the Great Leap and the apparent madness of the Cultural Revolution, the appeal of a Chinese "model" has largely evaporated in the rest of Asia and in Africa.

Just as Peking's early successes brought international stature to China, so have the regime's later failures made China seem less threatening. These reversals have also raised questions about the appropriate criteria for measuring Chinese performance. During the first decade and through the height of the Great Leap everyone seemed to agree that China should be measured by the pace of its economic, and especially industrial, development. The Chinese themselves boasted of their statistical achievements, and Mao Tsetung led the nation in declaring that China would industrially catch up with Great Britain in fifteen years. Since the Cultural Revolution scholars have suggested that Mao's China should not be evaluated by conventional economic standards. Presumably Mao is concerned primarily with equality and not mere growth, and therefore progress in China is geared to advancing the lowest levels of the society and economy. "Success" in China should be determined not by the growth of the economy but by leveling that will ensure equal distribution of poverty and improvements. Mao has never gone so far in discounting the importance of conventional standards of economic performance, and so this view seems to be more that of some sympathetic westerners anxious to find a rationale for economically inexpedient policies. In any case the issue is not important because evaluating Chinese performance according to both criteria is quite easy. Equalization may be as elusive an objective as conventional economic growth, but it can be evaluated just as readily. Furthermore, since the reestablishment of order after the Cultural Revolution Chinese spokesmen, particularly Chou En-lai, have returned to the practice of citing with pride economic statistics as a way of suggesting China's progress.

More serious is the problem of obtaining reliable information. The Chinese have shrouded their policies with layers of secrecy and frequently have indulged in glowing and uncritical propaganda. In no country in the world do government statements give a complete picture of national life. The Chinese government is not unique simply because it has been so secretive. However, before 1956 Peking and even provincial authorities did release figures that Chinese planners used. Since the Great Leap, we have almost no figures.

OVERVIEW OF ECONOMIC PERFORMANCE

Most economists agree that during the first decade of the Communist regime the Chinese economy made significant strides, first in rehabilitation from wartime disruption and then in substantive growth, particularly in the industrial sector. Since 1959, however, the economy has suffered severely and has generally stagnated. Whereas during the first decade China's industrial growth rate was second only to that of Japan and Pakistan in Asia, it dropped nearly to the bottom of the list during the 1960's. Only in 1970 did the economy begin to revive.

In part the achievements of the first decade reflect a natural pattern of Chinese history. The establishment of political order after a period of chaos was always accompanied by vigorous economic activity. During the war years millions of Chinese were learning new skills that would be invaluable when attention could be given to industrial and economic development. In Japanese-occupied territories the conquerors extensively used Chinese labor for their war-related industries. This was particularly true in the industrial centers in Manchuria and also in Tientsin, Hankow, Shanghai, Canton, and even in secondary centers such as Taiyuan and Tsinan.

China thus had a potential for development in its large and well disciplined labor force, which had steadily grown during each decade since the 1911 revolution. In contrast to many underdeveloped countries whose populations have had little experience in factory life, China did not have to create a responsible and hardworking labor force. The new government, however, did play a critical role in moving quickly to counter the effects of inflation stimulated by the weakening Nationalists. By reuniting the urban and rural economies of China and introducing strict fiscal controls, the new Communist regime set the stage for sober economic activities.

Peking's initial commitment to emulate the Soviet model of economic development resulted in benefits and costs to China that are still difficult to appraise. An immediate consequence of the policy of "leaning to one side" and following the Soviet example was that China obtained a source of credit and technical assistance. During Stalin's lifetime it was common in the West to say that the Russians drove a hard bargain with the Chinese and that China was in some respects being exploited through Soviet "aid." It is now far less clear that this was the case. Alexander Eckstein made a detailed examination of this complex question and arrived at the cautious conclusion that although Russian aid took different forms, it was on balance probably more generous toward China than toward the Eastern European socialist states.[1] The Russians bought commodities from the Chinese for which they had little need and sold to the Chinese things they could have used for the rehabilitation of their own economy. The Chinese got things their planners valued greatly and exported low-priority items to Russia. Negotiations for Russian aid were difficult and protracted, but the technical questions were exceedingly complex.

The importance of Soviet aid to China may be deduced from the fact that when it ceased in 1960 and Soviet technicians were withdrawn, the Chinese economy began to falter. With the end of Soviet aid Chinese planners had to give up their dream of rapid industrialization and think instead of developing agriculture.

---

[1]Alexander Eckstein, *Communist China's Economic Growth and Foreign Trade* (New York: McGraw-Hill, 1966), pp. 168–82.

The extent of Russian technical assistance can be seen from the fact that between 1950 and 1960 at least 10,800 Soviet and 1,500 Eastern European specialists and technicians were sent to China.[2] Joint-venture firms were established in which Russian blueprints and factory plans were followed under Soviet guidance in order to establish quickly new manufacturing industries in China. Furthermore, various Soviet scientific and technological academies, institutes, and organizations made available to China great quantities of technical knowledge. Through such assistance the Soviets provided the atomic reactor and the diffusion plant that were critical in China's development of the atomic bomb.[3] When Soviet technicians were suddenly withdrawn under the heat of Sino-Soviet ideological polemics, they took with them the plans for many unfinished plants. With great difficulty the Chinese were able to finish some but had to abandon others. On balance the Chinese unquestionably benefited greatly from Russian technical assistance. After the Korean war China had no other source of foreign assistance.

It is considerably more difficult to evaluate the relative costs and benefits of China's fundamental commitment to follow the Soviet planning model, which emphasized heavy industry at the expense of consumer goods. A strong case can be made that by 1950 China was on the threshold of the normal stage of industrial development, comparable to where Japan stood in the early 1920's, at which Chinese industries could have produced light consumer goods and textiles for the world market. Even before the war with Japan China was one of the three largest textile producers in the world, mainly supplying its huge domestic market but about ready to export. (Now China is the world's largest textile producer even though the regime has tended to favor heavy industries over light ones.) The industrial centers of mainland China thus had the skilled labor force and the technical competence to become a series of "Hong Kongs." According to this argument, if the Chinese had exploited their comparative advantages in international trade, they could have been producing the textiles, plastics, and light electrical goods for the rest of Asia and Africa, and they could have filled the gap

[2]*Ibid.*, p. 169.

[3]William L. Ryan and Sam Summerlin, *The China Cloud* (Boston: Little, Brown, 1967).

created when Japan began to produce technically sophisticated commodities for the American and European markets.

In any case, regardless of what might have been, the Chinese missed this opportunity and focused on heavy industry, at least until 1960. Without Soviet aid the Chinese had to turn to agriculture. By 1971 China was showing more interest in exporting light consumer goods, but world conditions in the 1970's were quite different from what they were in the 1950's. Seeking to enter world markets twenty years late, the Chinese have encountered intense competition. Almost all the other underdeveloped countries have their own textile industries and many aspire to become producers of light manufactured goods.

At present the Chinese can produce limited quantities of acceptable consumer merchandise, which, with internal subsidization, they can export below world prices in order to obtain foreign exchange. These goods are available in Hong Kong, Singapore, and some African cities, and in a sense they represent a form of Chinese subsidy to these economies, given in return for providing China with foreign exchange and a sense of prestige. Chinese exports are priced low partly because factories do not have to recover their costs through sales and partly because Chinese laborers are paid below world levels.

If the Chinese were to expand such production for larger markets and continue to underprice their items, then, of course, Chinese workers and peasants would be paying the difference in price. Conceivably, the Chinese will try to do precisely this, but probably the cost to Chinese labor will be much greater than it would have been if China had recognized its comparative advantage much earlier. By 1970 textiles and clothing accounted for a quarter of China's exports; next in importance came light manufacturing. In contrast, during the 1950's China sold mainly soybeans, food products, and metal ores.

The social consequences of the Communists' economic policies may be more significant than the economic consequences. The early stress on the development of heavy industries favored the urban labor force and in many respects made the Chinese worker an advantaged citizen in comparison with other groups in the society. Factory workers were given job security, and their wages generally were higher than rural laborers could hope to obtain. The regime sought to universalize the prewar practice of elite industries whereby workers were provided with housing near their jobs at nominal rents.

During the 1950's the Chinese factory worker felt that he was relatively well off. His consumption demands were quite limited. He had little information about conditions in other countries and could compare his lot only with the previous state of affairs — the hyper-inflation of the civil war years, the disruptions of the Japanese war period, and the prewar world depression. The average worker and his family considered themselves fortunate to have a single-room apartment and a luxury item such as a radio. Some could look forward to saving enough to buy a bicycle.

These favorable conditions tended to attract people from the countryside to the cities, so that by the late 1950's the regime had to initiate several programs for moving populations back to the rural areas and discouraging growth of the large industrial centers. By refusing to provide work permits and by insisting that young people prove their revolutionary dedication by going into the interior, the regime hoped to diminish the number of unemployed urban people looking for a way to become a part of the favored industrial working class. The problem of a large unemployed urban population increased during the period of economic depression that followed the failure of the Great Leap. The need for administrative controls to prevent urban population expansion from completely outstripping employment opportunities has continued to grow.

In the meantime, however, the regime has continued to give the urban industrial worker economic rewards great enough to keep him satisfied. As a result Chinese workers have become a conservative force, in support of the status quo, ready to employ the rhetoric of revolution and the routines of Communist indoctrination and not anxious for any fundamental changes. The conservative character of the industrial workers was clearly demonstrated during the Cultural Revolution when they resisted the revolutionary demands of the Maoists and clashed with the Red Guards who sought to disrupt their factories.

The satisfaction of the industrial workers has produced high morale in Chinese factories. Chinese managers maintain reasonably close contact with their laborers, and there is evidence that they pay more than lip service to the Communist ideal that those who engage in manual labor may have constructive ideas about improving production. The fact that all managers and executives must spend one day a week engaging in physical labor may also contribute to a sense of unity among the different factories.

Since the mid-1960's, when the focus of Chinese economic planning shifted from heavy industry to agriculture, public attention to labor has declined but material advantages still remain. The shift, however, has brought to light some fundamental problems, which deal with issues that have plagued the Chinese ever since they sought to modernize.

CENTRALIZATION VERSUS LOCAL AUTONOMY

The first and possibly most fundamental issue for Chinese development has been the question of how centralized China's economy and society can become without great reductions in efficiency. During the 1950's the Communist Party imposed totalitarian controls on the great diversities of China and sought to influence decisions throughout the country. Yet every time the leaders tried to achieve total mobilization they seem to have weakened national unity.

During the first years of Communist government the need for national unity and recognition of the legitimacy of the regime became confused with the belief that centralized direction would accelerate Chinese economic and political development. Foreigners in particular were impressed with the appearance of Chinese monolithic rule and assumed that centralized direction would cause China's economy to develop more rapidly than economies in the rest of the underdeveloped world. Yet during the 1960's the Chinese leaders, particularly Mao Tse-tung, indicated that efforts at strong centralization were creating problems. Most serious were the difficulties of excessive bureaucratization. Centralized control meant domination by officials in Peking who were generally out of touch with local problems and the attitudes of workers. Mao's attack on bureaucracy, which reached its shrillest notes during the Cultural Revolution, was in fact an assault on what had once been considered China's optimal form of development — a highly centralized and rationalized model.

Yet giving power to local authorities would have been tantamount to giving sovereignty to all the various regions of China. Some areas are rich, industrialized, urban, and sophisticated; others are pathetically backward. To do away with the concept of uniformity and standardized growth would be to legitimize gross inequalities. If growth rates were allowed to become dramatically different from region to region, the result would be a challenge to national integration, and in time some parts of the country would probably be exploiting others.

Either freezing the country under a single set of standards, with Peking declaring uniform policies for the whole country, or decentralizing authority might set back national growth. The dilemma of where to concentrate power first appeared during the last days of the Ch'ing dynasty when the Manchu rulers had to deal with the introduction of the railroad and telegraph. It remains a problem in the modernization of China. It has turned up in various guises regardless of the type of regime, ever since the Chinese sought to replace the peculiar balance of the imperial bureaucratic system, in which the pretensions of centralized authority were combined with local accommodations. The dilemma, however, has become particularly acute under communism because it exposes an ideological contradiction. Theoretically communism provides standardized and "scientific" policies for an entire society — that is, it supports centralization. But communism is supposed to be sensitive to the creative spirit of the working class and not dominated by officials — that is, it should support decentralization and local initiatives.

In coping with the question of centralization versus autonomy, the Chinese Communist regime has vacillated. In the early years propaganda stressed centralization, but regional authorities continued to exist. With the Hundred Flowers and the Great Leap, although the appeal was for spontaneity, there was a movement toward greater standardization. In the early 1960's bureaucratization increased, but local officials had more autonomy. During the Cultural Revolution the ideological theme was strongly against centralization, but the destruction of the Party left the political and administrative scene to the mercies of the army, an institution with considerable central direction.

Of all the institutions that have emerged in modern China, the People's Liberation Army comes the closest to balancing centralization and local autonomy. The army gives the appearance of being a standardized organization and it certainly is capable of reacting in defense of the national interest, yet at the same time its regional field armies are remarkably autonomous. The People's Liberation Army may become a model for the civilian institutions of China. In the meantime, however, China's desire for unity and need to recognize local differences will continue to create tensions and divide the leadership.

THE ISSUE OF MATERIAL INCENTIVES

A second basic issue, which emerged from economic policies and has influenced most areas of Communist domestic policy making, has been how far the regime should go in offering material rewards in order to increase the efforts of the people. Chinese communism is ambivalent toward material as opposed to moral rewards. The acceptability of material rewards is implicit in the goal of achieving national power and prestige, both of which will raise standards of living. Chinese Communist propaganda dwells on tales of the bitterness of life before liberation and holds out the confident hope of improved conditions under communism. Whenever the Chinese can claim that they have advanced the material lot of their people, they do not hesitate to publicize the facts, thereby suggesting that people should properly desire to be better off.

But also basic to Maoist ideology is the value of equality in austerity and a belief that only people infected with the evils of bourgeois materialism could want an improved standard of living. According to Maoism, a true Communist is willing to work hard for the glory of Communism with no expectation of personal benefits. Traditionally in China the ultimate sin was selfishness, and therefore the government was not to design policies that would encourage self-betterment of officials. Long before Maoism, both Confucianism and Taoism suggested that spiritual incentives were more honorable than material ones.

These abstract issues of the right and wrong of material incentives have become concrete matters in several fields. In industry the policy of allowing modest material rewards has resulted in urban workers' becoming an elite and conservative element of Communist China. Although their material rewards might seem to be modest when compared with what is expected in other societies, Chinese workers have proved to be extraordinarily responsive to the benefits they have received. Consequently Chinese planners have substantial evidence that material incentives can be extremely useful to the government. Political loyalty and economic performance have directly followed upon the receiving of material rewards. Yet the country does not have enough resources to materially reward all who work hard for the national goals. People must be encouraged to respect self-sacrifice and seek moral or spiritual rewards.

In agriculture the problem of incentives has been more difficult than in industry. Should rewards for production gains be collective? For example, if a unit (a commune, cooperative, brigade, county, a province) increases production by ten percent, should that unit be given a ten percent increase in rewards? Doing so would mean that increases in production would benefit those who caused them, and the regime would be unable to transfer surpluses from one area to another. If, on the other hand, those who increase their production are not proportionately rewarded, they may be less inclined to work harder the next year. The Chinese Communists have been perplexed with the question of where justice lies and what the most desirable policies for dividing the fruits of increased production are. Yet the early successes of the regime in countering food shortages lay precisely in taking from the productive areas to supplement the less well-off ones.

The most acute problem of incentives goes beyond collective rewards to the question of justice in individual returns. The issue became particularly critical during the high point of the communes, when Peking briefly sought to enter a condition of true communism by providing many things, including meals and haircuts, to commune members at no expense and without keeping strict records of who did what work for how much pay. Very soon Chinese peasants enthusiastically sought to get all that they could for nothing and to do the least amount of work possible. The regime had to reestablish a system of work points, whereby individuals were rewarded in proportion to the significance of their contributions. The experience brought out into the open the question of how it is possible to justify differential rewards for different forms of labor. Without any basic market mechanism to demonstrate relative earning powers, it proved to be exceedingly difficult to justify some people's receiving more than others for a particular kind of work.

Above all the regime discovered that in agriculture the principle of material incentives had to be maintained in the form of the private plots of land on which families could raise vegetables, pigs, chickens, and ducks to sell in the open market for their own income. Even during the extreme radicalism of the Cultural Revolution the principle of private plots was not challenged.

The Communists continue to seek to increase production without allowing an increase in consumption. Only by doing this will they be able to gain savings necessary for greater investments in a growing economy. Constantly they appeal to people to be selfless and to accept nonmaterial rewards instead of improved material conditions. Up to a point nationalistic appeals have been effective, but basically the Chinese people are poor and, like peasants throughout the world, suspicious of those who would talk them out of their just rewards.

The Chinese probably will become impatient with postponements of material rewards. During the first years of the revolution they were willing to make personal sacrifices for the collective goals of the revolution, but after two decades the appeal for further sacrifices can produce cynical reactions and a rising suspicion that they are being exploited by the regime. This problem, cast in ideological rhetoric, becomes the question of declining revolutionary spirit, a matter that increasingly haunts Mao.

THE SOCIALIZATION
OF NEW GENERATIONS

Instilling ideological awareness and enthusiasm in new generations is another basic policy issue for the Chinese. Presumably the reason for indoctrinating people in Mao Tse-tung's Thought is to improve their effectiveness in all fields, yet concern over the erosions of revolutionary fervor can make ideological indoctrination an end in itself and not just a means for improving performance. Leaders' concern for maintaining a revolutionary outlook can become counterproductive in the very things that the revolution is supposed to achieve.

A fundamental issue for Chinese communism is the question of whether resources devoted to raising the level of ideological commitment might be more effectively devoted to pragmatic goals. Mobilizing the Chinese public in various campaigns and drives has required huge investments of talent and resources. The best organizational abilities in the country have gone into these mass efforts, but it has not been clear that they have benefited development as much as would the application of the same talent to actual problems. Some of the brightest and most energetically committed people in China have been the propaganda cadres who have directed all their efforts to influencing popular views rather than to carrying out substantial development projects. Yet if the spirit of the revolution disappeared with the succeeding generation, history would judge the Communists failures.

The basic problem, of course, is that national policies in different fields have not been sufficiently successful to convince the leaders that their revolutionary achievements have earned public enthusiasm. Mao in particular continues to believe that special effort must still be made to win people to the correct revolutionary outlook.

Until the Chinese Communist system is substantially institutionalized, people will not be automatically inspired by what is taking place, and special effort to indoctrinate each generation in the revolutionary ethic will continue to be needed. Yet once the system is institutionalized, people are likely to be routinized into supporting ongoing processes. To some, including apparently Mao, this means that they will no longer be truly revolutionary because they will be acting out of habit. From this point of view the success of revolution is likely to be self-defeating if it means that enthusiasm has become routinized. The need for institutionalization and fear of its consequences have been major factors producing the vacillations of the Chinese Communist leaders.

THE PROBLEM OF PRIORITIES

Determining priorities among different objectives, particularly between sectors of the economy such as industry and agriculture, has affected the Communists' policy choices. The essence of policy

MODEL HEROES

The campaigns to raise political awareness and inspire revolutionary order have customarily involved appeals to emulate the personal qualities of specific model heroes. The following are some of the most famous models.

Lei Feng was the first major hero. His most famous exploit occurred when he was working at the Anshan Iron and Steel Works in 1958. He rushed out in the rain with his own clothes, quilt, tarpaulin, etc., to cover up bags of cement that had been left outside. An emulation campaign was carried on by written media, and a color film and even a popular song about Lei Feng appeared. Lei Feng texts were used in teaching students, particularly in primary school. Lei Feng's four ideals were, "Be merciless to your class enemies, be warm as spring toward your comrades, be enthusiastic and conscientious in your work, and sweep away all selfishness."

Ou Yang Hai, a twenty-two-year-old People's Liberation Army squad leader, died when he pushed a horse laden with artillery parts off a railway track out of the path of an oncoming train, thus saving both the train and the lives of his own squad members. This story was more heroic than Lei Feng's and appealed especially to young people.

Wang Chieh, another army hero, threw himself on a faulty mine during an exercise, saving the lives of nearby comrades.

Chiao Yu-lu, Party secretary of Lan Kao county (a very barren area), struggled to increase agricultural output and became a "production hero." He died at the age of forty-two from an incurable liver disease. He was married and had children. This emulation cam-

making in any society is setting of priorities, but the problem has been particularly acute for Chinese Communists because they lack a political process in which conflicting interests can struggle over priorities. Instead of openly acknowledging that different interests may exist not only within the society but among the leaders and that power conflicts must be tolerated, the Communists presume that every problem has a correct ideological solution. Mao has made the point that struggle within the Party is desirable and that certain forms of contradiction will continue to exist even in a classless soci-

paign was aimed at middle-level Party members in the countryside. Chiao Yu-lu was not as great a hero as the former ones. Among young people, though, it was carefully emphasized that his sacrifice was at least equal to those of the army heroes.

The Cultural Revolution produced a new kind of hero (no longer were there production heroes); model soldiers became politically more dynamic. For example, there was Mai Hsien-te, a twenty-one-year-old engine-room technician who received a serious head wound during a fight with "U.S.-made Chiang Kai-shek ships." This story used the appeal of a struggle against an external enemy and transferred it to a domestic context. Red Guards were told to struggle against "ghosts and monsters."

Men Ho, an army hero more mature than Lei Feng (forty years old, married, and with children) and more political, was deputy political commissar of an army unit in the Tibetan minority area of Chinghai province. He died by throwing himself on a homemade rocket. Those whom he saved were carefully described as "class brothers." His story stressed the theme of loyalty to Mao. Men's biography shows him consistently making correct decisions in his attempts to "support the left" and correctly judging which of the Red Guard factions in his area were legitimate. Presumably his story was directed toward middle-level cadres, especially army members, emphasizing that the army should support the "Party center" headed by Mao.

Liu Hsueh-pao was an army hero remarkable because he did not die. He was praised for his courage in "fighting a vicious counter-revolutionary single-handed and risking his life to save a bridge from this saboteur's charge of explosives."

---

ety. His view, however, has to do with his assumptions about the virtues of conflict and the dangers of the revival of bourgeois attitudes in even a fully Socialist society. He has not suggested that elite decision making on priorities might follow the logic of a political process.

Yet conflicts do have to take place, and indeed over the years the vacillations generally have reflected the instability of alliances and coalitions among those struggling to advance their preferred policies. Specific issues of priority have ranged from questions about the extent to which the armed forces should be supplied with modern technology to the balance of investment in industry and agriculture. Under communism when all priority problems become matters of ideology, they tend to be elevated into issues of legitimacy, and it is nearly impossible to treat them as matters of opinion among well meaning men. Those who lose out on questions of priority tend to suffer severely. Often they must be purged from the Party or be reeducated.

The Chinese Communist style of single-mindedly pursuing objectives also makes changing priorities a profound event that can cause reverberations throughout the system. During the years when the Communist leaders, particularly Mao, developed their style of tenacious concentration on particular objectives, such an approach was highly productive because the circumstances called for persistence in the single goal of gaining power. Once the Communists were in power, however, circumstances were altered and more often occasions have required flexibility in priorities rather than rigid commitment.

The difficulty of shifting priorities and the tendency toward single-mindedness have produced a recurring pattern of exaggerated zigzags in policies. Programs soon gain a momentum of their own and go beyond the limits intended by their initiators, and the only way to check the activities is to call for a complete reversal of emphasis.

THE COLLECTIVE PROBLEMS
OF MODERNIZATION

The general problems in Chinese Communist decision making involve far more than just the distinctive qualities of the regime and are inherent in the modernization of Chinese society. Choosing between heavy and light industry, industrial and agricultural investment, would trouble any leaders anxious to speed China's economic development. The problem of centralization versus local autonomy is age old in Chinese dynastic history but would disturb any government trying to introduce modern rule into the diverse Chinese regions. The question of material and moral incentives is common to all poor countries in which there is the hope that nationalism may work to inspire self-sacrifice when resources are insufficient for giving substantial rewards. The task of socializing new generations is also of course a universal problem in countries seeking rapid change.

All these problems quite naturally tend to create conflicting attitudes among leaders who see the specific problems from different perspectives. Quite understandably the problem of priorities has tended to blur into issues of factional strife. To appreciate these problems it is necessary to examine some specific policy areas in detail.

CHAPTER FIFTEEN

The Search for Specific Solutions

Ideology, personality, and the structural problems of decision making have shaped the general trends in Chinese Communism. The clash between factions has been most intense when the problem in dispute is concrete and focused. Agriculture, education, socialization, and military affairs have presented important problems for the future of China. The history of policies in these areas tells much about the causes of conflict among the leaders and the developmental crisis that overtook the Chinese during the Cultural Revolution.

AGRICULTURE:
FROM LAND REFORM TO COMMUNES

China has always been an agrarian country. Through the decades, regardless of industrial advances, about eighty-five percent of the Chinese people have been rural. Therefore government agricultural policy has been important to the well-being of the largest proportion of the population. Although not always appreciated by planners in Peking — especially during the years when Soviet assistance made possible concentration on urban, industrial developments — the basic economic fact of China is that the modernization and growth of its economy depends on the success of its agricultural sector, which produces seventy percent of the country's exports and over half of its gross domestic product.

Even before communism, Chinese farming was more sophisticated and more productive than agriculture in most underdeveloped countries. The Chinese farmer by the middle of the twentieth century had enough skill and knowledge so that quick increases in production could not be readily achieved by routine introductions of scientific information. During the last three hundred years Chinese agricultural production improved its efficiency at a rate consistent with China's population growth. Farmers in the north rotated their crops and used fertilizer, largely in the form of human waste. In short by the time the Communists came to power the Chinese had advanced about as far as they could without radical changes either in technology or in the structural organization of agriculture.

Improved technology calls for heavy capital investment for research, the development of better crops, and the use of more and better fertilizers. Altering the structure of Chinese agriculture — that is, making the units of land more efficient by combining small holdings into larger ones and by increasing the efficiency of the marketing and distribution system — can have only a marginal impact. The Communists have chosen to emphasize the second approach. Their record to date is very uneven. At times their policies nearly produced disaster; at best they have been sufficient only to keep up with population growth, which Chinese agriculture had been doing with no help from national planning. In a few more years the Chinese will have to face the problem of greatly increasing the capitalization of their agriculture. Until now most capitalization has been in irrigation and terracing, a form of investment the Communists have also followed in seeking to reclaim land and expand the acreage in production. Since their break with the Soviet Union, the Chinese have begun to make significant investments in agriculture. For example, at the time of the Soviet termination of aid, China was importing less than one million tons of fertilizer a year, but by 1968 China was purchasing six million tons, and Chou En-lai spoke of the need for thirty to thirty-five million tons of chemical fertilizer by 1975.

Basically, however, Chinese agricultural policy has been similar to Soviet and Eastern European Communist policies of moving from a "land to the tiller" phase toward collectivization. Chinese agricultural policies have been misinterpreted in several ways. There was a widely held view that the Chinese Communists, being closer to the peasants than other Communists, would not be inclined to move toward collectivization but rather would be agrarian reformers. Even when this turned out to be untrue, it was still widely believed that they had moved more slowly toward collectivization than other Communists and had used techniques unknown to the Russians. This view, however, overlooks the policies introduced by the Russians to the Eastern European countries after World War II. The Chinese Communists used precisely the same policies a few years later when they came to power. Thus, although the Chinese did not follow Stalin's policies of the late 1920's, they did follow his views of the late 1940's. In fact a comparison of the number of years taken at each stage of collectivization shows that the Chinese actually moved faster, and, with the communes, further than the Russians did.[1]

	In Russia	In China
Confiscation of landlord properties and redistribution among the peasants	1917–1920	1950–1953
"New Economics Policies" with greater liberties for peasants	1921–1928	No counterpart
Transitional stage with early forms of cooperation	No counterpart	1953–1955
Formation of the kolkhozy or advanced producers cooperatives	1928–1935	1955–1957
Introduction of communes		1958

The significance of the initial stage of land reform was more political than economic. During the period of land reform probably few changes in production level could be related in any way to changes in ownership. The restoration of peace after World War II and the civil war brought an improvement in the distribution system, which gave the country food. Land reform was important, however, in building loyalty to the regime. Those who had been dispossessed were members of the new elite, and their interests lay in supporting the government, even as its policies changed.

Chinese peasants who received land were quite willing to give

[1]Derived from Klaus Mehnest, *Peking and Moscow* (1962), p. 149. Copyright © 1964 by G. P. Putnam and Sons and George Weidenfeld and Nicolson, Ltd.

it up in a few years to the requirements of collectivization — unlike Russian peasants, who, having benefited from confiscation, fought hard to hold on to what they had gotten. The Chinese peasant never developed a strong sense of the legitimacy of the title that came to him through land reform. Although awarded his land by the decisions of people's courts, he generally felt that he was on to a good thing that could not possibly last. Long-time residents of a village recognized the ancestral lands of their neighbors and though willing to benefit from someone else's bad fortune, perhaps did not really believe themselves the legitimate owners of their new property. They were prepared to meekly follow Party dictates calling for the first steps of collectivization. Mao Tse-tung testified to the Chinese peasants' distrust of the confiscation and redistribution of land by government when he described how the farmers in his home district refused to recognize the legality of the Kuomintang's redistribution of his family lands when in 1930 he was declared a "bandit."

During the summer of 1952 the Party began collectivization by introducing mutual aid teams. Peasants retained their land and the produce from it but cooperated with each other during busy periods. The operations of the mutual aid teams were practically identical with age-old traditions in any of the rice-growing areas of China; only in the northern regions were they novel. The important variation on tradition was the introduction of the Communist cadre who helped supervise "cooperation" and adjudicate disputes, which were apparently numerous and generally took the form of debates over whether particular individuals had "cooperated" as much as they should.

Even as the mutual aid teams were being set up, there was pressure from the cadres to move on to the next stage of collectivization — the lower producers cooperatives. According to this arrangement, the equivalent of three or four mutual aid teams were brought together, labor was pooled, and all the land was managed according to government plans. However, the original owners were paid rent for the use of their land, draught animals, and implements. About five percent of the land was left in private plots. In the summer of 1955 all mutual aid teams were brought into lower producers cooperatives. By the following summer the whole country was caught up in the establishment of advanced producers cooperatives, in which all distinctions with respect to previous ownership of land, animals, and tools were obliterated, and payment was made only on the basis of labor.

The advanced producers cooperatives were considerably larger units, involving as many as three hundred households at the level of the total collective. They were, however, subdivided into production brigades, which usually coincided roughly with the earlier lower cooperatives and consisted of twenty to forty households. These were further subdivided into production teams, which generally coincided with the original mutual aid teams and consisted of seven or eight households.

These changes reflect conflicting goals. The tendency toward forming larger and larger units was in response to the goal of greater managing efficiency and consistency. It was easier for the Party leaders to ensure that centralized planning was being implemented if the farm lands were brought together in huge holdings. Problems of marketing, storage, and distribution were also generally eased by using large units. On the other hand, efficiency in raising crops has generally been achieved in China only by moving the decision-making level closer to the group that observes at first hand the right moment to start planting and harvesting. Control and planning were facilitated by large units, while sensitive and correct decisions could be made only by those on the spot. In a strange way the basic problem of organizing agriculture has been a replica of the national dilemma between centralization and local autonomy.

In practice emphasizing the creation of larger units gave the impression of rapid change although development did not accelerate. Whenever production became the most critical consideration, the tendency was to stress the small, intimate group where specialized knowledge of conditions and a sense of solidarity among those who .had to "cooperate" produced better results than management through the larger and more impersonal organization.

This difference was dramatically demonstrated at the next stage of collectivization when in August 1958 the people's communes were introduced. These were massive organizations, covering whole counties and involving generally from five thousand to eight thousand households. In the communes everything was to be planned from above, not just agriculture but also rural industries, schools, and even defense in the form of the commune militia. During the communes' first year or so the regime attempted to control all the means of production, which meant the elimination of the private plots. At the same time, the planners hoped to compensate the peasants for their losses by offering free meals at commune mess halls and other free marginal services. The peasant's reaction was to take as much as he could for nothing while doing as little work as possible in return.

By the spring of 1959 the regime was in retreat. Private plots were restored, and the system of mess halls largely abandoned. The communes were gradually decentralized, so that by 1960 they were really little more than paper organizations. Instead, the production brigades became the accounting units. They kept records of how many work points each member had earned and "paid" him accordingly. Decentralization was carried even further by making the production team — the subdivision of the production brigade — the prime unit of decision making in production matters.

The regime made a firm public commitment to respect the private plots, which, although consisting of only five percent of the land, soon were producing most of the country's meat, vegetables, and fruits. Despite the radicalism of the Cultural Revolution there have been no centrally directed attacks on the private plots, and after the near-famine that followed the extreme commune effort, Mao himself apparently became reconciled to the fact that collectivization in China must fall short of the elimination of private landholdings. During the period when the regime did seek to abolish them, the peasants reacted very much as the Russian kulaks had and slaughtered their pigs and poultry rather than give them over to the commune.

Kenneth R. Walker, after a most detailed study of Chinese agriculture, concluded:

> In the current state of China's political and economic development, a private sector of agriculture, composed mainly of private plots, is a "necessary adjunct to the socialist economy."[2] There are two reasons for this. The first is that the peasants have shown themselves unwilling to surrender all private ownership of land, presumably until they have enough confidence that the collective economy will supply their needs. . . . The second reason is that the

[2]Editorial, "Under the Premise of Prior Development of the Collective Economy Develop Commune Members' Household Subsidiary Industries," *Renmin Ribao* (November 5, 1961).

Government found that a private sector was needed to make up the deficiencies in the public sector. . . . A division of responsibility was, therefore, needed, between the collective and private sectors, the former concentrating on the important food and industrial crops, while the latter produced vegetables and pigs.[3]

After the collapse of agriculture that followed the effort to establish the communes in 1958 and 1959, the countryside gradually was brought back to normal by reinstating former institutions and encouraging the peasants to realize their self-interest. By the early 1960's the regime was talking about "agriculture as the base" for economic development, but the government still had no clear idea about how to modernize agriculture. The effort to open up new lands, particularly in the northwest, is not really a new program and it offers no hope of even making agricultural production keep up with population growth, to say nothing of providing the surpluses necessary for industrialization or raising living standards.

The near-famine conditions of 1960–1962 were a result of mismanagement and natural disasters and caused Peking to take much more seriously its agricultural policies. Massive quantities of wheat were imported. Nearly half of China's foreign exchange earnings from 1962 to 1964 were used to purchase grain, mainly from Canada and Australia.

The population of China is growing at the alarming rate of between 2 percent and 2.5 percent a year. The population of some 750 million will be doubling every thirty-six or, if the higher rate is correct, every twenty-seven years. So far, the regime has not been able to find an agricultural policy that will push production significantly ahead of population growth and provide surpluses for export. Collectivization has not brought about greater efficiency or greater investment in farming. Calculations based on Communist figures suggest that the amount of cultivated land per person declined from about 0.47 acres in 1952 to about 0.41 acres in 1956.[4] Peking's concern over the danger that China's urban population will grow faster than industrial development can provide jobs means that most of the growth of population has been squeezed into the countryside.

[3]Kenneth R. Walker, *Planning in Chinese Agriculture: Socialization and the Private Sector, 1956–1962* (London: Frank Can, 1965), p. 93.

[4]Pi-chao Chen, "The Political Economics of Population Growth," *World Politics*, 23:2 (January 1971), p. 255.

Ultimately the Chinese will have to advance the technology of their agriculture by making massive capital investments in the research necessary to develop new strains of rice and wheat and in the chemical industry for fertilizer production. During the mid-1960's Peking began to make greater investments for agriculture, and by the time of the Cultural Revolution the importation of chemicals and chemical plants for making fertilizers was, next to wheat, China's largest import. In the meantime, however, some of the leaders are hoping that they can substitute human effort for capital investment. Although seeking greater personal exertion, they feel they cannot offer material incentives and hope they can inspire peasants to work harder for fewer rewards by infusing them with ideological commitment to revolution. Yet the effort to instill a greater sense of ideological awareness takes peasants away from their work and reduces their productivity. Also, much of the ideological discussion has made them more rather than less aware of whether they are being treated justly and are receiving appropriate rewards.

With the introduction of the advanced producers cooperatives and even more with the people's communes the peasants have been exposed to questions about the appropriate rewards for different tasks. Historically, peasants simply worked hard and did their best because hard work was their lot and suffering was the nature of life. With the introduction of work points and the principles of egalitarianism they began to ask why some people were paid more than others.

Ever since 1958 there has been a problem of declining incentives in Chinese agriculture. Inexorable population pressure, which is keeping the country poor, is also keeping the peasant working. At the production level the peasants are still concerned with growing enough food to feed their families. Population pressure is bringing into the rural areas large numbers of young people who have been sent to the countryside. These unemployed youth have been educated but because the urban, industrial society has no place for them they are being shipped back to the agricultural sector. The leaders expect that these intelligent, educated, and presumably politically motivated young people will be able to infuse the rural people with a desire to work without material incentives. Such labor is necessary in order to dramatically raise agricultural production.

It is too early to say whether the infusion of youth into the countryside will significantly alter Chinese agriculture or whether it will only produce a generation of frustrated and cynical people resentful of being condemned to farming, when at school they had dreamed of being at the forefront of the modernization of China.

The linkage of Chinese agriculture to problems of overpopulation and educated young people with no careers in the modernized sector of the Chinese economy indicates that China's educational system has problems.

EDUCATION: RED AND EXPERT
OR EQUALITY VERSUS QUALITY

One of Confucianism's most profound influences on Chinese culture was its emphasis on education, which encouraged a vulgarized but strong belief that schooling should be materially rewarding. Even with the lessening of Confucian influence and the introduction of Western knowledge, the Chinese continued to value education. Parents at all levels of society want their children to receive as much schooling as possible.

When the Communists first came to power, they immediately called for the elimination of Western educational practices and the introduction of Russian procedures and textbooks. From the beginning the Communists distrusted "bourgeois" learning and wanted proletarian education. In the early 1950's this meant that students had to display correct political enthusiasm and study ideologically oriented subjects. By May 1957, when Mao Tse-tung initiated the Hundred Flowers Campaign, the leaders were assuming that the Chinese academic and intellectual community had been fully won over to proletarian thinking. Mao believed that if he gave intellectuals freedom to express their inner thoughts and to criticize the regime the results would be constructive. When the criticism turned out to be fundamental and divisive, Mao turned on the educational establishment and gave vent to deep-seated anti-intellectual sentiments. He stressed the need for educating only the proper "revolutionary classes" and rejecting bourgeois education.

Politically the outcome of the Hundred Flowers Campaign shocked Mao and reinforced his distrust of intellectuals; it also signaled the emergence of dilemmas that have dominated educational policy in Communist China. The solution of them has on occasion nearly destroyed the entire Chinese educational system.

There have been three major issues: first, a belief that there is an inherent conflict or tradeoff between political loyalty in the form of ideological commitment and technical competence and intellectual skills; second, awareness that academic selection and competition tend to work against the lower classes, which are supposed to be benefiting from the revolution; third, a serious problem of inadequate opportunities for getting an education and finding appropriate employment after leaving school.

The intellectuals' challenge to the government, which surfaced during the Hundred Flowers Campaign, also illuminated what the Communists call the "red and expert" problem. In China as in all other Communist countries, increasing intellectual sophistication produces "revisionism" because the scientific mode of thinking is not consistent with ideological indoctrination. Students and researchers busy with their intellectual work find the Party study sessions in ideology tedious and a waste of time. Most Party officials have far less schooling than the intellectuals. Party cadres who are not intellectuals have felt that the students and university communities have lost touch with the workers and peasants and are trying to become an isolated elite much as the Confucian mandarin class once was. The Party view has been that people should strive to be equally "red" (that is, ideologically committed) and "expert" (that is, technically skilled). It is hoped that intellectuals striving to be both will not become vulnerable to anti-Party views.

Professors at one point tried to argue that the more expert a person became the less time he had to give to "redness." Such an approach would concentrate ideological training in the early years and in the least specialized fields, while those working in complex areas, such as developing the atomic bomb and working in advanced physics and engineering, would not have to participate in endless meetings about the Thoughts of Mao Tse-tung.

The leaders in Peking were unlikely to sanction such a position because the colleges and universities were populated almost entirely by people without worker or peasant backgrounds. However, the Party bureaucrats were willing to reduce the ideological demands on China's scientists because they appreciated these men's contributions to the development of weapon systems and industry. In terms of announced policies, however, the Party has continued to stress the primacy of politics and the need not only for extensive indoctrination programs but also for the education of students of the proper classes.

A frustrating irony for the Communists was that until 1966 the longer they had been in power the greater had become the predominance of children from bourgeois backgrounds in colleges and universities. The explanation for this odd fact is that competition for places in China's limited higher education establishments has become intense. Population growth has run far ahead of college expansion, and the children from culturally disadvantaged families, from rural and working-class families, lose out to those from families with a tradition of educational involvement. Leaders, like Mao, with strong equalitarian feelings have been disturbed by the failure of a Communist educational system to help the children of peasants and workers get ahead.

The Communists are also beset by the choice between quality education for modernization and mass education for equality. Limited resources have ruled out both expansion in quality higher education and general education for all children. Early in the planning process the central government took over responsibilities for higher and technical education, leaving primary and secondary education to local authorities. This decision widened the gulf between the two, with the universities focusing on research and the advanced skills necessary for economic development, while the local authorities lacked the funds to provide effective primary schooling.

The central government was not unconcerned about primary education in the rural areas; it has just lacked the resources to do much about it. In fact, in the realm of policy guidance, one of Peking's proudest formulations was the concept of the "part-work, part-study" schools, which were supposed to capture Mao's ideal of combining practical and academic work. In practice the concept allowed rural areas without professional teachers to believe that they were providing appropriate and even progressive education for their children by allowing them to attend part-time, informal one-room schoolhouses while also working in the fields during the busy periods.

The easy mobility that had always existed in China, making it possible for ambitious and bright rural children, such as Mao Tse-tung and numerous other Communist leaders, to leave home to attend inexpensive boarding schools, largely disappeared under Communist rule. Peasant children who received primary education in the new rural setting generally were not able to get examination scores qualifying them to enter the urban secondary schools.

From 1955 to 1958 expansion of primary schools in China was considerable, but the quality of instruction did not keep up with it. More children were getting some education, but fewer rural children were getting schooling good enough to allow them to continue in the more competitive secondary schools. During the Great Leap twenty-two million more students were "enrolled" in primary schools. But all these schools were supported by the local communes, and when agricultural disaster struck, most of them disappeared.

During the 1960's the trend was back in the direction of favoring quality education. For over four years, from 1960 to 1964, almost no new schools were constructed in China, even though population growth was increasing the number of school-age children.

As a consequence of the vacillation between school expansion and school contraction and of the continuing and unrelenting population pressure, truly disturbing problems began to confront the Peking leaders. On the one side, growth in the number of potential students and the limited number of openings were creating deep disappointment and frustration among those not able to continue their schooling for as long as they wanted. Yet by 1962 the universities and secondary schools were beginning to produce more graduates than the sluggish Chinese economy could absorb. Students who had expected that they would be working in the historic reconstruction of their country discovered, after the Tenth Plenum of October 1962, that they were going to be caught up in the Go to the Countryside Campaign (*Shan-san Hsia-hsiang Yun-tung*). This campaign was another effort of the regime to de-urbanize China. By sending millions of energetic and ambitious young people into the countryside, the leaders hoped to revive the backward parts of China. The practice only increased students' restlessness.

All these problems created a feeling among authorities and students that little was right either with the educational system or with the employment prospects for intellectuals. The stage was thus set for the Cultural Revolution and for Mao's massive attack on the bourgeois character of the educational system. By 1965 Mao could argue that none of the major objectives of education that he had sought in 1949 had been realized. His goals had been to educate the masses, to combine practical and theoretical work and eliminate bookish and abstract knowledge, and to put politics in command of knowledge. During the Cultural Revolution extensive criticism from Mao's point of view was made of the educational system. It was charged that the system discriminated against children from poor families because the examinations and the methods of grading favored the culturally advantaged. It was also argued that Mao's desire for practical education had been violated by teachers stressing scholarship and abstract knowledge.

The Cultural Revolution closed down the entire Chinese educational system, and from 1966 until the fall of 1970 there was complete paralysis. When the country began to emerge from the Cultural Revolution, one of the last areas to regain order was education, because the basic problems still had not been resolved. Changes introduced by the Cultural Revolution tend to favor the equalitarian and anti-intellectual predispositions of Mao. Time will tell whether they will greatly damage China's prospects for economic development.

The present educational system has been severely abbreviated and given a much narrower focus. In the past the Chinese system involved six years of primary school, three years of junior middle school, and three years of middle school before four years of college — essentially the same system as in America. Now primary and junior middle school have been merged into six years. There are no examinations and the emphasis is on elementary skills of reading, writing, and arithmetic, with a heavy dose of political instruction. In the urban areas less than half of those in the new schools can expect to go on to what is to be two years of high school, or senior middle school. In the rural areas even fewer can expect to continue. At this next stage emphasis is on practical work on farms and in factories and on raising ideological understanding. Because schools will continue to be locally financed, there will be great differences in quality.

The universities are experiencing the most radical changes. Entry to higher education is no longer to be by examination. Instead, students will be selected by the masses, which means by the people of the community in which they live and work. They must also be approved by the local authorities. Political qualifications have replaced scholarly merit. Thus when Peking National University opened after the Cultural Revolution in the fall of 1970, ninety percent of the twenty-five hundred new students came from poor families of workers and peasants, and the remainder were children of cadres, that is Party, army, and government officials. The political strain in making selections has apparently already raised suspicions that various forms of corruption will determine who gets into college.

The new curriculum calls for only two or at the most three years of work. The emphasis is on rather narrow technical subjects. The universities themselves are supposed to become directly involved in applied economic and technological affairs, instead of research laboratories, and creativity is supposed to be carried to the point of full production and manufacturing for distribution. The idea that universities should be primarily technical institutions and should blend into the realm of the factory is matched by the idea that factories should establish schools and colleges. Students in such factory-colleges receive on the job training and attend classes where they are taught technical and political subjects. At present it is thought that such educational innovation will more successfully achieve Mao's goal of breaking down the distinction between practical and theoretical knowledge than earlier part-work, part-study schools. In fact, the phrase "part work, part study" has been denounced because it implies a distinction between the two that should be obliterated.

It is too early to judge the durability of these innovations, but past experiences suggest that the Chinese have not yet found a satisfactory approach to their massive education problems. The problems are not just those of economics, population growth, and tension between quality and quantity and between universal scientific knowledge and political indoctrination. They combine with problems of social policy, cultural heritage, and the desire to bring about changes in basic Chinese values.

SOCIAL POLICY: CHANGING VALUES AND IDENTITIES

Economic development, agriculture, and education present problems for any government, not just one that seeks to radically and rapidly change China. Social problems are in some respects more amenable to change, although in this area the Communists are so ambitious that many question whether their goals lie within the realm of the possible.

The Communists have been most successful as social revolutionaries. Peking's rulers would unquestionably have achieved greater success in other areas, particularly with economic policies, if they had not generally placed the highest value on social and revolutionary change. Much of the reason for the costliness of the leaders' approach to other problems can be understood by recognizing their commitment to the creation of a socialistic and eventually a communistic society.

To a degree the Chinese Communists' drive for fundamental social and cultural change coincided with historical trends in the modernization of Chinese society. The decaying of the old institutions, the weakening of family bonds, and the declining vitality of religion and traditional morals had long been taking place in China. Change was accelerated by the war and Japanese occupation. Therefore the Communists up to a point could harness the momentum of history.

Social change must have a particular character, yet there was nothing inevitable about the specific forms, emphases, and policies that the Communists chose. Indeed, in most of their social and cultural policies the Communists were not merely responding to basic social changes but were initiating their own preferred changes.

Appropriately, the Communist assault on the old social order began with the family, the primary social unit of traditional China. The marriage law was the first major law passed when the Communists came to power. Even before land reform began, the Party initiated its campaign against the feudal status of women. The law itself was consistent with the trends in China. It abolished parent-planned marriages, set the age of consent at twenty for boys and eighteen for girls, decreed economic and political equality for women, and gave women the right of divorce.

In letter and spirit little was revolutionary in the law. Even the Chinese Nationalists had passed laws directed toward free choice in marriage and the abolition of concubinage. What was revolutionary was the Communist campaigns to spread the word about the law and their efforts to implement it. During 1950 and 1951 cadres organized endless meetings that frequently called for confrontation between wives and husbands as wives were urged to denounce their husbands for their feudal attitudes. There was a steep rise in divorce rates. There was also an almost equally spectacular rise in suicides as wives reacted to the humiliation of what they had done to their husbands in the emotionally charged atmosphere of the cadre-organized meetings.

Yet, in spite of the overzealousness of the cadres, the marriage law and the campaign supporting it were to change significantly the Chinese family. The subordination of women lessened, and the power of the family was greatly reduced. The authority of the father, which had once been almost absolute, was drastically weakened, and children gained independence. As part of the attack on the family tradition children were urged to correct their parents' behavior and to report misdeeds to the authorities. The objective was the establishment of a new morality in which traditional family obligations would be replaced by Party loyalty. Young people were expected to help bring into being a society in which their basic identity would be determined by peer and political associations rather than by family.

In seeking to create a new society, the Party's assault on traditional sentiments soon reached beyond family relationships. The Chinese had always deeply valued personal friendships and the loyalty that goes with personal association. The Communists attacked such sentiments as "feudal" and called for a new spirit of public obligation and impersonal comradeship. The spirit of the dedicated revolutionary, which was supposed to inspire the Party, was declared to be the ideal for all society.

The new social ethic was proclaimed to be especially binding to youth. Students were instructed to eschew individual fulfillment and dedicate themselves to selfless service to Party and country. In place of special friendships, everyone was expected to treat everyone else as a comrade. Romance and personal affection were declared to be vile bourgeois attitudes. Boys and girls were to work together without personal feeling. By the mid-1950's it was widely assumed abroad that the new ethic was taking hold, partly because drabness pervaded the country, with boys and girls dressing alike in blue cotton clothes.

During the first years of the regime the champions of the new ethic seemed to be Liu Shao-ch'i and the other Party organization leaders. They were tireless in their efforts to make both the Party and the larger Chinese society models of revolutionary virtue. During these early years Mao appeared to be more relaxed and tolerant than the fanatically dedicated Party workers. It was Liu and the Party officials who urged the Chinese to admire above all the activist Party cadre who humorlessly and unrelentingly strove to be a revolutionary hero. But after the "Hundred Flowers" Campaign Mao became increasingly concerned with whether the Chinese people were adequately committed to the new ethic. His concern was heightened by the Great Leap effort when he, more than the Party administrators, took up the belief that human commitment could triumph over all else. By the time the Cultural Revolution was beginning to take shape, Mao was the unqualified champion of the powers of the new morality. Liu Shao-ch'i and the regular Party bureaucrats were less inspired by the spiritual aspects of the revolution.

The contrast between the new morality and the discredited feudal morality of traditional China is part of the larger problem of how a revolutionary Communist regime, seeking to revive Chinese national power, should treat the cultural traditions of ancient China. Since the beginning of the twentieth century, Chinese intellectuals have been perplexed over how to reconcile their national traditions with their commitment to modern science and technology. During the Yenan period Mao Tse-tung began to deal with the question of how a revolutionary movement striving to bring about the new world of socialism should treat the history of a great civilization. The Communists' initial approach to the problem, which they called that of China's "cultural legacy," was to make a sharp but rather arbitrary distinction between the feudal aristocratic culture of the oppressive ruling classes and the popular democratic culture of the common people. By this formula the Party could denounce the higher culture of China, its art, literature, philosophy, and above all its Confucian ideals of the amateur gentleman, and stress folk culture. During the first years of the regime, peasant folk dancing and woodcuts were treated as the essence of traditional Chinese culture, and the major art forms of landscape painting and classical opera were labeled "feudal."

By the mid-1950's more and more of the cultural legacy was

gradually being accepted. Peking opera was again popularized, and new themes were presented in the old opera forms. Mao Tse-tung himself repeatedly revealed his personal liking for traditional poetry and produced numerous verses in the old forms. Since feudalism was presumed dead, it was possible to use old forms without fear that doing so would encourage the revival of old social views. The Hundred Flowers period was the high point of tolerance for the old. Communist intellectuals freely talked about "developing the new out of the old" (t'ui-ch'en ch'u-hsin).

With the anti-rightist movement that followed the Hundred Flowers, and particularly with the Great Leap, tolerance for the cultural legacy sharply declined. During the height of the Great Leap there was no place for cultural purists, and all who valued the old had to suppress their interests. During the bleak years of economic depression and slow revival in the early 1960's, cultural interests gradually reemerged, possibly as an escape from the intolerable present. In any case, the Party, particularly Mao, became suspicious that the revival of features of the cultural legacy was working against revolutionary sentiments.

The cultural legacy issue became one of the triggering elements of the Cultural Revolution. It is significant that this upheaval, which rocked the Communist system to its foundation, is called by the Communists a "cultural" revolution. Culture, for the Chinese Communists, comprises the basic orientations of a society. Indeed, Mao was disturbed that the new revolutionary ethic was not taking hold.

At a more immediate level the Cultural Revolution was initiated by a clash over an apparently cultural matter. In November 1965 a relatively obscure Shanghai critic, Yao Wen-yüan, attacked the historian and playwright Wu Han for his new play, The Dismissal of Hai Jui. The charge was that it displayed feudal and bourgeois influences because it told of an official in the Soochow area in 1569 to 1570 who was dismissed from office because he showed sympathy and understanding for the lot of the peasants. Wu Han was denounced for suggesting that class differences did not matter and for upholding bourgeois ideals of humanitarianism and "loving the people." The Party stated that such ideals have no place in a proletarian society in which the true class interests of the workers are respected and the illusion that class lines can be overcome by mere goodwill is rejected. Moreover, Wu Han's references to the past were considered a cover for criticism of the present. When he made the sympathetic figure of Hai Jui support the policy of returning land to the peasants, he was really suggesting the worth of private plots of land, thereby condemning Mao's communes and policies of total collectivization. Sophisticated Chinese audiences were expected to see Hai Jui as symbolizing P'eng Te-huai, whom Mao had dismissed for criticizing his commune policies. Because Wu Han was a leading Communist writer, he presumably had the support of some powerful figures in the Party — he was seen as a protegé of P'eng Chen, the mayor of Peking.

In the spring of 1966 China's cultural establishment was shaken by further exposés and charges that historical forms were being used to criticize Mao's revolutionary ideals. Teng T'o, a secretary of the Party's Peking branch and close associate of P'eng Chen, Politburo member as well as mayor of Peking, was charged with veiling profoundly counterrevolutionary ideas in his newspaper column "Evening Talks at Yenshan," in which he had followed an almost Confucian style of relaxed and judicious observation about the human condition. Teng T'o was also linked with Wu Han and a third literary figure, Liao Mo-sha, in vicious attacks upon their "Three Family Village" essays, which had conveyed a greater sense of humanity and less devotion to class struggle than the dedicated Maoists would accept.

As the Cultural Revolution finally proved, the Communists' not inconsiderable performance in social policies and in changing human attitudes has not brought satisfaction to Peking's rulers, particularly Mao, who still see a gap between their revolutionary ideals and the realities of Chinese society.

The Red Guards took it upon themselves to destroy irreplaceable cultural and artistic works and to violate museums and art collections. Yet clearly the Chinese will not be able to end the problem of their cultural legacy so easily. Ironically Madam Mao Tse-tung, Chiang Ch'ing, during the height of the Cultural Revolution advanced the strange thesis that the piano was a cleansing agent. She reasoned that if Peking operas used piano music rather than traditional Chinese instruments the feudal and bourgeois elements of opera would be eliminated. Even in such a strange formulation the old would live and haunt the builders of a new world.

MILITARY AFFAIRS:
THE ARMY AS MODEL FOR SOCIETY

The Communists came to power out of a civil war, and in the first years of the regime administration was through the army structure. The Korean war provided the Chinese Communist army not only with a major challenge but also with the opportunity to become fully modernized with Soviet assistance. During the Korean war the People's Liberation Army was transformed from a guerrilla force into a conventional force with modern equipment and firepower.

With this transformation came major issues that have in some ways continued to plague the Chinese leadership. The basic division was between military leaders who welcomed the modernization and technological transformation of the army and those who felt that guerrilla traditions were more appropriate in a poor country committed to a social revolution. Those favoring modernization wanted close association with the Soviet Union, the development of airpower, and increased mechanization of all forces. Their views on organization and doctrine represented professionalism and sensitivity to international military trends. Other Chinese leaders continued to see the army in terms of its nonmilitary functions and wanted to increase its ability to help the country with the tasks of economic development. In the views of these officials the army was more important as a domestic institution than as a security force.

The clash was somewhat muted during much of the first decade of the regime, partly because of the existence of the Public Security Forces and the militia, which met many of the domestic objectives of the second group of leaders. With each year in power the Communists expanded the size of the militia until in 1958 during the Great Leap and in conjunction with the establishment of the communes the Party launched the Everyone a Soldier Movement. This drive was supposed to help prepare the country for any danger of international war — a danger heightened by the Quemoy and Matsu crisis of 1958. However, the drive was also apparently inspired by the belief that the heroic ideals of soldiering and the experience of military drill are beneficial in creating the revolutionary ethic and spreading enthusiasm.

The trend against professionalization of the People's Liberation

Army was intensified in 1958 when Mao denounced an attempt to establish "bourgeois military thinking" in the Chinese army. The following year Defense Minister P'eng Te-huai, who had been a hero in the war with Japan and the civil war, was purged from office, probably because his concerns for maintaining the professional character of the army brought him into conflict with Mao Tse-tung. P'eng apparently opposed Mao's policy of pursuing the ideological split with the Soviet Union. A military man, P'eng argued that China needed modern supplies and equipment, which were obtainable only from the Soviet Union. In August 1959 the military affairs commission "thoroughly settled accounts" with P'eng Te-huai and Lin Piao replaced him.

Lin Piao's emphasis was on "giving prominence to politics" and raising the ideological level of the army. In this approach he was fully in accord with Mao's views that "men are more important than materials." In supporting Mao's slogan "human factor first," Lin Piao pushed indoctrination and created a set of model heroes for emulation not only by all the soldiers but by the entire Chinese population. Professional officers accepted parts of Lin Piao's program because they improved discipline and dedication, but they continued to worry about what China would be able to do if invaded. Some, like P'eng Te-huai, thought security considerations called for greater caution in any ideological challenge to the Soviet Union.

During the period after the Great Leap when the Chinese economy was in a state of severe depression and agriculture was experiencing three consecutive years of crop failure, morale in the army was also down. In part the problem reflected the fact that the Chinese army was still a peasant army, and the men were mirroring the attitudes and moods of the civilian population. But the problem was also one of continuing uncertainty about strategic doctrine. The idea of people's war was not only repugnant to men just beginning to dream of China as at last having a modern military force but it also seemed to offer little hope for victory in case of a major war. Lin Piao and his associates, however, developed a counterargument that tried to put a military touch to Mao's requirements:

> In accordance with our situation, if there is a war within three to five years, we will have to rely on hand weapons. As to how to defeat the enemy with hand weapons, Chief Lin [Piao] has found a way, and it has to do with the question of distant war or close

war. Distant war means to fight at a distance of several tens, several hundred, or even several thousand kilometres. Close war means to fight at a distance between several metres and two hundred metres, or face to face. The enemy is stronger than we are in a distant war, but short distance fighting, and especially face to face fighting, is where our strength lies. We have to avoid the strengths and take advantage of the weaknesses of our enemy. In face to face fighting there can only be used hand grenades, bayonets, or flamethrowers. We have to use close fighting, night fighting, or trench warfare to defeat the enemy. . . . In the event of war within the next few years we can defeat the enemy by using close combat although we have no special weapons.[5]

Ironically, just as Chinese military doctrine was moving in the direction of discounting technology, Chinese scientists on October 16, 1964, detonated China's first nuclear device. China was in the strange position of being a nuclear power with an underequipped guerrilla force. Although the Chinese sought to gain whatever prestige they could from their nuclear success, they recognized that one bomb did not change basic power realities. Mao and Lin continued their pressure to use the army for its nonmilitary dimension and above all to hold it up as a model for other institutions in the society. They gave added weight to the Learn from the People's Liberation Army Movement. All organizations and individuals, especially Party cadres, were expected to regard the army as a means of solving all problems.

In the fall of 1965, Lo Jui-ch'ing, army chief of staff, was purged, apparently because he continued to doubt the effectiveness of the old Yenan guerrilla methods for the defense of China. The American escalation in Viet Nam was the immediate issue of the purge. Lo Jui-ch'ing favored a conventional buildup and the repairing of relations with the Soviet Union so that military assistance would be assured if the Americans invaded. Mao and Lin advocated a people's war strategy based on political mobilization, a withdrawal into a defensive and essentially guerrilla posture, and the avoidance of a massive military confrontation with any foreign enemies.

The elimination of Lo Jui-ch'ing compromised the position of Party pragmatists and technicians who also wanted to restore better

[5]Yeh Chien-ying, speech at Military Affairs Committee Conference on Training, January 1961, in *Kung-tso T'ung-hsun* (February 20, 1961).

relations with the Soviet Union, not just in case of war but because they felt that Soviet aid was essential for any significant industrial and economic development. The issue within the army between technology and the human will, between technical and scientific competence, and political mobilization and dedication divided the entire Communist leadership and set the stage for the Cultural Revolution.

CONVERGING THEMES

By the late 1960's, in one policy area after another, fundamental problems were beginning to arise. They had certain common dimensions, and men, probably equally dedicated to rebuilding Chinese power and glory, became more and more consistent in their approaches to them. No single issue was enough to divide men who had gone through so much together, but cumulatively the differences were enough to create lines for deeper and more personal divisions.

Some men, whether the problems were in agriculture, industrial development, education, social mobilization, or military policy, tended to stress rational and technical considerations, believed that skill and knowledge mattered and that power and efficiency were essential in strong, disciplined organizations. Others were inclined to believe that China's problems of development could be overcome only by political dedication, spiritual selflessness, and the initiative of all individuals working spontaneously together.

The leading spokesman for the latter view was, of course, Mao Tse-tung, who, not deeply enmeshed in administrative responsibilities, had been devoting himself to questions of history and ideology and to contemplating what had gone wrong with the Soviet Union. As his disagreements with Soviet policies under Khrushchev intensified, his statements about revolutionary spirit became more shrill. Domestically Mao was irritated at the prospect of technicians and specialists dictating all policies. He felt obligated to speak out against the idea that a lifetime of revolutionary effort should be reduced to no more than allowing economists and engineers to run affairs and to waiting for compound interest to bring about the accretions of power and wealth that would finally add up to China's destiny of renewed greatness. In his mind this would be no different from development under a nonrevolutionary system, for to Mao the sciences of the economist and of the engineer were bourgeois. His mood became one of impatiently wanting to assault all targets with massive outpourings of human effort and discarding the cautious advice of those who sought incremental development. The stage was set for the drama of the Cultural Revolution.

SLOGANS AND PHRASES

The Chinese Communists' ideological instruction emphasizes slogans and catch phrases. Chinese language facilitates the use of pithy statements, and catch phrases are useful in providing political instruction to a largely rural population that at best has had only a few years of schooling. Slogans are used freely at all times but particularly during campaigns and drives such as the Cultural Revolution. Just to read these slogans is to capture the spirit of Chinese communism through its catechisms.

"Class line" *(Chieh-chi-lu-hsien)*.

Party policy must be carried out according to orthodox division of classes. For example, in organizing, agricultural cooperatives and communes should rely on poor and lower middle class peasants and should unite middle class peasants and oppose rich peasants.

"Contending and blooming" *(Ming-fang)*.

This is a shortened version of, "Let a hundred schools of thought contend, let a hundred flowers bloom."

"Contradictions" *(Mao-tun)*.

Contradictions among the people are reconcilable; contradictions between the enemy and the people are irreconcilable.

"Unity-criticism-unity" *(Tuan-chieh-p'i-p'ing-tuan-chieh)*.

This is the Communist method of conducting ideological struggles within the ranks of the Party.

"Walking on two legs" *(Liang-t'iao-t'ui-tsou-lu)*.

The reference is to the policy of using modern and primitive methods of production at the same time, as in backyard steel production.

"Firstly poor, secondly blank" *(I-ch'ung-erh-pai)*.

This refers to China, which is economically underdeveloped but, like blank paper, "well-suited for writing the newest pictures" (a saying by Mao Tse-tung).

"Give prominence to politics" (T'u-ch'u-cheng-chih).

This means that "politics is primary; it is the soul, the commander."

"Left deviationists" (Tso-ch'ing-fen-tzu).

Those who are too radical are so called.

"Right deviationists" (Yu-ch'ing-fen-tzu).

Those who are too conservative are so called.

"Lay grip on production" (Chua-sheng-ch'an).

Pay close attention to production.

"Grasp revolution and promote production" (Chua-ke-ming, ch'u-sheng-ch'an).

This slogan was prominent in late 1966 when the Cultural Revolution was extended to involve factories and the countryside.

"Monsters and ghosts" (Niu-kuei-she-shen).

People to be attacked during the Cultural Revolution were so called.

"Learn and apply with vigor" (Huo-hsueh-huo-yung).

Learn Mao's ideology or the People's Liberation Army's political and ideological work from various angles in order to lay a firm grip on its essential spirit, apply it to each individual case in practice.

"March to mountainous areas" (Hsiang-shan-ch'u-chin-chun).

In 1957 this slogan was used to persuade people to reclaim wasteland.

"Slight the enemy strategically; take full account of him tactically" (Chan-lioh-shang-miao-shih-ti-jen; chan-shu-shang-chung-shih-ti-jen).

This slogan was used as guerrilla warfare theory and in speaking of difficulties that come up in daily work.

"Paper tiger" (Chih-lao-hu).

Meaning any person who is fierce outwardly but weak inwardly, this phrase was used by Mao to refer to U.S. imperialism and reactionaries.

"East wind prevails over west wind" (Tung-feng-ya-tao-si-feng).

This statement was first used by Mao in 1957 to say that Communist forces were growing stronger than those of Western countries.

"Remember bitterness and think of sweetness" (I-k'u-szu-t'ien).

Remember past sufferings and think of what the Party has done to relieve them.

"Regard agriculture as the main factor and let subsidiary production nurture agriculture" (I-nung-wei-chu; i-fu-yang-nung).

Use subsidiary production of vegetables, pigs, and fowl to accumulate capital for development of main agricultural grain production.

"Turn the table over" (Fan-shen).

This slogan was used extensively during early Communist years to signify that workers and peasants had turned the tables on the capitalists.

"Traverse the passes" (Kuo-kuan).

The "passes" include the political pass, family pass, livelihood pass, the pass of conceit.

"Hold the pass" (Pa-kuan).

To win a battle against bourgeois ideology takes vigor, but to guard it demands constant and unremitting vigilance.

"Capitalist roaders" (Tsou-tzu-p'ai).

Followers of Liu Shao'ch'i were so called. The phrase was used during the Cultural Revolution.

"Apparently obedient, but inwardly defiant" (Yang-feng-yin-wei).

This is an old Chinese four-character phrase used during the Mao study movement of the Cultural Revolution in somewhat the same sense as "waving the red flag to oppose the red flag."

"Bourgeois reactionary line" (Tzu-ch'an-chieh-chi-fan-tung-lu-hsien).

Liu was criticized for following this line.

"Hit hard at many to protect a handful" (Ta-chi-i-ta-p'ai; pao-hu-i-hsiao-ts'o).

Reactionary leaning cadres during the Cultural Revolution, using slogans that seem leftist but are in fact rightist, have incited the masses to attack cadres indiscriminately in order to protect their own group.

"Independent Kingdom" (Tu-li-wang-kuo).

Any official who runs an area according to his own will and for his own interests, disregarding the central government, is accused of having an "independent kingdom."

"Poisonous weeds" (Tu-tsao).

This phrase was used in 1957 to describe writings that did not conform to Mao Tse-tung's thought.

"Rectification campaign" (Cheng-feng-yun-tung).

First tried in 1942, rectification uses criticism and self-criticism to purify Party members' working style and ideological viewpoint.

"Barefoot doctors" *(Ch'ih-chiao-i-sheng)*.

Young people of poor and lower middle peasant classes who receive elementary medical training and practice in the countryside are so called.

Not surprisingly a considerable number of slogans refer to red and uphold redness as an ultimate virtue. The following is a brief sample of such slogans.

"Becoming 'red' naturally" *(Tzu-ran-hung)*.

Many young workers and peasants in China think that they do not have to go through ideological reform to become "red" because they have grown up under communism. Communists say this is wrong.

"Hoist a red flag" *(Ch'a-hung-ch'i)*.

Hoisting a red flag to salute a certain group is a form of praise for advanced achievement.

"Red flag unit" *(Hung-ch'i-dan-wei)*.

Often used in emulation drives, this phrase refers to a production team of a commune or a workshop of a factory that achieves a better output than others.

"Red and expert" *(Hung-yu-chuan)*.

"Red" means politically reliable; "expert" means trained in some branch of knowledge.

"Red successors" *(Hung-se-chieh-pan-jen)*.

Children, "young pioneers" in particular, are so called.

"Waving the red flag to oppose the red flag" *(Ta-che-hung-ch'i-fan-hung-ch'i)*.

This phrase was used by the Mao-Lin group in the Cultural Revolution to describe tactics used by their opponents who, while actually working against Mao, pretended they were on his side.

"Red Guards" *(Hung-wei-ping)*.

These were the guards, mainly students, organized during the Cultural Revolution to overthrow "those in power who follow the capitalist road" and "to destroy the four olds."

"Three reds" *(San-hung)*.

This phrase refers to the "proletarian headquarters," the People's Liberation Army, and the Revolutionary Committees.

"Red sentries" *(Hung-shao-ping)*.

These were teams to promote Mao Tse-tung and fight against his ideological enemies in factories and enterprises.

NUMBERS IN SLOGANS

A striking characteristic of the Chinese Communists' slogans is their use of numbers. Much of Communist ideological instruction involves memorizing various numerical quantities of ideological significance.

One

"One guides two" (I-tai-erh).

One advanced production team should lead two backward teams in production and turn them into advanced teams. In this way the whole commune will eventually be made up of advanced teams.

"Divide one into two" (I-fen-wei-erh).

This refers to the Marxist method of dialectical analysis. One must look at the positive and negative aspects of a person or work; good features and defects must be considered. The struggle of one against the other brings progress in a person and uninterrupted development in work.

"With one assisting another, a couple will become 'red' " (I-pang-i, i-tui-hung).

The underlying idea is for the progressive to help the backward, so that everybody will be progressive. "Red" signifies political stability and reliability.

"One red heart; two preparations" (I-k'o-hung-hsin; liang-chung-chun-pei).

This phrase is used to persuade students to stand ready either to enter a higher school or go to the country and become farm laborers.

"Get to the bottom by one pole" (I-kan-tsu-ch'a-tao-ti).

In tackling problems or making investigations, one should go straight to the depths to arrive at fundamental solutions or find out conditions.

"One specialty and many abilities" (I-chuan-to-neng).

An ordinary worker is expected to specialize in one line of work but also be able to do several other jobs.

"One tenth of one cent" (I-li-chien).

In production any material worth a fraction of one cent should be saved. The so-called I-li-chien spirit has been promoted in connection with the campaign for increasing production and practicing economy.

"One struggle, two criticisms, and three reformations" *(I-tou, erh-p'i, san-kai).*

The purposes of the Cultural Revolution, as determined by the Party's Central Committee on August 6, 1966, were to struggle and bring down power-holders traveling the road of capitalism, criticize reactionary academic authorities and the bourgeoisie, criticize the ideologies of the bourgeoisie and all the exploiting classes, reform education, reform literature, and reform all the upper structures that do not harmonize with the socialist economic foundation.

Two

"Struggle between two roads" *(Liang-t'iao-tao-lu-ti-tou-cheng).*

The two roads are capitalism and socialism. This phrase was used frequently during the Anti-Rightist Campaign in 1957.

Three

"Three antis" *(San-fan).*

In early 1952 a campaign was started to stop corruption, waste, and bureaucracy among Communist Party and government officials.

"Three-anti, double-reductions" *(San-fan-shuang-chien).*

Anti-rebellion, anti-corvée, anti-slavery, reduction in land rent, and reduction in rate of interest — these were to improve conditions of Tibetans after suppression of the 1960 rebellion.

"Three big mountains" *(San-tso-ta-shan).*

According to Mao, imperialism, feudalism, and bureaucratic capitalism had oppressed the Chinese people like mountains.

"Revolutionize the three" *(San-ke-ming-hua).*

Put a revolutionary spirit into enterprises, government groups, and people in order to achieve greater progress.

"Three changes" *(San-hua).*

During formation of communes the changes were militarization of the organization, combat readiness and collectivization of life.

"Three combined" *(San-chieh-ho).*

The three are the leading cadres, experts, and the masses. The leading cadres should provide political guidance and authority, the experts provide technical know-how; and the masses use their collective wisdom and determination to carry out the innovation.

"Three comparisons" *(San-tui-pi).*

Peasants should compare the present with the past, good and

bad features of present-day life, and the socialism of today with the promise of full communism in the future.

"Reckon three accounts" *(Suan-san-chang)*.

Peasants and workers are urged to consider their political, economic, and cultural progress.

"Three-eight working style" *(San-pa-tso-feng)*.

This is a reference to the three phrases and eight characters written by Mao to describe the working style that officers and men should adopt. The three phrases are correct political direction (capitalist or socialist), a simple and arduous working style, and flexible strategy and tactics. The eight characters are for the words unite *(t'ung-chieh)*, tense *(chin-chang)*, stern *(yen-suan)*, and lively *(huo-p'o)*.

"Three elders" *(San-lao)*.

The young generation should learn from the experiences of elderly poor peasants, elderly Party members, and elderly cadres.

"Three fixes and one substitution" *(San-ting-i-ting)*.

Cadres should report for work at fixed hours, labor for a fixed length of time each day, assume fixed responsibilities toward production and take fixed posts in a productive force. They should also learn to be able to do the jobs of the regular workers in order to become qualified to take their places.

"Three participations and one improvement" *(San-ts'an-i-kai)*.

To improve the operation and management of commercial enterprises, cadres should take part in physical labor, workers and staff in administration, and the masses in supervision.

"Three freedoms and one contract" *(San-tzu-i-pao)*.

The three freedoms are the extension of plots of land for private production, free markets, and increase of private enterprises. One contract means allowing each household to assume contractual obligation to the state for producing a fixed quantity of grain.

"Three reconciliations and one reduction" *(San-ho-i-shao)*.

Used by Chou En-lai in 1964, the phrase refers to the 1959–1962 period, in which there was a demand to make peace with the imperialists, with reactionaries, and with modern revisionists and to reduce aid to other peoples in their revolts.

"Three great viewpoints" *(San-ta-kuan-tien)*.

These are political viewpoint, production viewpoint, and mass viewpoint.

"Three histories" *(San-shih)*.

For peasants, this refers to histories of families, villages, and communes. For workers it refers to histories of families, factories (mines), and revolutionary struggles. Writing these three histories reveals how poor peasants and workers suffered before liberation.

"Three no-fear spirit" *(San-pu-p'a-ching-shen).*

Athletic trainees should not fear hardship, fatigue, or injury.

"Three 'passing' concepts" *(San-kuo-szu-hsiang).*

Intellectuals working on science and technology have advocated taking a passive attitude toward politics, acquiring excellent professional skills, and living comfortable lives. These three concepts are wrong.

"Three red flags" *(San-mien-hung-ch'i).*

The red flag is a symbol of victory. Three red flags represent the general line for socialist construction, the big leap forward, and the people's commune.

"Three summer, three autumn" *(San-hsia, san-ch'iu).*

The reference is to summer harvesting, planting, and hoeing and autumn harvesting, ploughing, and sowing.

"Support three things and carry out two military tasks" *(San-chih-erh-chün).*

After the People's Liberation Army was called on to intervene in the Cultural Revolution in January 1967, it was told to support the leftist masses, industry, and agriculture. The army was also supposed to exercise control over every phase of the people's life and to carry out military training for the Red Guards.

"Three anti-elements" *(San-fan-fen-tzu).*

The reference is to Liu Shao-ch'i and his followers, who are anti-Party, anti-Mao Tse-tung thought, and anti-socialism.

"Three calamities" *(San-hai).*

Factionalism, anarchism, and economism are said to be weapons used by Liu Shao-ch'i to obstruct the work of the revolutionary committees.

"Three capitulations and one abolition" *(San-hsiang-i-mieh).*

This phrase sums up crimes committed by Liu in foreign affairs and has the same meaning as "Three reconciliations and one reduction."

"Three check-ups campaign" *(San-ch'a-yun-tung).*

The campaign is to check up on diehard capitalist roaders, renegades, spies, unreformed landlords, rich peasants, counter-revolutionaries, bad elements and rightists, and to eliminate them all.

"Three emptying and four no-retaining" *(San-kuang, szu-bu-liu).*

This slogan says that Liu encouraged peasants in the communes to divide up everything, eat up everything, and use up everything; to reserve no commune fund, no welfare fund, no food grain, and no production fund. These evils were fought with the Combat Selfishness and Repudiate Revisionism Campaign.

"Three-family village" (San-chia-ts'un).

This was the column title of a series of articles jointly written by Wu Han, Teng T'o, and Liao Mo-sha, published in *Front Line Magazine*, Peking. It was criticized at the opening of the Cultural Revolution as anti-Party and anti-socialist.

"Three loyalties movement" (San-chung-yü-yun-tung).

This movement launched in spring 1968 urged the masses and the People's Liberation Army to be forever loyal to Chairman Mao, Mao Tse-tung's thought, and Chairman Mao's revolutionary line.

"Three main tasks" (San-ta-jen-wu).

The tasks are to grasp revolution, promote production, and promote the preparation for war.

"Three much-read articles" (Lao-san-p'ien).

These articles were written by Mao before 1949: "Serve the People" (1944) "In memory of Norman Bethune" (1939), and "Old Man Yu Kung Removed the Mountains" (1945).

"Three old cadres" (San-lao-kan-pu).

Old and sick cadres, old and good cadres, and old cadres over the age of sixty — these cadres, being old and not of high prestige, are regarded as harmless and are to be included in the great revolutionary alliance and the three-way alliance.

"Three recollections and three comparisons" (San-i-san-pi).

Peasants should remember the bitterness of the old society and contrast it to the sweetness of the new society, remember the nurture and education given them by the Party and compare these with their own contribution to the Party, remember the crimes committed by the power-holders and compare them with the tremendous achievements of the Cultural Revolution.

"Three-way alliance" (San-chieh-ho).

Revolutionary mass organizations, leading members of local People's Liberation Army units, and revolutionary leading cadres of Party and government organizations should join together in setting up provincial revolutionary committees.

Four

"Four category (bad) elements" (Szu-lei-fen-tzu).

These are landlord's, rich peasants, reactionaries, and local bad people, referred to in abbreviated form as *ti, fu, fan,* and *huai.*

"Four firsts" *(Szu-ke-ti-i)*.

Lin Piao first said at October 1960 military affairs committee meeting, "Human factor is first, political work first, ideological work first, and living idea first."

"Four fixes" *(Szu-ku-ting)*.

Land, manpower, draught cattle and farm implements assigned to production teams should be permanently used by them.

"Four-good company" *(Szu-hao-lien-tui)*.

The reference is to companies of soldiers good in political ideology, in three-eight working style, in military training, and in management of the living conditions of men.

"Four modernizations" *(Szu-hsien-tai-hua)*.

Agriculture, industry, national defense, and science and technology should be modernized.

"Four transformations" *(Szu-hua)*.

They are agricultural mechanization, electrification, spread of irrigation, and fully using chemical fertilizers.

"Four pests" *(Szu-hai)*.

They are flies, mosquitoes, rats, and bedbugs. The last category was originally sparrows.

"Four the-sames" *(Szu-ke-i-yang)*.

Factory workers and personnel should do their work in the same way whether by night or day, whether in fine or bad weather, whether with or without supervision, whether their work is examined or not.

"Four togethers" *(Szu-tung)*.

Cadres sent to farms or factories are not to remain aloof from farmers or workers. They must eat together, live together, toil together, and consult together.

"Four do-nots" *(Szu-pu)*.

During the Cultural Revolution, people were asked not to say or do anything, hold any meeting, put forth any slogan or big character poster unfavorable to the formation of the great Revolutionary alliance.

"Four 'Everything' " *(Szu-ke-i-ch'ieh)*.

Think of Chairman Mao in everything, obey Chairman Mao in everything. Follow closely Chairman Mao in everything. Everything for Chairman Mao. These were guiding principles of Men Ho, an emulation hero who sacrificed his life to save others.

"Four Great" *(Szu-ta)*.

There are four methods to carry out the "struggle by reasoning"

— great contending, great blooming, big character posters, and great debate.

"Four great freedoms" *(Szu-ta-tzu-yu)*.

This slogan, alleged to have been advanced by Liu Shao-ch'i during the land reform period, refers to freedom to engage in usury, hire labor, sell land, and run private enterprises.

"To destroy the four olds" *(P'o-szu-chiu)*.

The mission of the Red Guards is to destroy old thought, old culture, old custom, and old habits.

Five

"Five factors into one body — quintuplicity" *(Wu-wei-yi-t'i)*.

Used when communes were first established, this slogan describes the combination of agriculture, industry, commerce, education, and military affairs.

"Five-good soldiers" *(Wu-hao-chan-shih)*.

Soldiers should be good in political ideology, military techniques, the three-eight working style, carrying out assigned tasks, physical training.

"Five-good woman" *(Wu-hao-fu-nü)*.

A woman is considered good when she maintains good relations with her neighbors, keeps her family in good health, is good at cleaning, helps her family live well, and is good in studies.

"Five guarantees" *(Wu-pao)*.

Food, clothing, fuel, children's education, and funeral services are guaranteed to members of higher agricultural cooperatives. These guarantees are supposed to remain valid for commune members.

"Five loves" *(Wu-ai)*.

They are love for motherland, the people, labor, science, and public property.

"Five years to try it; ten years to popularize it" *(Wu-nien-shih-yen, shih-nien-tui-kuang)*.

This slogan, devised in December 1965, refers to the cautious introduction of the half-work and half-study education program.

"Do five things in each other's company" *(Wu-t'ung)*.

In carrying out educational revolution (during the Cultural Revolution) teachers should do five things together with students: study, combat, military drill, labor, and recreation.

"The five-men group" *(Wu-jen-hsiao-tsu)*.

The group, formed in late 1965 and later dissolved because of errors during the Cultural Revolution, consisted of P'eng Chen, Lu Ting-i, Lo Jui-ching, Yang Shang-k'un, and K'ang Sheng.

"Old five articles" *(Lao-wu-p'ien).*

These are the "three much-read articles" plus "On the rectification of Erroneous Thought in the Party" and "To Oppose Liberalism." The two added articles were chosen for the Red Guards to read after "combat selfishness and repudiate revisionism" was launched in October 1967.

(Compiled by Alison Huey.)

CHAPTER SIXTEEN

The Great Proletarian Cultural Revolution

One of the most extraordinary events in Chinese history, indeed in the history of any nation, was the Great Proletarian Cultural Revolution, which tore China apart during 1966 and 1969. The oddity of the Cultural Revolution lay not just in the bizarre conduct of an aging leader calling upon millions of young people to engage in a children's crusade but also in the fact that Mao was seeking to destroy the Party, presumably the most valued object in his political life. The Cultural Revolution brought together madness and reason in a peculiar blend of idealism and sly calculation.

UNCERTAIN TRENDS

The Cultural Revolution can be thought of as the product of a variety of men acting to resolve their differences about how best to deal with intractable historical problems. We cannot be sure about exactly what happened or why. The Cultural Revolution defies full explanation, and many interpretations of it are possible. Some scholars have seen it as an ideologically inspired event in which those who shared a Maoist vision set out to destroy all who did not. Others have treated the Cultural Revolution as a power struggle over succession to Mao's leadership. The truth no doubt is that the Cultural Revolution is a blend of ideological and power considerations, but in what proportions and in what forms it is impossible to say.

The Chinese Communist craving for secrecy has meant that

the inner facts of the Cultural Revolution are obscure, though the effects are dramatically obvious. All the world was able to see that the Chinese were in turmoil. The most central and vital institution of their political system, the Communist Party, was decimated, and the image of China as a model for developing countries was shattered by what seemed to be a fit of madness.

Unquestionably the Cultural Revolution altered the history of Chinese communism, for it compromised the mystique of authority of the Chinese leaders. Whether it accomplished any constructive objectives is still questionable. If Mao's interest was to urge a more rapid pace for domestic and economic development, he failed. The Cultural Revolution damaged Chinese progress, and it may take several years to make up for the losses of the upheaval. If Mao's objective was to raise the level of ideological commitment, he may also have failed. It is likely that instead of making the Chinese, particularly the younger generation, more radical and dedicated to the vision of a new society, the experience of the Cultural Revolution encouraged cynicism. Those who had been most enthusiastic found themselves in the most dismal situations; idealistic youths were called upon to follow the lot of the peasant and accept the isolation of rural China. Finally the Cultural Revolution ended in military rule and a foreign policy that included an invitation to President Nixon to visit Peking and Chinese support for the military rulers of Pakistan in their suppression of the Bangladesh movement in East Pakistan — hardly idealistic or revolutionary policies.

The one unquestionable consequence of the Cultural Revolution was the elevation to power of the military. The People's Liberation Army was put in charge of managing China. In this respect the ultimate charismatic act of Mao Tse-tung has been little different in its effects from that of most of the lesser charismatic leaders of other Afro-Asian states, men such as Sukarno and Nkrumah, who in their turn were succeeded by military rule. The only difference is that Mao is still at least formally in charge; the others were pushed aside. Perhaps an iron law of political development holds that military predominance is a likely outcome of all attempts by charismatic leaders to press the mystique of revolution beyond the pace that the society is prepared to accept. In China the acceptance of the ruling role of the army has been modified by a continuing purging of the top military leadership after the termination of the open turmoil of the Cultural Revolution.

Why did the Cultural Revolution occur? There is no definitive answer. The range of acceptable accounts reaches from the one extreme that Mao was driven by his radical, revolutionary vision to the other extreme that Mao, desperately fighting elements that were about to push him aside, had to unleash all his political forces even if he would achieve no more than a Pyrrhic victory.

The first interpretation suggests that Mao and his followers believed that the failure of the Hundred Flowers Campaign and Great Leap was caused by the ideological and spiritual weakness of those who represented Chinese communism. They did not acknowledge that anything could be wrong with their policies but rather insisted that those promulgating them lacked ideological commitment. The policy problems of the regime and the disappointing performance of the Party made these true believers feel that eventual success simply required renewed dedication and increased moral commitment.

Equally plausible, however, is the interpretation that Mao and his wife Chiang Ch'ing sensed that they were being disregarded and that real power was gravitating into other hands. According to this view, the fact that Mao was following the traditional Chinese imperial pattern of confusing ruling and reigning meant that they had not been in full control of events and by trying to intervene had created great tensions. As a reigning figure he had allowed others to manage affairs, yet when Mao tried to rule again he seemed as arbitrary as any Chinese emperor. Communist ideology and Party discipline were not designed to cope with Mao's vacillations. Any shift from reigning to ruling was interpreted as a direct challenge to those who had been ruling while Mao reigned.

The range of interpretations of the causes of the Cultural Revolution is matched by differing judgments of its consequences. Some observers insist that the Cultural Revolution strengthened Communist China by eliminating people with bureaucratic tendencies and elevating those of radical spirit. By destroying cadres who were careerists, elitists, and prone to revisionism, Mao was able, according to this view, to revitalize the Chinese revolution. Others feel that the Cultural Revolution was at best interrupting for a few years

Chinese progress and at worst setting the country back several decades and destroying one or maybe two generations of committed revolutionaries.

At present it is possible only to identify the various themes and currents that have emerged as contributing causes of the Cultural Revolution and to identify some of its main events. We must be careful not to overemphasize any particular cause or motive, and we must also recognize that in such a complex historical episode events frequently run ahead of planning and in a fundamental sense no one is in charge.

THE CONVERGENCE OF POLICY ISSUES AND THE DIVERGENCE OF LEADERS

Foreign analysts of China generally agree that by 1963 the country was beginning to move ahead. The economy had to a large extent recovered from the disruptions of the Great Leap and from the subsequent years of depression. Orderly advances were being made on several fronts. Within the Chinese ruling circles these developments were the cause of tensions rather than satisfaction. Some of the leaders were pleased by progress from disciplined action, guided by specialized and technical knowledge. Others, particularly Mao Tse-tung, were offended by such progress. Mao's view was that the Communist revolutionary vision was debased and made irrelevant if the consequence of revolution was merely to allow technicians and economists to dictate national policy. If progress depended on rational economic policies, how did China differ from other developing countries also being guided by the logic of engineers and economists, by technocrats and scientific specialists? Mao felt that China had to return to the spirit that had inspired the Great Leap.

In Mao's opinion the Great Leap had failed not because it was poorly planned and did not make sense but because those who directed it and participated in it lacked revolutionary ardor. What was needed was a higher degree of commitment. At the Lushan Conference of July 1959, when decisions were taken that eased the commune movement and slowed the Great Leap, Mao passionately defended his policies against the charge of reckless impatience: "In regard to speed, Marx also committed many errors. He hoped every day for the advent of the European revolution, but it did not come. . . . It was only by the time of Lenin that it came finally. Wasn't this impetuousness? Wasn't this bourgeois fanaticism?"[1] Mao, in making his plea, which apparently failed to move the conference, indicated his own frustration and helplessness by referring to the fact that he would have no posterity. (One son had been killed in battle and the other had been declared insane.) He also indicated his determination to fight back, in the spirit of the guerrilla days, with the help of the People's Liberation Army. At Lushan, having made the point that only in bourgeois nations do newspapers act so foolishly as to publish bad news, he said:

> Suppose we do ten things, and nine of them are bad and are published in the newspapers. Then we are bound to perish, and should perish. In that event, I would go to the countryside to lead the peasants to overthrow the government. If the Liberation Army won't follow me, I will then find the Red Army. I think the Liberation Army will follow me.[2]

As a consequence of Mao's efforts at Lushan his influence increased and there was a brief revival of the Great Leap during the fall of 1959. Yet by the next year Mao's influence had again declined. The fluctuations in Mao's authority, apparent in 1958 and 1959, foreshadowed the Cultural Revolution and revealed the fact that tensions within the leadership extended beyond domestic issues to include military affairs and foreign policy. At the Lushan Conference P'eng Te-huai criticized the commune policy. He charged that it was demoralizing the soldiers who had close peasant ties and went on to point out that the country was weakening itself through its isolation from the Soviet Union. The linkage of domestic and foreign policy helped to sharpen the lines of disagreement among the different factions of the Chinese leadership. P'eng, however, was fighting against determined Maoist opposition, for Mao not only wanted to defend his commune policies but felt strongly about the folly and revolutionary evils of closer associations with the revisionist Soviet Union.

[1]"Speech at the Lushan Conference," *Chinese Law and Government*, 1:9 (Winter 1968–1969), p. 42.
[2]*Ibid.*, p. 35.

During the brief upsurge of Mao's influence at Lushan he was able to have P'eng Te-huai purged from command of the army and replaced by Lin Piao; General Lo Jui-ch'ing became the new chief of staff. The concepts of the "human wave assault" on the economy, the superiority of willpower to technical expertness, and nearly total collectivization of agriculture were thus joined with Lin's view that military policy should depend on people armed and prepared for guerrilla warfare, rather than on a modernized and professional force. The combination of these attitudes became increasingly the views of Mao and his immediate associates.

Early in the 1960's the tensions among the leaders seemed to have lessened. After Mao had relinquished the ceremonial office of the chairman of the People's Republic, he disappeared for several months and the Party and state bureaucracies appeared to be managing domestic affairs with reasonable competence. During the Cultural Revolution it was revealed that Mao felt at the time he had been pushed aside. He claimed that Liu Shao-chi and Teng Hsiao-p'ing had treated him after 1958 like "one of their parents whose funeral was taking place." During this period Mao was engaged in polemics with the Soviet Union. He probably devoted less attention to domestic matters because he was so absorbed with his almost personal conflict with Khrushchev.

The tempo of the Sino-Soviet controversy, which had begun slowly after the death of Stalin in 1953, picked up momentum after Khrushchev's dramatic attack on the memory of Stalin at the Twentieth Congress of the Soviet Communist Party. The clash radically intensified in the spring of 1958 when the Soviets criticized the Great Leap, refused to support China in the offshore islands confrontation with the United States, and finally supported India in its border controversies with China. By 1959 the controversy had reached the point of no return, and Mao was convinced that Khrushchev was China's mortal enemy. Not only had he refused to give China aid, he also was undermining the very spirit of communism by seeking détente with the United States and encouraging revisionism at home.

In Mao's polemics, particularly in his Ninth Comment, entitled "On Khrushchev's Phoney Communism and Its Historical Lessons for the World," he began to reveal clearly and coherently a set of attitudes on domestic and foreign affairs that may be characterized as the ideological basis of the Cultural Revolution. He showed his great concern with maintaining and transmitting to the next generation the spirit of true revolution:

> The question of training successors . . . is one of whether or not there will be people who can carry on the Marxist-Leninist revolutionary cause started by the older generation of proletarian revolutionaries . . . whether or not we can successfully prevent the emergence of Khrushchevite revisionism in China . . . a matter of life and death for our Party and our country.[3]

Organizationally the stage was set for the Cultural Revolution at the Tenth Plenum, in the fall of 1962, when Mao pointed out that there had not been a mass campaign since 1958 and that a renewal of class struggle was needed. The result of the plenum was the Socialist Education Campaign of 1963, aimed at rural cadres, who were generally the best-educated members of village society and hence quite often the sons of "rich" rather than "poor" peasants.

Because the propaganda ministry found it difficult to reach the rural population, by 1964 they had to devise a new approach — the Learn from the People's Liberation Army Movement. The result of this effort was the introduction of political departments into most civilian agencies — and considerable confusion over the division of authority. Most civilian agencies already had a dual hierarchy of administrative-bureaucratic officials and the parallel Party arrangement. In addition they were to bring in the equivalents of the army's political commissars.

Confusion between administrative controls and ideological education increased tension and a sense of the inadequacy of the intellectual leadership of all groups. The Maoist response was to declare that publicists and writers, who set the intellectual and ideological tone for the entire society, had been lax and had fallen into the misguided ways of revisionism. They were accused of being concerned more with technical questions than with ideological dedication.

As Mao became increasingly obsessed with revisionism, he saw more signs of it at home, and in foreign affairs even imperialism seemed less menacing. In 1964 as the Viet Nam war intensified, there was in China considerable concern about war with the United

---

[3]"On Khrushchev's Phoney Communism and Its Historical Lessons for the World," in William E. Griffith, *Sino-Soviet Relations, 1964–1965* (Cambridge: M.I.T. Press, 1967), p. 349.

States. Some army leaders began to feel again the need to reduce tensions with the Soviet Union in order to gain material assistance if war broke out. In the ensuing debate on military affairs Chief of Staff Lo Jui-ch'ing took practically the same position that P'eng Te-huai had taken in 1959. The point at issue was whether the Communist states should prepare to unite in support of North Viet Nam. America's decision to bomb North Viet Nam and to commit major forces to the war forced the Chinese leaders into an intense debate in which foreign policy, particularly the balancing of American against Soviet dangers, merged with domestic issues. In taking a stand on these pivotal questions, the various factions tested their power, and the scene was set for the Cultural Revolution.

On the eve of the Cultural Revolution there were four major groupings among the Chinese leaders. First were Mao and the "court" that surrounded him and ceaselessly eulogized him, idolizing his every word and deed. The small inner group consisted mainly of ideologues and propagandists who stressed "uninterrupted revolution," "red over expert," and the need for a politically conscious "nation in arms." The key figures were Mao's wife Chiang Ch'ing, who felt that she had been denied proper recognition and had a deep grudge against Liu Shao-ch'i's wife; Ch'en Po-ta, a long-time personal secretary of Mao and the drafter of many of his works; and K'ang Sheng, a shadowy figure long close to Mao but never holding a separate command.

The second group consisted of the leaders of the Party apparatus who were strong Leninists and believed in hard-headed and pragmatic policies for national development. They accepted the cult of Mao's personality because it posed no threat to them and was useful in mobilizing the Chinese people, but they distrusted Mao's romantic style. The most important members of this group were Liu Shao-ch'i and Teng Hsiao-p'ing. (During the Cultural Revolution Liu would be called "the top Party person in authority taking the capitalist road" and "China's Khruschev.")

The third group was made up of government officials, particularly Chou En-lai, who were administratively oriented. This group seemed to have much in common with the pragmatic Party apparatus men, but when the conflict became intense Chou chose to support Mao. The decision may have been influenced by personal considerations and by Chou's long-recognized propensity to side with the winner in any controversy. Chou may have recognized that he and his administrators would be essential to the Maoists if they won because the Maoists lacked managerial talent. The Liu-Teng faction would have less need for Chou's talents because of the administrators supporting it.

The fourth group, which was divided into two factions, was the military. Lin Piao led those who accepted a national strategy based on low-level technology and strong ideological motivation. Increasingly during the course of the Cultural Revolution this group identified with the Maoists, but eventually, when the army was called in to actively help them, the military leaders tended to be concerned more with order than with revolutionary ardor. The other military faction was that of Lo Jui-ch'ing, whose commitment to technology and better relations with the Soviet Union made him an ally of the civilian Liu-Teng faction.

In early 1965 Lo Jui-ch'ing spoke out very sharply against the United States and by implication called for better relations with the Soviet Union. Teng Hsiao-p'ing also urged a limited rapprochement with the Soviet Union, for economic and political reasons. He went so far as to say that the rapid modernization of the Chinese economy required aid from the advanced Communist countries. Initially it was not the Maoists who responded to these comments. P'eng Chen, mayor of Peking and a Politburo member, bitterly denounced any suggestion of unity of action with the Soviet Union to help North Viet Nam. His thesis, later to be Lin Piao's, was that wars of national liberation call for self-reliance. In short, China should not cooperate with the evil forces of revision even to oppose imperialism, and China should allow others to fight their guerrilla wars without becoming directly involved. In September 1965 Lin Piao issued "Long Live the Victory of People's War," a pronouncement that people's wars should be fought throughout the underdeveloped areas in opposition to Western influences but that self-reliance was required by the guerrillas and not extensive Chinese aid.

Late in September 1965 Mao began to press his case for a cultural revolution at a meeting of the standing committee of the Politburo. The outcome of the debate was inconclusive, but a group of five was formed to supervise an intensification of ideological training. P'eng Chen was made chairman of the group, which also included K'ang Sheng, Wu Leng-hsi (editor of the *People's Daily*), Lu Ting-yi (head of the Party's propaganda bureau), and Chou Yang (a Party specialist in dealing with intellectuals).

Hardly had the group of five been designated when Mao began to show his distrust of its members, apparently believing that they were not as loyal to or enthusiastic about his ideological commitment to uninterrupted revolution as they should be. This revealed the extent to which Mao's approach was subjective and somewhat fearful. He repeatedly suspected people who professed their loyalty to him.

At this juncture Mao began his move to attack all who he believed opposed him. In November 1965 Lo Jui-ch'ing disappeared from public view, and in February 1966 it was announced that he had been arrested. Also in November Mao left Peking for Shanghai, where he had the newspaper *Wen Hui Pao* publish "The Dismissal of Hai Jui," an attack on an opera of the same name by Wu Han, a close supporter of P'eng Chen. Thus the direct attack on Wu Han for his presumed esoteric defense of the purged P'eng Te-huai was also an attack on P'eng Chen and his "independent kingdom" in Peking. P'eng Chen was the member of the Politburo most directly responsible for cultural and ideological education, but Mao was increasingly disturbed that he was too permissive toward writers. P'eng Chen was also a quasi-military figure, in command of the Peking garrison. The combination of his strategic location and his blend of ideological and military roles made him a potential power in the Party.

Why Mao Tse-tung left Peking and went to Shanghai and Hangchow to launch the opening diatribes of the Cultural Revolution is unclear. Presumably he knew he could command the support of the radical Shanghai branch of the Party, and there is evidence that he had trouble persuading the editor of Peking's *People's Daily* to publish his statements. Also, there was the matter of military force. Apparently during the winter there were significant troop movements around Peking; it was later claimed in Red Guard publications that in February 1966 P'eng Chen had attempted a coup. Mao later claimed that Peking was "already under P'eng Chen's complete control" and that he had no room even "to put in a needle."[4]

---

[4]Quoted in Gene T. Hsiao, "The Background and Development of the Proletarian Cultural Revolution," *Asian Survey*, 7:6 (June 1967), p. 397.

On the surface the conflict was confined to questions of cultural and propaganda affairs, but behind the scenes fundamental struggles were taking place. In April 1966 Chou En-lai associated himself with Mao's demands for a fierce and protracted struggle to wipe out "bourgeois ideology in the academic, educational, and journalistic field, in art, literature, and all other fields of culture." In May, Teng T'o, a member of the Central Secretariat of the Party in Peking, was viciously denounced, and later so was Liao Mo-sha, another high official in Peking. It became clear that P'eng Chen could not defend his subordinates. By June the heads of most of the major universities and other academic institutions were purged. P'eng was specifically charged with failing to carry forward with appropriate vigor the Socialist Education Campaign and for sympathizing with the prejudices of intellectuals.

While these attacks in the cultural and educational fields were taking place and distinguished Chinese officials were being denounced for bourgeois leanings, Liu Shao-ch'i, who was soon to become the principal target of the Cultural Revolution, made a goodwill visit to Pakistan and Burma. China's prestige in Asia had seriously deteriorated since the failure of a Communist coup attempt in Indonesia and the removal of Sukarno from office in late 1965. A case might therefore have been made for a state visit by the Chinese chairman of the People's Republic to strengthen Chinese influence. The effect of Liu's absence from Peking for two weeks was to greatly weaken the anti-Maoist forces.

By May 1966 Mao felt confident enough to return to Peking and in the name of the Central Committee declare the official opening of the Great Proletarian Cultural Revolution. P'eng Chen was ousted, and on June 1 the Maoists took over the *People's Daily*. Although Chou En-lai was out of the country on a trip to Albania, he threw his prestige behind the concept of a Cultural Revolution. Even Teng Hsiao-p'ing made a militant speech for Mao (he was later to be charged, as were many other reluctant radicals, of "waving the red flag to oppose the red flag" — that is, an apparently pro-Maoist act being declared inspired by an enemy simulating revolutionary dedication). T'ao Chu, secretary of the Central-South Region based at Canton, was moved to Peking to take charge of the propaganda apparatus, only to be purged later for being insufficiently radical.

On the surface the cult of Mao's personality seemed to be all-

The Actors in the Cultural Revolution

	Mao Tse-tung	Liu Shao-ch'i Teng Hsiao-p'ing	Chou En-lai	Lin Piao	Lo Jui-ch'ing	P'eng Chen
Power Position Resource	Propaganda; personal stature; and legitimacy	Party bureaucracy	State administration and personal stature	Party organization in the army	Professional military	Party personnel
Constituency	Disgruntled youth; Shanghai	Most of established party cadres; factory workers	Most established administration officials	Guerrilla-minded military; Manchuria; and Central-South	Military	Party bureaucracy; Peking
Basic orientation	Anti-revisionist; revolutionary ideal	Pro-technology; professionalism; strong organization and class leadership	Pragmatic; not worried about the West; distrusts Party bureaucracy	Political military leader; pro-militia; champion of guerrilla warfare	Professional soldier; technologically oriented; feared both U.S. and U.S.S.R. threats	Sought to straddle both party and bureaucracy, and military and civilian organizations
Tactical coalitions	Temporary coalition with P'eng leading to a coalition with Lin	Coalition with Lo	Maneuvering coalition with Mao	Coalition with Mao	Coalition with Liu and Teng	Ready to be opportunist

Policy Issues						
Collectivization, farm organization, and incentive policy	Moral incentives; not disturbed by 1958 failure of Great Leap; faith in communism	Recognized failure of 1958; favored material incentives	Recognized failure of 1958; but accepted importance of moral incentives	Favored moral incentives and saw the value of communes for militia	Not salient; but concerned about morale of soldiers with rural backgrounds	Recognized failure of 1958; favored material incentives
Institutional structure	Nonspecialized, nonregularized, guerrilla-type	Specialized, regularized, functional system	Specialized, regularized, functional system	Guerrilla-type army	Technologically based army	Specialized, regularized, functional system
Mass and elite revolution education propaganda	Hostile to established privileged cadres	Accepted Mao cult; but detached, and valued professional skills	Accepts Mao cult; taking advantage of it to make rule easier	Red army as model for society	Expert army	Accepted Mao cult; took advantage of it, but protected critics of Mao cult
Economic policy and industrialization	Agriculture dominant	Industry dominant	Balanced growth	Less reliance on industry	Heavy industry	Balanced growth
Defense and foreign policy	Anti-U.S.S.R.; ready for tacit agreement with U.S.	Tactical rapprochement with U.S.S.R.; used preparation for possible war with U.S. to strengthen technicians	Tactical rapprochement with U.S.S.R.; but also strongly anti-U.S.S.R.	Anti-U.S.S.R.; tacit agreement with U.S.	Most ready to accept rapprochement with U.S.S.R.	Most anti-U.S.S.R. and accepted rapprochement with U.S.
Order of Being Purged		3		4	1	2

☐ Stands for salient to actor

pervasive. Everywhere he was being extolled, and the power of his Thoughts was associated with all manner of achievements, from the raising of better watermelons to the winning of table tennis matches. Mao contributed to this frenzy by carrying out what was supposed to have been a spectacular nine-mile swim down the Yangtze River in world record time.

Yet in most of the country Mao had not been able to dislodge the forces of Liu and Teng from the Party bureaucracies. The removal of P'eng Chen had started the process of purges at the top level of the Party, but Mao had to move also against the great bulk of the Party professionals. To do this he sought out extremely unlikely allies — the young people and the students of high school age. Initially his theme had been that the propaganda ministry had to ensure that the next generation would be imbued with proletarian revolutionary ardor so that China could avoid revisionism. As the power struggle intensified, he saw youth as a source of power for attacking the entrenched Party officials.

THE EMERGENCE OF THE RED GUARDS

No aspect of the Cultural Revolution was quite so colorful, chaotic, or bizarre as the Red Guards. Millions of high school age students poured over the land, shouting down distinguished leaders, destroying precious art objects, and extolling puritan virtues. The movement spanned two symbolic acts of Mao Tse-tung. On August 18, 1966, at the first rally of nearly half a million ecstatic students in Peking he accepted a red armband from a Red Guard. Two years later, on August 5, 1968, he dramatized the end of his sympathy for youth by presenting a "treasured gift" of mangoes to a group of industrial workers who represented the first Worker-Peasant Mao Tse-tung Thought Propaganda Team and had been active in opposing all the conflicting Red Guard factions at Ch'inghua University. The first gesture demonstrated that Mao personally backed the Red Guards and that students throughout the country ought to emulate them. The second gesture showed that Mao's patience with the antics of the Red Guards was exhausted and that he believed that the working class must exercise leadership over all.

When the Cultural Revolution began with the attacks on Wu

Han and his play, *The Dismissal of Hai Jui,* there was no indication that students might be particularly involved in the controversy. However, a central committee circular on May 16, 1966, alerted the students that more than cultural matters might be dividing the nation's leadership:

> The present struggle centers around the issue of implementation or resistance to Comrade Mao Tse-tung's line on the Cultural Revolution. ... It is necessary at the same time to criticize and repudiate those representatives of the bourgeoisie who have sneaked into the Party, the government, the army, and all spheres of culture, to clear them out or transfer them to other positions. Above all, we must not entrust these people with the work of leading the Cultural Revolution.

Soon afterward the masses were called upon to sweep out the "monsters and ghosts" in their organizations. In schools throughout the country Party committees began to attack the "monsters and ghosts" among the teachers and administrators, and before long students were denouncing all who were in any positions of authority, including the very Party committees that had mobilized them. The movement picked up momentum when the students at Peking National University turned on their officials and accused them of trying to limit criticism and preserve academic order.

In early June 1966 the Party sent work teams into the schools with the mission to overthrow the school Party committees and to manage the election of preparatory Cultural Revolution small groups, one for each class and one for the whole school. A representative of each work team stayed behind to serve as liaison with preparatory small groups. The process of organizing students at this stage was still orderly, and a hierarchy extended from the Provincial Party Committee to the Work Team liaison member to the All-School Preparatory Committee and then to the Class Preparatory small group. Later in the fall, however, the work teams were denounced as the work of Liu Shao-ch'i, the man who was to become the prime target of the entire Cultural Revolution. This was an early example of "waving the red flag to oppose the red flag."

The attack on the work teams created great confusion on the campuses, particularly at Peking National University. Government officials appeared at large meetings with the students but seemed unable to provide definite guidance until the Central Committee's Eleventh Plenum, which in its sixteen-point decision called for direct attacks on the Party hierarchy. The students were told to organize into Red Guard units and leave their campuses to confront the Party headquarters in their locations and denounce the Party leaders in their communities.

Mao had called for the meeting of the Eleventh Plenum of the Central Committee, but when it met on August 1, 1966, his forces seemed to be a minority so he quickly mobilized supporters, including army representatives. Finally he packed the meeting so that he could get backing for his sixteen points for intensifying the Cultural Revolution and directing it against specific Party officials.

At this stage there was new confusion because many of the most activist students were sons and daughters of the cadres who had benefited the most from Communist rule. Suddenly they were being called upon to attack the established Party people whom they were associated with either directly or through their families. Such students were reluctant to act and were quickly replaced by more aggressive students who often turned out to be the sons and daughters of lower-level cadres who had not been able to advance very far in the Communist hierarchy because the middle and top ranks had been filled ever since 1949 by older cadres.

In schools throughout the country the Red Guard movement quickly picked up emotional momentum. Every day students were gathered together and harangued by their leaders on how Mao Tsetung personally was counting on them to save the revolution. Mao worship became almost hysterical. The rallies throughout the country but particularly in Peking were great outbursts of emotion involving waving, singing, and often crying students.

Initially the focus of the Red Guards was on "destroying the four olds" (old ideas, old culture, old customs, and old habits). This resulted in violent destruction of art objects in museums and private homes. The widow of Sun Yat-sen had her lovely home in Shanghai ransacked by Red Guards bent on destroying anything relating to traditional Chinese culture or to bourgeois practices. To protect their homes families with anything of historic value painted on their doors slogans by Mao Tse-tung in the hope that this might save them from destructive visitations by Red Guards.

"Destroying the four olds" soon merged into "great exchanges of revolutionary experiences," in which the Red Guards began to travel all over the country and converge on Peking to discuss "revolutionary experiences." Initially only "five kinds of red" students (poor peasants, middle peasants, workers, revolutionary soldiers, and revolutionary cadres) were supposed to travel, but by late fall of 1966 millions of students were moving about, taking over the railroads, and not paying for either the railroad travel or their accommodations.

Since nearly eleven million Red Guards eventually visited Peking, wishing to see Chairman Mao in person and proclaim to him their undying affection, clearly a great deal of behind-the-scenes logistical support must have been provided. In time it became apparent that the People's Liberation Army was making the "spontaneous" actions of the Red Guards possible. The army produced food, trucks, housing, medical care, and general guidance. On November 16, 1966, the central committee issued a circular calling for the end of the traveling by the Red Guards, but the students continued to move about throughout the winter. Transportation was seriously disrupted, and this affected production. Factories could neither obtain raw materials nor ship out their products.

Meanwhile in the schools and campuses conflicts were increasing among the various Red Guard factions. Different Red Guard headquarters were set up, each insisting that it represented the true spirit of Maoism. The splits among students led to a decline in the role of high school students, who had made up the bulk of the Red Guards, and gave greater initiative to college age activists. Leadership thus shifted from the Red Guards to the Revolutionary Rebels. The Revolutionary Rebels were generally older students with a greater sense of political purpose and enough sophistication not to dissipate their energies by attacking the diffuse evils of bourgeois thought and culture. They focused on destroying the old cadres who had succumbed to "economism," and they were ready to take on the serious task of seizing power.

The Revolutionary Rebels quickly sought to establish alliances with the workers and peasants, but in light of the behavior of the Red Guards they were, not surprisingly, rebuffed. The Chinese working class had seen enough of the follies of student activism and were suffering because of the disruptions of the economy by the Cultural Revolution. In December 1966 and January 1967, workers in Shanghai, Hankow, and elsewhere began to hit back by taking over the railroads in order to visit Peking, by initiating strikes, and by spending the money in factory treasuries on personal consumer items. Probably anti-Maoist forces were behind these actions of the workers, especially the decision for factory managers to hand over large sums of money to their employees and encourage them to buy bicycles, watches, and radios. The loyalties of the workers were thus held by the Liu-Teng professionals while the economy, which was the responsibility of the Maoists, was seriously threatened by inflation.

By the spring and summer of 1967 the activities of the Red Guards and the Revolutionary Rebels had brought China to the brink of anarchy. Dramatic scenes of hundreds of thousands of Red Guards parading before their revered Chairman Mao in Peking gave way to ugly scenes of angry mobs attacking teachers, civic leaders, and foreign diplomats. The violence of the Cultural Revolution was first systematically directed against not only all symbols of authority but also all that was foreign and different and nonconformist. The attacks on authority were matched by attacks on all who in the slightest way deviated from the Guards' view of correct behavior. People whose hair was too long, who wore clothes that seemed strange, whose speech was not filled with the right clichés, were all violently attacked.

Things had gotten out of hand. Mao himself had little sympathy for "petty bourgeois romantic revolutionary fervor." He believed deeply in revolution, but he knew that it called for discipline and leadership. He had to look for a new vehicle for his cause, and the obvious one was the People's Liberation Army, a force committed to revolution but not undisciplined behavior.

THE ARMY TAKES OVER

As early as 1958 during the Lushan Conference Mao had indicated that if necessary he would call up the army to enforce his position. During the clash with P'eng Chen in the winter of 1965, Mao started to use the *Liberation Army Daily* to express his views, and even after his associates took over the *People's Daily* in 1966, the *Liberation Army Daily* continued to be the most authoritative source of Maoist opinion.

The importance of Lin Piao rose steadily. By August 1966, at the Eleventh Plenum of the Central Committee, he was officially designated Mao's "closest comrade in arms" and the heir-apparent. While the Red Guards dominated the central scene in China, the prestige of the army quietly rose; it had been remarkably successful in keeping the Cultural Revolution out of its own ranks. Of course behind the scenes the army provided essential logistical support for the Red Guards and even more unobtrusively provided cadres who were politically active among the Red Guards.[5]

At the beginning of 1967, during the "January revolution," the Red Guards reached their high point and began to carry out the slogan of "seize power." The People's Liberation Army experienced a near-crisis. The "January revolution" was a direct attack on the Party structure at the provincial and the Peking levels. The Red Guards demanded that all Party officials who could in any way be accused of being counter-revolutionary should be removed. Because most of the officials had been in office for nearly twenty years and many functionaries beneath them had been frustrated by lack of promotion and mobility, it was not hard to find people to prefer charges against officials.

There was utter confusion. All manner of leaders were suddenly under attack, and the Red Guards and the Revolutionary Rebels were engaged in "revealing" all kinds of secrets in their various newspapers and wall posters. Every day Red Guards at the various headquarters designed posters indicting specific leaders and explaining Party decisions. The explanations generally revealed that for many years there had been intensive and extensive factions and clashes among the Chinese Communist leaders. Many of the charges were false, but there were many significant reverberations. People trying to defend themselves would make countercharges and reveal other secrets. The excitement of public demonstrations gave way to the excitement of intense factional struggle and of character assassination. Leaders throughout the country as well as in Peking were disappearing and many suicides were reported.

[5]Ellis Joffe, "The Chinese Army in the Cultural Revolution: The Politics of Intervention," *Current Scene*, 8:8 (December 7, 1970), p. 8.

In this atmosphere the army's Cultural Revolution group was reorganized, and Chiang Ch'ing, Mao's wife, was made an adviser to it. It appeared that the army would have to support fully the seizures of power by the Revolutionary Rebels. However, when the Red Guards ran into severe opposition from the workers, it was natural for the army to retreat and become the arbitrating force responsible for basic order. The Maoists in Peking realized that the momentum of the Cultural Revolution would decline if the Red Guards and the Revolutionary Rebels failed to get the backing of the army. On January 23, 1967, they ordered the army to intervene to support the "seizure of power." At this crucial juncture, however, the army refused to follow the revolutionary course and instead acted as a stabilizing force, seeking order rather then partisan support of the rebels.

Tension between the Maoists and the army was resolved by formalizing the balance among the key factions through triple alliances, which led to the formation of Revolutionary Committees. The triple alliance involved the Revolutionary Rebels, including the Red Guards, the Revolutionary Cadres (former Party members who had "remolded" themselves and were certified as loyal Maoists), and army representatives. In February 1967 the first Revolutionary Committee was established in Heilungkiang, and Peking declared that it (rather than the Paris Commune, which the Red Guards had been extolling) was to be the model for the rest of the country. Many of the Red Guards complained that the triple alliance formula for establishing the Revolutionary Committees provided a mask behind which the old cadres and the pragmatic soldiers could reestablish themselves without any real change of heart. The charge that people were "waving the red flag to oppose the red flag" became more widespread because judgments about subjective commitments were to be decisive in determining who was to have power in China.

Although Chiang Ch'ing and the other extreme radicals continued to call for revolution, Chou En-lai and the moderate Maoists seemed to go along with the idea that the army should gradually restore order. The creation of Revolutionary Committees proceeded very slowly because of the difficulties in deciding who should represent the Revolutionary Rebels and the Revolutionary Cadres. Factions in the provinces contended with each other and were firm in not yielding. They knew that exclusion from the Revolutionary Committees would mean political, if not physical, death.

In mid-July the delicate balance in the army between its central command and its regional authorities was dramatically strained by the most significant event of the Cultural Revolution, the Wuhan incident.[6] A high-level delegation from Peking led by two Central Committee members, Hsieh Fu-chih, vice-premier and head of the Peking City Revolutionary Committee, and Wang Li, a member of Chiang Ch'ing's revolutionary group, went to Wuhan to try to settle the factional fighting between two huge rival Red Guard organizations. The local military commander, Ch'en Tsia-tao, had backed the more "conservative" faction, but Peking insisted that the other faction be recognized and Ch'en publicly withdraw his support. The two emissaries were physically attacked in their hotel and were finally saved by the dispatch of troops toward Wuhan. Ch'en was dismissed from his post, and Hsieh Fu-chih and Wang Li were welcomed back to Peking by a massive parade of over one million people.

The immediate consequence of the Wuhan incident was a stepup of radical Red Guard actions under Chiang Ch'ing's leadership. But more fundamentally the incident propelled the army into a more active role in controlling developments. The other regional commanders decided that they should be more rigorous in managing the formation of Revolutionary Committees and not permit the factional strife to get out of hand as it had in Wuhan. Chiang Ch'ing in the meantime had demanded that the army be purged and that the Maoists should "drag out the handful of power holders in the army." By mid-August the army had counterattacked, and Wang Li, the hero of Wuhan, was purged for being excessively anti-army. On September 5, 1967, Chiang Ch'ing dramatically called for universal support of the army and denounced the Red Guards who had been attacking the military.

The army thus gradually came to the fore as the principal instrument of public rule. In September 1967 only six provinces had

[6]For a detailed discussion of the Wuhan incident see Thomas W. Robinson, "The Wuhan Incident: Local Strife and Provincial Rebellion during the Cultural Revolution," P-4511 (Santa Monica, Calif.: Rand, December 1970).

Revolutionary Committees, and in twenty-two provinces the army ruled directly. Thereafter even when Revolutionary Committees were established, they were clearly under the domination of the army. Indeed, the triple alliances were in many cases little more than facades for army control.

From April through July 1968 there was a last effort to revive the revolutionary processes. The Maoists were successful in obtaining the dismissal of the army's acting chief of staff, Yang Ch'eng-wu, as well as of the commander of the Peking garrison and the political commissar of the air force. Apparently these men had moved too early in expressing their opposition to Chiang Ch'ing and the radicals, and the radicals could attack them without creating a general confrontation with the army.

By August, however, Mao had appointed envoys and organized the Worker-Peasant Mao Tse-tung Thought Propaganda Teams to disband the Red Guards and had presented the first team with his famous mangoes. Mangoes were distributed throughout the country, and meetings were held to revere Mao's "gift" and to learn that the chairman no longer favored the Red Guards but honored the more conservative workers and peasants. By September the last Revolutionary Committees were established and the army was fully in control behind the scenes. Peking declared that the country was finally "all red." In practice China, like so many other newly developing countries, was dependent on its military to maintain order and to manage public affairs. The regional commanders set about breaking up Red Guard units and sending the youth to the countryside to adjust to the rural life of the peasant.

The Maoists were no doubt unhappy with this development, but they could at least formalize their successes at the top of the hierarchy even if they had lost power in the regions and the provinces. Thus in April 1969 they called for the meeting of the Ninth Party Congress, at which Lin Piao was formally designated Mao's successor. Forty percent of the members of the congress were army officers, and of the 279 members of the new Central Committee, 123 were military men.[7] The end of the Cultural Revolution had brought a form of military rule to China.

[7]Richard Baum, "China: Year of the Mangoes," *Asian Survey*, 9:1 (January 1969), p. 4.

The surface of political life was tranquil, but behind the front of military rule struggles continued and Mao continued his restless purges. During the next four years leaders who seemed to have been rising in favor would suddenly disappear and later were denounced indirectly. Mao first turned against his long-time personal associate and spokesman of the most radical cultural revolutionary group, Ch'en Po-ta. No sooner had this been done and the army appeared to be in full command, than the world was amazed to learn that Lin Piao and the military chiefs had fallen from favor. Although by 1972 the manifest revolutionary currents had run their course in China, the issues of succession and policy choices had not been resolved and Mao's revolution was still a fragile thing.

THE DAMAGE OF THE
CULTURAL REVOLUTION

Evaluating fully even the short-term consequences of the Cultural Revolution is impossible. Although the Party machinery was almost totally destroyed, the concept of the Party was never attacked and the Maoists maintained the traditional Leninist view that the Party is the most effective force for revolution. Attack was directed toward men holding Party offices. Men vilified and "dragged out" for public humiliation were at times rehabilitated, even during the course of the Cultural Revolution. On the other hand some leaders, including even those most hated by the Maoists, such as Liu Shao-ch'i and Teng Hsiao-p'ing, were for a long time not referred to by name.

The damage, however, was tremendous, and it did not end merely with the purging of those who were initially identified with enemy factions. The Cultural Revolution, like so many other revolutions, tended to devour its own. Of the group of five that was originally placed in charge of the Cultural Revolution in September 1965, four were subsequently purged. Of the eighteen members of the central Cultural Revolution group, which replaced the "group of five" in the summer of 1966, thirteen were purged. Possibly most amazing of all is the fact that Ch'en Po-ta, Mao's private secretary and confidant of many years, disappeared from public sight in August 1970, and K'ang Sheng, an equally close associate especially throughout the Cultural Revolution, dropped from sight in October 1970. Possibly these "purges" will not be permanent, however, for in March 1971 Hsieh Fu-chih reappeared to head the Peking Party committee after being out of sight for a year. The process of purge and rehabilitation continues.

A comparison of the Party office holders of the Eighth Central Committee, of March 1966, with those of the Ninth Central Committee, of April 1969, shows that only three members of the Politburo standing committee remained, seven members of the Politburo survived, and 54 out of 180 Central Committee members survived.[8] Of the 67 secretaries and alternative secretaries of the six regional bureaus, only 13 survived. Twenty of 28 provincial Party secretaries were purged, 2 were severely criticized, and 1 committed suicide.[9]

Generally the elimination of the older cadres did not result in the elevation of radicals or members of the Red Guard. Most of the openings provided by the purges were filled by military men and by subordinate regular Party officials. In the Eighth Congress twenty-seven percent of the delegates were military men; forty-one percent were military men at the Ninth Congress.[10]

The destruction of the Party apparatus at the province and county levels was even more profound. With the Revolutionary Committees replacing the Party organization, the structure of the Party and even its physical headquarters were generally totally eliminated. Only the abstract ideal that there should be a pure Party remained.

Damage to the government structures was somewhat uneven. The ministries and departments responsible for nuclear developments and advanced scientific work were relatively untouched. Other ministries were brought to a complete standstill. For example, the Red Guards occupied the offices of the foreign ministry, destroyed files, and brought China's diplomacy to a complete halt during most of 1966. All but one of Peking's foreign ambassadors were recalled so that they could be put through the ordeal of the Cultural Revolution and be "remolded." For nearly two years China had only

[8]Gordon A. Bennett, "China's Continuing Revolution: Will It Be Permanent?" *Asian Survey*, 10:1 (January 1970), p. 4.

[9]Richard Hughes, "Mao Makes the Trials Run on Time," *New York Times Magazine* (August 23, 1970), p. 67.

[10]*Ibid.*, p. 3.

one ambassador abroad, in Cairo. In this xenophobic spirit the Red Guards attacked various embassies in Peking, threatened the lives of French and British officials, and beat up Indian diplomats — to the extent that Indian mobs attacked and caused the hospitalization of Chinese diplomatic personnel in New Delhi.

The State Council ceased to operate, and of the sixteen deputy premiers, eight were completely purged, five were criticized and demoted, and one died. Only two survived politically. After the Cultural Revolution the size of government was reduced; ministries were combined. The result was to reduce the power of the central authorities and to leave the direction of many economic activities to provincial officials.

Possibly, Chinese universities and schools were the institutions most severely damaged by the Cultural Revolution. Universities that closed down in 1965 and 1966 did not begin to reopen until the fall of 1970. High schools were, of course, disrupted during the Red Guard days, but even after the Red Guards were disbanded the schools were slow to begin operations again. Teachers were afraid to return to their classrooms, and no one was sure what could be legitimately taught. By fall of 1970 most schools were only gradually and quite experimentally reopening.

When the new structure of education was announced in the fall of 1970, it was apparent that an important consequence of the Cultural Revolution was a drastic reduction in the amount of schooling for Chinese students. Elementary and junior high school years were to total seven, and only sixty percent of the young people in the cities and thirty percent of those in rural areas would go on to a two-year high school. There would be a three-year period of work before students could become candidates for two or three years in a technically oriented college.

The effects of the Cultural Revolution on the economy are exceedingly hard to evaluate because of inadequate data. Industrial production probably dropped as much as ten percent during 1966 and fifteen percent during 1967. Foreign trade also dropped but not to the same degree. Factory discipline was disrupted and workers began to question the purpose of their activities. Chou En-lai admitted in an interview with Edgar Snow that the economy had been temporarily hurt but that the political gains more than compensated. In the same interview he gave some statistics on production that generally exceeded those outside analysts had assumed to be likely.

The People's Liberation Army has had to pay a heavy price for the Cultural Revolution. Its expanded political and administrative roles have no doubt weakened its prime military capabilities. Regional commanders have had to become more sensitive to the conditions in their regions, and thus the tendency toward regionalism within the military has been strengthened.

The Chinese had to pay a very high price in foreign prestige for the Cultural Revolution. The fact that China seemed to be tearing itself apart while the Viet Nam war was raging made it apparent to all the world that the Chinese lacked the capability to intervene and need not be feared by the United States. Disruptions in transportation slowed the flow of aid to Hanoi, and indeed the Chinese at critical junctures prevented military supplies from the Soviet Union from passing through China. Most of the world assumed that the Chinese were possessed of some form of madness. The status and prestige of China and the Chinese revolutionary model diminished in the opinion of nearly everyone, except for marginal revolutionary groups who romanticized what they thought Mao was doing but were so politically impotent that they could do nothing to further China's national interests. Within the Communist world China lost ground and the Soviet Union was able to recover influence and authority. Communist parties all over the world found it hard to justify Peking's behavior.

The final consequences of the Cultural Revolution are hard to imagine. Much will depend on what China looks like after the rehabilitation of the Party is completed. The Maoists recognized that there would be short-term costs but believed that they were necessary to achieve ultimate objectives. Were these objectives achieved? Are they achievable?

Presumably Mao accepted the likelihood that the Chinese economy would be damaged. He believed that the trauma of revolutionary disorder was essential to produce new generations that would resist the temptation of revision and would steadfastly adhere to a world view that he had found for himself in the 1920's and 1930's. Did the Cultural Revolution truly produce a new generation of revolutionaries? Evidence suggests that it did not. The result has been to raise the level of cynicism and to leave a generation frustrated and scattered in the rural countryside. Two years after the height of the turmoil the Red Guards were disbanded. Youths have been sent to rural labor, and power at all levels is gradually reverting either to old cadres or to soldiers. The rhetoric of populism is declining and the practices of a law and order regime are being docilely accepted. Although Mao Tse-tung is still at the top of the Chinese government, the spirit of revolutionary Maoism seems to have lost out, and the advocates of pragmatic policy have reasserted their authority.

THE RETURN TO ORDER
AND THE PROBLEMS OF PARTY BUILDING

The destruction of the Party apparatus by the Cultural Revolution had the consequence of dramatically weakening the central authorities and allowing power to be transferred to the provinces. Army rule meant regional and provincial rule. The authority that remained at the top lacked the instruments necessary for implementing policy. During the Cultural Revolution Peking learned that it could issue commands and proclamations but that it would have to depend on the willingness of local authorities to enforce them. So it has been since the Cultural Revolution.

Mao's decision to disband the Red Guards and to hail the Worker-Peasant Mao Tse-tung Thought Propaganda Teams with his gift of mangoes was a signal to military officials throughout the country that they could use greater force to repress the Revolutionary Rebels. In the Revolutionary Committees the military men, who were generally the chairmen, steadily countered the influence of the radicals.

In large cities orders went out to send the youth away. In the countryside orders appeared to accept the young people and teach them how to work in the fields. Somewhat more than twenty million young people were transferred. This was one of the great migrations in history. Within a year many were beginning to drift back to the urban centers, where they had to live a semi-legal existence because they lacked work permits and food quota books. Many became criminals, but many more were simply called criminals by the regime because they preferred the cities to rural isolation.

During 1969 and 1970 in the larger cities extensive public

trials were followed by public executions of young people. During the first six months of 1970 more than five thousand people were tried and more than one thousand were executed.[11] The repressions were harsh because many of the local authorities felt it necessary to counter tendencies to lawlessness engendered by a period of near-anarchy.

In the main, however, the problems of restoring order in the cities and the countryside were not as great as might have been expected given the extent of the breakdown of public authority during the Cultural Revolution. Workers generally were anxious to keep their jobs, and peasants felt compelled to follow their traditional routines regardless of what the authorities were up to.

The real problem of restoring order was the political one of rebuilding the Party. On Halloween night, October 31, 1968, Mao Tse-tung revealed that Liu Shao-ch'i, the "number one Party person in authority taking the capitalist road," the leader of the "demons, freaks, and monsters," was officially expelled from the Communist Party. Teng Hsiao-p'ing was never officially expelled as secretary-general; the Central Secretariat of the Party was merely eliminated. The task of restructuring the Party machinery turned out to be exceedingly difficult.

The country had already experienced considerable difficulties in establishing the Revolutionary Committees based on the triple alliances formula, and it was necessary to make further selections of people at the provincial, county, and city levels to decide who would hold office in the new Party structure. In April 1969 the new Party Constitution, which explicitly designated Lin Piao as Mao's successor, was promulgated at the Ninth Party Congress. It called for a reconstituted Party that would combine the principles of the earlier triple alliance with a three-way alliance of old, middle-aged, and young people, along with the classic Maoist concept of the mass line and the principle "from the people, to the people."

Progress in Party consolidation and reconstruction was exceedingly slow. Six months after the Ninth Congress only thirty-seven county Party committees had been established in the more than two thousand counties in China, and no provincial or autonomous region committees existed. The Struggle-Criticism-Trans-

[11] *Ibid.*

formation Campaign kept alive the tensions between the young Maoists who wanted power and the older cadres who could claim that they were purified and should retain office. In this process the army had to decide how far it should go in making decisions or in allowing the contending factions to fight out their disagreements.

By late 1970 and early 1971 there seemed to be a tacit agreement between the army and the Maoists in Peking to side with the moderate elements in rebuilding the Party in return for maintaining the rhetoric of the Cultural Revolution. Thus "ultra leftists" were purged and "Party core groups" in the Revolutionary Committee — older cadres and army representatives — were made the new Party committees at various local levels. The chairmen of the Revolutionary Committees generally became the new secretaries of the Party committees. On December 13, 1970, the first provincial Party committee was established in Hunan, and in two weeks committees were set up in Kiangsu, Kwangtung, and Kiangsi. Yet when the Hunan Party committee was established, only 15 of the 82 counties in the province had Party committees, and in the country as a whole only 180 county Party committees existed. By April 1971, 14 of 28 provincial and special areas committees had been formed, and all except the Shanghai committee were under moderate old cadres or military officers. The goal of reconstructing the Party for its fiftieth anniversary was not met. On July 1, 1971, there were still four provinces without committees — Szechwan, Tibet, Ningsia, and Heilungkiang. Finally, on August 26 these committees were organized. Yet at the county level fewer than four hundred committees had been identified for the entire country.

The relationship between the Revolutionary Committees and the Party committees is still obscure. It was initially assumed that the Revolutionary Committees might disappear once Party committees were established, but this has not happened. However, announcements have been made that the two committees are not "on an equal footing" and that the Party should be the "leader." Possibly the Maoists at Peking welcomed the confusion in relations between the two because it was desirable for encouraging a continuing clash of opinions and inner-Party struggle.

Except in education, the pattern of consolidation since the Cultural Revolution has been one of reestablishing order much along the lines of the pre-Cultural Revolution system, but using more radical rhetoric. If this continues to be the case, the Cultural Revolution is likely to have few lasting effects. The basic problem of the Chinese Communist system of rule is that it has provided little possibility for mobility. Once the leadership was established and the institutions of Party and government were finalized in 1949, there was a general freezing of people in their respective offices. The system has not been dynamic. Consequently, young people have had few opportunities, and senior members of the bureaucracy and the Party organization have appeared to be obstacles to advancement. This rigidity, basic to a Communist-run society, was a major contributing cause of the Cultural Revolution. The intense struggle to form the Revolutionary Committees and the Party committees suggests that most Chinese believe that the post-Cultural Revolution system is likely to be just as rigid and lacking in advancement opportunities as the previous system. Those not appointed to committees are likely to be permanently excluded from the inner system of rule.

Mao has recognized the rigid and undynamic character of the Chinese system. His proposed solution has been to urge all individuals to adopt a more dynamic and revolutionary cast of mind. This in itself is not likely to alter the basic character of Chinese communism. What is needed is for the system to allow for greater institutional flexibility, for new officers in support of new activities to appear in response to new needs, for the relative status and power of officers to fluctuate with the flow of events, and for social and economic changes to be mirrored more readily in institutional changes.

The way in which the Chinese Communist system has institutionalized its structures has left the massive purge, such as the Cultural Revolution, as the principal method for shaking up personnel and bringing new blood into the order. It is not clear how well such purges have worked at the lower levels because many of the older cadres have displayed remarkable survival ability. Chou En-lai has even brought into question the value of the Cultural Revolution as a technique for bringing new blood into the Party. He has said that only one percent of the membership was actually purged.

Yet, if we discount the extreme and essentially romantic interpretations of Mao's objectives, it does seem that the Cultural Revolution produced measurable changes. Above all the Chinese system is likely to remain far more decentralized. Instead of administrative controls emanating from the capital and reaching into every county and commune, the leaders in Peking are likely to content themselves with providing general guidelines.

Initiative is supposed to come out of the local setting. However, the relaxation of central control has not produced much vigor at the local levels, largely because the cadres have been burned too often, charged with being too "rightist" as the Cultural Revolution began and "ultra leftist" as it died down. There are no guarantees that they will not again be accused of going either too fast or too slow. By the spring of 1971 for the first time in the history of the Communist regime people were reluctant to become local leaders and cadres.

Decentralization has also been legitimized by the Tachai system, presumably devised by peasants in a barren county of Shansi who demonstrated that their community could take care of all their needs. Peking has called upon all communities to emulate the Tachai system, in which everyone works for the production brigade and all are paid by a system of work points. The points include rewards for political work such as attending meetings, engaging in criticism, and studying the Thoughts of Mao Tse-tung. The system is probably most meaningful for the most backward areas, which cannot hope to produce a surplus but which if made content with self-sufficiency would free the surpluses of other areas for investment.

This development is entirely consistent with Mao's objective of moving the young into the countryside to provide the peasants with propaganda for the regime. His goal no doubt is that these young people will gain a sense of leadership similar to that which he developed out of his personal experiences leading peasants. As a result of the Cultural Revolution, the current generation of Red Guards, however, has a sense of frustration and disappointment, which Mao himself never knew.

By 1970 the pendulum had swung away from revolution and in the direction of a firm return to law and order. Gradually leaders of the Cultural Revolution came under attack for their excesses or simply disappeared. On May Day in 1971 several were noticeably absent from the public celebrations. Ch'en Po-ta had disappeared in the fall of 1970, and at the time of the fiftieth anniversary celebration, on July 1, 1971, there were ominous attacks on "the type of person who claims to be humble little men of the people," a reference to Ch'en, who once referred to himself in such deprecatory terms.

As Chou En-lai assumed control of the remnants of administration after the shattering effects of the Cultural Revolution, attacks were made on groups who had presumably been excessively destructive. In particular, announcements were made that the destruction of the foreign office and the recalling of all but one of China's ambassadors had been the work of the ultra-leftist "five one six clique." (This group was inspired by the Central Committee Circular of May 16, 1966 — hence 5-16.) The purge against this clique, and in particular the trial and execution of Yao Ten-shaw, signaled the return to bureaucratic order in government administration.

Behind the scenes the fall of Ch'en Po-ta apparently alerted Lin Piao to the dangers of an aging Mao constantly turning against those closest to him. In particular Mao's personal possessiveness of the Chinese revolution made him hypercritical of those designated to carry on after he passed from the scene. Therefore, instead of Lin Piao's official designation as heir-apparent giving him security, he became increasingly vulnerable. The outside world still does not know precisely what may have happened in the fall of 1971, but strange events did happen: the October 1st National Day celebrations were canceled, foreign embassies were told not to mention Lin Piao by name, and finally Party cadres spread the amazing story that Lin Piao had made three attempts on Mao Tse-tung's life and had sought contacts with a foreign power, presumably the Soviet Union.

The disappearance of Lin Piao was followed by the equally mysterious disappearances of Huang Yung-sheng, chief of staff of the armed forces; Wu Fa-shien, the air force commander; Li Tso-peng, the naval political commissar; and nearly two hundred other senior officers.

Politically the fall of Lin Piao was matched by a rise in influence of Chou En-lai and his close political associates. Thus, Chou, who had always played a balancing role in the hierarchy, became in 1972 the heir-apparent to Mao. Whether he will have greater longevity in that role than his two immediate predecessors, Liu Shao-ch'i and Lin Piao, only time will tell.

The restoration of the administrative order did not, however, signify the reestablishment of stable and trusting leadership relations. In contrast to the collegial band that ruled China during the regime's first decade, the post-Cultural Revolution Politburo was a diverse and uncongenial group, who represented more regional than national interests, who favored the military, and who conspicuously underrepresented the state bureaucracies. The process of purging and interparty struggle would have to continue.

CHAPTER SEVENTEEN

China and the World

As China came out of the Cultural Revolution and gained domestic order, it began again to look outward in foreign affairs. One of the first priorities of the officials after reestablishing internal stability was to counter the worldwide image of China as having been torn apart by revolutionary folly and anarchy.

IMPROVEMENTS IN UNITED STATES–CHINA RELATIONS

In the spring of 1971 the Chinese surprised the world by inviting the American table tennis team to tour China after the world championship matches in Japan. "Ping-Pong diplomacy" was accompanied by the admission of select Western correspondents who could report to the world that order had been reestablished and revolutionary spontaneity no longer held sway. By allowing the world to have first-hand reports on developments in China, the forces for administrative order and political stability strengthened their hands and compelled the remnants of the revolutionary elements to stay on their best behavior and not embarrass the country before foreign visitors.

Far more fundamental than short-run considerations in the aftermath of the Cultural Revolution were certain basic historical trends that called for China to take a more active interest in foreign relations as the decade of the 1970's began. Indeed, for the first time since 1949 both China and the United States, for separate and different reasons of national interest, found it desirable to seek greater mutual accommodation. The speed with which "Ping-Pong diplomacy" was followed by presidential adviser Henry Kissinger's secret trip to Peking and the invitation of the Chinese to President Nixon to visit China is dramatic evidence of the extent to which change was in order in what had been one of the most rigid relationships in the post-World War II era.

In the United States the combination of frustration over the Viet Nam war and the perception of China as severely weakened by its relations with the Soviet Union and by domestic upheavals made China seem less of a danger to world peace. During the period of the close alliance between the Soviet Union and Communist China, especially as a result of the Korean war, there had been considerable substance to the view that China was a growing threat to world peace. The successes of the Communist leaders in establishing domestic order and providing economic growth during the 1950's had made China seem increasingly formidable. Chinese revolutionary rhetoric had contributed to the view that Peking was a danger to neighboring countries and to the stability of any country faced with revolutionary insurgency.

The Sino-Soviet split and the debilitating effects of the Great Leap and the Cultural Revolution fundamentally changed Chinese power. Until Stalin's death there had been substance to the concept of a monolithic Communist world, but by 1969 Russian and Chinese soldiers were shooting at each other and Mao was preaching that Russian revisionism was a greater threat to China than American imperialism.

In some respects American policy was slow to respond to the implications of the Sino-Soviet split, and certainly it can be argued that the United States would probably not have become so deeply committed to the Viet Nam conflict if it had been possible to more accurately predict Chinese behavior. Certainly there was no evidence in the *Pentagon Papers* or in the statements of any of those who participated in making the Viet Nam decisions that any American decision maker foresaw the possibility that the Chinese would ignore such a potential threat as nearly half a million American troops in South Viet Nam and would turn inward in order to destroy their Communist Party and tear apart their administrative order.

Hindsight reveals that although the inexorable trend throughout the 1960's was toward the isolation and weakening of China, events were also contributing to maintaining earlier views of the danger of China. The Quemoy-Matsu crisis of 1958 flushed out the fact that China could not count on the Soviet nuclear umbrella. In 1959 the harsh suppression of Tibet kept alive the picture of aggressive and dictatorial China. In 1960 the Soviets recalled their technicians and canceled all industrial aid projects, a decision that nearly brought Chinese economic growth to a standstill. However, the weakening impact of this development was soon obscured by the Sino-Indian border war of 1962. The simultaneous fall of Khrushchev and the detonation of China's first nuclear device in October 1964 increased anxieties that the Sino-Soviet conflict might be reversed and China might practice nuclear blackmail against its Asian neighbors — considerations that apparently influenced the American decision to hold firm in Viet Nam. Chinese revolutionary rhetoric reached new heights in relation to events such as plans for a Second Afro-Asian Conference in Algiers in 1964 and the establishment of the Djakarta-Peking axis in 1965. Above all Lin Piao's speech of September 1965, ambiguous as it was, suggested to many that China was about to take an active interest in "revolutionary wars" wherever they might appear. (Many careful analysts interpret his stress on "self-reliance" to mean that China would not be directly involved in supporting insurgencies.) Because Maoist enthusiasts throughout the world welcomed the speech as heralding an era of Chinese leadership in toppling existing governments, it was not surprising that Washington decision makers also took Lin's words at face value.

The basic trend in American perceptions in the 1960's was that China indeed had become less threatening. Given President Nixon's determination to withdraw from Viet Nam and seek a lower level of American military commitment in Asia, it was logical that he would also want to safeguard his withdrawal of forces with a program of greater contact with Peking in the hope of reassuring the Chinese that they had no reason to fear the United States.

China, coming out of the Cultural Revolution, faced far more than just the need to gain international respectability. After the border incidents of the summer of 1969 the Chinese were dramatically confronted with a growing Soviet military buildup along one of the longest borders in the world. Numerous public hints were given that elements in Moscow were contemplating the desirability of a preemptive strike against the Chinese nuclear capability. The implied Soviet threat carried a particularly ominous note of credibility because the year before Russian troops had occupied Czechoslovakia in support of the Brezhnev Doctrine, according to which the Soviet Union had the right to use force to prevent a socialist country from abandoning its place in the Communist world. The threat was possibly made more explicit in the fall of 1969 when Kosygin pressured the Chinese into inviting him to visit Peking after his trip to Hanoi for Ho Chi-minh's funeral. The Soviet leaders did meet Chou En-lai at the Peking airport, and he might have pointed out how close the two countries were to war.

Regardless of what may have happened in private, the fact is that since 1969 the Soviet Union has engaged in a massive military buildup in its far eastern and central Asian territories; the buildup was continuing in 1972. By the spring of 1971 more Soviet forces were being deployed against China than the Soviets had deployed against NATO in Europe. Indeed, the Soviet buildup represented what may be the largest more or less permanent deployment of forces capable of effecting the world balance of power that has ever occurred without a major war.

The deployment on their northern frontier means that the Chinese have lost the great good fortune of being able to leave their northern border relatively underguarded. As a consequence of allowing their ideological disagreements with the Russians to get out of hand and cause a rift in state-to-state relations, the Chinese are once again prisoners of their historical problem of having to mobilize massive forces along their northern frontiers. China must guard its extensive inner boundaries — the problem that led to the construction of the Great Wall, the costs of which contributed to the fall of great dynasties such as the Han, T'ang, and Ming.

Surrounded by enemies or countries that deeply distrusted Chinese intentions, Peking was ready to seek an easing of tension with the United States as early as 1964. Through the Warsaw talks, Americans had made it clear that they had no aggressive designs on China or North Viet Nam. Although the pledge the United States gave to Peking — an assertion that the United States did not seek to destroy North Viet Nam — precluded effective subsequent threats against Hanoi, it did set the stage in the post-Cultural Revolution environment for Peking to respond positively to President Nixon's statement in favor of better relations with "one quarter of mankind."

Under the leadership of Chou En-lai, China in the summer of

1971 sought to break out of its isolation and to separate its various foes by blending diplomacy and propaganda in order to create distrust between the superpowers — the Soviet Union and the United States. Peking combined its invitation to President Nixon with a vigorous campaign against Japan, charging that the Japanese militarists and industrialists were seeking to replace the United States in controlling Taiwan and South Korea. In part the Peking leaders reflected China's deep-seated, historic fear of Japan, a fear particularly strong in the generation that had experienced the years of Japanese conquest of the mainland. In part, however, Peking also was apparently eager to intimidate the Japanese so that whenever the normalization of Chinese and Japanese relations became appropriate, Tokyo would be in a defensive position and in negotiating a peace treaty Peking could thus make extremely high reparation demands for damages during the Sino-Japanese war of 1937–1945. The possibility of such reparations may become important for Peking because they may constitute China's only source of aid from an industrialized country on concessionary terms.

THE LONG PERSPECTIVE

While the Chinese Communist political system recovers from the trauma of the Cultural Revolution and the leaders cope with foreign policy issues, many of the basic modernization problems that China faced a century ago await solution. The turmoil of modern China has not ended, for the new has not been reconciled with the old. Modernization still eludes the Chinese in spite of their willingness to pay the price of revolution.

The Chinese have always had a civilization that in contrast to the cultures of its immediate neighbors largely justified their belief that China was indeed the center of the universe. Early contacts with the West reinforced this "Middle Kingdom complex." The Chinese world view involved more than just a sense of cultural superiority; it was premised on a strong sense of superior moral virtue. The Confucian government embodied the wishes of heaven, which were based on ethical principles. Divine sanction was accorded to China's dealings with foreigners, who were believed to be easily impressed with the merits of Chinese authorities.

Much happened to Chinese institutions and patterns of thought since the collapse of the imperial system. The changes in contemporary China are possibly more significant than the remaining strands of continuity. Yet there is much truth in the idea that Mao Tse-tung and his revolutionary colleagues share in some degree the old spirit of China as the Middle Kingdom. In seeking to reassert Chinese power and influence and in striving to regain what they feel is China's rightful place in the world, the Peking leaders display a strong sense of moral righteousness. Although their rhetoric has suggested that they seek influence in order to advance revolutions, the underlying reason is to spread virtue.

Other countries tend to rationalize their policies as being virtuous, to assume that there is a conflict between power and morality and that policy may require masking power considerations with moralistic statements. The Chinese, however, have tended to assume that virtue produces power and thus influence. A need to assert virtue continues to inspire China's foreign policy and to complicate relations with other societies.

International opinion of China has vacillated greatly. Europeans first found the Chinese strange and exotic, with a civilization that both attracted and repelled. From earliest times China seemed to tap the most avaricious instincts of Westerners, and Chinese practices have easily provoked in foreigners feelings of arrogance and contempt. However, some Westerners have been captured by a blend of awe, sympathy, and respect for the Chinese. Western images of the Chinese have fluctuated between sympathy and hostility, largely responding to the currents of international relations.[1]

During the latter part of the nineteenth century and the early decades of the twentieth century American sentiments toward China were increasingly sympathetic, with strong paternalistic overtones. Americans felt that China needed their help and that they should assist China into the modern world. Therefore, when China fell to the Communists, Americans felt betrayed. When the formerly friendly Chinese declared themselves implacable foes of the United States, Americans responded with bitterness. In spite of years of ideological antagonism, Americans have generally reacted favor-

---

[1]The classic study of Western biases toward China is Harold R. Isaacs, *Scratches on Our Minds* (New York: Day, 1958).

ably to the prospect of better relations with the Chinese people, and Washington's view of Communist China has been influenced less by ideological than by power considerations. Although ideologically the Chinese have not appreciably altered their revolutionary and their anti-American views, the simple fact that China isolated after the Cultural Revolution is less powerful than China unified and allied to the Soviet Union has fundamentally altered Chinese and American relations.

As welcome as the thaw in relations between the world's most powerful and the world's largest nations has been, it would be premature to assume that full normalization of relations is likely soon. It is not easy to forecast the direction of Chinese foreign policy. Chinese diplomatic approaches to the outside world during the past twenty years have shifted as much as domestic policy. During the first years when China was "leaning to one side," Peking adopted a hard line toward all governments not on "its side." Then after the Korean war the Chinese, imbued with the Bandung spirit, discovered that an apparently benign China had appeal in neutralist countries anxious to avoid the conflicting pressures of the cold war giants. During this period the Chinese were extremely active, inviting all manner of Afro-Asian groups and government officials to visit Peking and see the progress of the new regime. These efforts seemed to be inspired by the Chinese sense of the importance and power of virtue, but some were also directed toward more pragmatic objectives, such as winning support for United Nations membership.

After the Hundred Flowers and the shock of the Hungarian revolution, the Chinese shifted toward a more radical posture. The Indian border war of 1962 drove them into a harsher approach toward neutrals. Then competition with the Russians over leadership of the world Communist movement forced them into ever more radical positions in foreign affairs.

Wavering between a benign approach and the hard line, in addition to the general historical trend toward greater radicalization of rhetoric, left the Chinese with relatively little sympathy in foreign governments. In the early 1950's India and many other Afro-Asian states were prepared to sponsor the Peking regime in international groups, but by the end of the 1960's China had few champions, aside from Albania, among the Communist states, and Pakistan, among the non-Communist states.

China's determined participation in the Korean war established the idea that the new regime was inclined to be aggressive and would have to be contained. The weakness of the various newly independent countries of Southeast Asia and the importance of overseas Chinese communities in most of them suggested in the 1950's that there was indeed great danger that a strong and unified China would soon be extending influence well beyond its frontiers. The rising tempo of Chinese rhetoric, largely in response to the polemics of the Soviet Union, gave further credence to the view that China was becoming aggressive. Governments in Asia became increasingly convinced of the difficulties of dealing with Peking and tended to be slow in seeing either the decline in Chinese power as a consequence of the Sino-Soviet antagonism or the extent to which China had to turn inward to cope with problems of domestic development.

Many scholars believe that China's behavior has not been particularly aggressive and that Chinese actions have frequently been misunderstood. They contend that the Chinese entered the Korean war only because they felt that their territory in Manchuria was threatened by General MacArthur's march toward the Yalu River. In Tibet the Chinese were reasserting control of traditional Chinese territory. The Quemoy-Matsu crisis also was an internal affair — the continuation of the Chinese civil war. In the border controversy with India, the Chinese had something of a case in international law, particularly because the Indians had not complained earlier of Chinese activities in what they were later to claim as their territory. And in the border clashes with the Russians in the summer of 1969 the Soviets had been provocative. According to this view the Chinese have not been threatening in foreign relations in spite of their ominous rhetoric. They have championed the idea of people's wars and insurgencies against non-Communist governments, but they have also preached self-reliance to such insurgents and have not sent their own forces across international borders in support of such wars.

The truth is that Peking has not been so benign, nor has it been so aggressive as many governments have pictured it. China's capabilities have lagged behind the thrust of the revolutionary rhetoric, and even when the Chinese have had capabilities they have generally shown considerable caution. However, the Chinese have acted in ways that have alienated most governments with which they have had dealings. They have often appeared rather insensitive to how others might interpret their policies, and they have seemed willing to use force more readily than others have felt appropriate. For example, if during the Korean war the Chinese had felt threatened in Manchuria, they might have sought the assistance of their close ally the Soviet Union, or they might have used more than esoteric warnings before intervening militarily. Furthermore they seem to have grossly underestimated the cost of their intervention in producing prolonged American hostility. Similarly, whatever the merits of the Chinese and Indian cases in international law, there is no questioning the political fact that the Chinese decision to use force did affect the world's image of China. While the Chinese succeeded in shattering Nehru's foreign policy and destroying India's claims to leadership in world politics, they also frightened many countries into becoming more distrustful of them. In short, the Chinese leaders' determination to seek a direct solution of the impasse with the Indians made them insensitive to the long-range consequences of their actions. To the degree that they were concerned with the broader implications of their policies, they apparently placed a higher value on humiliating the Indians than on the costs of appearing to be militaristic.

Much the same point can be made of the manner in which the Chinese escalated their ideological controversy first into border problems with the Russians and then into military clashes. In this case the Chinese were apparently willing to take the tactical initiative, firing on Russian forces with little regard to consequences. The immediate Soviet responses came during the summer of 1969 when the Russians initiated incidents that bloodied the Chinese. The longer-range Soviet reaction has involved a massive deployment of Russian forces into Soviet Asia as a permanent threat to the Chinese. The question of whether the Chinese have been or are likely to be aggressive in their foreign relations may be somewhat beyond the point, for their actions, however interpreted, have caused both the United States and the Soviet Union to build up their forces around China and thus have increased China's sense of encirclement.

In the years immediately preceding the Cultural Revolution

much of China's foreign policy was concerned with competition with the Soviet Union, and quite naturally the Chinese sought to identify themselves not only with the most revolutionary Communist parties or factions but also with those governments that were prepared to be both anti-American and distrustful of the Soviet Union. At that time the most serious and concerted diplomatic effort of the Chinese was their attempt to bring both Sihanouk's Cambodia and Sukarno's Indonesia into a coordinated foreign policy with China in opposition to the United States and the Soviet Union. In both countries domestic coups shattered Chinese efforts.

In Africa the Communist Chinese also made major commitments, with some successes. Their objective in seeking influence in that distant continent has been mainly a function of their competition with the Soviet Union, the United States, and the Nationalist Chinese on Taiwan. In their competition with the Soviets they sought to gain favor with the radical African regimes, such as Nkrumah's Ghana, Sékou Touré's Guinea, and Ben Bella's and Boumedienne's Algeria. In this competition the Chinese were handicapped by their limited resources. In seeking to inspire insurgent movements against the white redoubts in southern Africa, the Chinese were also seeking to place themselves ahead of the Russians as a revolutionary force, but their resources were limited. In east Africa China was anxious to establish itself as a natural and logical competitor with the United States and thus enhance its prestige. In this case the urge for competitive advantage led the Chinese to offer substantial help in the construction of a railroad from Zambia through Tanzania to the sea, an enterprise that may eventually cost them nearly half a billion dollars. In Africa the Chinese Communists also actively competed with the Chinese Nationalists to obtain support for their campaign for a seat in the United Nations. They offered the African states a variety of technical assistance programs.

The Cultural Revolution compromised the diplomatic campaigns of the Peking regime, and the extreme xenophobia of the Red Guards set back the country on all fronts. The prospect now is that the Chinese will seek to return to their earlier positions. In many cases, such as the construction of the Tan-Zan Railroad, they will be able to pick up where relations were broken by the Cultural Revolution, but in other cases making up for what was lost will be hard.

However, in the post-Cultural Revolution period Peking is also interested in new and potentially more constructive departures in foreign policy. China has shown a renewed interest in foreign trade. Indeed it is likely that as China comes out of its isolation one of the strongest means of contact with the rest of the world will be through economic relations. Paradoxically, the regime that likes to think of itself as the archetypal proletarian revolutionary government will find it more important to deal with bourgeois capitalists than with scientists or even liberal politicians.

In seeking a reduction of tension with the United States and working for United Nations membership, the Chinese since the Cultural Revolution were apparently striving to improve the range of their state-to-state relations and to gain recognition as a major world power. A weakened and significantly decentralized China seemed to be allowing much of its foreign policy to be handled by professionals in its ministries of trade and foreign affairs. The links between domestic developments and foreign policies may become as tenuous as they were during the warlord period, when China was domestically weak and divided but managed a remarkably effective program of foreign relations. The Chinese accomplished this because of the competence of their specialists in foreign relations and because other states' interests in China happened to coincide with Chinese interests. At a time when the process of rebuilding the Party must be completed and further internal struggles may be in store, it will be necessary for China to carry out rather delicate foreign policy maneuvers.

The foreign policy of the weakened Chinese central government will be determined by three factors. First, Peking will have to respond to the more or less permanent fact of a massive Soviet military presence on China's northern borders. Eventually, therefore, Chinese diplomacy may become more receptive to maneuvering in a triangular balance of power involving Washington and Moscow. Second, Peking's foreign policy makers are likely to be caught in the dilemma of needing to maintain respectable state-to-state relations, for reasons of security and trade, while seeking for China the political role of a revolutionary force. Thus Maoist hopes for China are likely to be constantly compromised by foreign policy calculations that appear to favor stability over revolutionary fervor. Third, it is likely that Chinese foreign policy will continue to be erratic. Domestic pressures will take precedence at some times; the demands of ideology cannot be entirely ignored; and Mao himself is likely to intervene from time to time to disrupt the plans of the professionals. Since the power base of those responsible for foreign affairs is impermanent, their policies can be easily compromised and idiosyncratic developments are likely to be frequent.

However, these are all matters of a passing nature. The fundamental consideration of Chinese foreign relations is the century-old question of the path China should take in emerging into the modern world. Eventually the nation will be acknowledged as a member of the modern international community. But for China to gain such acceptance, the Chinese must first come to terms with themselves. Before China can determine its proper international role, domestic problems must be solved. Is China on the verge of such a development? Could it be that after nearly a century of internal conflict and revolution the Chinese are at last prepared to take a more balanced, a more relaxed and pragmatic approach to their problems of modernization?

A vision of China on the verge of sustained progress is tempting. Since early in the twentieth century observers of China have many times been seduced by the illusion that China was about to find its full measure of greatness and become an "awakened giant," a modern nation-state. Immediately on the heels of the revolution of 1911 Western friends were forecasting that the inherent good sense and good humor of the Chinese people would speed the growth of republican institutions. The victory of the Nationalists and the establishment of the Nanking regime stimulated another rash of optimistic predictions and emotion-laden descriptions of the leadership virtues of the Kuomintang. In the first years after the Communists came to power some observers pictured China as certain to make dramatic progress because the country was firmly organized, well disciplined, and its leaders united and given to a pragmatic approach. Since the Great Leap and the Cultural Revolution another group of supporters of China has forecast imminent progress for precisely the opposite reasons: Instead of discipline and pragmatism the Chinese road to success will be spontaneity and an anti-technocratic, anti-elitist spirit.

Now that order is emerging out of the Cultural Revolution, once again a common expectation is that moderation and rationality are about to guide Chinese developments, and professional analysts are returning to what might be called the "prudence model" of Communist China.[2] This "model" for Chinese action is a most natural one. In trying to predict what the Chinese are about to do, Westerners are inclined to assume that China's decision makers will recognize the fundamental elements of Chinese development and eventually deal with them efficaciously — that is, that they will have to follow the dictates of good sense. Westerners are also inclined to expect prudence and rationality from China simply because in seeking to make predictions it is easier to think in terms of trends and incremental progress than to foresee the extraordinary and unexpected. The tendency to expect the routine to dominate China's future persists in spite of the fact that two decades of Communist government have been filled with the unexpected. Before the event who would have imagined that China would attack India or carry the split with Russia to the point of border clashes or engage in either the Great Leap or the Cultural Revolution? The fact that after the event we can find "reasons" for what happened does not mean the occurrences were predictable.

The "prudence model" should be treated skeptically not only because of the record of past Chinese behavior but also because there are compelling reasons to believe that tensions rather than stability are likely to characterize the future. Additional changes are in the offing for Communist China. First of all, in spite of the Cultural Revolution, China's national leaders are the oldest in the world, and with the death of Mao and others in his circle Chinese politics will be fundamentally changed. Although Mao Tse-tung has been peculiarly sensitive to the prospect of change after his death and created a cult of his own personality as extreme as the Stalin

[2]The view that analysts were in danger of being misguided by the interpretation of Communist China that treated ideological extremism as an aberration and assumed that the Chinese leaders are "capable of learning" — that is, the danger of the "prudence model" of Communist China — was advanced before the Cultural Revolution in Lucian W. Pye, "Coming Dilemmas for China's Leaders," *Foreign Affairs*, 44:3 (April 1966), pp. 387–403. The analysis here follows the central thesis of that article. The situation in China since the Cultural Revolution contains most of the problems that dominated the pre-Cultural Revolution scene.

cult, there is no assurance that the grip of the Thoughts of Mao Tse-tung will long survive him. Never in history has a leader of Mao's proportions passed from the scene without a major upheaval.

Moreover, the Cultural Revolution revealed the profound divisions among the Communist leaders. Thousands of cadres and senior leaders have been severely damaged by the Maoists, and powerful forces will be seeking revenge when the opportunity arrives. Because Chou En-lai lacks the strength of character of Mao Tse-tung there probably will be few inhibitions among those seeking to destroy him once he loses the protection of Mao.

Another round of feuding among the Communist leaders after the death of Mao could raise in the popular mind serious questions about the legitimacy of the post-Mao authority. The Chinese people were unquestionably shocked by the spectacle of leaders being attacked and degraded during the Cultural Revolution, and already cynicism about government has increased. If there is another power struggle in the near future, confidence in the Communist system could be further undermined.

Although Mao is apparently convinced that his revolutionary style will produce stability needed for his goals of socialism and communism, another judgment based on historical experience might forecast precisely the opposite result. A system that in twenty years has done so little to institutionalize and routinize authority is not likely to be long enduring without the charisma of its founder. To an extraordinary degree government in China continues to be of a quasi-revolutionary nature, depending on ad hoc campaigns and drives rather than on standardized procedures and basing its claims of authority on the mystical powers of Mao and his Thoughts. China is an almost pure example of a system based on charismatic authority that is not being transformed into rational-legal authority. In a sense the Cultural Revolution was Mao's resistance to the notion that his charismatic authority should become institutionalized.[3] The practice

[3]This would be almost the exact opposite interpretation from Robert Lifton's thesis that Mao was seeking "revolutionary immortality" by wanting to inspire in all Chinese his own revolutionary ardor so that the spirit would last after his death. However, if Mao had allowed authority to become institutionalized, it would have more readily endured after his death. By insisting on the preservation of his charismatic authority, he may have achieved the unconscious wish of proving that he is indispensable and thus ensured that the system will not last long after he passes from the scene.

of relying on mass mobilization and the personal dedication and energy of individual cadres means that any major changes at the center could demoralize and immobilize the entire system.

The relative absence of institutionalization and the need to rely on mass mobilization campaigns to achieve most objectives has also made the contemporary Chinese political system quite inflexible and unable to deal with a number of problems simultaneously. Massive assaults have to be made on selected problems. Other fields are neglected, and even modest changes in priorities call for major remobilization. There is thus a continuous sense of crisis, not only because the mobilization style requires a sense of urgency but also because problems generally do not get much attention until they reach crisis proportions.

These considerations point to the basic fact that the Cultural Revolution did not solve the inherent problems of Chinese modernization, and in a sense the effort to recapture the earlier sense of revolutionary élan may only have further delayed China's progress. A final source of potential instability in China is the passing of the revolutionary mystique and the need for the regime and the people to learn to live without the elation of their earlier dreams. At all levels, people have had to give up their expectation of miracles, and the Party itself now recognizes that there is no shortcut to transforming society. The only course is hard work and gradual improvement. At one time the mystique of communism, the esoteric doctrines of Marxism-Leninism, and the Thoughts of Mao were expected to contain miraculous answers to China's problems. Now, however, the Chinese have to settle for the potency of compound interest and the prospect of slow incremental improvement.

The one institution that has survived the Cultural Revolution and is likely to be the key to all future developments even after the death of Mao is the army. Most likely the army will seek to institutionalize the charisma of Mao and strive to produce the union of technical competence and revolutionary dedication that Mao himself has failed to give China. Army rule will give China an era of disciplined order and sacrifice, which may turn out to be strikingly similar to features of Stalin's rule, but without the purges and terror.

Although most speculation on the future of China centers on the death of Mao Tse-tung, it is conceivable that Chou En-lai is more indispensable. Indeed, among the ranks of the younger Chinese leaders no one has his diplomatic and administrative skills. Instead of a generation of imaginative and cosmopolitan leaders, the current candidates for future leadership in China appear to be dedicated Party workers with little subtlety of mind or breadth of vision.

Ultimately the Chinese will have to work out political arrangements that will make it possible for them to live with each other and with the modern world. Historically, their genius was to provide themselves with an enduring form of government. It is not yet clear that they will be able to adapt communism to their needs.

CHAPTER EIGHTEEN

Communism and the
Traditions of China

Many people still find it hard to believe that the Chinese are really Communists and that Mao Tse-tung, for all his dramatic efforts, can possibly change the character of a unique and historically great people. Is not Chinese civilization the oldest, the most self-contained, and the most stubbornly enduring and unchanging the world has ever known? How can people with such a heritage lose their heads over communism, a new and unstable phenomenon that is constantly changing from year to year and from leader to leader?

Because of the profound differences between the humanistic traditions of Chinese civilization and the materialism and dogmatism of communism many people once argued that communism would not endure in China. Yet more than twenty years have passed since the Communists came to power in Peking, and clearly there is still vitality in Mao's version of communism. At some deep and obscure level of Chinese culture there is a reason for China's affinity for Communism.

Exploring the relationships between traditional Chinese culture and communism, we must remember that there were many contradictions in Confucian China and that in speaking of Chinese civilization we are not speaking of something that was homogeneous. Confucianism was the official philosophy of the Chinese. Its demanding rules of filial piety and its stern virtues of correctness, rectitude, obedience, and hard work, dominated Chinese culture. Yet Taoism, with its awareness of relativity, its cult of effortlessness, and its belief in nonaction, also reflected and affected the Chinese people. Paradoxically, the upper-class Chinese gentry preached the stern and demanding doctrines of Confucianism, yet practiced the arts of leisure and sought an effortless existence more consonant with Taoism. Lower-class Chinese championed Taoism and professed to believe that nonaction could bring results, yet their lives were filled with hard work and the need to practice the Confucian virtues. What amazing examples of that strange human capacity to adopt ideologies that conflict with day-to-day behavior!

Chinese tolerance of contradiction and conflicting philosophies suggests that an analysis of Chinese civilization must go beyond the content of specific doctrines and philosophies and include less formal cultural attitudes and feelings that determined the basic style of Chinese behavior. By recognizing the distinction between Confucianism and Taoism on the one hand, and what we might call basic Chinese culture on the other, we can see how the Chinese could disregard Confucianism and still preserve qualities of their basic culture.

Under communism there have been ceaseless attacks on much of Confucianism. Filial piety, respect for ancestors, deference to age, and much else have been condemned. Nevertheless Mao's revolutionary campaigns contain much of the essence of Confucianism. His moralistic approach and stress on revolutionary sincerity and rectitude in revolutionary behavior are closer to the underlying qualities of Confucianism than to the materialism of Marxism-Leninism.

Mao and the Chinese Communists have reflected some elements of traditional Chinese culture in their attacks on other features of traditional China. The Red Guards shockingly violated the proprieties of old China, yet Mao based his exhortations to them on ethical appeals about the proper conduct of authority, the most significant concern of Confucianism. Thus even though the Chinese Communists under the leadership of Mao Tse-tung declare that they will rid China of its traditional qualities, they cannot escape reflecting the style and tone of Chinese culture.

The relationship between communism and the Chinese personality is complex. Mao has consciously attacked some traditions while unconsciously reflecting other traditions. He has claimed to be supporting new developments when in fact he is acting according to old patterns of behavior. Mao believes he is trying to change the place of China in the world. Yet in his appeals to Chinese nationalism and in his assertions that China is the center of world revolutionary affairs, he is tapping at the subconscious "Middle Kingdom complex" of the Chinese people. Similarly Mao speaks optimistically about the possibility of a constantly improving situation in China. But he displays a typically Chinese mood about the inevitability of deterioration in human affairs. He repeatedly acts as though all he has accomplished will fade away unless he heroically struggles against the inevitable.

The articulate Chinese view of time is that history is cyclical; there is a rise and fall in all affairs. The Chinese expect political decay not only because of the historical cycle but because of the inescapability of human corruption, which they believe comes from selfishness. Long before Mao Tse-tung Chinese moralists dwelt on the dangers of selfishness. Why is Chinese culture so sensitive about selfishness? Both Confucianism and communism require the individual to submerge his ambitions into group concerns, yet both expect that people will become selfish. Under both Confucianism and communism, Chinese parents strove to develop in their children strong egos and willpower, as well as willingness to yield to the collective interest — the family in the past, the Party and nation at present. Thus in Chinese culture there is an unstable balance between the desirability of willpower and the demand that an individual defer to the group. The two parts of the balance provide a basis for suspecting that anyone who excels is too egocentric and thus selfish.

These attitudes were common to traditional China, and they are apparent in Mao's attack on the Party during the Cultural Revolution. They help to explain why the Chinese are inclined to suspect that selfishness and corruption, either material or spiritual, will ultimately bring decline to most institutions.

COMMUNISM AND
MONOLITHIC AUTHORITY

Historically the Chinese have always preferred a single, unambiguous authority. Two thousand years of Confucian government was an uninterrupted era of authoritarian rule. From about 200 B.C. to 1911, the Chinese developed a remarkably stable system of government and a political culture that continues to influence the Chinese political mind.

The Confucian political order was hierarchical. Society was divided between superior and inferior people, and everyone had a sense of rank, which progressed upward toward the supreme ruler — an emperor supposedly embodying the greatest virtues and deserving unqualified respect. For the Chinese the ideal condition was one in which there was no confusion about the structure of the hierarchy. They have always thought of their evil days as the times when there was open competition for power and when there was political pluralism. Historically they idealized the periods of dynastic stability and decried those when there was uncertainty about who was supreme. In modern times this attitude resulted in widespread distress over the complex balance of power that characterized the early Republic and warlord period. A ceaseless craving for one-party rule contributed to an exaggerated faith in the Kuomintang and then in the Communist regime.

The Chinese have never been comfortable talking about politics in pure power terms. Instead they have preferred to obscure power considerations by emphasizing ideological and ethical matters. In many fields the Chinese have been realistic and pragmatic, but not with respect to political power. They have always sought to clothe naked power with the fig leaf of ideology. In traditional Chinese political thought, questions about political power were always approached through the language of the Confucian ideology. Confucianism as a political philosophy was essentially an ethical system, and for the Chinese the ultimate issues of politics and government have been questions of right and wrong, good and evil.

The Chinese have generally felt that the only right way to analyze public life was from the perspective of Confucian or some form of moral philosophy. In modern China the tendency to accentuate ideology, first in terms of the *San Min Chu I* and then in terms of Communist ideology and the Thoughts of Mao Tse-tung, has been apparent. At every stage the Chinese have insisted on the supremacy of ideology and have denied the significance of power considerations.

In the Chinese mind the virtues and vices of rulers have been decisive in determining their success and failure. In modern times neither the Nationalists nor the Communists had any doubts about the importance of making their rule appear to be consonant with the highest ethical considerations, and both groups have acted as though a prime obligation of government was to raise the moral standards of the people. This stress on morality is related to the traditional Chinese view that good government depends on superior men and not necessarily on workable institutions or efficient procedures. The essence of the Confucian doctrine was that superior men, guided by their inner sincerity and ruling by moral example, provided the best government, far superior to rule by impersonal laws and abstract principles. The cult of Mao is a continuation of this belief, and Mao reflects the traditional view about the importance of the inner sincerity of officials in his constant preaching about the need for the proper revolutionary spirit and the unimportance of administrative procedures.

The traditional Chinese view of government emphasized the importance of teaching all citizens the rules of proper conduct, particularly within the family context. The Chinese early appreciated the fact that governing a country was made a great deal easier if all children were taught to be dutiful and obedient and if families and clans assumed major responsibilities for regulating the behavior of their members. Thus education was seen as a powerful force supporting government. If the rulers could provide the right environment for teaching proper sentiments and correct rules of behavior, the remaining tasks of government would be relatively easy. Needless to say, in Mao's China there is still a powerful faith in the power of indoctrination and in the benefits of bringing up young people with the right ideals and ideas. The highest priorities in the allocation of resources and energies in Communist China have gone to molding and remolding attitudes and sentiments.

The Chinese system of government, both past and present, has tended to be hierarchical, stressing the importance of monolithic authority and emphasizing the role of ideology and particularly moralistic considerations. Many scholars of Chinese affairs, noticing these continuities, have suggested that the Communist system is not a radical break from the past but rather represents only the establishment of a new dynasty. According to this view the basic forces of Chinese history are still operating. The fall of the Ch'ing dynasty ushered in the typical period of confusion and contending forces, represented by Republican China and the warlords. Then came the great conflict between the Nationalists and the Communists to unite the country, and Mao Tse-tung, out of his success in this conflict, became the equivalent of the first emperor of a new dynasty.

POLITICAL REVOLUTION
AND CULTURAL CONTINUITY

The theory that Communist China under the rule of Mao Tse-tung represents a new dynasty and thus a repetition of the standard cycle of Chinese history illuminates elements of continuity in Chinese political history. There are many similarities between the current Communist system and the traditional imperial system — a pretension to centralized bureaucratic rule, the reality of local accommodation, reliance on an official ideology that is supposed to guide the conduct of all officials and that makes the Chinese state superior to all others, and at the top a supreme single figure, an "emperor" who reigns more than rules and issues pronouncements from a relatively secret inner world or Forbidden City.

The theory, however, does not take into account the revolutionary changes that have come to China as a consequence of the Western impact and exposure to the modern world. The consequences of a hundred years of drastic social change have produced confusion and tensions that exceed those in any of the periods of disorder that historically accompanied the fall of one dynasty and the establishment of another.

In short, there have been some decisive breaks and discontinuities in modern Chinese history. In some cases the discontinuities have meant that the Chinese can probably never again use some of the institutions and practices on which they once relied heavily. For example, the Chinese family, even before the Communists' attack on it, had been so weakened that it probably could never again have served as the prime focus for the lives of most Chinese.

On the other hand, the disorders of modern times have apparently made the Chinese look again toward monolithic authority for salvation. In this respect the Chinese people's reaction to disorder has been their classic response of placing their faith in one ruler, one party, and one ideology.

The Chinese revolution of the last hundred years has destroyed many traditional social values, including possibly the most basic value of traditional government — harmony. In all affairs harmony and balance, the avoidance of extremes and the acknowledgment of compromise, once dominated Chinese life. The goal of government was to bring peace and tranquility; and the basic principle of social life was the avoidance of conflict. Under Mao class conflict and ceaseless struggle are the themes of government and social life. Slogans that express hostility and even hatred have replaced the older appeals for harmony. This suggests that in China's transition from a traditional order to a modern state a distinctive problem has been to control and express aggression.

The basic features of traditional China — the stress on moralistic ideologies, the need for strict order and hierarchical relationships, the emphasis on the moral virtues of leaders, the need for education in correct conduct, and the importance of proper manners and etiquette — combined to suppress any manifestations of aggression. Harmony, the ultimate ideal of old China, likewise worked to check aggression. Modernization has meant the weakening of many of the old bonds that controlled people's behavior and compelled them to suppress their aggressive feelings. Above all, the emergence of popular politics and the need to mobilize the entire population has resulted in extensive appeals to the people's long-suppressed emotions of aggression.

Not surprisingly there is ambivalence in China over this new possibility for expressing aggression. Because for most Chinese personality formation emphasized the dangers of expressing aggressive sentiments, most Chinese find considering anything that is regarded as a dangerous issue quite exciting. However, most Chinese still feel the traditional cultural abhorrence of violence and aggression. Consequently there is a strong tendency to reduce the dangers of explicitly expressed aggression by the psychological device of ritualizing these expressions. Thus there is a trend in modern China of using extreme language in politics but of controlling sentiments, of symbolic violence that becomes routinized action. One of the secrets of Mao's success in achieving power was that through the rhetoric of communism he discovered that by appearing to be fearless and even reckless about the great Chinese dread of disorder, of seeming to welcome conflict and struggle, and by giving vent to sentiments of aggression, he made himself appear to have heroic qualities of leadership that set him above most Chinese.

Mao's tragedy is that the psychological qualities that made the Chinese admire his fearlessness about disorder have given them their great capacity to ritualize their sentiments, particularly if they approach too closely the area of aggression. Mao is constantly troubled because although the people are prepared to verbally accept revolution their emotions readily become controlled and passive. For this reason Mao can never be quite satisfied that the Chinese people truly feel the revolutionary emotions his rhetoric demands.

Before the arrival of Mao and the Communists the theme of modern Chinese politics was already that of revolution. Since 1911 the Chinese have talked incessantly about the need to "complete the revolution." Yet what they have had in mind has not been the need to destroy more authorities in order to liberate more of life. They have called for stronger and more competent authorities. Instead of seeing revolution as the weakening of authority, China's concern has been that existing authorities are too weak and that the country needs more powerful and more complete authority.

The strange relationship between explosive appeals for revolution and a craving for stronger authority calls for a deeper analysis of the Chinese view of authority.

REVOLUTION AND AUTHORITY

Modernization has brought a crisis of authority to the Chinese. In most African and Asian countries the process of change in modernization has caused crises of identity. People are torn between the old and the new, between scorning their traditions and asserting that their traditions contain the essence of modern culture. The Chinese, however, have been less troubled by questions of identity because of their powerful sense of historical greatness.

The Chinese have been disturbed that they have not been more powerful and more effective in world affairs. Out of their agony of frustration over no longer being the Middle Kingdom, the Chinese have tended to find fault with their leaders and to dream of having a more complete and absolute form of government, strong enough to bring China back to its rightful place in the eyes of the rest of the world.

It is not hard to see why the Chinese have tended to place such importance on authority and why they want to turn to strong leadership whenever they are in difficulty. Traditionally a child's fundamental experience in growing up was to learn filial piety and to defer completely to the authority of the father. Filial piety was extremely severe, and the child learned that he could never give expression to any of his feelings of aggression against his father. He learned that he should never complain to those above him and to accept much suffering in silence. This is clearly the psychological basis of the Chinese people's suppression of aggression.

There was, however, a positive side to filial piety — the comforts of dependency and the satisfaction of achieving moral standards. If one placed one's faith in the parental figure, acted dutifully, sought always to meet expected standards of conduct, and generally displayed a supporting and cooperative spirit, one could expect to receive the few psychic rewards that parents were prepared to give to children.

Thus in Chinese culture individuals learned from their earliest experiences with authority that, in spite of its uncompromising demands, correct behavior and dependency would provide psychic security. The Chinese tended to extend this view to authorities beyond the family and thus created a cultural ideal of authority as being absolute and stern on the one hand and protective and concerned with the well-being of subjects on the other. The model of government was both authoritarian and paternalistic.

Although a remarkably high proportion of the leaders of Communist China rebelled against their own fathers, including Mao Tse-tung, they generally accepted the propriety of the authoritarian dimension of their parents' behavior and charged that their fathers in particular had not been supportive enough and were therefore unjust. This points to a tension that has always existed in Chinese culture — the tension between the acceptance of the substance of authoritarianism and the requirement that the form and the spirit of paternalistic support also exist. The right to rule was not questioned, but the people expected the benefits of dependency. In return for the right to absolute authority, the ruler was supposed to worry about the welfare of the people.

Widespread social change and political revolution have not fundamentally altered this view of authority. There have been some modifications in content but not much in substance. For example, there is in Communist China less extolling of the traditional view that age should command authority. Yet it is significant that the Chinese Communist leadership is at present the oldest ruling class in the world, and certainly Mao's advanced age has given him considerable protection from open criticism and counterattack from his colleagues. Authority is still supposed to be based on knowledge — now, of Marxism and the Thoughts of Mao Tse-tung. The cultural ideal that authority should be based on virtue and should command a system of morality still appears to remain intact. Ever since the Cultural Revolution the dominant theme in Communist China has been Mao as the fountainhead of all morality. According to Chinese cultural concepts the fact that Mao is depicted as the ultimate authority on morality makes him also the supreme political authority.

In most societies moralizing about the behavior of others is considered a potentially aggressive act. Most people are permitted to express their displeasure at being preached at, and those who perform the social role of moralizers are usually protected by being given a clear, somewhat isolated, position. They are priests or ministers and are removed from exposure to violence. In Chinese culture there has always been a close linkage between the holding of power and the right to moralize. This has contributed to exaggerated expectations of what authority can do if it wants to, and to deeply suppressed hostility toward the source of moralizing.

THE VULNERABILITIES OF LEADERSHIP

A century of change in Chinese civilization and prolonged social revolution have not greatly altered the profound Chinese faith in authority. They have only made the Chinese dissatisfied with existing rulers and anxious for more perfect government. Expecting so much of their leaders, the Chinese are prone to see failures of authority. Hence, in modern times they have been experiencing a peculiar crisis of authority.

In the Chinese view political authority should be able to deal with all problems in the society. Traditionally rewards and prestige were to be gained by careers in government, and the Confucian mandarinate contained not just men interested in public administration but those interested in wealth, learning, leisure, and all civilized pursuits.

The Chinese never had a stage of highly developed feudalism. They were not exposed to the institutionalized division of labor that Western Europe and Japan knew. Thus the Chinese did not develop distinctions between economic, social, and political systems. Instead of believing that economic relationships called for a separate set of "laws" and specialized skills, the Chinese assumed that ultimate authority should be equally competent in all matters. Faith in the supreme mastery of the political domain predisposed the Chinese to accept the Communists' idea that Party and government should run all aspects of society. It also prepared them for the idea that the supreme leader, Mao Tse-tung, was fully qualified and competent to determine all policy.

In all societies, however, modernization has involved specialization and differentiation. Modern industrial societies need many different kinds of specialists who must be allowed to apply their particular knowledge. Specialization calls for divisions of authority. Political authorities have to recognize the legitimate domains of the specialists if they are to benefit from the advances of technology and modernization.

This basic trend fundamentally conflicts with the traditional and persisting Chinese faith in the need for omnipotent authority. This is the basic problem Mao confronts when he talks of the "red and expert" issue. He continues to insist that the specialist must be the complete servant of the political authority and that no form of specialized knowledge can be allowed to compromise the authority of his revolution, which is embodied in his own person.

If specialization causes any compromise of his revolutionary authority, Mao is prepared to forego the benefits of technological advances. He tends to see any diminution of ideological authority as revisionism. Thus the clash between ideological purists and pragmatic specialists during the Cultural Revolution was also a clash between traditional Chinese sentiments about the omnipotence of authority and the requirements of modernization.

For the Chinese it is not easy to divide authority. They believe that any separation will inevitably produce conflict that can be resolved only by the reestablishment of a monopoly of authority. It is not just those in official positions who tend to be anxious about competing authorities. The people as a whole believe their supreme leaders should have dominion over all problems and protect the people from all hardships.

This blend of authoritarianism and dependence on authority means that when the government appears to be weak and failing, the people are inclined to turn against it. Usually they continue to have faith in the supreme figure but see evil in those who surround him and act in his name. Historically, the Chinese, needing to believe in the existence of an almost magical authority, tended to believe that the emperor was good but separated from the people by bad officials. In Communist China there is continuing faith in Mao but aggressive criticism of lesser officials.

In spite of the authoritarian tradition, officialdom has always been vulnerable, particularly to moral criticism. Whenever things are not going well, the Chinese suspicion is that the root problem is probably the personal immorality of officials. Historically, these sentiments were expressed in the concept of the Mandate of Heaven. It was assumed that disasters and national misfortune were heaven's way of showing displeasure over the behavior of officials, including even the emperor. That tradition continues in the practice of blaming troubles on the personal behavior of cadres and leading Party members.

In a strange way much of Chinese politics, both traditional and contemporary, has involved confrontations over morals and correct behavior between officials and subjects. When things go wrong, the people point to the moral laxity of the rulers and the officials stress the immoral behavior of the population. At times the supreme ruler might ally himself with the people and charge that the trouble stems from the improper behavior of subordinate officials. At other times he might support his officials and demand that the population as a whole improve its behavior. This pattern is apparent in much of the behavior of Mao. During the Cultural Revolution he identified himself with the lowest ranks in attacking the existing hierarchy of officialdom, yet at other times he has called on the people as a whole to improve their conduct and revolutionary spirit.

The assumptions that authority figures should ceaselessly concern themselves with moral matters and that the welfare of the society depends on the morality of officials and subjects are the bases of the Chinese belief that rulers have the right and the duty to concern themselves with controlling and improving the thoughts of the people. Thus there exists in Chinese culture a rationale that provides implicit support to all the efforts of the Communist regime to concern itself with thought reform.

THOUGHT REFORM

How effective have the Peking regime's efforts been in changing Chinese ways of thinking and replacing Confucianism with the Thoughts of Mao Tse-tung? Certainly one of the most distinctive and startling characteristics of the Communists when they first came to power was their endless enthusiasm for remolding the thoughts of all the Chinese people. In the 1950's most of the attention of loyal and skilled Party members was given to organizing study groups in every location and place of work. Self-criticism and mutual criticism sessions and techniques touched the lives of millions of Chinese. These attempts to change the attitudes and psychology of the Chinese people produced the concept of brainwashing as cadres sought to eliminate improper views and instill the new correct ones.

By the mid-1960's much of this activity had become standardized, and people's attention focused more on other matters, causing Mao to feel that the revolution was losing its dynamic force. To counter this trend he called for the Socialist Education Campaign and the Learn from the People's Liberation Army Movement, which culminated in the Great Proletarian Cultural Revolution.

In the early years of the regime the technique of thought reform seemed to be remarkably effective. Millions of Chinese learned in a very short period the lexicon of the Communist ideology and the slogans and attitudes that pleased their new rulers. Several characteristics of Chinese personality and culture help to explain why the Chinese responded as they did to the efforts to give them a new world view and a new morality. Traditional Chinese concern for harmony, good manners, and the need to suppress aggression tended to make the Chinese anxious to please their superiors and to conform to their peers' expectations. They always appreciated the importance of adjusting to the realities of any situation and of being guided by the condition in which they found themselves.

Sensitivity to conformity and the need to adjust to circumstances is probably related to the importance of shame in the training of children. Chinese culture has often been described as a shame culture, rather than a guilt culture. The Chinese are extremely sensitive to what others may think of them and are less troubled by deep inward or private feelings of conscience about their own behavior. Children are taught to behave by being shamed, and it is assumed that the individual will go to great lengths to avoid being publicly humiliated.

The Chinese try to behave correctly in every situation and to avoid situations in which they cannot cope. In any new situation they are anxious to learn what they can do to make themselves either inconspicuous or the objects of praise. Thus many Chinese reacted positively to the Communists' efforts at reforming their thoughts because they thought the Communists were being helpful in teaching them how to behave in order to reduce social risks and gain greater security in their relations with others.

On the other hand, the psychological sensitivity to shame that facilitated thought reform also makes the Chinese careful about expressing their real feelings. Communist rulers always are in some doubt about how changed the people really are. Shame, if unaccompanied by guilt feelings, means that the individual adapts readily to outward conditions without making great emotional commitments. The traditional Chinese practice of using shame and teasing in bringing up children teaches the child to be careful about showing his emotions and act according to cues outside of himself, rather than being guided by his inner feelings. Thus the Chinese are taught early to conceal their true emotions and always appear to have the feelings required by the situation.

Mao Tse-tung's frustration is that he cannot truly tell how effective his efforts at thought reform have been. He finds that the Chinese can repeat from memory what is expected of them, but he does not know whether the people have internalized the new spirit or whether they are merely responding as they always have by trying to please those with power. He has no way of knowing how enduring his regime will be.

Mao's concern over the state of mind of the Chinese people

is heightened by his need to believe in the importance of enthusiasm because he rejected the benefits of technological specialization for fear that division of authority would compromise the ultimate political authority of the regime. Thus, Mao, out of his notions about authority, has been forced to demand more control over the inner thoughts and sentiments of the Chinese people than probably is necessary for the maintenance of communism or even desirable for the modernization of China. Indeed, Mao has probably set impossible goals, trying to change the character and personality of the Chinese people. Perhaps the greatest danger to his dream of a Communist society for China is that he will waste his resources trying to change things that do not matter and fail to use effectively the advantages he does have.

THE FUTURE OF CHINESE COMMUNISM

It is extremely difficult to forecast the future of Chinese communism because at no point since the founding of the Peking regime in 1949 have its operations been more obscure. Mao Tse-tung seems to have emerged from the Cultural Revolution as the supreme figure, yet as has so often been his practice he has drifted away from the day-to-day administration of his government. At this time there is no solid Party hierarchy to manage affairs. Instead China, like so many underdeveloped countries, has seemingly backed into military rule, and there seem to be no command decisions to give direction to the Chinese people, who are always anxious and ready to do the right thing as enunciated by established authority.

This is an ironic outcome of the extreme anti-organizational radicalism of the Cultural Revolution. Out of his distrust of divided and hence competing authorities Mao sought to eliminate the Party and all that stood between the authority of his thoughts and the Chinese masses. But to carry out the functions of governing he has had to turn to the most hierarchical of institutions, the army.

In an odd fashion, however, this development may reveal much about the limits of modernization under Mao Tse-tung. The People's Liberation Army under Lin Piao, ever since the purge of P'eng Te-huai and the more technologically oriented commanders, achieved a balance between spiritual discipline and a low grade of technology.

Such a balance may be the goal Mao has for Chinese society, except in a few isolated and self-contained fields such as nuclear physics and missile development.

Given the character of the Chinese people, can Mao's faith in human willpower produce significant national development, and are other, more promising, approaches available to the Chinese? In many economically backward countries there is a serious need to shake the people out of their traditional inhibitions and give them the inspiration to strive for new goals. In the case of China, however, this need is less apparent. Although China in Mao's formative years was indeed retarded by outmoded customs, the Chinese people have in recent years experienced a great deal and they are now remarkably energetic and hard working.

The question is whether the Chinese people will continue to have the necessary drive and motivation to carry out the demanding work of building up their country. Mao's belief is that the necessary, and probably only available, motivation has to be moral and spiritual. Moral appeals do have great meaning to the Chinese people, but they also know of the need to control their emotions, to feign sentiments, and to calculate their circumstances in order to achieve maximum benefits. Moral appeals can easily lose their potency and cause the Chinese to become cynical and distrustful of an authority that does not gratify their desire for dependence.

Thus excessive reliance on moral appeals can be a two-edged sword, helping authority when all is going well but undercutting authority when the leaders seem to be faltering. Turning his back on the advantages of modern technology and rejecting material incentives and the pragmatic considerations that have always been important to the Chinese and have influenced much of their behavior, Mao Tse-tung is on a reckless course.

There is no inherent reason why Chinese civilization should not effectively adapt to modern life. Other peoples who have been historically influenced by Chinese civilization, such as the Japanese and Koreans, have demonstrated that the heritage can be of great advantage in supporting the drive toward modernization. Indeed, it is clear that in Asia the peoples who were most influenced by the basic qualities of traditional China have been the leaders in successful modernization. Furthermore, large populations of Chinese in Taiwan, Hong Kong, Singapore, and the overseas Chinese communities of Southeast Asia are proof that Chinese culture produces the intellectual genius and spirit necessary for adapting and developing modern ways.

China's tragedy has been that none of its rulers, from the last of the Ch'ing through Mao Tse-tung, has been able to give the nation's very talented people the kind of government that could maximize their great capacities. However, each of these rulers has in a different way expressed peculiarly Chinese qualities. The Chinese expect much of those in authority, and the rulers feel compelled to fulfill ideals that cannot be realized and are not necessarily relevant for national development. Although Chinese culture has emphasized filial piety, the role of the ideal father is quite unattainable. Because an ideal ruler should embody the traits of an ideal father in addition to political expertise, superhuman demands press down on any conscientious ruler. It is noteworthy that the Chinese have felt compelled to glorify beyond human recognition all their leaders from their emperors to Sun Yat-sen to Chiang Kai-shek and Mao Tse-tung.

The Chinese tendency to regard the ruler as a superman may arise from the fact that throughout Chinese history the all-powerful ideal figure was mortal, not divine. Chinese culture has been infused with the teachings of Confucius, a man who had an influence as great as that of gods in other cultures. Chinese rulers must measure themselves against a fellow mortal whose cultural significance approached that of divinities. In other cultures rulers try to do their best and know that they cannot meet the cultural ideals attributed to divine figures. Mao Tse-tung, in his heroic effort to put China on a new course of historical development, cannot escape his own human limitations, which embody so much of Chinese culture. Yet he must at least subconsciously feel that his success will depend on his becoming more significant than Confucius. This goal cannot possibly be accomplished in his lifetime. But Mao feels compelled to try; he knows that after his death he cannot control his own image.

Chinese culture will persist and steadily change in accordance with the historical processes that govern the modernization of traditional societies. Even as China modernizes the Chinese will continue to reflect much of their heritage, as have all societies that have advanced into the industrial era.

Sources and Suggested Readings

In recent years there has been a great increase in the number of scholarly monographs on China. The writers of most of them presume that the reader is somewhat familiar with the subject. Probably the best guide to this literature is the bibliography in John K. Fairbank, *The United States and China* (Cambridge, Mass.: Harvard University Press, 1948, 1958, 1971). A more detailed bibliography is in Charles O. Hucker, *China: A Critical Bibliography* (Tucson: University of Arizona Press, 1962).

In preparing this book, I consulted and relied on the following works. They can be profitably read by all who wish to further explore Chinese history and culture

GENERAL INTRODUCTIONS

The most masterful overview of Chinese history and social evolution is the above-mentioned study by Fairbank. For a more detailed analysis see Edwin O. Reischauer and John K. Fairbank, *East Asia: The Great Tradition* (Boston: Houghton Mifflin, 1960); and John K. Fairbank, Edwin O. Reischauer, and Albert M. Craig, *East Asia: The Modern Transformation* (Boston: Houghton Mifflin, 1965). An introduction that balances political developments with cultural and artistic ones is C. P. Fitzgerald, *China: A Short Cultural History*, 3d ed. (New York: Praeger, 1961).

THE CONFUCIAN TRADITION

The richest single source of translations of traditional Chinese thought is William Theodore de Bary, Wing-tsit Chan, and Burton Watson, comp., *Sources in China Tradition* (New York: Columbia University Press, 1960). The standard translation of the Confucian classics is James

359

Legge, *The Chinese Classics* (Oxford, Eng.: Clarendon Press, 8 vols., 1893–1895). For a more sensitive and literary translation see Arthur Waley, *The Analects of Confucius* (London: Allen and Unwin, 1938). The standard textbook on Chinese philosophy is Fung Yu-lan, *A History of Chinese Philosophy,* trans. Derk Bodde (Princeton, N.J.: Princeton University Press, 2 vols., 1952). The most detailed study of Confucius is H. G. Creel, *Confucius: The Man and the Myth* (New York: Day, 1949). The best introductions to Taoism are Arthur Waley, *The Way and Its Power* (London: Allen and Unwin, 1938); and Holmes Welch, *The Parting of the Way: Lao Tzu and the Taoist Movement* (Boston: Beacon Press, 1957).

THE CHINESE LIBRARY

The best general introduction to Chinese literature is Burton Watson, *Early Chinese Literature* (New York: Columbia University Press, 1962). For a technical review of Chinese historical scholarship see Charles S. Gardner, *Chinese Traditional Historiography* (Cambridge, Mass.: Harvard University Press, 1938). The character of the official dynastic histories is revealed in the following translations: Homer Dubs, *The History of the Former Han Dynasty of Pan Ku* (Baltimore: Waverly Press, vol. 1, 1938; vol. 2, 1944; vol. 3, 1955); Burton Watson, *Records of the Grand Historian of China* (New York: Columbia University Press, 2 vols., 1961); and Achilles Fang, *The Chronicle of the Three Kingdoms* (Cambridge, Mass.: Harvard University Press, 2 vols., 1952, 1965). For a detailed review of other aspects of Chinese classical literature see James Robert Hightower, *Topics in Chinese Literature: Outlines and Bibliographies* (Cambridge, Mass.: Harvard University Press, 1953). Introductions to Chinese poetry include James J. Y. Liu, *The Art of Chinese Poetry* (Chicago: University of Chicago Press, 1962); and Arthur Waley, *Ballads and Stories from Tunhuang: An Anthology* (London: Allen and Unwin, 1960).

THE TRADITIONAL CHINESE SYSTEM

Among the most informative and readable discussions of life and institutions in traditional China are Michael Loewe, *Imperial China: The Historical Background to the Modern Age* (New York: Praeger, 1966); Derk Bodde, *China's First Unifier: A Study of the Ch'in Dynasty as Seen in the Life of Li Ssu 280?–208 B.C.* (Leiden, Neth.: Brill, 1938);

Arthur F. Wright, ed., *Studies in Chinese Thought* (Chicago: University of Chicago Press, 1953); John K. Fairbank, ed., *Chinese Thought and Institutions* (Chicago: University of Chicago Press, 1957); David S. Nivison and Arthur F. Wright, eds., *Confucianism in Action* (Stanford, Calif.: Stanford University Press, 1960); Arthur F. Wright and Denis C. Twitchett, eds., *Confucian Personalities* (Stanford, Calif.: Stanford University Press, 1962); Charles O. Hucker, *The Traditional Chinese State in Ming Times, 1368–1644* (Tucson: University of Arizona Press, 1961); E. A. Kracke, Jr., *Civil Service in Early Sung China, 960–1067* (Cambridge, Mass.: Harvard University Press, 1959); Derk Bodde and Clarence Morris, *Law in Imperial China: Exemplified by 190 Ch'ing Dynasty Cases* (Cambridge, Mass.: Harvard University Press, 1967); T'ung-tsu Ch'ü, *Local Government in China Under the Ch'ing* (Cambridge, Mass.: Harvard University Press, 1962).

CHINA'S FOREIGN RELATIONS

Classic studies of Chinese relations with nomadic "barbarians" are Franz Michael, *The Origin of Manchu Rule in China: Frontier and Bureaucracy as Interacting Forces in the Chinese Empire* (Baltimore: Johns Hopkins Press, 1942); Wolfram Eberhard, *Conquerors and Rulers: Social Forces in Medieval China*, 2d. ed. (Leiden, Neth.: Brill, 1965); and John K. Fairbank, ed., *The Chinese World Order: Traditional China's Foreign Relations* (Cambridge, Mass.: Harvard University Press, 1968).

Early Western contacts are described in Hosea Ballou Morse, *The International Relations of the Chinese Empire* (London: Longmans, Green, 3 vols., 1910, 1918); John K. Fairbank, *Trade and Diplomacy on the China Coast: The Opening of the Treaty Ports* (Cambridge, Mass.: Harvard University Press, 2 vols., 1953); Immanuel C. Y. Hsü, *The Rise of Modern China* (New York: Oxford University Press, 1970).

A rich storehouse of documents that reveal Chinese attitudes is Ssu-yu Teng and John K. Fairbank, *China's Response to the West: A Documentary Survey, 1839–1923* (Cambridge, Mass.: Harvard University Press, 1954); and the most stimulating and subtle treatment of Chinese intellectual developments as a consequence of the Western impact is Joseph R. Levenson, *Confucian China and Its Modern Fate*: Vol. 1, *The Problem of Intellectual Continuity*, 1958; vol. 2, *The Problem of Monarchial Decay*, 1964; vol. 3, *The Problem of Historical Significance* (Berkeley: University of California Press). The spirit of the Confucian

mandarin in the face of the Western Challenge is best conveyed by Mary
C. Wright, *The Last Stand of Chinese Conservatism: The T'ung-Chih
Restoration, 1862–1872* (New York: Atheneum, 1966).

CHINESE SOCIETY

A lively general introduction to the Chinese rural society and
economy is Fei Hsiao-t'ung, *China's Gentry*, ed. Margaret Park Redfield
(Chicago: University of Chicago Press, 1953). For studies of Chinese
social structure and social mobility questions see Chung-li Chang, *The
Chinese Gentry: Studies on Their Role in Nineteenth Century Chinese
Society* (Seattle: University of Washington Press, 1955); for a master-
ful blending of sociological and historical analysis see Ping-ti Ho, *The
Ladder of Success in Imperial China: Aspects of Social Mobility, 1368–
1911* (New York: Columbia University Press, 1962). Also see Etienne
Balazs, *Chinese Civilization and Bureaucracy*, trans. H. M. Wright, ed.
Arthur F. Wright (New Haven, Conn.: Yale University Press, 1964);
Morton H. Fried, *Fabric of Chinese Society* (New York: Praeger, 1953);
E. A. Kracke, Jr., *Civil Service in Early Sung China, 960–1067* (Cam-
bridge, Mass.: Harvard University Press, 1953); Max Weber, *The
Religions of China: Confucianism and Taoism*, trans. Hans Gerth,
(Glencoe, Ill.: Free Press, 1951).

RURAL ECONOMY AND VILLAGE LIFE

An exceptional economic history study that demonstrates that
Chinese agricultural production kept pace with population growth is
Dwight H. Perkins, assisted by Yeh-chien Wang, *Agricultural Develop-
ment in China, 1368–1968* (Chicago: Aldine, 1969). A systematic review
of both Japanese and Chinese data on rural economics is Ramon H.
Myers, *The Chinese Peasant Economy: Agricultural Development in
Hopei and Shantung, 1890–1949* (Cambridge, Mass.: Harvard Univer-
sity Press, 1970). The classic anthropological study is Francis L. K. Hsu,
Under the Ancestors' Shadow: Chinese Culture and Personality (New
York: Columbia University Press, 1948). Also see Martin Yang, *A
Chinese Village: Taitou, Shantung Province* (New York: Columbia
University Press, 1945); Lin Yüeh-hua, *The Golden Wing* (London:
Kegan Paul, Trench, Trubner, 1948). Studies that focus on changes
with the Communist takeover include C. K. Yang, *Chinese Communist
Society: The Family and the Village* (Cambridge, Mass.: M.I.T. Press,
1965); William Hinton, *Fanshen: A Documentary of Revolution in a*

Chinese Village (New York: Monthly Review Press, 1966); and Jan Myrdal, *Report from a Chinese Village* (New York: Pantheon Books, 1965).

THE CHINESE FAMILY

A classic empirical study of the Chinese family is Olga Lang, *Chinese Family and Society* (New Haven, Conn.: Yale University Press, 1946); and the classic theoretical study is Marion J. Levy, Jr., *The Family Revolution in Modern China* (Cambridge, Mass.: Harvard University Press, 1949). More recent studies include Maurice Freedman, *Chinese Lineage and Society: Fukien and Kwangtung* (London: Athlone, 1966); Maurice Freedman, ed., *Family and Kinship in Chinese Society* (Stanford, Calif.: Stanford University Press, 1970); Margery Wolf, *The House of Lim: A Study of a Chinese Farm Family* (New York: Appleton-Century-Crofts, 1968); Ida Pruitt, *A Daughter of Han: The Autobiography of a Chinese Working Woman* (Stanford, Calif.: Stanford University Press, 1967).

THE WARLORDS AND THE NATIONALIST PERIOD

The 1911 revolution has most recently been analyzed in Mary C. Wright, ed., *China in Revolution: The First Phase, 1900–1913* (New Haven, Conn.: Yale University Press, 1968). The warlord period is covered in O. Edmund Clubb, *Twentieth Century China* (New York: Columbia University Press, 1964); James E. Sheridan, *Chinese Warlord: The Career of Feng Yü-hsiang* (Stanford, Calif.: Stanford University Press, 1966); Donald Gillin, *Warlord: Yen Hsi-shan in Shansi Province 1911–1949* (Princeton, N.J.: Princeton University Press, 1967); Lucian W. Pye, *Warlord Politics* (New York: Praeger, 1971); and Ralph L. Powell, *The Rise of Chinese Military Power, 1895–1912* (Princeton, N.J.: Princeton University Press, 1955); and Arthur N. Holcombe, *The Spirit of the Chinese Revolution* (New York: Knopf, 1930).

Little has been written on the Nationalist period. The formal system of Kuomintang rule is described in Ch'ien Tuan-sheng, *The Government and Politics of China, 1912–1949* (Cambridge, Mass.: Harvard University Press, 1950); William L. Tung, *The Political Institutions of Modern China* (The Hague: Nijhoff, 1964); Paul M. A. Linebarger, *The China of Chiang K'ai-shek: A Political Study* (Boston: World Peace Foundation, 1943).

THE RISE OF COMMUNISM

In contrast a great deal has been written on the early years of the Chinese Communist Party, the most important being Edgar Snow, *Red Star over China* (New York: Random House, 1938); Harold Isaacs, *The Tragedy of the Chinese Revolution* (Stanford, Calif.: Stanford University Press, 1938, 1951); Benjamin Schwartz, *Chinese Communism and the Rise of Mao Tse-tung* (Cambridge, Mass.: Harvard University Press, 1951); Shanti Swarup, *A Study of the Chinese Communist Movement* (Oxford, Eng.: Clarendon Press, 1966); Stuart Schram, *Mao Tse-tung* (New York: Simon and Schuster, 1966); Jerome Ch'en, *Mao and the Chinese Revolution* (New York: Oxford University Press, 1967); Richard C. Thornton, *The Comintern and the Chinese Communists, 1928–1931* (Seattle: University of Washington Press, 1969). The thesis that nationalism and reactions to the Japanese occupation were more important than landlord-peasant relations in explaining the rise of the Communist Party is impressively developed in Chalmers A. Johnson, *Peasant Nationalism and Communist Power: The Emergence of Revolutionary China, 1937–1945* (Stanford, Calif.: Stanford University Press, 1962).

THE COMMUNIST SYSTEM

Probably the most authoritative and illuminating single source for understanding the Chinese Communist system is the writings of A. Doak Barnett, in particular: *China on the Eve of Communist Takeover* (New York: Praeger, 1963); *Communist China and Asia: Challenge to American Policy* (New York: Harper, 1960); *Cadres, Bureaucracy, and Political Power in Communist China* (New York: Columbia University Press, 1967); and *Communist China: The Early Years, 1949–55* (New York: Praeger, 1964).

The early years of the regime are covered in W. W. Rostow, *The Prospects of Communist China* (New York: Wiley, 1954); Richard L. Walker, *China Under Communism: The First Five Years* (New Haven, Conn.: Yale University Press, 1955).

The organizational discipline of the early Communist regime is stressed in Franz Schurmann, *Ideology and Organization in Communist China* (Berkeley: University of California Press, 1966). The best study of mass organizations is James R. Townsend, *Political Participation in Communist China* (Berkeley: University of California Press, 1968).

IDEOLOGY AND THOUGHT REFORM

The classic and rather grim study is Robert J. Lifton, *Thought Reform and the Psychology of Totalism: A Study of "Brainwashing" in China* (New York: Norton, 1961). Others that stress more the problems of intellectuals include Theodore H. F. Chen, *Thought Reform of the Chinese Intellectuals* (Hong Kong: Hong Kong University Press, 1960); Roderick MacFarquhar, *The Hundred Flowers Campaign and the Chinese Intellectuals* (New York: Praeger, 1960); and Merle Goldman, *Literary Dissent in Communist China* (Cambridge, Mass.: Harvard University Press, 1967). On the role of the mass media see Frederick T. C. Yu, *Mass Persuasion in Communist China* (New York: Praeger, 1964); Franklin W. Houn, *To Change a Nation: Propaganda and Indoctrination in Communist China* (Glencoe, Ill.: Free Press, 1961); Alan P. L. Liu, *Communications and National Integration in Communist China* (Berkeley: University of California Press, 1971).

General treatment of Communist ideology and Mao's Thoughts include Stuart Schram, *The Political Thought of Mao Tse-tung* (New York: Praeger, 1963); Arthur A. Cohen, *The Communism of Mao Tse-tung* (Chicago: University of Chicago Press, 1964); James Chieh Hsiung, *Ideology and Practice: The Evolution of Chinese Communism* (New York: Praeger, 1970); Chester C. Tan, *Chinese Political Thought in the Twentieth Century* (New York: Doubleday, 1971).

POLICY AREAS

A good introduction to a wide range of Chinese Communist policies is to be found in Franklin W. Houn, *A Short History of Chinese Communism* (Englewood Cliffs, N.J.: Prentice-Hall, 1967). Agricultural policy is presented in Kenneth R. Walker, *Planning in Chinese Agriculture* (London: Can, 1965); Chao Kuo-chun, *Agrarian Policy of the Chinese Communist Party* (Bombay: Asia Publishing House, 1960). The most detailed treatment of the economy is Audrey Dannithorne, *China's Economic System* (London: Allen and Unwin, 1967). See an excellent general analysis in Alexander Eckstein, *Communist China's Economic Growth and Foreign Trade* (New York: McGraw-Hill, 1966). See also Barry M. Richman, *Industrial Society in Communist China* (New York: Random House, 1969); C. Liu and K. Yeh, *The Economy of the Chinese Mainland* (Princeton, N.J.: Princeton University Press, 1965); Alexander Eckstein, Walter Galenson, and Ta-chung Liu, eds.,

Economic Trends in Communist China (Chicago: Aldine, 1968); and Dwight H. Perkins, *Market Control and Planning in Communist China* (Cambridge, Mass.: Harvard University Press, 1966).

PERSONALITIES AND BIOGRAPHIES

For biographical information that covers Communist leaders as well as pre-Communist figures see Howard L. Boorman, *Biographical Dictionary of Republican China* (New York: Columbia University Press, 4 vols., 1967, 1968, 1970, 1971). For Communist figures alone see Donald Klein and Anne B. Clark, *Biographical Dictionary of Chinese Communism, 1921–1965* (Cambridge, Mass.: Harvard University Press, 1971). For more general treatment of the main leaders see Robert S. Elegant, *China's Red Masters* (New York: Twayne, 1951); Martin Eban, *Lin Piao* (New York: Stein and Day, 1970); Nym Wales, *Red Dust: Autobiographies of Chinese Communists* (Stanford, Calif.: Stanford University Press, 1952); Robert Payne, *Mao Tse-tung* (New York: Abelard-Schuman, 1962).

PARTY POLITICS

See A. Doak Barnett, ed. *Chinese Communist Politics in Action* (Seattle: University of Washington Press, 1969); John M. H. Lindbeck, *China: Management of a Revolutionary Society* (Seattle: University of Washington Press, 1971). For policies and politics as reflected at the local level, see Ezra F. Vogel, *Canton Under Communism* (Cambridge, Mass.: Harvard University Press, 1969). See also John W. Lewis, *Leadership in Communist China* (Ithaca, N.Y.: Cornell University Press, 1963); Roderick MacFarquhar, ed., *China Under Mao* (Cambridge, Mass.: M.I.T. Press, 1966); William T. Liu, ed., *Chinese Society Under Communism: A Reader* (New York: Wiley, 1967).

FOREIGN POLICY

The classic study is still A. Doak Barnett, *Communist China and Asia* (New York: Harper, 1960). For a detailed analysis see Harold C. Hinton, *Communist China in World Politics* (Boston: Houghton Mifflin, 1966); and the same author's *China's Turbulent Quest* (New York: MacMillan, 1970). On Chinese military policy see John Gitting, *The Role of the Chinese Army* (London: Oxford University Press, 1967);

Alice Langley Hsieh, *Communist China's Strategy in the Nuclear Era* (Englewood Cliffs, N.J.: Prentice-Hall, 1962); Samuel B. Griffith, II, *The Chinese Peoples' Liberation Army* (New York: McGraw-Hill, 1967). On the Sino-Soviet dispute see two studies by William E. Griffith, *The Sino-Soviet Rift* (Cambridge, Mass.: M.I.T. Press, 1964); and *Sino-Soviet Relations, 1964–1965* (Cambridge, Mass.: M.I.T. Press, 1967); and Robert S. Elegant, *Mao's Great Revolution* (New York: World Publishing, 1971).

THE CULTURAL REVOLUTION

Several major studies are now in preparation by knowledgeable men such as Edward E. Rice, Stanley Karnow, and A. Doak Barnett. Specialized studies include Philip Bridgham, "Mao's 'Cultural Revolution': Origin and Development," *China Quarterly*, no. 29 (January 1967); Philip Bridgham, "Mao's Cultural Revolution in 1967: The Struggle to Seize Power," *China Quarterly*, no. 34 (April 1968); Harold Hinton, "The Beginning of the Cultural Revolution," in Lucian W. Pye, ed., *Cases in Comparative Politics: Asia* (Boston: Little, Brown, 1970); Richard Baum, "China: Year of the Mangoes," *Asian Survey*, 9:1 (January 1969); Chalmers Johnson, "Lin Piao's Army and Its Role in Chinese Society," *Current Scene*, 4:13–14 (July 1 and 15, 1966); Charles Neuhauser, "The Chinese Communist Party in the 1960s: Prelude to the Cultural Revolution," *China Quarterly*, no. 32 (October 1967); Michel Oksenberg, "China: Forcing the Revolution to a New Stage," *Asian Survey*, 7:1 (June 1967); Thomas W. Robinson, "The Wuhan Incident: Local Strife and Provincial Rebellion During the Cultural Revolution," P-4511 (Santa Monica, Calif.: Rand, 1970).

SUMMARY INTERPRETATION OF MODERN CHINA

A provocative comparative interpretation of China and Russia is Klaus Mehnert, *Peking and Moscow* (London: Weidenfeld and Nicolson, 1963). A very imaginative and solid interpretation of Maoism and Chinese culture is Richard H. Solomon, *Mao's Revolution and the Chinese Political Culture* (Berkeley: University of California Press, 1971). Also see Lucian W. Pye, *The Spirit of Chinese Politics* (Cambridge, Mass.: M.I.T. Press, 1968).

Index

369